Richard Wagner

Oswald Georg Bauer

Richard Wagner

The Stage Designs and Productions
from the Premières to the Present

Foreword by Wolfgang Wagner

RIZZOLI
NEW YORK

Editorial Consultant for English Language Edition:
Michael Sonino

Translated from the German:
*Richard Wagner – Die Bühnenwerke von der Uraufführung
bis heute*
Copyright © 1982 Office du Livre S.A.
Fribourg, Switzerland

English translation: Copyright © 1983 Office du Livre S.A.

English edition published 1983
in the United States of America by:

𝓡*IZZOLI INTERNATIONAL PUBLICATIONS, INC.*
712 Fifth Avenue/New York 10019

Library of Congress Cataloging in Publication Data

Bauer, Oswald Georg.
Richard Wagner.

Bibliography: p.
Includes index.
1. Wagner, Richard, 1813–1883. Operas.
2. Wagner, Richard, 1813–1883 – Dramaturgy.
3. Opera – History and criticism.
4. Opera – Dramaturgy. I. Title.
ML410.W13B23 1983   782.1'092'4   82-42889
ISBN 0-8478-0478-X

Photolithographs: Schwitter AG, Basle
Set, printed and bound: Freiburger Graphische Betriebe,
Freiburg im Breisgau
Design and production: Emma Staffelbach

Printed in Germany

Table of Contents

Acknowledgements

One might imagine that everything there is to say about Wagner has already been said and written. The secondary literature on Wagner has grown over the years to a point where it is scarcely possible any longer for a single individual to come to terms with it all. There is hardly a single aspect of his life, work and thought which has been ignored by Wagnerian scholars, with one major exception – the theatre. Until now only a few isolated attempts have been made to write a stage history of Wagner's works; there is still the need for a comprehensive study. Richard Wagner was first and foremost a man of the theatre, a librettist and composer, who wrote for the theatre and for whom a work was not finished and completed until it emerged into life in performance on stage. For this reason a performing history not only makes sense: it is absolutely essential for anyone who concerns himself with Wagner's works, inasmuch as such an account can form the basis for a discussion about the problems of staging those works.

An attempt has been made in the chapters which follow to trace Wagner's intentions back to the conception and genesis of each of his stage works and to see how they relate to the planned performances and then to examine his efforts to achieve as faithful a performance as possible at the time of each particular first production. The unique role of Bayreuth is described here, as are some of the many interpretations which have been seen in various opera-houses up to the present day, each one of which has been shaped by an individual and artistic stylistic intent.

It goes without saying that, given such a wide-ranging subject, it was necessary to be selective in the choice of examples. It was none the less important to include not only the prestigious, spectacular and influential solutions to staging the works in question, but also examples of that theatrical routine which has created what might be called registered designs.

In the photographic captions to the individual productions the date of the première has been given wherever possible. There are occasions, however, where, in spite of intensive investigations, it was not possible to obtain all the details in as complete a form as desired. The laborious attempts to trace generally out-of-the-way pictorial and textual records of past performances, many of which have long since been forgotten, would have been impossible without the willing co-operation which I have received both from individuals and from institutions. I should like to thank in particular Herbert Barth, Bayreuth; Dr Oswald Bill of the Theatre Collection of the Hesse Regional and University Library in Darmstadt; Sergio Castagnino, Milan; Carlo Clausetti, Archivio Ricordi, Milan; Peter Dannenberg, State Opera, Hamburg; Jaroslav Dlask, Library of the Bavarian State Opera, Munich; Dr Martin Dreier, Swiss Theatre Collection, Berne; Pavel Eckstein, National Theatre, Prague; Dr Manfred Eger, Richard-Wagner-Museum, Bayreuth; Francesca Franchi, Archive Office of the Royal Opera House, Covent Garden, London; Reinhard Heinrich, Munich; Dr Wilhelm Hermann, Theatre Collection of the Municipal Reiss-Museum of Mannheim; José Manuel Infiesta, Barcelona; Martine Kahane, Library and Museum of the Paris Opéra; Arthur Kaplan, San Francisco; Dr Roswitha Karpf, Graz College of Music; Dr Peter Kehr, State Theatre, Stuttgart; Dr Robert Kittler, Picture Archives of the Austrian National Library, Vienna; the staff of the Theatre Museum in Cologne-Wahn; Peter Lehmann, State Theatre of Lower Saxony, Hanover; Dr Edda Leisler, Institute for Theatre Studies, Vienna; Montserrat F. Mateu, Barcelona; Karol Musiol, Warsaw; Dr Peter Nics, Theatre Collection of the Austrian National Library, Vienna; Roberto Oswald, Teatro Colón, Buenos Aires; Michel Pazdro, Paris; Matthias Rank, State Opera, Dresden; Lamberto Scotti, Teatro Comunale,

Florence; Kurt Söhnlein, Hanover; Dr Geza Staud, Budapest; Gloria Tanzini, Teatro alla Scala, Milan; Giampiero Tintori, La Scala Theatre Museum, Milan; Robert Tuggle, Metropolitan Opera Archives, New York; Sigrid Wiesmann, Bayreuth. My most cordial thanks to them all.

My special thanks are due to Gudrun and Wolfgang Wagner, who encouraged me to write the present book and who followed its progress with such close personal interest. On the basis of the wealth of experience gained during almost forty years' activity in the theatre and of his continuous involvement with his grandfather's works, Wolfgang Wagner was in a unique position to point me in the right direction on more than one occasion and to provide me with a great number of informative insights.

Bayreuth 1982   Oswald Georg Bauer

Foreword by Wolfgang Wagner

Theatre is an art form which takes place in space and time. For that reason it is determined by the moment of its creation: unlike works of graphic art and literature, no theatrical experience can ever be captured and preserved. It emerges briefly into life between the rise and fall of the curtain. Wagner's scenic demands are laid down in his scores and are thus an essential component of any realization of his works which is intended for the stage. Even with the technical media of films and television, the experience of 'theatre' can be captured in only a very limited way. These media, it is true, may be a form of documentation, but they can never be the work of art in its actual impact. The theatre, like life itself, is subject to a constant process of change, which is why it, too, is of necessity changeable.

The present work similarly deals with documents about the 'art work of the theatre', in the form of illustrations, texts, reviews, production ideas, reconstructions and personal impressions, in other words with actual eyewitness reports. But the history of the theatre is not merely a history of the relevant dates and facts; it is also a history of the ideas by which the theatre was and is both sustained and informed. And these ideas remain continually and constantly vital, being handed on and preserved for each new generation. In the pages which follow, Wagner's stage works are described as interpreted in performance on the international stages of the world. On the basis of his own knowledge and awareness of a particular tradition and in the light of his own experiences, Wagner attempted a renewal and conceptual reappraisal of the operatic theatre of his own time. To regard the theatre as a major form of entertainment for contemporary society was meaningless for someone with Wagner's artistic aims.

For him the theatre was to be once again a means of conveying ideas, as it had been in classical antiquity, in the Middle Ages, in the Baroque and, finally, during the age of German classicism. His artistic ambition was to continue the great Western tradition which had started with Aeschylus and continued through Shakespeare and Calderón right down to the time of Goethe, a tradition in which, as far as Wagner the music dramatist was concerned, the great operatic composers were of equal stature to the names already mentioned. He was not concerned with a purely optical or acoustical appeal or with those merely superficial effects which had always fascinated audiences, but rather with an intensive interaction between stage and auditorium, an interaction which served to provide an intellectual stimulus and to provoke discussion. Like Gluck and Weber before him, he hoped that, by writing exemplary works of art, he would be able to breathe new, and hence authentic, life into the rigidified form that this genre had become. In this way he sought to satisfy other demands than those which had by now become traditional and expected. With Wagner's music dramas there began a new theatrical phenomenon, a newly defined interaction of music and drama. This was Wagner's central concern, a point which he underlined when describing his profession in the Bayreuth directory as that of a word- and tone-poet.

The present volume investigates, amongst other things, those conditions which Wagner found already existing in his own day for the stage realization of his works; and it indicates the decisive extent to which he himself was involved in preparing them for performance. There is no doubt that the operatic stages of his own time could meet his artistic requirements only to a very limited degree, partly because the demands which he made of his singers required a completely different type of performer from the one which then dominated the operatic stage, partly because his production standards stretched to their limits the capabilities of all concerned, and partly because of the problems of scenery involved in staging the works. If the level of the performances which he himself attended and conducted frequently fell below the lofty aims which he had set himself, the reason for that may well have been that he only rarely had at his disposal fellow workers who shared his own views and that the right artistic, administrative and technical conditions were not always available. It is hardly surprising, therefore, that Wagner, with his elevated artistic demands, was the bane of all theatre managers, who were most reluctant to see their well-ordered routine disrupted by such an outsider as he. Audiences, used to what was expected, were bound on the whole to regard Wagner's demands on them and his attempts at stylistic innovation as an affront; and they reacted with violent opposition which occasionally ended in scandal. For, as he himself wrote, Wagner felt the need to 'spur on' and to rouse people from their state of philistine contentment, and to provoke a fruitful sense of intellectual disquiet. It was a goal which he certainly achieved during his own life-time.

Not least of the consequences of these inadequate conditions in the theatre was the founding of Bayreuth, although Wagner was of course not always successful in entirely overcoming all the difficulties mentioned above. This is particularly true of the first complete performances of the *Ring* in Bayreuth, which took place against the background of the earlier productions of *Das Rheingold* and *Die Walküre* in Munich, where they had been staged against Wagner's wishes. Not even these productions, he felt, had been a success, in spite of the immense technical and material outlay involved. In the same way, his remarks about the first production of *Parsifal* in Bayreuth in 1882 reveal that, although these performances were the best which could be possibly staged in his own theatre, Wagner was fully conscious of the fact that, in the final analysis, there were very many of his theatrical ideals which could not be realized and that the audience's reaction in particular was of a kind such as he had neither hoped for nor anticipated. The problems of Bayreuth are no doubt in part due to

the fact that the works which Wagner staged there – the *Ring* and *Parsifal* – were considerably more difficult to mount than, for example, *Tristan* or *Die Meistersinger,* whose Munich premières had turned out to Wagner's satisfaction. It can only be described as tragic that a lack of financial means prevented a revival of the *Ring* in 1877, when a reappraisal of the production difficulties encountered during the first Festival of the previous summer would have been possible. 'Next year we'll do it all differently': Wagner's intention unfortunately remained a beautiful but unrealized dream. The results of such a reappraisal of the staging methods of this most important of all Wagner's works, together with the intended changes in its musical realization, would have provided vital information for today's performing practice. Such information would have reinforced the view that, for a practical man of the theatre such as Wagner, a work could evolve its active and immediate conceptual meaning only when realized on stage. That explains why not even Wagner himself was able to establish a fluent tradition nor a Wagnerian style which would have committed others to the same decisive sense of authenticity.

It is regrettable, although understandable, that with her own new productions in Bayreuth Cosima sought simply to reconstruct all those performances which Wagner himself had supervised and that, in the area of stage scenery in particular, the course which she adopted led not forwards but back into the past. This is particularly striking in the case of her 1896 production of the *Ring,* a full twenty years after the first production of the work in Bayreuth. This is something which overshadows her very real achievements in the area of production techniques and of the development of a performing style which sought a unified expression of gesture and music, an area in which Cosima undoubtedly exercised a formative influence at the time in question.

The style of stage presentation which, on the whole, prevailed throughout the nineteenth century had been that of a naturalistic narrative, but even before the end of the century a sense of unease was beginning to be felt by certain sections of the audience who saw more in Wagner's works than simply a series of superficially interesting but firmly prescribed settings and a wealth of often exciting detail. They missed the presence of an intellectual element in this powerful life's work. They were no longer satisfied by an exclusive preoccupation with the fable but demanded to know the meaning behind it. The fact that it was at precisely this time that Adolphe Appia's ideas, for example, first found expression and proved to be both fruitful and necessary was bound to appear almost as a matter of course, given the reappraisal of Wagner's works which was then taking place. Appia demanded that the purely two-dimensional theatrical realism of a system of flats and soffits should be abandoned as being stylistically inappropriate to the work and that, on the basis of the particular dramaturgy of the *Ring*, ideas might be developed which would make use of various new technical possibilities, including those of lighting and the fully three-dimensional stage. These were of course means of expression which unfortunately had not been available to Wagner in his own day. It is sufficient in this context to mention the single example of what Appia termed the 'hieratic' style of *Das Rheingold*, the preliminary evening of the tetralogy, with its cast of gods, giants and dwarfs. Such an interpretation no longer had any use for nineteenth-century set-painters, but called instead for a designer whose work was neither exclusively decorative nor illustrative but independent and artistic, being the result of his analysis of the piece in question and his insights into its inherent laws. In this way there was set in motion one of the greatest revolutions in the history of the theatre: the replacement of illustrative scenery by interpretative designs. This is a revolution which, in principle, has continued in force right down to the present day. It was sparked off in and

through Wagner, before spreading to the remaining works of the music theatre and of drama. In the years following the turn of the century, many young designers saw in Wagner's works a particular challenge to them to realize their own independent artistic ideas and, with the help of various individual means of expression, to transform their own interpretation of the work into visual terms on stage. A wealth of creative talent was released. This was important for the interpretative history of Wagner's works because of the counter-reaction which set in following the end of the First World War and, in particular, during the 1920s: the immense popularity which these works had enjoyed around the turn of the century now gave rise to a sense of satiety. The intelligentsia of the period dismissed 'Wagner' as the art form of Wilhelminianism and as something which 'belonged to the past'; or else he was given the non-committal status of a classical composer.

This reappraisal of the visual element in the staging of Wagner's works brought with it of course the danger that the sets were no longer what Wagner himself called 'the silently facilitating background of the action' but that they won an autonomy which seriously impaired what for Wagner was the crucial balance between music, action and scenery. Often enough, moreover, the ideas contained in the set-designs went far beyond what was technically possible at the time and, in their stage realization, they lost a great deal of the bold expressive force they were intended to convey. This is a statement of fact, not an attempt to disparage such achievements: it merely serves to confirm that, in the theatre, limits are often set on ideas by technical considerations. The opposite of course may equally be true, namely that technology may get in the way of a genuine artistic statement, if it is employed purely out of a pleasure in technical effects.

The misunderstandings which surround not only the figure of Wagner himself but also his works and influence, and which recur at clearly defined intervals in time, made it a matter of pressing concern that, particularly in the period following the Second World War, there should be a reconsideration and a closer analysis of all that had gone before; and this in turn led to a productive phase of critical re-evaluation. Since the reopening of the Bayreuth Festival in 1951, my brother Wieland and I have attempted to lay bare the intellectual and humane heart of Wagner's work, to penetrate to its archetypal substance, to strip away all those elements which limit it to a particular period and to bring into focus what my grandfather always characterized as 'the purely human' aspect. Wagner himself did not remain bound by his literary ambitions but sought increasingly to fathom the depths of human behaviour and actions and to return there, rather than to allow himself to be limited by those patterns of thought and action which were conditioned by the particular age which produced them. Within those depths there opened up to him an undistorted picture of man in all his contradictory qualities, his fears, hopes, desires, ideals, dreams and longings, his greed and his cruelty and everything which in every age has motivated man in his actions – in a word, those situations in life which are still with us today. When seen from a certain distance in time, Wagner's works once again assumed a remarkable topicality; and this experiment, which took Bayreuth as its starting-point, not only proved to be essentially correct but also achieved a 'festival-like' importance within the framework of a theatrically vital attempt to come to terms with Wagner. Other operatic stages have taken over these ideas in their own Wagnerian productions.

Amongst other things, present-day productions have encouraged a historical reappraisal of the nineteenth century, following the recognition that many of our own current intellectual, cultural and social conditions have their roots there. The turbulent interpretative history of Wagner's works both inside and outside Bayreuth is assimilated into each new interpretation and may even come to be regarded as an integral part of the work itself. As long as audiences throughout the world use the medium of the theatre as a means of coming to terms with those problems which are of concern to the whole of humanity and of seeking there a stimulus to rational debate, performances can provide a constructive contribution towards forming the individual consciousness; and it will always be necessary to find ever new forms of interpretation and presentation which of course may, and indeed should, carry a variety of artistic trade-marks but which must be communicated to the audience with the help of the chosen means of theatrical expression.

I myself am not a theatre historian but a producer and festival administrator. My task is not to document but to keep alive, which is why a further group of theatre workers deserves to be mentioned here, a group which could equally well be called 'the silently facilitating background of the action'. These are the stage technicians, and their colleagues in the costume and make-up departments, as well as in the workshops and offices. All these professional groups do the preparatory work necessary for the performance on stage and, together with the singer-actors, the orchestral musicians and the members of the chorus, make it possible for the art work of the theatre to take place night after night. What is so wonderful, but also so problematical, about the theatre is that, basically, it is still made and determined by people rather than by machines. These people all work together so as to create 'life' on stage during the performance and a 'living experience' for the audience.

If the present volume is seen not simply as a record of historical events but also as a contribution which stimulates a lively discussion about the Wagnerian stage and the theatre in general, then it will not have failed in its objective.

K. Hof- & National-Theater.

München, Freitag den 29. Juni 1888.

Zum ersten Male:

Die Feen.

Romantische Oper in drei Aufzügen von Richard Wagner.

In Scene gesetzt vom k. Ober-Regisseur Herrn Brulliot.

Personen:

Der Feenkönig	Fräulein Blank.	Lora, seine Schwester	Fräulein Weiß.
Ada,	Fräulein Dreßler.	Drolla, deren Dienerin	Fräulein Herzog.
Zemina, Feen	Frln. P. Sigler.	Harald, ein Heerführer	Herr Bauserwein.
Farzana,	Frln. M. Sigler.	Ein Bote	Herr Schlosser.
Arindal, König	Herr Mikorey.	Des Zauberers Groma Stimme	
Gunther, seine Freunde und	Herr Herrmann.	Arindal's und Ada's Kinder	
Morald, Gefährten	Herr Fuchs.	Edelfrauen, Dienerinnen, Volk und Krieger.	
Gernot,	Herr Siehr.	Feen und Geister, eherne Männer.	

Die im ersten und dritten Aufzuge vorkommenden Tänze sind arrangirt vom k. Balletmeister Herrn Fenzl und werden ausgeführt von den Fräulein Jungmann, Spegele, Capelli und dem weiblichen Ballet-Corps.

Nach dem ersten und zweiten Aufzuge finden Pausen von je 15 Minuten statt.

Neue Dekorationen:

Erster Aufzug:	Feengarten,	
Zweiter Aufzug:	Vorhalle eines Palastes,	Sämmtliche Dekorationen sind von den
	Festliche Halle,	k. k. Hoftheatermalern Herren Brioschi
Dritter Aufzug:	Klüfte des unterirdischen Reiches,	und Burghart in Wien.
	Feen-Palast.	

Das decorative Arrangement, Maschinerie und Beleuchtung vom k. Obermaschinenmeister Herrn Karl Lautenschläger.

Costüme und Requisiten nach Angabe des k. Professors Herrn Josef Flüggen.

Textbücher sind zu 50 Pf. an der Kasse zu haben.

Preise der Plätze:

Ein Parketsitz	6 M. — ₰	Ein numerirter Vorderplatz im		
Ein numerirter Balconsitz (I. Reihe)	8 M. — ₰	III. Rang	5 M. — ₰
Ein numerirter Balconsitz (II. Reihe)	6 M. — ₰	Ein Rückplatz im III. Rang	4 M. — ₰
Ein numerirter Vorderplatz im		Ein numerirter Vorderplatz im		
I. Rang	6 M. 50 ₰	IV. Rang	4 M. — ₰
Ein Rückplatz im I. Rang	6 M. — ₰	Ein Rückplatz im IV. Rang	3 M. 50 ₰
Ein numerirter Vorderplatz im		Parket-Stehplatz	4 M. — ₰
II. Rang	6 M. 50 ₰	Parterre-Stehplatz	2 M. — ₰
Ein Rückplatz im II. Rang	6 M. — ₰	Galerie	1 M. — ₰

Die Kasse wird um halb sieben Uhr geöffnet.

Anfang um 7 Uhr, Ende um ½ 11 Uhr.

Freier Eintritt: Classe I.

Samstag den 30. Juni: Im k. Hof- und Nationaltheater: Othello, Oper von Verdi.

Auf dem Repertoire: Sonntag 1. Juli: (Hof) Zum ersten Male wiederholt: Die Feen.

Montag 2. Juli: Der zweite Stamm der Gesellschaft.

Unpäßlich vom Schauspielpersonal: Herr Herz.

Nachdruck verboten.

Die Feen
('The Fairies')

Wagner's formal musical education dates from 1828, when he began to take lessons with Gottlieb Müller, a member of the Gewandhaus Orchestra; it was completed four years later, in the spring of 1832, under Theodor Weinlig, the cantor of St Thomas's Church in Leipzig. The works which he composed during these years, the fruits of that formal training, include a number of overtures and a piano sonata in D major, but they were little more than a way of preparing the ground for his real field of activity, which was to be opera. He wrote his only symphony, in C major, within a period of six weeks during the early summer of 1832. As he tells us in his *Autobiographische Skizze* ('Autobiographical Sketch') of 1842, the most determinative influence at this time, after Beethoven, was that of Wolfgang Amadeus Mozart, and above all the latter's Symphony in C major. In spite of 'many strange aberrations', as he later wrote, he had endeavoured here to achieve 'clarity and strength'. He wrote the libretto of his first opera *Die Hochzeit* ('The Wedding') in Prague in November of the same year (1832) and began work on the score; but the latter was never completed, since Wagner's sister Rosalie, an actress at the theatre in Leipzig and, during this period, not only the head of the family but also, as far as Richard was concerned, the last word in all matters concerning the theatre, found herself out of sympathy with the work. The young composer had conceived his first tragic opera as 'a perfect nocturne of the blackest hue' and scorned 'every ray of sunlight', every 'operatic embellishment' which at that time he regarded as 'inappropriate to the gravity of the subject'. But it was precisely this that Rosalie missed, preferring 'that the relatively simple story be embellished and elaborated so as to produce more varied situations which should be as cheerful as possible' (*Mein Leben* ['My Life']). Without further ado Wagner destroyed the libretto, partly to prove to Rosalie how important her opinion was to him.

In his second operatic venture, *Die Feen* ('The Fairies'), Wagner showed how much he had learned from Rosalie's criticisms. As was to be the case with all his later works, Wagner once again wrote his own libretto, since even by this date it had become clear to him that an opera libretto was something special, something intimately linked with the music, which a man of letters or even an experienced librettist could not necessarily produce. In writing the words of *Die Feen*, he felt himself first and foremost a musician and a composer, and, 'as far as the poetic diction and versification were concerned', he set about his task 'with an almost intentional carelessness'. What mattered for Wagner was not fame as a poet but simply the production of a 'suitable libretto' *(Mein Leben)*. And in this he was entirely successful.

Once the text had been finished, he set off in January 1833 for Würzburg, where his brother Albert was engaged as a tenor. He wanted to put to belated practical use the musical abilities which he had acquired and he had ample opportunity to do so in Würzburg. The 'top administration' of the town's theatre offered him the position of chorus-master for the remainder of the season. Since he was not yet of age, his brother Albert, together with Rosalie and his mother, had to stand surety for his 'punctuality and good behaviour'. According to the terms of his contract, he undertook in addition 'to make himself useful where necessary as an actor in speaking and silent roles in plays and tragedies as well as miming roles in ballet, if so required.' The most important new productions during these months were Heinrich Marschner's *Der Vampyr* ('The Vampire'), Giacomo Meyerbeer's *Robert le diable* ('Robert the Devil') and Ferdinando Paër's *Camilla.*

Wagner began the orchestral sketch of *Die Feen* on 20 February 1833 and completed the orchestral sketch of Act III on 7 December. 'It was just midday – 12 o'clock, and the bells were ringing in all the church-towers, as I

Court Theatre, Munich,
29 June 1888
Playbill announcing the first
performance.

wrote *Finis* at the foot of the last page; – – that gave me a lot of pleasure,' he wrote with a sense of pride and joyful excitement to his sister Rosalie, before continuing, 'May God grant that I do not disappoint you in your joyful expectations; – but I know that this will not be so, for the whole work has poured from my innermost soul – and people say that, if that is so, the work will pass into the souls of others' (11 December 1833). This letter, with its numerous dashes and exclamation marks, accurately reflects Wagner's mood of almost ecstatic excitement on completing the work. He wanted to prove to himself and his family that his musical studies had not been in vain. The work was completed on 6 January 1834 with the addition of the overture.

Die Feen. Romantische Oper in 3 Acten ('The Fairies. Romantic Opera in 3 Acts') was based upon *La Donna serpente* ('The Serpent Woman'), a fantastic fairy tale by Carlo Gozzi (1720–1806). Gozzi's tragicomic and fairy-tale plays were written as a reaction to Goldoni's realistic comedies, reinterpreting afresh the popular elements of the degenerate *commedia dell'arte.* They left their mark on all the German Romantic writers, including E. T. A. Hoffmann, and it is highly probable that Wagner's attention was drawn to the subject-matter when he read Hoffmann, whom he admired greatly. Hoffmann had mentioned 'the magnificent Gozzi' in his dialogue 'Der Dichter und der Komponist' ('The Poet and the Composer'), part of the *Serapionsbrüder* ('The Serapion Brethren'), where he had noted 'how inconceivable it was that this rich vein of excellent operatic subjects has until now been so little exploited.'

Wagner was chiefly interested in the conflict between the world of men and that of fairyland, such as had been depicted in Hoffmann's opera *Undine* and in Marschner's *Der Vampyr,* which had been first produced in Leipzig in 1828. It was above all Hoffmann's 'musical mysticism', as he called it, which made so deep an impression upon the young Wagner while he was still at school.

Arindal (the name, like that of a number of the other characters, is taken from the fragmentary *Die Hochzeit*) is a young prince, who, while out hunting, comes upon Ada, the daughter of the king of the fairies, in the form of a beautiful hind. He falls in love with her and they live together in her underground fairy palace. But she can only truly become his wife if for eight years he refrains from asking her who she is. Before the final year has passed, he breaks his vow and is transported by magic to a desolate, rocky landscape where he rediscovers his friends Gunther and Morald. They turn themselves into an old priest and into the ghost of Arindal's father in order to convince him in this guise that his love is merely an illusion and the result of his obsessive belief in witches, and that he must return to his own kingdom which has been laid waste by enemies during his absence. This act of deception on the part of his two friends is accompanied by thunder and lightning, whereupon the scene changes back to the delightful fairy garden, in which Ada now appears. Her fairies proclaim her queen. If Arindal wishes to win her back, he must swear never to curse her whatever may befall him at her hands. As though as a matter of course, Arindal's companions are also present at this ceremony: they express their amazement at the magnificence of the fairy garden and then conduct Arindal back to his war-torn kingdom.

Arindal's warriors and people assemble in the entrance hall of his palace and prepare to march against the enemy, which has surrounded the capital. Totally unexpectedly Ada appears in the midst of this world of men, leading her own and Arindal's two children by the hand. At a sign from her, a fiery abyss yawns open before them and into it she hurls her children, like some latter-day Medea. Worse is to come, for the chorus of warriors now returns, defeated by a woman in armour who was none other than Ada herself. In the depths of despair and madness Arindal curses his perfidious wife and in a great lament she reveals to him her fate: herself immortal she longed to become mortal through her love for Arindal, which is why he himself had to undergo such trials, which for her, too, have meant unspeakable suffering, in order to demonstrate the constancy of his love. Because he doubted her love and cursed her, she will now be turned to stone for a hundred years and remain immortal for ever. Their two children return, cleansed by the fire from the taint of their birth. The enemy has been defeated since Ada had opposed Arindal's false friends and all who had conspired against his kingdom. The fairies are triumphant now that Ada is once more one of them. Arindal predictably goes mad. In the distance he hears the voice of Ada coming to him through the stone. A second voice, that of the kindly disposed magician Groma, directs him to a shield, a sword and a lyre with the help of which he may still be able to win back happiness, if love and courage remain by him. The scene changes once again to a 'fearsome ravine in the subterranean kingdom.

Court Theatre, Munich,
29 June 1888
Producer: Karl Brulliot.
Designers: Carlo Brioschi,
Hermann Burghart. Conductor:
Hermann Levi
The famous closing scene in the
first performance, the
magnificent fairy palace. The
lavish sets were designed by the
Viennese team of Brioschi and
Burghart; the complicated
technical installations and
lighting equipment, some of
which was electrically operated,
were the work of Karl
Lautenschläger. This 'fairy
enchantment of flowers and
crystal', with hundreds of
magically glowing stars, electric
flowers and illuminated swans,
was the greatest attraction of
the first performances. On the
steps to the left one can see
Ada, the spell on her having
been broken; Arindal is to the
right, their children are between
them and high above them on
his throne is the fairy king.

Earth spirits with hideous masks fill the air with bustling flight'. The chorus of earth spirits and of bronze men bar his entrance to the gates of terror but his magic shield and sword are stronger. The severest trial still lies ahead, his meeting with Ada, now completely turned to stone. His singing and the sound of the lyre melt the stone and restore Ada to him. The scene changes to a 'magnificent, cloud-girt fairy palace'. The 'infinite power of love' has made Arindal immortal and fit to reign over fairyland. His friends 'are brought in'; he hands over his temporal realm to his sister and to Morald, promising at the same time to protect them. The final chorus sings in jubilation:

Ein hohes Los hat er errungen,
dem Erdenstaub ist er entrückt!
Drum sei's in Ewigkeit besungen,
wie hoch die Liebe ihn beglückt!

('Striving, he won a lofty fate
and passed beyond this earthly pale;
and so let men for ever sing
how deeply love has gladdened him.')

There is a quite remarkable sureness about the way in which Wagner seems already to have discovered a number of his most important later themes in this first of his completed operas. Redemption through love, the forbid-

den question, the woman's self-sacrificing love and the demand for unconditional trust already point the way to the 'real' Wagner. In his *Mittheilung an meine Freunde* ('A Communication to my Friends') of 1851, he wrote that 'an important element' of his entire later development was already evident here 'in embryo'.

In spite of the demonstrable weaknesses, which Wagner himself admitted, and in spite of its multiplicity of thematic motifs, the libretto is astonishingly concentrated. The exposition is concise and straightforward and the ensuing action avoids any major digression. Only the matter-of-fact way in which fairies and mortals pass to and fro between each other's worlds is somewhat difficult for our modern sensibilities to accept.

Wagner is stating no more than the truth when he claims in *Mein Leben* to have furnished the text with 'every conceivable kind of device, however incompatible they may all have appeared.' Virtually every one of the then traditional operatic effects is paraded here, including chorus of spirits, mad scene, ballad (about the witch Dilnovaz), the Undine theme, chorus of warriors and so on. The influence of Mozart's *Die Zauberflöte* ('The Magic Flute'), which, according to contemporary taste, was a Romantic opera, is evident in the trial-scenes, in the chorus of bronze men guarding the gates of terror, in

15

Court Theatre, Munich,
29 June 1888
Costumes: Joseph Flüggen
The fairy king: costume design
for the first performance. The
fairy king is depicted as a kind
of water sprite in the traditional
style of Neptune and Baroque
river gods. His attributes are a
crown and a sceptre-like staff
decorated with coral.

the conception of the character of Arindal, clearly modelled on Tamino, and in the duet of the *buffo* couple Gernot and Drolla. Of significance for Wagner's later development is the fact that here, in spite of the dismissive attitude by his friend, the German writer and journalist Heinrich Laube, he has chosen a subject which he could invest with mythological and legendary motifs: Ada and the men whom she turns into animals remind one of the sorceress Circe, and the fairy garden has clear parallels with the Venusberg, while particular emphasis is laid on the Orpheus theme. In Gozzi's version the fairy is turned into a serpent and her prince rescues her by kissing the snake; in Wagner's version redemption comes through song and the sound of the lyre, in other words through love and art.

The music, too, shows a mixture of borrowings and wholesale appropriation, beside passages of unmistakable originality. Wagner himself was honest enough to admit that Carl Maria von Weber (whom he had known from his Leipzig days) and especially Heinrich Marschner, who succeeded Weber as the leading exponent of German Romantic opera and who held an appointment in Leipzig from 1827 until 1832, 'induced him to imitate them' *(Eine Mittheilung an meine Freunde).* Weber's *Euryanthe* and Marschner's *Der Vampyr* provided the model for the musical structure of *Die Feen,* which consists of eighteen musical numbers, some of which are self-

contained, while the others are all linked together. Marschner's opera was one of those which Wagner had had to rehearse in Würzburg and it interested him sufficiently to 'make his miserable job appear rewarding' *(Mein Leben).* He also wrote the words and music for an additional aria for this opera, at the request of his brother Alfred. For Ada's great *scena* in Act II, Leonore's aria in *Fidelio* was both textually and musically the principal source of inspiration, while the a *cappella* scene in Act III for chorus and soloists looks forward on the other hand to the end of Act II of *Tannhäuser* and to the scene in Act I of *Lohengrin* which follows the king's prayer.

Even in his first opera we find Wagner already placing heavy demands on the human voice, as we might expect to be the case in a work whose gestures are so inflated. He himself was subsequently to realize that the individual vocal numbers lacked 'any freely independent melody which is the only means the singer has of impressing the audience; instead, the composer has used small-scale, detailed declamation as a means of depriving the singer of any independent effectiveness'; this, Wagner concluded, was 'an evil committed by almost all the Germans who write operas' *(Autobiographische Skizze).* He returned to Leipzig in a confident and buoyant frame of mind and presented his family with the 'three massive volumes' of his latest score. The director of the Leipzig Theatre, Friedrich Sebald Ringelhardt, was not opposed to a performance of the work, or that at least was the impression he gave. But difficulties soon arose over the question of scenery and costumes. The theatre administration had plans for oriental costumes, whereas Wagner had intended to give the whole piece 'a Nordic character', as was self-evident from his choice of names for the leading characters, all of which were modelled on Ossian. Against this it was argued that there were no fairy-tale themes in northern Europe and that in any case Gozzi's original had been set in the Orient. Bristling with indignation, Wagner refused to accept all the 'insufferable turbans and kaftans' and instead vigorously demanded 'costumes from the days of early medieval chivalry' *(Mein Leben).* But now Wagner had gone too far. The singer and producer Franz Hauser, with whom the ultimate decision lay, explained to the young composer that the latter's whole outlook was at fault and how regrettable it was that J. S. Bach had not written any operas.

Wagner examined Hauser's objections in a long letter of March 1834, in which he supported his own point of view with a number of highly factual and rational arguments: he was aware of the inadequacy of his opera but shared the opinion of his teacher Weinlig that even a young, immature composer should be given the opportunity to see his works performed, since only in that way was it possible for him to develop and progress. In answer to Hauser's objection that the demands made of the singers were inordinate, Wagner pointed out that, in the course of composition, his brother had drawn his attention to the impracticality of some of the vocal parts and that he had altered the passages in question under his guidance. In the end Hauser and Wagner agreed to disagree. The performance was postponed initially until August but by the autumn Wagner had given up all further attempts to have the work staged. He no longer felt any 'sense of contentment' with the piece and now that Leipzig was no longer interested in it, he resolved 'not to trouble himself any further with it' *(Autobiographische Skizze)*. He was already working on a new opera.

Wagner did not live to see a complete performance of *Die Feen,* although excerpts from it were given at concert performances in Würzburg in December 1833 and also in Magdeburg. The first complete performance took place in Munich on 29 June 1888, after the death not only of Wagner himself but also of King Ludwig II to whom he had presented the orchestral score. In a letter to Felix Mottl on 21 October 1889, Cosima described the event as 'one of the most unpleasant acts ever to be committed by a Court Theatre', claiming that it was never Wagner's intention that his first opera should ever be performed in public. Wagner's heirs had ceded the performing rights of both *Die Feen* and *Das Liebesverbot* ('The Ban on Love') to Munich in 1887. The Court Theatre retained the rights to *Die Feen* with the result that, apart from a performance in Prague mounted by Angelo Neumann, the opera was not given again outside of Munich, until it was performed in Zurich during the 1913/1914 season as part of a cycle of all Wagner's works. The organizers in Munich were convinced that *Die Feen* could only be successful if staged as a theatrical spectacular and so no expense was spared on its realization. The Viennese firm of Brioschi und Burghart provided a number of the fantastic sets and Joseph Flüggen designed the costumes. The conductor was Hermann Levi who six years previously had been in charge of the first performance of *Parsifal.* Karl Lautenschläger was the stage technician and he lavished all his skill on the production, creating a particularly striking impression with his electric lighting effects. In Act III the change of scene was achieved by means of a transformation scene. The critics were somewhat at a loss to know what to make of this youthful work: what could they say about it in the light of *Tristan,* the *Ring* and *Parsifal?* On the other hand, the work enjoyed an outright success with the general public, thanks no doubt to the sets. During the 1888 season alone, *Die Feen* received no fewer than twenty-five performances.

The revivals of 1895 and 1899 were mounted during the summer as a tourist attraction, at a time when the city was packed with foreign visitors. The organizers counted on the novelty value of a work which could be seen nowhere else but in Munich. In the 1895 revival the part of Ada was sung by Richard Strauss's wife, Pauline de Ahna; in 1899 by Berta Morena. In spite of all the efforts it received, by 1899 the work was playing to half-empty houses. A new production was mounted in 1910 at the Prinzregententheater as part of the Munich Summer Festival. The conductor was Felix Mottl. A society audience which included the city's assembled aesthetes did not lift a finger to applaud a work on whose scenery and musical preparation so much care and expense had been lavished. Even by this time the opera had come to be regarded as a historical monument incapable of maintaining itself in the repertory.

Stuttgart mounted a production of the work during the 1932/1933 season, on the occasion of the fiftieth anniversary of Wagner's death. It was again produced as a stage spectacular. The part of Ada was taken by Margarete Teschemacher. The performance of 6 January 1933 was broadcast on the radio. The only other performances of *Die Feen* during the 1930s were a handful given in Wagner's birth-place of Leipzig within the framework of a commemorative cycle of his works, after which the opera finally disappeared from the repertory, not to re-emerge until 1967, when a production was given as part of the Bayreuth Youth Festival. The most recent attempt to restore the work to the repertory took place in Wuppertal in 1981, an event which aroused considerable attention. The producer (Friedrich Meyer-Oertel) and designers (scenery by Hanna Jordan and costumes by Reinhard Heinrich) made an interesting attempt to distance themselves ironically from the opera and to show it as a typical product of nineteenth-century art. A number of concert performances of *Die Feen* are planned for 1983 as part of the various celebrations to commemorate the hundredth anniversary of Wagner's death.

Das Liebesverbot

oder

Die Novize von Palermo

Große komische Oper in 2 Aufzügen

von

Richard Wagner

Music-Director des Stadt-Theaters

in

Magdeburg.

Das Liebesverbot oder
Die Novize von Palermo ('The Ban on Love')

In May 1834 Wagner set out from Leipzig in the company of Theodor Apel, a long-standing acquaintance of his who had tried his hand at being a poet and composer. Their goal was Wagner's beloved Bohemia and their mood was one of 'Young German fanaticism'. The two men would gladly have plunged into some 'wild adventure' but were prevented from doing so not only by their circumstances but 'by the whole of the bourgeois world around them'. In the course of their journey they discussed E. T. A. Hoffmann, Beethoven, Shakespeare and Heinse's *Ardinghello*. In Teplitz (Teplice), where they remained for several weeks, Wagner would occasionally get up early and creep away in order to breakfast alone on the Schlackenburg and to sketch out the preliminary draft of a new opera. His source was Shakespeare's *Measure for Measure,* although the opera's basic mood, as he later said, was set by Young Germany and by Heinse's *Ardinghello.*

Wagner had renewed his friendship with Heinrich Laube while in Leipzig the previous spring, where he had gone to await the first performance of *Die Feen.* Laube, who was one of the leading voices of the literary movement known as Young Germany, had in the meantime become editor of the influential *Zeitung für die elegante Welt* ('Gazette for Elegant Society'). The first part of his epistolary novel *Das junge Europa* ('Young Europe'), which had appeared in 1833, had had 'an extremely stimulating effect' upon Wagner 'in the context of all the hopes which he then cherished' *(Mein Leben).* The work was a kind of Young German manifesto, full of liberal and democratic ideas, which resulted in Laube's being thrown into prison before the year was out; in it he pleads for 'the improvised establishment of a new social and religious community' opposed to 'all forms of authority'; he condemns philistinism, speaks of the inevitability of social revolution and generally holds forth on the subject of free love and marriage. In much the same way the

Sturm-und-Drang poet Johann Jacob Wilhelm Heinse had presented the outlines of an ideal state on the Aegean islands of Paros and Naxos in his *Ardinghello und die glückseligen Inseln* ('Ardinghello and the Blessed Isles') which had appeared in 1787. Here mankind was able to realize itself, under the leadership of the artist Ardinghello, in classically abandoned sensuality, in beauty and in freedom. Wagner, it may be added, considered Laube's *Das junge Europa* to be 'a reworking' of *Ardinghello.* He transformed Shakespeare's serious drama into an *opera buffa,* taking over principally the figure of the puritanical governor and discovering in him 'the wickedness of hypocrisy and the unnaturalness of ruthless moral censorship'. Justice emerges triumphant in Shakespeare's play, 'free sensuality' in Wagner's. He transferred the action from Vienna to Palermo, to 'torrid Sicily', and a neat contrast between the cold, moralistic and puritanical North, on the one hand, and the hot, sensual South, on the other, informs the whole of the text. Even though his plans to visit Italy with Apel came to nothing, his poetic imagination none the less conceived the vision of a Mediterranean world imbued with Young German idealism.

Upon his return to Leipzig, he learned from his family that he had been offered the position of director of music with Heinrich Bethmann's theatre company in Magdeburg. During the summer months Bethmann toured around, visiting first of all Bad Lauchstädt, where they performed at the spa theatre, then at the Vogelwiese in Rudolstadt, with its fair and shooting match, and finally in Bernburg, after which the troupe returned to Magdeburg. It was at this time that 'care' first entered Wagner's life, as he ominously noted in his autobiography. And yet Wagner's descriptions of the eternally bankrupt theatre manager and his seedy company are among the most delightful accounts to be found in the pages of *Mein Leben* which, were written in 1865 with the hindsight and superior view of an artist who had finally found his way in life.

Title-page of the libretto with a note added by the Magdeburg censor's office: 'Permission for performance granted.'

It was in Rudolstadt that he now wrote the libretto of *Das Liebesverbot* or *Die Novize von Palermo* ('The Ban on Love'). He himself stressed that he created and devised the situations 'with incomparably greater awareness' than had been the case with *Die Feen*. The 'Grand Comic Opera in 2 Acts' begins with a good, old-fashioned riot and a gathering of people in the course of which 'tables, chairs, bottles and so on' are hurled through the air. A crowd of guards, under their captain Brighella, arrest the landlord of one of the low taverns on the edge of the town, since the governor, Friedrich, has recently decreed that all the inns on the island are to be closed; in addition, the local carnival is to be abolished and – as the very last straw – a general ban has been placed on free love within the precincts of Palermo. Claudio, a young nobleman, is brought on in chains, having failed to observe the ban. He is now threatened by sentence of death. His friend Luzio resolves to inform Claudio's sister Isabella, a novice in the Convent of St Elizabeth, of her brother's imprisonment and to implore her help. The scene changes to the courtyard of the convent. Isabella learns from her fellow novice, Mariana, that the latter is in fact secretly married to the governor, Friedrich, but that she has been rejected by him. Luzio arrives at the convent to see Isabella and from the very first sight of her is overwhelmed by her beauty. Without further ado he offers her his hand in marriage. A further change of scene takes us to the court-room where, in the governor's absence, Brighella acts out a comic court scene in which he passes sentence on the servants of Danieli's tavern. He falls in love on the spot with the pretty serving wench, Dorella. But when the townsfolk surge into the court-room, Brighella's stern demeanour gives way to fear and he 'takes comical steps to defend himself'. Friedrich now enters and categorically refuses to accede to the townspeople's request that the carnival be allowed to go ahead. He condemns Claudio and his lover Julia to death. Isabella, dressed as a novice, begs for her brother's life, singing a Song of Songs to love and love's pleasures. It scarcely needs to be added that Friedrich falls in love with the young nun and promises to free her brother if she agree to a secret meeting. She pretends to do so, having already formed a secret plan of her own.

Act II begins in prison. Isabella meets first Claudio and then his friend Luzio. The latter reasserts his undying love, but his train of thought is repeatedly broken by Dorella, to whom he is already promised. The scene changes to Friedrich's palace. Dorella hands the governor Isabella's letter, summoning him to appear that evening on the Corso, wearing a mask. He stifles his initial doubts, physical desire finally triumphing over his puritanical principles. In much the same way, Brighella, who is still infatuated with Dorella, allows himself to be persuaded to meet her on the Corso: he is to appear disguised as a pierrot and she is to come as Columbine. The last scene takes place on the Corso where, in spite of the ban, the carnival is in full swing. Luzio sings a boisterous carnival song to the clicking of castanets, while the rest of the company dances. All then go and hide in the bushes, where they remove their masks and watch the others arriving. Brighella in his pierrot costume meets Dorella disguised as Columbine and the masked governor, Friedrich, meets his wife, Mariana, who is disguised as Isabella. Comic confusion reigns, inspired by jealousy and followed by a general unmasking, which is made worse for Friedrich inasmuch as he has sentenced Claudio to death in spite of the promise made to Isabella; only her interception of the warrant prevents the sentence from being carried out. Friedrich is exposed as the hypocrite he is and Claudio is brought on in triumph. Brighella is paired off with Dorella and Luzio with his novice Isabella. All join in the final chorus,

Reisst alle Trauerhäuser ein,
Für Lust und Freude lebt allein!

('Tear down all the houses of mourning
And live only for joy and pleasure!')

The king's arrival is proclaimed and the revellers form a masked procession to welcome him. Bells ring out, shots are fired in celebration, and with that the opera ends.

An astonishing transformation has taken place between *Die Feen* and *Das Liebesverbot,* and that in the space of barely two years. There is no doubt that in 1834 Wagner had moved decisively away from the 'brooding seriousness' which had earlier encouraged in him 'a mood of sentimental mysticism'; what now attracted him was 'the beauty of the subject, its wit and spirit'. The political idealism and social criticism of the other Young Germans are absent from this work; Wagner interpreted their ideas in an entirely personal way as the advocacy of an autonomous and eccentrically fancy-free life-style in contrast to a life of hypocritical philistinism. He is not interested in putting forward an 'ideal state' in the sense that Laube or Heinse would have understood it. One reminiscence of his read-

Bayreuth International Youth
Festival, 1972
Designer: Roland Aeschlimann
Act I, scene 2, courtyard of the
monastery. The scene between
Isabella and Mariane. In the
centre is a triptych based on a
painting by Max Ernst, showing
the Madonna chiding the Infant
Jesus.

ing Gozzi is the masks and the *commedia
dell'arte* elements of the swaggering but comi-
cally fear-stricken figure of Brighella and of
his Columbine, Dorella. As in *Die Feen*, there
are three couples left at the end of the work:
Friedrich and Mariana, the 'real life' pair of
Isabella and Luzio and the *buffo* pair of Brighella and Dorella. In his choice of scenes,
Wagner similarly follows well-tried models:
court-room, prison, convent courtyard and
the Corso at carnival time. Criticism of
worldly power in the Young German tradi-

tion is directed only at the person of the puritanical and frigid governor, Friedrich, while
the monarchy itself remains above such disre-
spect. Indeed, the king is welcomed as a lib-
erator.

We should certainly be guilty of overinter-
preting the work if we attempted to see the
convent scenes and the two novices, one of
whom is actually married, as a Young German critique of the Church. It would be
nearer the mark to assume that Wagner has
set one particular scene in a convent church-

21

yard and that he has used a chorus of nuns and the pealing of bells as a means of generating atmosphere, just as Meyerbeer had done in *Robert le diable*, and that he hoped to raise a smile when, at the end of the opera, the novice of Palermo herself decides in favour of love, since

Palermos Frauen sind bereit
Zu teilen jede Lustbarkeit
('Palermo's women are ready
To share in every amusement')
(Act II)

A guest appearance in Leipzig by Wilhelmine Schröder-Devrient as Bellini's Romeo had left a deep impression upon Wagner and this, together with his experiences as director of music in Magdeburg, had convinced Wagner that the solidness and seriousness of German music were not calculated to win success. Shortly before Schröder-Devrient's guest appearance, Wagner had seen Weber's *Euryanthe* in a performance which had made strenuous attempts to do justice to the work's 'classical demands' and which had undermined his 'youthful enthusiasm even for Weber's music'. If Bellini's opera, in spite of its 'thoroughly insignificant music', seemed to Wagner to be 'happier and more likely to spread a sense of warmth than the anxiety-ridden conscientiousness with which we Germans have achieved no more than a sham and tormented truth' *(Mein Leben)*, then it was no doubt largely because of Schröder-Devrient's performance in the title-role. The means by which one might achieve a major success on the operatic stage, Wagner felt, were in the hands of the Italians and the French. The easy success enjoyed by a piece which he had cobbled together for the New Year celebrations in Magdeburg in 1835 encouraged him in his view that 'to give pleasure to others, one need not be over-scrupulous about one's choice of means' *(Autobiographische Skizze)*. He abandoned himself completely to 'the trumpery of the stage', as he described it in a letter to Theodor Apel of 26 October 1835. And even as late as 1851 he was prepared to admit in *Eine Mittheilung an meine Freunde* that 'My way led me first of all to a frivolous view of art [...] Rehearsing and conducting those fashionable, light-weight French operas with their shrewd and showy orchestral effects, I often felt a sense of childish pleasure when I stood on the conductor's podium and was able to unleash the full battery of effects to my right and to my left'. In composing *Das Liebesverbot*, he 'did not make the slightest effort to avoid French or Italian musical reminiscences' *(Autobiographische Skizze)*. Quite

the opposite: the music of *Das Liebesverbot* is 'no more than a reflection of the influences of modern French and (as far as the melody is concerned) even of modern Italian opera' on his 'violently aroused sensual perceptivity' *(Eine Mittheilung an meine Freunde)*.

The first performance of *Das Liebesverbot* took place in Magdeburg on 29 March 1836, an event which also marked the end of Wagner's career as director of music in the town. Since the manager of the theatre, Heinrich Bethmann, continued to find himself in 'a state of perennial bankruptcy', the various members of the company had already begun to go their separate ways before Easter. Wagner had to speed up the rehearsals for his new work and have the whole opera ready for its first performance within the space of ten days. In spite of intensive rehearsals and in spite of the fact that Wagner himself 'gave constant prompts, joined in audibly with the singers and was even reduced to shouting his instructions at them', he was incapable of helping them to master their roles in the short time available. In such circumstances there could be no question of their remembering their moves. The result was that, when the curtain went up on the first performance, what took place on stage was 'a musical shadow play, while the orchestra obliged with musical effusions and a frequently exaggerated level of noise' *(Mein Leben)*. Freimüller, who was singing the tenor role of Luzio, attempted to underline his effectiveness by wearing 'an excessively large and garish plume, which fluttered every time he moved'. The audience failed to understand what was going on, which, in Wagner's view, 'was perhaps to its advantage', given 'the questionable nature' of the libretto. The Magdeburg police had instructions not to allow comedies to be performed during Holy Week but Wagner had somehow managed to persuade them that they were dealing with a serious Shakespearean subject, with the result that his copy of the text was returned to him by the censor's office with the note, 'Permission for performance granted.' Presumably it had not been read.

It was, however, the second performance which was the real catastrophe. It was the last of the season and intended as a benefit performance for Wagner himself, which meant that he was to have received the box-office receipts. There were precisely three people in the auditorium, Madame Gottschalk, 'a trusting Jewess' who was one of Wagner's creditors, her husband and 'a Polish Jew in full regalia'. But even before the performance began, a brawl broke out on stage among the singers, in the course of which the tenor who was singing Claudio was so badly beaten that he had to leave the stage with blood streaming down his face. Nor was the soprano who was to sing Isabella spared by her jealous spouse, as a result of which she suffered a convulsion. General confusion ensued and it seemed as though the evening had been devised solely for the settling of old scores. The performance was finally called off 'due to unforeseen circumstances' *(Mein Leben),* thus bringing to an end the stage career of Wagner's second opera even before that of his first opera had ever begun.

During his stay in Paris, Wagner attempted to have *Das Liebesverbot* staged at one of the city's theatres, since the frivolous work seemed well suited to Parisian taste. On Meyerbeer's recommendation, Anténor Joly, the manager of the Théâtre de la Renaissance, accepted the work for performance. Wagner saw to a French translation, although, as he wrote in *Mein Leben,* he no longer had any respect for himself as the composer of *Das Liebesverbot.* However, he had nothing better to offer and he desperately needed a success. On 15 April 1840 he received the grim news that Joly was bankrupt and that his theatre had closed.

Ill fortune continued to dog *Das Liebesverbot* and it was never able to find a place for itself in the repertory. In Munich, where the first attempts were made after Wagner's death to mount a complete cycle of his works, the subject was found to be too *risqué.* The first performance accordingly did not take place until 24 March 1923 when, because of inflation, the tickets ranged in price from 18,000 marks to 750 for standing-room. Hamburg followed in 1925. Stuttgart was the first theatre to perform all of Wagner's works from *Das Liebesverbot* to *Parsifal,* in the course of the 1932/1933 season. During the same decade *Das Liebesverbot* was added to the repertory in Berlin, Leipzig, Magdeburg and Bremen. In Berlin, it may be noted, the producer was Franz Ludwig Hörth and the conductor Leo Blech. The cast included such well-known names as Käthe Heidersbach, Marcel Wittrisch and Theodor Scheidl. What was characteristic of all these productions was an exhilarating Mediterranean style including such typically Italianate accessories as balconies, striped awning and cypresses, all intended to create a bright and lively atmosphere. In the post-war period only two new productions have taken place in Germany, the first, a highly successful affair, in Dortmund in 1957, the second on the occasion of the 1972 Bayreuth Youth Festival. Munich has announced plans for a new production to mark the centenary of Wagner's death.

16te Vorstellung im ersten Abonnement.

Königlich Sächsisches Hoftheater.

Donnerstag, den 20. October 1842.

Zum ersten Male:

Rienzi,
der Letzte der Tribunen.

Große tragische Oper in 5 Aufzügen von Richard Wagner.

Personen:

Cola Rienzi, päpstlicher Notar.	Herr Tichatschek.
Irene, seine Schwester.	Dem. Wüst.
Steffano Colonna, Haupt der Familie Colonna.	Herr Dettmer.
Adriano, sein Sohn.	Mad. Schröder-Devrient.
Paolo Orsini, Haupt der Familie Orsini.	Herr Wächter.
Raimondo, Abgesandter des Papstes in Avignon.	Herr Vestri.
Baroncelli, römische Bürger.	Herr Reinhold.
Cecco del Vecchio,	Herr Risse.
Ein Friedensbote.	Dem. Thiele.

Gesandte der lombardischen Städte, Neapels, Baierns, Böhmens ꝛc. Römische Nobili, Bürger und Bürgerinnen Rom's, Friedensboten. Barmherzige Brüder. Römische Trabanten.

Rom um die Mitte des vierzehnten Jahrhunderts.

Die im zweiten Akt vorkommenden Solotänze werden ausgeführt von den Damen: Pecci-Ambrogio, Benoni und den Herren Ambrogio und Balletmeister Lepitre.

Der Text der Gesänge ist an der Casse für 3 Neugroschen zu haben.

Einlaß-Preise:

Ein Billet in die Logen des ersten Ranges und das Amphitheater	1 Thlr.	10 Ngr.
Fremdenlogen des zweiten Ranges Nr. 1. 14. und 29.	1	10
übrigen Logen des zweiten Ranges	—	25
Sperr-Sitze der Mittel- u. Seiten-Gallerie des dritten Ranges	—	15
Mittel- und Seiten-Logen des dritten Ranges	—	12½
Sperr-Sitze der Gallerie des vierten Ranges	—	10
Mittel-Gallerie des vierten Ranges	—	8
Seiten-Gallerie-Logen daselbst	—	6
Sperr-Sitze im Cercle	—	25
Parterre-Logen	—	25
das Parterre	—	15

Die Billets sind nur am Tage der Vorstellung gültig, und zurückgebrachte Billets werden nur bis Mittag 12 Uhr an demselben Tage angenommen.

Der Verkauf der Billets gegen sofortige baare Bezahlung findet in der, in dem untern Theile des Rundbaues befindlichen Expedition, auf der rechten Seite, nach der Elbe zu, früh von 9 bis Mittags 12 Uhr und Nachmittags von 3 bis 4 Uhr statt.

Alle zur heutigen Vorstellung bestellte und zugesagte Billets sind Vormittags von 9 Uhr bis längstens 11 Uhr abzuholen, außerdem darüber anders verfügt wird.

Der freie Einlaß beschränkt sich bei der heutigen Vorstellung blos auf die zum Hofstaate gehörigen Personen und die Mitglieder des Königl. Hoftheaters.

Einlaß um 5 Uhr.   **Anfang um 6 Uhr.**

Ende um 10 Uhr.

Rienzi

Court Theatre, Dresden,
20 October 1842
Playbill announcing the first
performance.

In May 1836 Wagner travelled to Berlin in the hope of being offered the post of *kapellmeister* at the city's Königstadt Theatre and of having *Das Liebesverbot* performed there. Situated at the edge of the city, the theatre was an extremely successful one, in spite of its being limited to local farces, *opera buffas* and comedies, since the royal theatres reserved for themselves the right to perform serious operas and plays. In this mood, with the failure of *Das Liebesverbot* in Magdeburg behind him, and the prospect of a further second-rate theatre ahead of him, Wagner, accompanied by Heinrich Laube, attended a performance at the Royal Berlin Opera of Gasparo Spontini's *Fernando Cortez* under the composer's baton. Spontini, who had once been the offical composer to the court of Napoleon and imperial Paris, was now director of music in Berlin and had written *Fernando Cortez* on the occasion of Napoleon's Iberian campaign. The first performance had taken place in Paris on 28 November 1809. Hector Berlioz went into raptures over the work, opining that 'Never has the enthusiasm of war been more brilliantly and poetically depicted.' This was probably the first time that Wagner had seen a 'Grand Opera' in its overwhelming musical and scenic splendour. Spontini's operas were performed in Berlin with extraordinary lavishness. Wagner described this performance as the most important artistic impression which Berlin had to offer him. He gained 'a new opinion of the real value of great theatrical performances which could be raised in all their parts by means of marked rhythm to the level of an original and incomparable artistic genre' (*Mein Leben*). This impression continued to have a 'profound' influence on him and played a leading role in his conception of *Rienzi*.

Wagner had got to know the source of the opera, Bulwer-Lytton's novel *Rienzi, the Last of the Tribunes* in Bärmann's translation (published in Zwickau in 1836) in June 1837, while he was staying at Blasewitz near Dresden. In July he wrote an extensive prose draft for a five-act opera, in which important sections of the dialogue were already cast in verse form. He completed the poem in August 1838, by which date he had taken up the position of *kapellmeister* in Riga; and he immediately set to work on the orchestral sketch to Act I. In drawing up the libretto he had neglected both poetic diction and metre, being solely concerned to write an effective 'musical play', his years as a *kapellmeister* having taught him that, however had their libretti, French and Italian operas enjoyed a great success provided only that the subject were itself effective and dramatic, whereas other operas failed to make any impact, for all their 'fine verses and elaborate rhymes'. Since Wagner himself longed desperately for a major theatrical success, he felt obliged to produce 'a decent play with music which should have nothing at all to do with musical sweet talk' (Preface to *Rienzi*). In order to pre-empt any possibility that this latest work of his might see the light of day in some 'out of the way provincial theatre', in conditions which depressed and inhibited him, he wrote so elaborate a draft, with so many complicated changes of scene, that only one of the leading theatres in Europe would be in a position to perform this 'Grand Tragic Opera'. He was already secretly dreaming of Paris, the world capital of opera, for it was here that, as he wrote to August Lewald on 12 November 1838, he wished his *Rienzi* 'to receive a decent entry into the world'. After all, had not Meyerbeer himself achieved his first major breakthrough here? While still in Riga he had prepared a French translation of the libretto. 'Just as, at the very moment of conceiving *Rienzi,* I had had in mind only the most magnificent of theatrical conditions, so I now resolved not to delay a moment longer but to make my way directly to the very heart of Europe's operatic life,' he wrote in *Mein Leben*.

In June 1839 he laid the plans for his departure from Riga and on 19 July set sail from Pillau in the schooner *Thetis*, finally arriving in Boulogne-sur-Mer on 20 August after an adventurous sea voyage of several weeks' duration. He remained there for some four weeks, completing the score of Act II of *Rienzi* so that on his arrival in Paris he might at least have something to show. While in Boulogne he met Meyerbeer, who cast an eye over his compositions and promised him his support. Disillusionment, however, was soon to follow. Meyerbeer's letter of recommendation to the director of the Opéra was worthless and the only suggestion which he received was that he should collaborate with a French composer and write the music for a short, one-act ballet, a proposal which he wasted no time in refusing. His money soon ran out, forcing him to eke out a miserable existence by means of paid work. Doubts began to assail him as to the course along which *Rienzi* was taking him and he broke off its composition for six months. In Paris he had got to know the works of all the upstart and successful operatic composers, and at the same time seen the possibilities offered him by a major stage and a superlative orchestra. Being barely twenty-seven years old, and with a score which, for all its vast proportions, still remained half-finished, Wagner was simply out of his depth. He was forced to come down to earth and realize that this was not the right course. As late as 1862 he was able to look back on these years, in a letter to Mathilde Wesendonck, 'I can still recall the time when I was about thirty and was driven by a sense of profound despair to ask myself whether I really possessed what it needed to achieve supreme artistic individuality; I could still detect the influence and style of other composers in my works and scarcely dare think of my own subsequent development as an original and creative artist.' In spite of these self-doubts Wagner completed the full score of *Rienzi* on 19 November 1840 and in doing so 'conceded the artistic claims' of a 'course' which had led him to Paris but which he now saw to be 'completely barred' to him (*Eine Mittheilung an meine Freunde*).

He had soon given up any thought of a first performance in Paris, his hopes having turned instead to Dresden, where the ensemble included ideal interpreters of the leading roles of Rienzi and Adriano in the tenor Josef Tichatschek and in Wilhelmine Schröder-Devrient. Additionally, a new and well-equipped opera-house was then in the process of being built in Dresden to designs by Gottfried Semper. It was opened on 12 April 1841 and already promised to be one of the best theatres in Germany. Wagner completed the score of *Rienzi* on 19 November 1840 and by the beginning of December had despatched it to Wilhelmine Schröder-Devrient in Dresden. Tradition has it that the money needed to post the parcel was lent to him by his employer, the publisher Maurice Schlesinger. In a letter to the king of Saxony, written at the same time, Wagner entreated his sovereign to issue a decree ordering that the first performance of this work by one of his subjects be mounted at the Court Theatre. On 23 March 1841 he sent the theatre intendant, August von Lüttichau, a second fair copy of the libretto, in which a handful of alterations had been made in order to dispel the censor's doubts, which Wagner must have assumed to be the main reason for Lüttichau's delay in acting. Ferdinand Heine, the producer and costume designer in Dresden and later one of Wagner's closest friends, had written to the painter Ernst Benedikt Kietz in Paris, 'There is not a single German Court Theatre, least of all one attached to a Catholic court, where stories about the Church, the papacy and the clergy will get past the censor' (28 February 1841). Having waited for seven months, Wagner finally learned from Lüttichau in June 1841 that *Rienzi* had been accepted, with the first performance planned for the following winter. Wagner now began a voluminous correspondence with the chorus-master Wilhelm Fischer, the conductor Carl Gottlieb Reissiger, with Tichatschek and with Ferdinand Heine, in the course of which he set forth his detailed wishes and suggestions for the performance. He intended to leave nothing to chance but to prepare everything right down to the very last detail, in the hope that *Rienzi* would finally be a success and a breakthrough.

He left Paris on 7 April 1842, hoping that he would never have to look on the city again.

Rienzi, der letzte der Tribunen. Grosse heroisch-tragische Oper in 5 Akten ('Rienzi, the Last of the Tribunes. Grand heroic-tragic opera in 5 acts') deals with the rise and fall of Cola di Rienzo in fourteenth-century Rome. Once the proud ruler of the world, Rome has grown poor and desolate under the reign of terror imposed by its aristocratic rulers. The pope has fled to Avignon. Rienzi, who is of lowly descent, is urged by the papal legate and by the Roman populace to assume the reins of power and he allows himself to be proclaimed tribune. He re-establishes peace and restores Rome to her former greatness. In his dealings with the *nobili,* he attempts initially to show magnanimity and clemency. The action of the opera reaches its climax in a great celebration of peace, accompanied by an elaborate pantomime. During the festivities the *nobili* carry out an abortive attempt on Rienzi's life, but he pardons them on hearing Adriano's impassioned plea. They continue to plot insurrection and rebellion, until finally defeated by Rienzi in battle. Their ringleaders Orsini and Colonna are killed. A group of conspirators emerges from among Rienzi's own supporters, suspecting him of striving to acquire for himself the absolute power formerly held by the *nobili*. When, following the battle, Rienzi is on the point of entering the Lateran church to the sounds of a solemn *Te Deum,* the door is barred to him and the papal legate reads out a ban of excommunication. The Roman people abandon him. Goaded on by the conspirators, they set fire to the Capitol, in which Rienzi and his sister Irene perish. Dramatically the most effective role is that of Adriano Colonna, the son of Stefano Colonna; he is in love with Irene and for a time supports Rienzi's political concept of popular government until overcome by the conviction that all Rienzi is really motivated by is his desire to avenge the old system of government and to acquire absolute power for himself. Adriano is destroyed by the conflict between, on the one hand, his ancestry and his obligations as a Colonna and, on the other, his infatuation with Irene and her brother's ideals.

Wagner indeed achieved his 'artistic ambition not simply of imitating grand opera in all its scenic and musical pomp, its cheap showmanship and its musically overblown passions,' but of 'surpassing every single previous example of it by virtue of the most utterly wasteful means available' *(Eine Mittheilung an meine Freunde).* His grand opera became so grand that not even Europe's largest theatres were able to perform the entire work without cuts. With all the youthful enthusiasm of a composer who understands the repertory, who knows the recipe for success and who is determined at all costs to outdo them both, he included finales, ensembles, huge choral scenes, the clash of arms, chorales, duets and trios and the whole gamut of passions, all of which were larger than life. It may be that with *Rienzi* Wagner had to approach the boundaries of what was feasible for himself and for the genre of grand opera, in order to discover the self-criticism necessary for him to find his own way.

There are obvious borrowings from the famous and successful operas of Auber, Halévy and Meyerbeer. In his freeing the Romans from the tyranny of the *nobili*, the popular tribune Rienzi reminds one of Masaniello, the revolutionary hero of Auber's *La Muette de Portici* (1828); his prayer in Act V takes as its model the prayer of Eliézer in Act II of

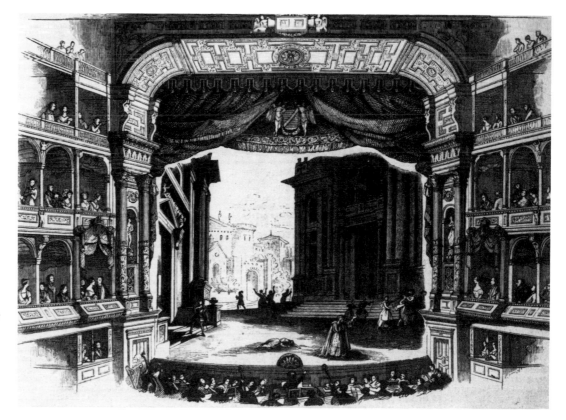

Court Theatre, Dresden, 20 October 1842
Conductor: Carl Gottlieb Reissiger
The square in front of the Church of St John Lateran, closing scene of Act IV, taken from the *Leipziger Illustrirte Zeitung.* The church is shown here in its Baroque form, rather than in the style of the fourteenth century, when the action of the opera takes place. The sets which were used in Munich continued to be Baroque in style until as late as 1900.

27

Halévy's *La Juive* (1835), just as Rienzi's excommunication by the papal legate in Act IV
is modelled on the curse of Cardinal Brogni
in the same work, while the conspiracy of the
nobili (Act V) is based upon the *bénédiction
des poignards* of Meyerbeer's *Les Huguenots*
(1836). And yet these outward similarities
should not be allowed to obscure a number of
basic differences. Wagner is already attempting to abandon the rigid schematization of
aria and ensemble and is moving instead towards larger dramaturgical units; it is true
that there are individual numbers such as
Adriano's aria, 'Gerechter Gott' ('Righteous
God') in Act III or Rienzi's prayer, 'Allmäch-
tiger Vater, blick' herab' ('Almighty Father,
look down on me'), but they are bound up in
the total dramatic context and do not stand
out on their own as separate numbers to be
applauded. Even the great pantomime ballet
in Act II is not simply the usual interlude but
is dramaturgically justified. The portrayal of
the rape of Lucretia and the Tarquins' expul-
sion from Rome is an allegory of the *nobili's*

own rule and a warning to the Romans to be
mindful of their task. In view of their importance, Wagner wanted the roles in this pantomime to be taken not by members of the *corps
de ballet* but by some of the company's leading actors. Even in this *soi-disant* grand opera,
it was Wagner's desire to achieve the greatest
possible unity of action, words and music.

Rehearsals began on 1 August 1842. The
singers and musicians started by complaining
about the difficulties of the score but, once
they had understood Wagner's ideas, their attitude soon changed and they set about their
new task with enthusiasm. Even for the conductor Reissiger, who himself wrote operas
and was bound to view Wagner as a rival, the
rehearsals were a time of unalloyed pleasure.
Tichatschek was happy at finally being given
a part in which he could show off his voice,
and Wilhelmine Schröder-Devrient, initially
somewhat piqued at not having been given
the main part, soon recognized the enormous
dramatic possibilities offered her by the role
of Adriano. All the favourite passages were

Court Opera, Berlin,
24. October 1847
Designer: Johann Karl Jakob
Gerst
'A Part of the Campo Vaccino':
Gerst's design for the Berlin
première, entirely within the
eighteenth-century tradition,
with its elegiac depiction of
architectural ruins. The
atmosphere of nostalgia for the
lost greatness of Rome and for
the decline of its former
classical beauty are well
captured here. Gerst's Church
of St John Lateran was a
medieval Romanesque basilica.

applauded at rehearsals and the whole cast was firmly convinced that the première was bound to be a success. All the 'minim-mongers and counterpoint-codgers' could be seen 'putting their heads together and declaring roundly that with this opera Wagner had earned a place for himself among the most worthy classics'; even the supporters of Italian opera declared that 'it was even better than the divine Donizetti' (Ferdinand Heine to Ernst Benedikt Kietz, 24 October 1842).

The whole of Dresden was agog; rumours ran rife about the extraordinary new work and Madame Schröder-Devrient did all the necessary publicity. 'All hell will be let loose on the 19th: I can honestly say that I'm immensely looking forward to the first night, because it will be so good! [...] Now may the Capitol collapse in ruins, and may my unlucky star fade with it,' Wagner wrote to his brother-in-law, Eduard Avenarius, on 8 October 1842.

The performance began at six o'clock on the evening of 20 October. Wagner was taken aback by the length of the piece. The third act which 'because of the tumults of war got off to a particularly stunning start' did not end until nearly ten, and the whole performance lasted until midnight. And – something which nobody had counted on – the good people of Dresden stuck it out until the end. The first night was the sort of unequivocal success which Wagner was never again to achieve. He was 'a shadow, not knowing whether to laugh or cry, hugging everyone who came up to his box and all the time cold sweat was running down his forehead. At the first "bravo", he refused to come on stage and I had to give him an enormous shove so that he literally flew out from the wings [...] but was then physically driven back by the thunderous cheers of the audience. Fortunately he has such an incredible nose that everyone sitting on the left of the auditorium could at least regale themselves at the sight of the end of it,' thus Ferdinand Heine reported the first night to Kietz in Paris (24 October 1842). The success of subsequent performances was every bit as great and for a number of years *Rienzi* remained the principal attraction of the Dresden Opera, attracting summer visitors from the surrounding health resorts. In January 1843 the work was split between two evenings because of its length, but since the Dresdeners did not see why they should pay twice to see the same opera, the management reverted to the practice of performing the whole work complete on a single evening.

After the initial wild applause had died down and the first performance of *Der fliegende Holländer* ('The Flying Dutchman'), which Wagner held to be the more important work of the two, had met with comparatively little enthusiasm, he tried to work out the reasons for this and was forced to conclude, 'with a strange sense of horror', that the success of *Rienzi* was evidently the result of a misunderstanding. Tichatschek had totally failed to bring out the 'dark demonic side of Rienzi's character' to which Wagner 'had given unmistakably clear emphasis at decisive points in the work [...]; not for a moment had the singer allowed himself to be distracted from his performance as the typical exultant and radiant *Heldentenor'*. The opera owed its success to Tichatschek's 'bright, unusually warm voice which he delighted in constantly showing off, to the novel effect of the choral ensembles and to the lively goings-on on stage' *(Mein Leben)*. What gave him particular food for thought was the success of the 'ballet' in the second act: 'Since there were no choreographic means available in Dresden for meeting my demand for classical tournaments and expressive, serious round dances, I had, most ignominiously, to settle for two tiny ballerinas performing ridiculous *pas seuls* and *pas de deux* for an eternity, before a company of soldiers finally marched on stage and lifted their shields over their heads to form a roof, evidently intended to recall the ancient Roman *testudo;* the choreographer and his assistants, dressed in nothing more than flesh-coloured tights, then leaped up on to the roof formed by the shield, where each of them in turn stood on his head a few times, presumably in the belief that this represented the gladiatorial games of ancient Rome. It was at this moment that the house always burst into thunderous applause and I had to remind myself that, when that moment arrived, I had reached the very pinnacle of my success' *(Mein Leben)*.

Hamburg was the second theatre to produce *Rienzi* on 21 March 1844, with Wagner himself conducting the first two performances. Once again he found himself face-to-face with his earlier bad experiences of 'ill-founded and shallow theatrical life'. He had to muddle through as best he could with 'badly organized conditions which were calculated to produce only the most vulgar theatrical glitter.' The director of the theatre, Julius Cornet, had assembled the costumes 'from all the fairy ballets in the repertory', convinced that success was assured provided only that the costumes were colourful enough and that sufficient people passed across the stage *(Mein Leben)*. This new production took place only three years after the great fire which had destroyed a large part of the city.

Wagner hoped that a new production in Berlin would allow him to repeat away from home the local success which he had enjoyed in Dresden, but for that he had to wait until 1847, the Berlin ensemble having no suitable tenor for the title-role. Dresden, in the meantime, had already witnessed the first performances of *Der fliegende Holländer* and *Tannhäuser* and Wagner himself was working on the score of *Lohengrin*. During the intervening period, he had already moved some distance away from *Rienzi* but was still in need of a success outside Dresden. Even the larger theatres held back from staging a work which had attracted to itself the reputation of involving huge sums of money. Wagner now spoke dismissively of the 'monster' which he no longer loved, and called *Rienzi* his 'screaming brat' (letters to Alwine Frommann of 27 October 1844 and 27 December 1845). The first performance in Berlin took place on 24 October 1847, at a time when *Rienzi* had 'long since been written off' *(Eine Mittheilung an meine Freunde)*. Wagner himself conducted the rehearsals and the early performances. While every attention was lavished on the new scenery and costumes, the rehearsals were noticeably lacking in any spirit of enthusiasm; *Rienzi* was considered as just another repertory opera. After all, the Berliners were only too familiar with grand operas. The king, on whose orders *Rienzi* had been staged, preferred to ride to hounds. The Berlin audiences, it is true, were impressed but unenthusiastic. Wagner had addressed the singers and musicians before the dress rehearsal and apologized for the fact that this 'youthful transgression in the field of art' had cost them all such effort, whereupon the press, as Wagner noted in *Mein Leben,* had described it as an affront to offer a youthful transgression to the artistically sophisticated Berlin public. The reactions of the press were largely negative and after the third performance Wagner returned to Dresden, convinced that he would not achieve a lasting or lucrative success in Berlin.

Théâtre Lyrique, Paris, 6 April 1869
Rienzi's great entry on horseback in Act III in the Paris première of the work. Here again there are classical ruins. The right-hand façade shows an attempt to reproduce an historically accurate fourteenth-century style, but the attempt is vitiated by Michelangelo's dome of St Peter's painted onto the back-cloth.

Court Opera, Vienna, 30 May 1871
Designer: Hermann Burghart
The great hall of the Capitol in the first Vienna production of the work. It was painted by Burghart in the style of a Romanesque basilica. Cosima reports that Wagner found the performance in the brilliant new opera-house to be 'ghastly'.

Teatro dal Verme, Milan
Designer: Hermann Burghart
Ricordi asked for Burghart's
designs for the Vienna Court
Opera to be sent to him in
Milan. They included stage
plans and precise details about
the positioning of the sets. The
illustration depicted here, which
is unsigned and undated, is the
work of a Milanese
set-designer. It belongs firmly
to the tradition of architectural
painting which had been
founded at La Scala by
Alessandro Sanquirico.

The sets for this production, of which three designs have survived, were created by Johann Karl Jakob Gerst. Wagner preferred the costumes and scenery of the Berlin production to those in Dresden. The reason for this may be due to the fact that Gerst's designs reproduced the architectural style of fourteenth-century Rome, his church of St John Lateran being a simple, Romanesque basilica with a clearly divided façade of columns and the Capitol a structure predating the later designs of Michelangelo.

During the 1860s *Rienzi* was given in a number of smaller theatres in Germany, including Weimar, Mainz, Schwerin and Würzburg, and this decade, too, saw the first foreign productions of the work, beginning with Prague in 1859, followed by Stockholm (1864), Rotterdam (1868) and, on 6 April 1869, Paris, the city for which Wagner had initially written the work. The last-mentioned performance, however, took place not at the Opéra but at the Théâtre Lyrique. Wagner kept well away from the rehearsals and the performances, not wishing to expose himself to the suspicion that it was with *Rienzi* of all works that he wanted to make up for the *Tannhäuser* fiasco of 1861. The first performance of *Rienzi* in Italy took place in 1874 at the Teatro la Fenice in Venice and was given in Italian in a translation by Arrigo Boito, Verdi's librettist and the composer of *Mefisto-fele.* Bologna followed in 1876. Other first performances include those at Budapest in 1874 (in Hungarian), Madrid in 1876, New York in 1878, London in 1879 (in Italian), St Petersburg in 1879 (in Russian) and Rome and Zurich, both in 1880. The American première was given at the Academy of Music in New York on 4 March 1878 by the Pappenheim Opera Company. A contemporary print of the London performance shows the pantomime ballet, with the ballerinas wearing traditional tutus and the whole style of the lavish production more reminiscent of the nineteenth century than the fourteenth. This was entirely in keeping with contemporary practice. In May 1872 Wagner and Cosima attended a performance of *Rienzi* in Vienna. The work had been first produced in the new opera-house on the Ringstrasse the previous year. Wagner was appalled by the style of the production and by the anachronistic sets. This production, designed by Hermann Burghart with all the magnificence of his typically ornamental style, remained for years a part of the programme of festivities regularly put on for visiting heads of state. And as a show-piece with large chorus and ballet *Rienzi* remained in the repertory of the larger opera-houses in Germany and Austria for decades, although it was never a success on the international stage. It has been performed during only three seasons (1885–1886,

Imperial Theatre, St Petersburg,
3 November 1879
Rienzi owed its popularity
throughout the nineteenth
century to those productions
which staged it as a theatrical
spectacular in the style of the
grand operas of Giacomo
Meyerbeer. Audiences were
particularly impressed by the
conflagration and collapse of
the Capitol, an anticipation of
the later *Götterdämmerung*.

Dietrich-Eckart Open-Air
Theatre, Berlin; 1939 Summer
Festival of the national capital
Sets and costumes: Benno von
Arent
Rienzi as a grand opera for the
masses. Sets and costumes by
the Reich's official designer von
Arent.

33

Teatro alla Scala, Milan,
4 June 1964
Producer: Herbert Graf.
Designer: Nicola Benois.
Conductor: Hermann
Scherchen. Rienzi: Giuseppe di
Stefano
Ruins and scaffolding have
become permanent motifs in the
intervening years.

1886–1887, 1889–90) at the Metropolitan Opera, New York. Leopold Damrosch was the General Manager. The cast included Lilli Lehmann, Marianne Brandt and Emil Fischer. All operas were sung in German.

For orthodox Wagnerians the popularity of *Rienzi* has always been something of an embarrassment, particularly in the decades following Wagner's death in 1883. Cosima, it is true, had an expurgated version of the score prepared, which attempted to recast the grand opera in the style of a music drama, and she herself produced *Rienzi* in Berlin in 1895 and supervised new productions in Karlsruhe and Munich, but audiences continued to regard the work simply as a good, old-fashioned opera.

In Germany, even smaller theatres mounted the costly work, in often very skilful productions, saving money by using Lautenschläger's reform stage with its fixed proscenium and interchangeable backdrops. Yet even in these relatively modest productions there was rarely any question of cutting out Rienzi's spectacular entrance on horseback in Act III. Some of the world's leading conductors have shown an interest in the work, including Felix Mottl, Bruno Walter and Hans Knappertsbusch in Munich, Gustav Mahler and Clemens Krauss in Vienna and Richard Strauss in Weimar; notable producers have included Oskar Wälterlin in Basle and Walter Felsenstein in Cologne. Alfed Roller designed new sets for the Vienna Opera's production,

turning the Capitol into a huge Italian citadel. A memorable achievement in stage design, contrasting favourably with the traditionally monumental style, was that of Johannes Schröder for Saladin Schmitt's production in Bochum-Duisburg during the 1926/1927 season: his 'Rome' consisted of a system of columns and arches, clearly well constructed and an eloquent symbol of power. But designs such as these remained the exception rather than the rule. The critic of the *Augsburger Postzeitung* in his review of the 1932 Munich production, with its conventional sets by Adolf Linnebach, felt that the audience's applause was 'a cry for ornamentation' such as had been abolished by modern art. Performances of *Rienzi* became more frequent during the Third Reich, a fact which the German writer Hermann Johannes Müller attributed to the opera's heroic element and 'the yearning for freedom, order and honesty in the state'. He suggested that the first part of the opera should be performed under the title 'Rienzi's Greatness' (but not the second part, 'Rienzi's Fall') at an official gala to celebrate the new state.

A footnote in the performing history of *Rienzi* is provided by the open-air performances which the work has received. One such performance took place in 1933 in the square in front of the Stuttgart Opera. The orchestra was located to one side. The whole undertaking was calculated to create the greatest possible impact, with huge crowd scenes and

State Opera, Stuttgart,
3 November 1957
Producer and designer: Wieland
Wagner. Conductor: Lovro von
Matacic. Rienzi: Wolfgang
Windgassen
Rienzi's Prayer. His hopes
shattered and the ban of
excommunication weighing
heavily upon him, Rienzi
communes alone with the figure
of the crucified Christ.

State Opera, Stuttgart,
3 November 1957
The gathering of the *nobili* (Act II, scene 1) in Wieland Wagner's production. The fixed positioning of the seats and the heraldic insignia embroidered on gold-braided cloth underline the ceremonial aspect of the scene. In the background hangs a panel depicting Guidoriccio da Fogliano, a Sienese commander, based on a fresco by Simone Martini in the Palazzo Pubblico in Siena.

State Theatre, Wiesbaden,
22 April 1979
Producer: Peter Lehmann.
Designer: Ekkehard Grübler.
Conductor: Siegfried Köhler.
Rienzi: Gerd Brenneis
Rienzi in the costume of a contemporary political activist. Here, too, the central visual element is a triumphal arch partially surrounded by scaffolding.

whole cavalcades of horses turning the event into an elaborate spectacle. Open-air performances were also given in 1934 in Augsburg by the Rote Tor, in Berlin in 1939, as a mass event on the occasion of the Summer Festival held in the Reich's capital, and at the 1967 Munich Festival, when it was performed in the Apothekenhof of the Residenz on a stage which was almost 150 feet in width. As the Capitol caught fire, the *nobili* plunged down on horseback on to the heads of the Roman plebeians below.

In 1906 a seventeen-year-old youth attended a performance of *Rienzi* in Linz. He was deeply stirred by the fate of the Roman tribune and after the performance, still overwhelmed by what he had seen, he went with one of his friends on to the Freinberg hill near Linz. 'Words poured out of him, like a flood-tide which had been held back and which now burst through the shattered dyke. In wonderful, rousing images he painted the way ahead for himself and his nation.' His name was Adolf Hitler. His friend, August Kubizek, went on to relate that as late as 1939 Hitler had told him 'That was the hour when it all began.' According to notes taken by Albert Speer, Hitler is reputed to have observed that it was not by chance that party meetings opened with the overture to *Rienzi*: Rienzi, a publican's son, had driven out the corrupt senate and restored the empire to its former greatness. 'When, as a young man, I first heard this divinely inspired music at the theatre in Linz, I realized that I, too, would succeed in uniting the German Reich and making it great.' It may be noted that Hitler fails to mention the destruction of the Capitol and the fall of Rienzi. In 1843 Wagner had explained the 'whole ideal' of his opera to be that 'the confusion inflicted on Rome by the *nobili*' is dispelled and that 'with calm and noble dignity, the hopes and inspired faith in Rienzi's ability to bring about a change in the direction of the *buono stato*' are clearly to be seen. Rienzi, he admitted, was a demonically inspired figure, but he is reformed in the course of the opera, renouncing personal vendetta and recognizing only 'Rome, his country and freedom'. His tragedy springs from the fact that 'the only truth is not the Roman people but Rienzi's own idealism' (letter to Albert Niemann of 25 January 1859). *Rienzi* deals with failure, although this fact is generally overlooked, so impressed are we by the clash of arms and blare of trumpets which the work contains. Rienzi's sense of mystical vocation, the constant and intense conjuration of 'Rome' as a political ideal has a rather sceptical ring about it nowadays, so that when, in Act V, Rienzi cries out that his bride is called Rome, the words strike us as ominously familiar. For a generation which had lived through the revolutions of 1830 and which had pinned its hopes on the *buono stato*, these words must have had an entirely different ring. Theodor Wiesengrund Adorno sees direct parallels between Rienzi, the 'first servant of a great whole', and the Fascist Adolf Hitler. Others, conversely, have argued that Wagner cannot be held responsible for the fact that Hitler saw himself vindicated by the example of Rienzi, the more so in view of the ending which Wagner gave the work.

What is incontrovertible is that the history of the interpretation of Wagner's works is also a history of their reinterpretation. On the whole *Rienzi* disappeared from the repertory after the end of the Second World War. Wieland Wagner produced it in Stuttgart in 1957 in order to find out whether it might not after all be possible to include the opera in the Bayreuth canon. Richard Wagner had always felt that his true style did not emerge until *Der fliegende Holländer* and was against the idea of the three earlier operas being performed on the Green Hill. Wieland's experiment was a failure. He staged the work as a grand opera with more than 600 costumes and a large number of sets, incurring production costs which were considered excessive by the standards of the day. Adriano was sung not by a mezzo-soprano but by a tenor, and Wieland also changed the ending of the piece. Rienzi was not buried beneath the ruins of the burning Capitol but struck down in broad daylight by the Roman people.

Peter Lehmann produced *Rienzi* at the Wiesbaden May Festival in 1979, staging it in the style of a modern revolutionary opera. He, too, altered the ending: after Rienzi's death, the *nobili* again assume control, thus restoring the *status quo*. Lehmann created the atmosphere of an election campaign by means of news-sheets, handbills and banners, inviting comparisons with the street riots which were then in the news. The production was broadcast on television, thus re-opening discussion about the work. Recently there have been a few performances in the U. S., including a pretty lavish one in San Antonio in 1977 (Act III had 250 people on stage). The conductor was John Mauceri and Robert Darling was the designer and director. The cast included John McCray (Rienzi), Janet Price (Irene) and RoseMarie Freni as Adriano. The opera was given at the Theatre for Performing Arts.

1ʰᵉ Vorstellung im vierten Abonnement.

Königlich Sächsisches Hoftheater.

Montag, den 2. Januar 1843.

Zum ersten Male:

Der fliegende Holländer.

Romantische Oper in drei Akten, von Richard Wagner.

Personen:

Daland, norwegischer Seefahrer.	Herr Risse.
Senta, seine Tochter.	Mad. Schröder-Devrient.
Erik, ein Jäger.	Herr Reinhold
Mary, Haushälterin Dalands.	Mad. Wächter.
Der Steuermann Dalands.	Herr Bielezizky.
Der Holländer.	Herr Wächter.

Matrosen des Norwegers. Die Mannschaft des fliegenden Holländers. Mädchen.

Scene: Die norwegische Küste.

Textbücher sind an der Casse das Exemplar für 2½ Neugroschen zu haben.

Krank: Herr Dettmer.

Einlaß-Preise:

	Thlr.	Ngr.
Ein Billet in die Logen des ersten Ranges und das Amphitheater	1	—
Fremdenlogen des zweiten Ranges Nr. 1. 14. und 29.	1	—
übrigen Logen des zweiten Ranges	—	20
Sperr-Sitze der Mittel- u. Seiten-Gallerie des dritten Ranges	—	12½
Mittel- und Seiten-Logen des dritten Ranges	—	10
Sperr-Sitze der Gallerie des vierten Ranges	—	8
Mittel-Gallerie des vierten Ranges	—	7½
Seiten-Gallerie-Logen daselbst	—	5
Sperr-Sitze im Cercle	—	20
Parterre-Logen	—	15
das Parterre	—	10

Die Billets sind nur am Tage der Vorstellung gültig, und zurückgebrachte Billets werden nur bis Mittag 12 Uhr an demselben Tage angenommen.

Der Verkauf der Billets gegen sofortige baare Bezahlung findet in der, in dem untern Theile des Rundbaues befindlichen Expedition, auf der rechten Seite, nach der Elbe zu, früh von 9 Uhr bis Mittags 12 Uhr, und Nachmittags von 3 bis 4 Uhr statt.

Alle zur heutigen Vorstellung bestellte und zugesagte Billets sind Vormittags von 9 Uhr bis längstens 11 Uhr abzuholen, außerdem darüber anders verfüget wird.

Der freie Einlaß beschränkt sich bei der heutigen Vorstellung blos auf die zum Hofstaate gehörigen Personen und die Mitglieder des Königl. Hoftheaters.

Einlaß um 5 Uhr.   Anfang um 6 Uhr.

Ende gegen 9 Uhr.

Der fliegende Holländer
('The Flying Dutchman')

According to Wagner's own testimony, it was through his reading of Heinrich Heine that he first became familiar with the legend of the Flying Dutchman, a familiarity which probably dates from Riga in 1838. As early as 1831, while he was still a student at Leipzig, he had read a number of Heine's books, including no doubt the *Reisebilder aus Norderney (Die Nordsee)* ('Traveller's tales from Norderney [The North Sea]'), published in 1826, in which Heine had first mentioned the legend of the Flying Dutchman as 'the most attractive of all the wondrous seafarers' tales'. A more detailed account of the legend followed in 1833 in the *Memoiren des Herrn von Schnabelewopski* ('The Memoirs of Mr von Schnabelewopski'), where it took the form of an imaginary play. The legend of the Flying Dutchman and his phantom ship had first appeared in literary form, in England, at the beginning of the nineteenth century, having led an exclusively oral existence up until then. This was all part of a general literary interest in legends and ghost stories.

Heine's version of the legend contains a number of discrepancies. In his imaginary memoirs, which are simply a pretext for Heine's delight in story-telling, Schnabelewopski, in the course of a sea voyage, recalls the tales once told him by his toothless old grandmother, about water-sprites and sea-nymphs, as well as the Flying Dutchman, forced to wander the seas on board his accursed vessel with its blood-red sails. This is the punishment he must suffer for having once sworn by all the devils in hell that he would round a certain cape, in spite of the violent storm which was blowing, though it should take him until the day of judgement. The devil took him at his word. Only the undying loyalty of a woman can release him from the curse. He is allowed to go ashore once every seven years 'in order to marry and by this means to achieve his release. The poor Dutchman! He is often happy enough to be released from marriage and be rid of his would-be redemptress [...]'. Schnabele-

wopski claims to have seen the Dutchman in person, on the stage in Amsterdam. A further seven years have passed; the doom-laden Dutchman goes ashore and meets a Scottish merchant, to whom he offers diamonds at an absurdly low price; when he learns that the Scotsman has a daughter, he demands her as his wife. The deal is concluded. Back at home, the merchant's daughter sits waiting for her bridegroom, repeatedly glancing wistfully at a large, decaying canvas which hangs on the wall. The painting shows a handsome man dressed in the style of the Spanish Netherlands. According to the grandmother, this is the Flying Dutchman, a man all young girls should beware of. When the Dutchman himself enters, both he and the girl are initially at a loss for words, but he soon succeeds in allaying her suspicions, making fun of the Flying Dutchman whom he calls 'the Wandering Jew of the ocean'; but his voice involuntarily takes on a melancholy accent as he describes the doom-laden man's unspeakable anguish. 'His pain is as deep as the sea on which he floats; his ship has no anchor, his heart no hope.' Katharina, his bride, is deeply moved and promises to remain faithful to him unto death. In the final scene, standing on the cliff-top, the Flying Dutchman's wife wrings her hands in despair, while her hapless spouse stands on deck and reveals to her his dreadful fate and the curse which weighs upon him and from which he vows to save her. But Katharina knows a simple way of remaining faithful unto death: she throws herself into the sea. The Dutchman is redeemed and sinks with his phantom ship beneath the waves.

This account must have appealed to Wagner greatly and occupied him a good deal, although he appears not to have followed his usual practice of sketching a short prose draft following his reading of the work in question. Other experiences of decisive significance were first necessary before he found a suitable form in which to work out the material in detail, a process which allowed him finally to realize himself as a lyric dramatist.

Court Theatre, Dresden,
2 January 1843
Playbill announcing the first
performance.

The first such experience was provided by his stormy sea voyage from Riga to London, which gave a characteristic colouring to the gloomy depictions of nature and to all that Eduard Hanslick was later to call, rather disrespectfully, the 'maritime' element of the piece. The sailors on board ship confirmed to him the details of the legend. Driven off course by a terrible storm along the Norwegian coastline, he again saw the pale figure of the Flying Dutchman rise up before him: 'My own situation lent him strength of purpose; his physiognomy and colour came from the storms, the billowing sea, the rocky Norwegian coastline and the bustle on board ship' *(Eine Mittheilung an meine Freunde)*. The rapid rhythm of the sailors' call which rebounded from the granite walls as they entered the fjord was later transformed into the main theme of the sailors' chorus. The 'awesomely sublime desolation' of the fjord and the 'terrible melancholy of the black marshy moorland' left a deep impression upon him. Even the name of the Norwegian fishing village, Sandwike, was taken over into the text of the opera, at the point where Daland sings, 'Sandwike ist's, genau kenn' ich die Bucht' ('It's Sandwike, I know the bay full well').

Wagner's years in Paris are generally regarded as a time of hunger and poverty, which is what they certainly were. But they were also decisive years in the development of his artistic personality, years of clarification and self-discovery. While the sight of the capital's musical life robbed him of any illusions he might have had, it also forced him to consider more closely his own position as an artist. In the final analysis, his self-doubts proved fruitful. Of significance here was an experience involving Beethoven's Ninth Symphony, which Wagner heard (minus the choral movement) being rehearsed by the Paris Conservatoire Orchestra under its leader François Antoine Habeneck: he was severely shaken by the technical perfection of the performance and particularly by the beguiling sheen of the strings. Until then he had had no idea of what a first-class orchestra was capable of achieving. The work stood before him 'as bright as the sun and as though physically tangible: where I had once seen only mystical constellations and toneless supernatural shapes, there now flowed, as though from innumerable springs, a stream of unending melody which drew my heart into the thrall of its ineffable power. The whole period during which my taste in music had been corrupted – a period which had begun at precisely the point when I first failed to grasp the meaning of Beethoven's late compositions, a

failure which became aggravated through my stultifying contact with the terrible world of the theatre – now sank down from sight as if into a deep abyss of shame and remorse' *(Mein Leben)*. Whether this orchestral rehearsal really did bring about a significant change in Wagner's outlook or whether, as is more plausible, he subsequently compressed a variety of experiences into this single incident, it remains undeniable that he found his way in Paris after years of uncertainty in matters of artistic taste and after years of running after outward success. One of his friends in Paris, the painter Friedrich Pecht, recalls in his autobiography the powers of critical discernment which Wagner showed in judging contemporary and earlier music; his familiarity with the whole literature of music seemed to him inconceivable in someone as young as Wagner. He soon gave up going to the opera, although he had initially admired its brilliant possibilities. He now knew how things stood and knew at least how he himself would or would not proceed. In his short story *Eine Pilgerfahrt zu Beethoven* ('A Pilgrimage to Beethoven'), written in 1840, he puts into

Court Theatre, Dresden,
2 January 1843
Producer: Ferdinand Heine.
Conductor: Richard Wagner
This wood engraving from the
Leipziger Illustrirte Zeitung
shows the final moments of the
first production. Senta throws
herself into the sea from a
rocky promontory stage right.
The Flying Dutchman's ship
then sinks beneath the waves.
Upstage left are Daland's house
and ship, with Mary, Daland
and Erik standing
terror-stricken at downstage.

Lyceum Theatre, London,
3 October 1876
First production in English, by
the Carl Rosa Opera Company.
The first time a Wagnerian
opera was staged in England
was on 23 July 1870 at the
Theatre Royal, Drury Lane,
when it was sung in Italian. The
apotheosis at the end of the
opera. By her act of
self-sacrifice Senta has
redeemed the Dutchman from
his curse. Both soar aloft 'in
transfigured form' in an aureole
of clouds. Daland's ship is on
the left. The Dutchman's vessel
had been moored alongside a
practicable dock stage right and
is now seen sinking beneath the
waves. It was from this dock
that Senta had leapt into the
sea.

41

Beethoven's mouth his own ideas on the future development of opera. There would be none of the usual 'arias, duets, trios and such like'; instead, the new opera would be a 'true musical drama', comparable to the plays of Shakespeare. Audiences would walk out of the theatre and call the composer a fool, because all they cared for was 'sparkling falsehoods, brilliant nonsense and sugar-coated boredom'.

The prose draft of *Der fliegende Holländer*, written in the spring of 1840, survives only as a fragment containing the second half of Act II and the whole of Act III. In this sketch, as in others, large passages of the dialogue, such as the duet in Act II between Senta and the Dutchman, are already very close to their final form. As in Heine's version, the action still takes place on the Scottish coast. Only after the completion of the full score was it transferred to Norway, the names of Donald and Georg being altered to Daland and Erik respectively. Senta is still called Anna in the prose draft.

'I reached an understanding on the subject with Heine himself,' Wagner wrote in the *Autobiographische Skizze.* Heinrich Laube had introduced Wagner to Heine in Paris. Unfortunately we have no further information about this understanding and do not know whether it was concerned with the question of authorship or with thematic considerations. Wagner hoped to receive a commission to write a one-act opera of the type then in fashion and given as a so-called *lever de rideau* ('curtain-raiser') before ballet performances. He drafted a short prose sketch in French, which he sent to Eugène Scribe, the most famous of all opera librettists, on 6 May 1840. Their collaboration, however, came to nothing. On 4 June and 26 July he wrote to Meyerbeer appealing for help and mentioning that he had already written words and music for Senta's ballad, the song of the Norwegian sailors and that of the Dutchman's crew. This had been done with a view to an audition at which individual numbers were performed and a decision taken as to the ultimate acceptance of the work. Meyerbeer arrived in Paris during the summer and introduced Wagner to the new director of the Opéra, Léon Pillet, to whom Wagner showed his sketch for *Der fliegende Holländer*. The subject certainly appealed to Pillet, but he had no confidence in an unknown composer such as Wagner. After months of waiting and false expectations, Pillet offered to buy the sketch from him and Wagner, rather than lose everything, agreed. He sold Pillet 'le sujet du Hollandais volant' for 500 francs under an

Teatro Comunale, Bologna, 20 November 1877
Designer: Tito Azolini
Set-design for Act I, probably for the Italian première, which was given in an Italian translation in Bologna in 1877. The gloomily charged atmosphere which surrounds the sudden appearance of the Dutchman's vessel in the wild and rocky bay has been well captured here. There is a clear attempt to express the drama of the music in the sets on stage.

agreement dated 2 July 1841; and with that he signed away his latest hopes for a Paris première. The proceeds of the sale, however, allowed him to keep his head above water for a little while longer and to take his time over the composition of his own version of *Der fliegende Holländer.* Pillet passed the sketch on to Paul Foucher who versified it. Foucher's libretto was then set to music by Pierre-Louis Philippe Dietsch whom we shall later find conducting the 1861 performances of *Tannhäuser.* Their joint collaboration, *Le Vaisseau fantôme,* was first performed on 9 November 1842; it ran for eleven performances and was praised by Hector Berlioz.

Wagner moved to Meudon on 29 April in order to complete the opera in peace. The poem was drafted within the space of ten days, between 18 and 28 May. When the piano he had hired arrived at the beginning of July, he was worried that he might have forgotten how to compose. He was beside himself with joy when ideas came to him for the steersman's song and the spinning chorus. The orchestral sketch of Act III was completed on 22 August, barely seven weeks after he had begun the work. The overture was written during November and the full score lay finished on his desk by 20 November.

What proved decisive in persuading Wagner to base his own version on Heine's account of the legend was the latter's 'genuinely dramatic treatment of the redemption

granted this Ahasuerus of the oceans.' 'Redemption', still only hinted at in *Die Feen,* is a theme which will preoccupy Wagner for the rest of his life. In Heine, it is true, redemption is parodied: the Flying Dutchman's wife throws herself into the sea in order to protect herself against infidelity. Wagner, on the other hand, was deadly serious in his handling of the theme: Senta, overcome by pity for the Dutchman's plight, which she knows from tales told by Mary, her nurse, sees it as her duty in life to sacrifice herself for his sake and to release him from his curse. Otherwise, Wagner has taken over Heine's plot in outline. The Dutchman's narration, which is introduced into the second act of Heine's version, has been recast as a great entrance monologue. Even the ending of the prose sketch follows Heine's account, with the Dutchman's vessel sinking beneath the waves. Only in the final version of the libretto is the apotheosis added by way of expansion: 'the sea rises up and then sinks back in a whirlpool. The Dutchman and Senta, in transfigured form, rise up out of the sea; he holds her in his embrace.' For Wagner, this scene was dramaturgically crucial, though it has caused major headaches for set designers and technicians.

Wagner's own invention is the dramaturgically important figure of Erik, the young huntsman who loves Senta and who warns her of her obsessions. There is no doubt that

Wagner invented this triangular relationship between Senta, Erik and the Dutchman in order to add dramatic weight to the substance of the legend. The solution of the conflict nevertheless remains unsatisfactory, being constructed along the lines of a traditional operatic intrigue: the Dutchman sees Senta alone with Erik, considers her to be unfaithful and believes himself betrayed. In order to spare her eternal damnation, which is the fate of all who are unfaithful to him, he sails away again. Senta resolves to prove her fidelity and throws herself into the sea. The two leading figures of the Dutchman and Senta are Wagner's first successful attempt to create dramatic characters with their own unique profile. The Dutchman is less the ghostly figure of the northern seas than an allegory of the lonely outcast, a tragic figure whom Wagner numbers among all the other 'hounded' exiles of western literature:

> In the bright Hellenic world we meet him in the wanderings of Odysseus and in his longing for homeland, house and hearth, and for his wife who, for this philanthropic son of old Hellas, was truly attainable and whom he finally attained. Having no earthly home, Christianity embodied this feature in the figure of the 'Wandering Jew': there was no earthly deliverance in store for such a wanderer as he, damned for ever and eternity to the living death of a life devoid of purpose and joy; the only yearning that remained for him was the longing for death, his only hope the chance

no longer to exist. As the Middle Ages came to an end, a new and active impulse drew the nations of the earth back towards *life,* an impulse which, within the context of world history, found its most successful expression in the urge for discovery. The sea now became the terrain of life, no longer the tiny inland sea of the Hellenic world but the earth-encircling ocean. This marked a break with the old world: Odysseus's longing to return to his homeland, hearth and wife, when nurtured on the sufferings of the Wandering Jew, had become a longing for death: it was now intensified in turn to the level of a desire for something new and unknown, something not yet present but already felt. This feature, with all its vast implications, is something we find in the myth of the Flying Dutchman, this epic poem of a seafaring nation from the period in world history of the great voyages of discovery. What strikes us here is a remarkable mixture, produced by the spirit of the people, of the character of the Wandering Jew with that of Odysseus. As punishment for his temerity, the Dutchman is condemned by the devil – a transparent image for the element of floodwater and storms – restlessly to roam the seas for all eternity. As an end for his anguish he longs, like Ahasuerus, for death; this form of release, denied to the Wandering Jew, may come through a woman who sacrifices herself to him out of love; yearning for such a woman thus drives the Dutchman to

Court Opera, Vienna,
18 August 1913
Designer: Anton Brioschi
Set-design for Act I. Rendering
by Brioschi from an original
design by Alfred Roller.
Although Roller retained the
traditional positioning of the
two adjacent ships, he
abandoned the usual Romantic
depiction of a Norwegian fjord.
The sets convey an impression
of barrenness, heaviness and
drama.

Regional Theatre, Eisenach,
after 1918
Scene from Act I. The
production shown here
remained the model for every
international stage for a number
of decades.

search her out. This woman, however, is no longer the Penelope of Odysseus, wooed by him in ages past and caring for him at home; it is woman in general, a woman who does not yet exist, who is longed for and foreseen, the woman who is infinitely womanly, in a word the woman of the future (*Eine Mittheilung an meine Freunde*).

Senta is this woman of the future. She has been alienated from her surroundings, from the girls of the village and from Erik; she is wistful, it is true, but inwardly strong and possessed by the idea of her duty in life. Once again we recognize in her the Leonore of Beethoven's *Fidelio,* the operatic character who was Wagner's great model. Senta's line, 'Wer du auch sei'st' ('Whoever you may be'), has been lifted word for word from Act II of *Fidelio.* Her wistful nature 'should not be interpreted in the sense of a modern, sickly sentimentality.' Rather is she 'a quite robust Nordic girl, who is utterly naïve even in her apparent sentimentality.' The impulse to redeem the Dutchman 'finds expression with her as a healthy madness such as can only be the case with people who are completely naïve' ('Bemerkungen zur Aufführung der Oper "Der fliegende Holländer"' ['Notes on performing the opera *Der fliegende Holländer*']).

The very core of the work is Senta's ballad which was also the first number to be written and composed. 'In this piece I unconsciously laid the thematic seed for the whole of the music of the opera: it was the condensed image of the entire drama, as it appeared in my mind's eye; and when the time came to choose a title for the finished work, I was sorely tempted to call it a "dramatic ballad",' Wagner wrote (*Eine Mittheilung an meine Freunde*). Of interest here is his comment that it was folk songs which provided him with the stimulation necessary to write the melodies of the ballad, the spinning chorus and that of the sailors. These three numbers have become his most popular pieces of music. However, the 'marked rhythmic vitality' of the folk song, which ultimately derives from the folk dance, is used only in the popular scenes. Where he had to express 'the feelings of the dramatic characters', such as 'were made known by them in expressive dialogue', he paid no heed to catchy tunes but reproduced the conversation in the music itself, 'in accordance with its emotional content'. The listener's sympathy was to be elicited not by 'the melodic expression on its own' but by 'the feeling which was being expressed'. 'The melody therefore had to emerge quite spontaneously from the

words'; Wagner was not trying to write an 'opera' in the modern sense, but to find music adequate to express the legend; and, since it was clear to him that 'the vast raging sea with its scattered legends could not be channelled sufficiently to produce a modern opera,' he allowed 'the whole aura of the legend to spread unimpededly over the whole work' and retold the legend in a single breath as though it were a poem. At least by 1851, when these observations were written down, it had become clear to Wagner that a good deal had remained no more than a wish and an idea and that the influence of traditional operatic melodies was only gradually lost. 'No longer and not yet. A work influenced at one and the same time by tradition and by change' is how Hans Mayer has described *Der fliegende Holländer.* The middle-class environment in which Senta lives – her father Daland, Erik, the steersman and Mary – all of these characters are depicted by means which musically, too, are conventional. Whether this happened consciously or subconsciously, it is nowadays interpreted as characteristic of this particular aspect of the work.

Wagner called the figure of the Flying Dutchman 'the mythical poem of the people', the 'first folk poem' to touch his heart. It was from this moment that he dated his true career as a poet 'and left behind him his career as a manufacturer of operatic libretti' *(Eine Mittheilung an meine Freunde).* He was convinced (and in this he was supported by contemporary scholarship) that what he described as a folk poem, legend or myth had not sprung from the reflection or intuition of a single individual. In its transmitted form, of course, it had to be expressed or written down by an individual person but what it expressed was in accord with the general conviction or general consciousness of a nation: it was common property. In the legends and popular poetry which have come down to us, ideas are expressed in which mankind can recognize himself and his world. General human archetypes can be perceived in this thematic store of common property.

By 27 June 1841 it had become clear to Wagner that he would not receive a commission for the work from the Paris Opéra and so he wrote to Count Redern, intendant of the Berlin Court Opera, offering him the first performance of *Der fliegende Holländer.* Meyerbeer, whose name he mentioned, would put in a good word for him. Wagner sent the finished score to Berlin on 20 November, and on 9 December Meyerbeer wrote to Redern, recommending the Court Opera's acceptance of it: the court theatres of Germany should

Municipal Theatre, Remscheid,
1937
Producer: P. Bargelt
The old familiar spinning-room,
a traditional sight for
generations of opera-goers. A
small, intimate room in a log
cabin, the hearth to the left, the
portrait above the door, Senta
to the right in her armchair, the
girls in traditional costume,
some of them wearing blonde
plaits.

not bar their doors to this notable tone-poet, who was being forced to live in the most appallingly straitened circumstances. Although Redern was not ill-disposed towards the idea, he was unable to make a definite commitment, being on the point of retiring and not wishing to impose any obligations upon his successor.

Dresden was determined to forestall Berlin over the question of who should be first to produce *Der fliegende Holländer,* once it had seen the success enjoyed by *Rienzi. Der fliegende Holländer* entered the repertory on 2 January 1843, two and a half months after the first night of *Rienzi.* This showed somewhat thoughtless planning on the part of the administration, given the diametrically opposed nature of the two works. The audience came along expecting the same sort of spectacle as that provided by *Rienzi,* but too much was being asked of them and, after the initial performances, they quickly lost interest in so austere and gloomy a work. In spite of this Wagner felt able to describe the first night as a success, he and the singers being called repeatedly before the curtain. We should certainly not be justified in speaking of a failure, still less of a total disaster; it was simply that the work was not calculated to meet with a loud and tumultuous success. Wagner in any case was prouder of the unexpected success of his sombre new work than of the predictable success of *Rienzi. Der fliegende Holländer* was removed from the repertory after four performances, the administration being only too

happy to replace it with *Rienzi,* which was still proving such a draw at the box-office.

Wagner himself conducted, his unusual power and precision being praised by no less a critic than Hector Berlioz. He himself was thoroughly dissatisfied with what the Court Theatre had managed to achieve, finding only Wilhelmine Schröder-Devrient's performance as Senta worthy of praise. She was 'a dramatic artist in the fullest sense of the word'; but around her there reigned only 'awesome desolation'. It was her performance alone which 'rescued the work from total misunderstanding'. Johann Michael Wächter, who sang the title-role, was totally unsuited to the part; his 'large corporation, and in particular his broad, round face and the peculiar movements of his arms and legs, which he waved around to look like physical stumps' turned his portrayal of the demonic seafarer into something approaching the ridiculous. Wagner reports that new sets had been commissioned, but the Dresden stage technicians evidently had an off-day. In the third act 'the full fury of the orchestra could not stir the sea from its slumbers nor the phantom ship from its secure mooring.' Even the ships' rigging was reputedly inauthentic and, according to a contemporary newspaper report, the aureole of clouds at the end of the work looked if anything like a nest of straw, which caused the audience a good deal of merriment. But what most surprised the Dresdeners was the fact that Wagner had presented them with 'such an utterly plain, impoverished and

Smetana Theatre, National
Theatre, Prague,
20 March 1959
Producer: Václav Kašlík.
Designer: Josef Svoboda.
Conductor: Jaroslav Vogel
The designer has attempted
here to break up the realistic
design model and to use a
collage technique, including a
powerfully expressionist
handling of light and shade
effects. There is a female figure
head (Senta ?) on the bow of
the Dutchman's vessel.

Bavarian State Opera, Munich,
23 October 1964
Producer: Hans Hotter.
Designer: Günther
Schneider-Siemssen. Conductor:
Hans Gierster
During the 1950s and 1960s,
the final apotheosis with Senta
and the Dutchman soaring
heavenwards was often replaced
by a kind of aurora borealis in
the night sky.

gloomy work' (*Eine Mittheilung an meine Freunde*). It was not until 1865 that *Der fliegende Holländer* was revived in Dresden. A performance in 1881 was attended by Wagner himself, in the course of a visit to the city.

The second theatre to stage the work was far-away Riga, on 22 May 1843. The first performance in Cassel on 5 June 1843, rehearsed and conducted by Ludwig Spohr, must have been a technically outstanding achievement: two impressive sailing ships passed easily over the stage, came to anchor, rocked to and fro and then tacked about; storm clouds, moonlight, transfiguring glow, everything was done with ease and as though by magic. Audiences expected as much from any new opera if it was to be successful. The Cassel production, which was backed by Spohr's authority, was of major significance for Wagner since it was the first time that a well-known theatre outside Dresden had risked performing one of his works.

Berlin did not follow until 7 January 1844. The new intendant, Karl Theodor von Küstner, who had refused to accept *Der fliegende Holländer* in Munich on the grounds that it was unsuited to the German stage and incomprehensible to German audiences (Wagner was of the opinion that the work was uniquely suited to German opera-houses) was finally forced to honour his predecessor's promise. Wagner had insisted on his doing so since early in 1842 since he feared that the Paris production of Dietsch's opera would forestall him. French imports always sold well on the German stage and there was the risk that his own opera would be dismissed as a secondary and inferior reworking of the story. Wagner himself conducted the first two performances, which took place in the theatre on the Gendarmenmarkt, the opera-house having recently burned down.

A sketch has survived from the Berlin performances, by the designer Johann Karl Jakob Gerst, which hitherto has always been incorrectly described as a set-design for the first Dresden production. The sheet is dated 24 September 1842 and bears Gerst's signature. He assembled the sets from whatever was available in the theatre store, making a note of whatever was missing. The 'bare rocks', for example, had to be specially built. The two ships came from the ballet *Der Seeräuber* ('The Corsair'), the cyclorama and masts from *Oberon*. Daland's front room was Gretchen's parlour in *Faust*, to an original design by Karl Schinkel, and had already done additional duty in the play *Columbus*. The house in Act III was a Swiss chalet from *Wilhelm Tell*. Writers on Wagner have often poked fun at this last example, claiming that it shows signal disregard for the Master's instructions. It should be remembered, however, that the practice of reusing sets was quite common throughout the nineteenth century: the number of works in the repertory was constantly changing and swelled by a dozen or more new productions every year, making it financially out of the question to prepare new sets for each new work. Thanks to the costume reforms of Count Brühl and to Karl Schinkel's work on set-design, the Berlin Opera was in a class of its own in matters of staging new works throughout the decades under consideration. Since the theatre store was destroyed in the same fire which gutted the opera-house, we can no longer be certain whether or not Gerst's sets were put together from the different elements described. The theatre playbill mentions only a 'new sea-set', so that the remaining sets may well have been assembled from whatever happened to be available. To judge from his report to Minna, Wagner at least was quite taken with the performance, which was well received by the Berlin public. The press, however, was critical of this first of Wagner's operas to be performed in the city. The work disappeared from the repertory after 25 February and was not revived until 1868, when the distinguished cast included Franz Betz as the Dutchman, Vilma von Voggenhuber as Senta and Albert Niemann as Erik, names which were themselves sufficient to ensure the work's acceptance.

For a number of years no other theatre was willing to risk a production of *Der fliegende Holländer*. Wagner in the meantime had fled from Dresden and settled down in exile in Zurich, where the director of the town's theatre, Wilhelm Löwe, persuaded him to produce and conduct the work in 1852. New sets were built and in spite of the fact that conditions were 'wretched, crude and cramped', everything was 'properly indicated and purpose-built' so that, in Wagner's view, these performances could serve as a model for larger theatres as well (letter to Wilhelm Fischer of 9 May 1852). Certainly, the Zurich performances gave him far more pleasure than the 'infinitely clumsy and lacklustre' achievement of the technically superior Dresden theatre. With the great revolutionary writings of these early years in Zurich already behind him and now that the 'limited facilities of the Zurich opera-house' had robbed him of 'all his illusions about drama', he was surprised to see how far the 'operatic' element of *Der fliegende Holländer* was shown off to advantage.

State Opera, Hamburg,
6 April 1966
Producer and designer: Wieland
Wagner. Conductor: Leopold
Ludwig. Daland: Arnold van
Mill. Dutchman: Theo Adam.
Steersman: Gerhard Unger
As was always the case, Wieland
Wagner not only produced the
work in question but also
designed his own sets. For him,
Der fliegende Holländer is a
'scenic triad of myth,
psychology and music'. The
fixed structure which
encompasses the whole
forestage is Daland's ship, over
which the Dutchman's vessel
towers threateningly. The
Dutchman is here the
'Ahasuerus (Wandering Jew) of
the seas', Daland a money-bags
and seller of souls. Wieland
realized these same production
ideas, with minor modifications,
in Bayreuth in 1959, Stuttgart in
1961 and Copenhagen in 1966.
The Copenhagen production
was sold to Sydney, Australia,
and was still on view there as
late as 1977.

Franz Liszt, who at this time was director of music in Weimar and who had claimed of *Der fliegende Holländer* that 'No poet since Byron has conjured so pale a phantom from the gloom of night,' hoped to follow the success of *Lohengrin*, which had received its first performance in Weimar in 1850, with a production of the earlier work. He wrote to Wagner, asking for detailed instructions about sets and production. Wagner drafted his 'Bemerkungen zur Aufführung der Oper: "Der fliegende Holländer"' ('Notes on performing the opera *Der fliegende Holländer*'), the first in a series of instructions for stage designers, producers and conductors. One can already sense here in embryo Wagner's desire for model performances such as he was later to attempt to achieve in Munich and Bayreuth. The Weimar production opened on 16 February 1853 and for years remained a model of its kind. As was the case with the Leipzig performances of 1846 and the Zurich production of 1852, Wagner revised the orchestration of the score, in particular reducing the brass. In later years he frequently told both Cosima and King Ludwig II that he intended revising the opera again so that it might be worthy of taking its place among all his subsequent works, but his plans for an extensive revision of the score came to nothing. What Wagner demanded above all else for the Weimar production was a realistic portrayal of the storm-lashed sea and of the two ships; the pitching of the ships should be lifelike and be in time with the music. For the storm scenes Wagner suggested gauzes and lighting changes.

Between 1853 and 1857 there were new productions of *Der fliegende Holländer* in Schwerin, Wiesbaden, Olmütz, Frankfurt, Hanover, Karlsruhe and Prague. It was, however, not until 2 November 1860 that it was first performed at the Vienna Court Opera and not until 1871 that it entered the repertory of the new opera-house on the Ringstrasse, which had been opened two years previously.

The first of the series of model performances of Wagner's works to be mounted at Ludwig II's Court Opera in Munich was the production of *Der fliegende Holländer* which opened on 4 December 1864 under the direction of Franz Lachner. Wagner, who was most anxious that the performance should be exemplary, wrote to Lachner, admitting that he had a particular weakness for this early work of his, since, unlike any of the later compositions, it contained popular elements which the conductor must seek to bring out. The new sets were designed by Heinrich Döll (Acts I and III) and Angelo Quaglio (Act II), with costumes and props by Franz Seitz. The National Theatre was sold out and five policemen were required to stop the crowd from storming the box-office when advance ticket sales opened. This was the first time the work was performed with the new ending of the overture and the third act, which had been revised to incorporate the redemption theme.

The Munich production created a pattern which remained valid for decades and which was frequently imitated elsewhere. In the bay in Act I, Daland's vessel was always on the right and the Dutchman's on the left. The approach of the Dutchman's ship from out of the distance was indicated by means of a small ship passing in front of the backcloth and then disappearing into the wings, whereupon the full-sized vessel appeared on stage in its place. The storm at sea was contrived by means of water-cloths.

Daland's front room in Act II was a middle-class living-room with whitewashed walls, a wooden ceiling, a fireplace with the usual 'maritime objects' such as a model ship, a globe, charts and fishing nets, the portrait of the Dutchman and Senta's 'fireside armchair'. A sketch which has survived from the first performance in Bologna in 1877 is a copy of the Munich interior. Any trace of a characteristically Norwegian style is still missing. It was only under the influence of the first Bayreuth production of 1901 that Daland's parlour became more rustic and more austere, a room built entirely of beams and reminiscent in style of a log cabin.

In Act III the position of the two ships was the reverse of that seen in Act I. The sides of the stage were filled, on the left, by the front of Daland's house and, on the right, the rocky ledge from which Senta plunges into the sea. During the sailors' festivities Daland's ship was hung with lanterns, creating an effective contrast with the Dutchman's pitch-black vessel. The closeness of the two ships, lying at anchor beside each other, caused a number of problems, since not infrequently there was insufficient room to move and the scale of the fully rigged sailing ships was bound to be out of proportion to that of the singers.

The Dutchman was slow to circumnavigate the globe. He reached London in 1870 as *L'Olandese dannato*. Performed in Italian, it was the first of Wagner's opera to be produced in England. An English-language version followed in 1876, before the opera was finally given in German in 1882. Stockholm audiences first heard the work in Swedish (1872) and those in Budapest in Hungarian (1873); the American première was sung in Italian (Philadelphia 1876) and the first Copenhagen production was given in Danish (1884). Performances then followed in quick succession in Barcelona (1885), Buenos Aires (1887), Mexico (1891), Lisbon (1893) and Moscow (1894). As an indication of how many of these productions failed to achieve the artistic level which Wagner considered indispensable to an understanding of the work, we may quote the example of the London revival of 1891, when, according to George Bernard Shaw's account, Daland's ship had been rooted 'so monumentally in the Shaftesbury stage that even I could ride out the storm in her without a qualm.' Apart from the two ships, 'there is one prima donna's spinning-wheel (practicable) out of Faust for Miss Damian, and three broken and incomplete ones (desperately impracticable) for the chorus' (*The World*, 4 November 1891). The first performance in French of Wagner's *Le Vaisseau fantôme* took place in Brussels on 6 April 1872, followed in 1897 by the Paris Opéra-Comique. The opera had to wait until 27 December 1937 for its first performance at the Palais Garnier.

Bayreuth Festival, 1969
Producer: August Everding.
Designer: Josef Svoboda.
Conductor: Silvio Varviso
Chorus scene from Act III.
Starkly expressionistic effects of
light and shade. The flight of
steps on the right was used for
the turbulent action of the
chorus. It was from here, too,
that Senta plunged into the sea.
To the left is the deck of
Daland's ship, which was used
in all three acts as a basic acting
area.

Chronologically the first of his works
which Wagner considered 'worthy of Bayreuth', *Der fliegende Holländer* was the last to
enter the festival repertory. Siegfried Wagner
produced it there in 1901, in collaboration
with Cosima. And with it the Bayreuth canon
was complete for the first time. The work was
performed without intervals, the sets being
changed behind a drop curtain. As was the
case with all of Cosima's productions, the sets
were designed by Max Brückner and painted
by him at his studios in Coburg. In their naturalistic style they in no way differed from the
then traditional standards. Cosima certainly
laid great emphasis upon Norwegian local colour, with carved beams and ornaments both
inside and outside Daland's house, Norwegian tools and Norwegian costumes for the
women. For Senta Cosima chose a traditional
Norwegian bridal dress. The final apotheosis
was achieved by having two life-size dummies
soaring upwards. In their facial expressions,
costumes and even their shoes, they were
realistic copies of the singers Anton van Rooy
and Emmy Destinn who for many years were
the most internationally sought-after inter-

preters of the roles of the Dutchman and
Senta. As a result, parts which had long been
considered thankless now became popular
among the great singers, with interpreters of
the title-role including Feodor Chaliapin and
Francesco d'Andrade. Later singers asso-
ciated with the part have included Michael
Bohnen and Friedrich Schorr, in New Bayreuth Hans Hotter, Hermann Uhde and
George London, and, most recently, Thomas
Stewart, José van Dam and Simon Estes. For
many years Maria Müller was the leading
Senta of the day; at the Metropolitan Opera,
New York, the role was notably sung by
Maria Jeritza and Kirsten Flagstad in the
1920s and 1930s, at La Scala by Maria Canig-
lia and then Birgit Nilsson, and in post-war
Bayreuth by Astrid Varnay, Anja Silja and Le-
onie Rysanek; the leading interpreters of re-
cent years have been Lisbeth Balslev and
Hildegard Behrens.

All new productions of the work have been
concerned on the whole with technical improvements, while the old scheme of production has generally been left unaltered. A use
was found for recent inventions such as films

State Theatre, Cassel,
15 February 1976
Producer: Ulrich Melchinger.
Designer: Thomas
Richter-Forgach. Conductor:
James Lockhart
The Dutchman's monologue
performed as a black mass; with
virgins and a naked girl
outstretched on a kind of altar.
The Dutchman, acting as a
priest of Satan, kills her by
driving his sword into her
vagina. Wagner's idea of
redemption is reduced to sexual
perversion. When, in addition
to all this, a hen was
slaughtered and its blood
poured over the girl, the
audience's limit of tolerance
was reached and riots broke
out.

and projections to solve the problem of the storm scenes and the final apotheosis, and the results were often visually impressive. The main emphasis was placed on the work's nautical aspects. But those producers and designers who made a serious attempt to show Wagner's contemporary relevance felt a sense of unease when confronted by repeated revivals of their own productions. In 1922 Oskar Fritz Schuh warned producers of *Der fliegende Holländer* that it was essential here, above all else, not to lose one's way in matters of nautical detail; what was more important was to grasp the gloomy balladesque atmosphere. For Schuh, as for Wagner, it was the sea which was central to the action and it should be visible even in Act II. The arrival of the Dutchman's ship should appear sudden and unexpected; the vessel should be very much larger than Daland's ship and inspire a real sense of dread. He also demanded that the usual apotheosis at the end should be relegated to the trap at the back of the stage and instead merely be hinted at by means of lighting techniques which might suggest, for example, a radiant dawn. Schuh further regarded it as an indispensable requirement that the work be performed without intervals. His most important ideas have really only found general acceptance since the end of the Second World War.

The greatest problems were posed by Act II. Senta's ballad was staged rather like a private concert with the spinning girls all dressed in identical costumes, with flaxen plaits and little bonnets, and arranged in a *tableau vivant* around Senta.

Various attempts were made during the 1920s to overcome these stage conventions. Two examples are worth elaborating to illustrate the point. In the 1926 production at the municipal theatre in Königsberg the arrival of the Dutchman's ship was staged in such a way as to appear unreal and terrifying. Daland's ship was consigned to the wings and the set consisted simply of black rocky ledges and a blood-red cyclorama on which flashes of lightning were projected. The blood-red sky disappeared and the Dutchman's ship, covering the whole width of the stage, rose up out of the trap, sinister and ghostlike.

The new production mounted by the Kroll Opera in Berlin on 15 January 1929 turned into something of a political affair. It had been entrusted to Jürgen Fehling, a producer from the straight theatre who had started his career under Leopold Jessner. The sets were designed by Ewald Dülberg and the conductor was Otto Klemperer. The chorus had been rehearsed by Hugo Rüdel, chorusmaster of the Bayreuth Festival. The version

Teatro alla Scala, Milan,
3 February 1966
Producer: Frank de Quell.
Designer: Peter Bisseger.
Conductor. Wolfgang Sawallisch.
Senta: Leonie Rysanek
Scene from Act II. During
Senta's Ballad, the wall of the
spinning-room flies open to
reveal the sky and the sea, the
Dutchman's two elements.
Senta's desire to break out of
her surroundings became the
dominant theme of all new
productions during the 1970s.

Bayreuth Festival, 1980
Producer: Harry Kupfer.
Designer: Peter Sykora.
Costumes: Reinhard Heinrich.
Conductor: Dennis Russell
Davies. Senta: Lisbeth Balslev
Scene from Act II. Daland's
house as a nineteenth-century
warehouse, with living
accommodation on the ground
floor. Senta is, as it were,
walled in by her surroundings.
A single window opens to the
outside world, a motif of
yearning from Romantic
iconography. It is from this
window that she plunges to her
death. In the course of her
visions of the Dutchman, the
walls of the house fly apart.

performed was the original Dresden Version without the later ending involving the theme of redemption, and a manuscript score was used from which Wagner himself had conducted the work in 1844. There was not a trace of Norwegian folklore. Senta was an unpretentious peasant girl, wearing a rough woollen pullover sweater and a tweed skirt, who looked as though she might have stepped out of a drawing by Käthe Kollwitz and the sailors looked like contemporary seamen in woollen jumpers, but without their usual slouch hats and beards. The spinning girls were no longer pretty dolls in traditional Norwegian costumes but tough and used to working in aprons and smocks. The Dutchman, finally, had neither a hat nor a beard.

Dülberg's sets were in the style of the 'New Objectivity' and did not attempt to create an illusion in the traditional sense; what they did instead was to translate the work's sombre balladesque nucleus into concrete imagery. The predominant colour was a dark slate-blue. Daland's parlour was transparent; changes of lighting brought the sea and the Dutchman's ship into view. Senta's ballad was the ecstatic outburst of a violent emotion causing consternation among the other girls. With the help of up-to-date stylistic means, the work's historical remoteness was overcome so that Wagner's elemental drama was able to achieve so stunning an effect that the audience was reduced to a state of bewilderment hitherto unknown in the opera-house. The work was distorted to the point where it became recognizable. The fact that the singers, too, were forced to rethink and correct their own interpretations is shown by a remark made by Moje Forbach, who sang the part of Senta in the production. Fehling told her that she had 'a flowing operatic walk' which made her look as though she were wearing a train to her dress. The expressionist style of acting which was being developed at that time in Berlin was now a required part of operatic training as well.

Critical reaction was not slow in coming. The various Wagner Societies protested publicly against such a 'sin committed against the spirit of Wagner' and called upon 'all who understand art' to rise up and protect Germany's threatened cultural inheritance. The state was asked to intervene as a force of order. In the discussions which followed, the counter-argument was quite rightly put forward that not a single hand had ever been lifted before now to protest against the slovenly treatment of Wagner's works at the hands of provincial theatres.

The mentality of the protesters was summarized by the Berlin newspaper *Der Montag Morgen*: 'What they understand by Wagner is the popular hero's pouting breast, a swastika in his buttonhole, ancient German discipline and morals, the grandiose meaningless gesture, full beards, heaving bosoms, long and flowing flaxen hair, ironclad fists and Long-Live-the-Emperor' (19 February 1929). A book written in 1935 with the characteristic title *Wachet auf. Ein Mahnruf aus dem Zuschauerraum für Richard Wagners Bühnenbild* ('Awake. A word of warning from the audience about Richard Wagner's scenery') observed with evident satisfaction that the 'illness of the day', which consisted in 'self-indulgent and irreverent experimentation', now seemed to be past and that 'what is truly good, what is genuinely Wagnerian', the creative artist's unadulterated spirit (whatever that may have meant), had once more been allowed to prevail. The totalitarian state had eliminated the individualist element in its midst. No one would deny for a moment that novelty and nonconformity purely for their own sake are worthless and that they may be no more than the pretext for a sense of elitism on the part of self-appointed connoisseurs and those in the know; but more important – and more numerous – are the examples when what is new arises from a genuine necessity and when it conveys topical insights. Wieland Wagner's remark that attempting to avoid change is tantamount to 'turning the virtue of fidelity into the sin of fossilization' is still valid today; and Gustav Mahler's observation that 'tradition is slovenliness' is more than just a witty turn of phrase.

The controversy has been allowed to range widely because it is symptomatic of the debate which has raged over Wagner not only during the years in question but in respect of all his other works as well. *Der fliegende Holländer* was subjected to an overhaul during the New Bayreuth era of Wieland and Wolfgang Wagner.

A new chapter in the stage history of the work was opened in February 1962 with Joachim Herz's productions at the Komische Oper in East Berlin, at Leipzig in October of the same year and at the Bolshoi Theatre in Moscow in May 1963. All three productions basically followed a single concept. The Komische Oper's set-designs were by Rudolf Heinrich and were revived for the Leipzig and Moscow productions by Reinhart Zimmermann. Herz, who studied under Walter Felsenstein and who supported his mentor's stylistic principle of a realistic music theatre, trans-

Metropolitan Opera, New York, March 1979
Producer and designer: Jean-Pierre Ponnelle.
Conductor: James Levine
Chorus scene in Act III. The ship's afterdeck provides a unit set for all three acts. Ghostly atmosphere with skeletons. At the front of the stage, the steersman lies asleep by the steering-wheel: the whole opera is a nightmare which he dreams.

Bavarian State Opera, Munich, 25 January 1981
Producer and designer: Herbert Wernicke. Conductor: Wolfgang Sawallisch.
Dutchman: Franz Ferdinand Nentwig
The Dutchman's entrance monologue delivered through an open window. The outcast longs to become a respectable citizen. The stage remains a unified space for all three acts. In the doorway at left is the gangway leading to Daland's ship. The furniture is shrouded in dust-sheets, which are removed for the spinning scene in Act II.

ferred the action to the time at which the work was written, in other words the bourgeois milieu of the period between 1815 and 1848. Daland's ship was a paddle-steamer and the meeting in Act II between Daland, Senta and the Dutchman took place in an entirely realistic manner around the living-room table. Senta longs for an element of unreality and eeriness to enter the closed confines of her present environment. The stormy sea, projected onto a gauze, formed the basis of the whole action. It flooded Senta's ballad and her duet with the Dutchman. Herz encountered problems over the ending. In Berlin he staged it as far as the figure of the Dutchman was concerned in the way Wagner himself had intended, with the Dutchman renouncing redemption out of his love for Senta. Senta no longer sacrificed herself by an act of conscious suicide but died 'of a sudden numbness in her heart'. According to Herz, 'The farewell is the farewell of two lovers'. For his film version (the first time one of Wagner's operas had been filmed) he evolved a different idea: confined by her bourgeois life, Senta dreams of the freedom of the sea and dreams her own death, before waking up, seizing the portrait of the Dutchman and running out of the house, like Ibsen's Nora, towards the sun as it lifts itself out of the sea.

In 1973 the opera was actually performed on water, its original element, on the floating stage of the Bregenz Festival. Daland's and the Dutchman's ships sailed as large as life across Lake Constance. In Nuremberg in 1977 Luca Ronconi attempted a simpler theatrical expedient of having the action of the opera develop out of water. His set-designer Pier Luigi Pizzi had lined the entire stage with grey cloths which could be set in motion like waves. The characters emerged from the water, had their say and then disappeared back into it. There were no ships, only a large, seductively golden model of one which the Dutchman offered to Daland in exchange for his daughter.

The 1976 Cassel production by Ulrich Melchinger, with sets by Thomas Richter-Forgach, took place on two narrative levels: on the one hand there was the cosy bourgeois mid-nineteenth-century world of Daland, in which Senta was bargained over as though she were a remunerative investment and which the Dutchman entered in the costume of a baroque nobleman; and, on the other, there was the world of darkness of jet-black Romanticism, with its mixture of superstition, fear and perversion. The Dutchman was a typically Romantic Dr Jekyll and Mr Hyde, being in reality a respectable citizen, but in the imagination of those who had invented this ghostly apparition, a miscreant, a sinner and a kind of Marquis de Sade, scandalously embodying the sexual repressions of bour-

Teatr Wielki, Warsaw,
12 April 1981
Producer: Erhard Fischer.
Designer: Roland Aeschlimann.
Costumes: Irena Biegańska.
Conductor: Antoni Wicherek.
Senta: Hanna Lisowska.
Act II as a scene from the working world. The spinning-room is a brick hall as in a factory and the spinning girls work at spinning machines, to which they are virtually bound by ropes.

geois society. The steersman dreamt the Dutchman's monologue as a black mass, the sailors' festivities were staged as a brawl and an outburst of mass hysteria in the course of which Erik stabbed Senta to death at the moment of her throwing herself between him and the Dutchman. The steersman, too, was murdered. Senta's desire to redeem the Dutchman was simply an *idée fixe,* a figment of her imagination; the Dutchman got up and left; the theme of redemption at the end of the work must have sounded like mockery.

The opera became a product of the *Sturm und Drang* in Harry Kupfer's production for the 1978 Bayreuth Festival (sets by Peter Sykora, costumes by Reinhard Heinrich). The production impressed first of all by virtue of its being performed at breakneck speed without intervals, with twelve changes of scene taking place during the action and requiring the utmost precision on the part of the technical crew; it impressed, too, by virtue of the quite stunning chorus scenes in Act III and the theatrical imagination of the staging. What took place on stage was Senta's psychodrama, her own vision of her duty in life and her life-long dream. It follows from this that the ballad became the starting-point for Kupfer's interpretation. Senta was on stage from the beginning of the opera until the very end; everything that happened took place in her imagination. Two hands formed the Dutchman's vast ship, opening and releasing the Dutchman (Simon Estes) from his golden-red prison. In the duet between Senta and the Dutchman in Act II, which both of them sang as though it were an inner monologue, the prison-ship was transformed into an imaginary vessel of flowers and blossoms, a kind of lovers' cave. Here, too, there was no question of redemption, but only suicide. The crowd stood gaping at Senta's body as it lay on the pavement, scarcely moved by what they had seen but shaking their heads in disapproval. The music admitted of no redemptive solution: the original Dresden Version of the score was used.

At the Metropolitan Opera, New York, the 1950 production, with its realistic, three-dimensional sets, designed by the famous Robert Edmond Jones and realized by Charles Elson, remained in the repertory until the 1970s. The new 1979 production by Jean-Pierre Ponnelle, for which he also designed the sets and costumes, provoked a lively con-troversy among audiences and critics. Ponnelle had already mounted the same production in San Francisco in 1975, and had interpreted the opera as the young steersman's nightmare. This was the time when directors were generally fond of producing all operas, including Wagner's, as dreams. During the redemption theme at the end of the opera, the steersman woke up and rubbed his eyes with visible relief: happily it had all been a dream. *Time* Magazine was scandalized by the fact that an anti-Wagnerian producer from among Europe's most radical revisionists had been invited to work at the Metropolitan Opera, and it noted that New York audiences preferred their Wagner to be conventional. Until now they had been spared extreme, experimental productions in Wagnerian matters. For them Wagner had been first and foremost a festival of fine voices.

The basic idea behind the designer Herbert Wernicke's production, first seen at the National Theatre in Munich in January 1981, was the various levels of meaning which can be imposed on a uniform space. For Wernicke, the space occupied by the entire action was first of all 'some archetypal room, confusing and undefined'; it was recognized by the Dutchman as 'the room he longs for' and finally shown to be, in Wernicke's words, 'the concrete world of Daland'. The Dutchman, a buccaneer, who has cut himself off from society, would once again like to be a part of some human community; Senta, on the other hand, in the bourgeois idyll of this room – with its piano, its fireside chair, even its toy railway and its 'traditional German' furniture – projects onto the Dutchman her liberating vision of a man who is not part of this bourgeois world. This 'failure to understand each other's expectations' leads to the catastrophe. Senta stabs herself with Erik's hunting-knife. She is not the redemptress but the victim. The Dutchman remains sitting in his armchair by the fireside.

What all these interpretations have in common is a deep sense of scepticism towards Wagner's belief in the possibility of redemption through love. In spite of this the opera has continued to fascinate producers, precisely because its ending can be interpreted in so many different ways. Central to their interest are a critique of bourgeois society and the interpretative possibilities inherent in the counter-world of the Dutchman.

Königlich Sächsisches Hoftheater.

Sonntag, den 19. October 1845.

Zum ersten Male:

Tannhäuser

und

der Sängerkrieg auf Wartburg.

Große romantische Oper in 3 Akten, von Richard Wagner.

Personen:

Herrmann, Landgraf von Thüringen.	—	Herr Dettmer.
Tannhäuser,		Herr Tichatschek.
Wolfram von Eschinbach,		Herr Mitterwurzer.
Walter von der Vogelweide,	Ritter und Sänger.	Herr Schloß.
Biterolf,		Herr Wächter.
Heinrich der Schreiber,		Herr Curty.
Reimar von Zweter,		Herr Risse.
Elisabeth, Nichte des Landgrafen.	—	Dem. Wagner.
Venus.	—	Mad. Schröder-Devrient.
Ein junger Hirt.	—	Dem. Thiele.

Thüringische Ritter, Grafen und Edelleute.
Edelfrauen, Edelknaben
Aeltere und jüngere Pilger.
Sirenen, Najaden, Nymphen, Bachantinnen.
Thüringen. Wartburg.
Im Anfange des 13. Jahrhunderts.

Die neuen Costüme sind nach der Anordnung des Herrn Hofschauspieler Heine gefertigt.

Textbücher sind an der Casse das Exemplar für 3 Neugroschen zu haben.

Montag, den 20. October: Richard's Wanderleben. Lustspiel in 4 Akten, von Kettel.
Hierauf: Tanz-Divertissement.

Das Sonntags-Abonnement ist bei der heutigen Vorstellung aufgehoben.

Erhöhete Einlaß-Preise:

	Thlr.	Ngr.
Ein Billet in die Logen des ersten Ranges und das Amphitheater	1	10
Fremdenlogen des zweiten Ranges Nr. 14. und 29.	1	10
übrigen Logen des zweiten Ranges	1	—
Sperr-Sitze der Mittel- u. Seiten-Gallerie des dritten Ranges	—	20
Mittel- und Seiten-Logen des dritten Ranges	—	12½
Sperr-Sitze der Gallerie des vierten Ranges	—	10
Mittel-Gallerie des vierten Ranges	—	8
Seiten-Gallerie-Logen daselbst	—	5
Sperr-Sitze im Cercle	1	—
Parquet-Logen	1	—
das Parterre	—	15

Die Billets sind nur am Tage der Vorstellung gültig, und zurückgebrachte Billets werden nur bis Mittag 12 Uhr an demselben Tage angenommen.

Der Verkauf der Billets gegen sofortige baare Bezahlung findet in der, in dem untern Theile des Rundbaues befindlichen Expedition, auf der rechten Seite, nach der Elbe zu, früh von 9 bis Mittags 12 Uhr, und Nachmittags von 3 bis 4 Uhr statt.

Alle zur heutigen Vorstellung bestellte und zugesagte Billets sind Vormittags von früh 9 bis längstens 11 Uhr abzuholen, außerdem darüber anders verfüget wird.

Freibillets sind bei der heutigen Vorstellung nicht gültig.

Tannhäuser

My first glimpse of the Wartburg, which we drove past during the only sunlit hour of the whole journey, afforded me a real gleam of hope. The sight of the mountain stronghold which, if one approaches from Fulda, has plenty of time to create a favourable impression, inspired within me an unusual feeling of warmth and excitement. There was a mountain ridge lying some distance away and to one side, which I immediately labelled the 'Hörselberg' and, as we drove along the valley, I saw before my mind's eye the relevant scene in Act III of *Tannhäuser,* an image which has been fixed in my mind ever since.

Thus Wagner reports in his autobiography his journey from Paris to Dresden in April 1842. As was the case with *Der fliegende Holländer,* literary reminiscences were again mixed with personal impressions whenever he was carrying around within him the idea of a new work.

Wagner had first become interested in the legend of Tannhäuser in Paris during the winter of 1841/1842. The subject had been popularized in a number of different versions published during the previous decades. The first account is that found in Ludwig Tieck's *Der getreue Eckart und der Tannenhäuser* ('The Faithful Eckart and Tannenhäuser') of 1793. Achim von Arnim and Clemens von Brentano printed the old Tannhäuser ballad of 1521 in the first volume of *Des Knaben Wunderhorn* ('The Boy's Magic Horn'), published in 1806. It tells of the knight Tannhäuser and his visit to the Venusberg, where he spends a year living with Lady Venus until longing and remorse drive him out of his mountain retreat and to Rome, where he implores the pope's forgiveness; but Pope Urban IV is unable to absolve him from his sin: just as the bishop's staff which he holds in his hand will never again put forth leaves, so can Tannhäuser never attain God's grace. With heavy heart he returns to the Venusberg. On the third day the staff puts forth leaves and Pope Urban sends out messengers in search of Tannhäuser, but the latter is nowhere to be found.

As a result, the pope, like Tannhäuser, will be damned for all eternity.

Goethe wrote a review of this edition, drawing particular attention to the 'great Christian Catholic motif' and rejecting as a later addition the final line of the poem with its reference to the pope's being damned. In 1816 the Brothers Grimm published a prose version of the Tannhäuser ballad in their *Deutsche Sagen* ('German Legends') and in 1837 there appeared Heinrich Heine's typically ironical account of the legend, as the final section of the *Elementargeister* ('Elemental Spirits'). According to this account, Tannhäuser leaves Venus and goes to Rome, where he sings her praises in the presence of the pope; without having been absolved (but did he even bother to ask for absolution?), he returns to Lady Venus, passes on the pope's kind regards and settles down to live with her in a state of blissful domesticity. Wagner must have known Heine's version in addition to the others already mentioned, even though the only sources which he himself names are Tieck's and the old ballad of Tannhäuser.

What provided him with a starting-point for his own dramatic reworking of the legend was a 'chap-book', as he himself called it, which linked, albeit in a tenuous manner, the legend of Tannhäuser with the tale of the Wartburg Song Contest. Research has shown that the chap-book in question must have been Ludwig Bechstein's collection of legends, *Die Sagen von Eisenach und der Wartburg, dem Hörselberg und Reinhardsbrunn* ('The Legends of Eisenach and the Wartburg, the Hörselberg and Reinhardsbrunn'), published in 1835; certainly, no 'chap-book' as such is known to exist. Wagner no doubt came to describe Bechstein's collection in this way since he assumed the legends to be folk poems rather than Bechstein's own invention. Bechstein also mentions that Tannhäuser lived at the time of Landgrave Hermann and that the latter gathered poets around himself at his court on the Wartburg, where he held song competitions. Wagner already knew of the Wartburg Song Contest from E. T. A.

Hoffmann's story 'Der Streit der Sänger' ('The Singers' Contest') in Volume II of the *Serapionsbrüder* ('The Serapion Brethren') of 1819. Hoffmann's version, it may be added, was based upon Johann Christoph Wagenseil's book *Von der Meistersinger holdseliger Kunst* ('On the Fair Art of the Mastersingers'), published in Altdorf in 1697, which Wagner was later to draw on in writing the libretto of *Die Meistersinger von Nürnberg* ('The Mastersingers of Nuremberg'). At that time he felt that Hoffmann's ideas about the legend were thoroughly wrong-headed and so he set about looking for the original version. This was the first time that Wagner had not followed a ready-made model in drawing up his own version; instead he began a philological study, researching various sources and linking thematically a number of different subjects which he brought together to create a new and characteristically individual form. It was the philologist Samuel Lehrs, one of Wagner's friends in Paris who stood by him in time of need, who wrote to his brother at the university in Königsberg and asked him to send Wagner a copy of C. T. L. Lucas's *Ueber den Krieg von Wartburg* ('On the Wartburg Feud'), a monograph published in 1838 by the Royal German Society of Königsberg. Lucas printed the original Middle High German text of the Song Contest, which is reputed to have taken place in 1207. The contestants were the minnesingers Wolfram von Eschenbach, Walther von der Vogelweide, Biterolf, Reinmar, Heinrich der Schreiber and Heinrich von Ofterdingen and the theme of the competition was whether Landgrave Hermann or Duke Leopold of Austria deserved to be more highly praised. The contest got so out of hand that whoever lost was to be executed. Heinrich von Ofterdingen so incensed all the others present that only the Landgrave's wife was able to shield him against their anger. The magician Klingsor of Hungary was summoned to act as arbiter. He became involved in an argument with Wolfram and prophesied to the landgrave that the daughter of the king of Hungary would one day be his son's wife. The girl in question was Saint Elizabeth. According to Lucas's thesis, Heinrich von Ofterdingen was to be identified with Tannhäuser, which was sufficient justification for Wagner to call his own leading character Heinrich Tannhäuser. Even though he 'was able to use practically nothing of any substance' from the original version of the Song Contest, the text nevertheless showed him 'the German Middle Ages in a succinct coloration' of which until then he had had no inkling.

In June 1842 Wagner returned to Teplitz (modern Teplice) in Bohemia in the company of his mother, who lost a night's sleep following his telling her the legend of Tannhäuser. On his own he visited the ruined castle of Schreckenstein near Aussig (modern Ústí), in its strikingly romantic setting. He spent the night on 'a bed of straw' in the restaurant there and during the day wandered through the mountains of Saxon Switzerland. It was in this lonely mood that he jotted down in his diary the great prose draft for a three-act opera *Der Venusberg* ('The Mount of Venus'). This was on 22 June. He considered it 'a total success' and on 10 September 1842 wrote to Kietz, telling him of his conviction that his new opera would be his 'most original product yet'. Once again, both personal experiences and natural occurrences played their part. On the Wostrai, the highest mountain of the region, he heard a shepherd piping a dance tune and saw the second scene of Act I in his mind's eye; he even saw himself as one of the chorus of pilgrims filing past the young shepherd. In the church at Aussig (modern Ústí) he asked to see a painting of the madonna by Adolph Mengs, copied from an original by Carlo Dolci. The painting caused him 'an extraordinary sense of delight; and if Tannhäuser had been able to see it, I could have fully understood how it was that he turned away from Venus towards the Virgin Mary, without the question of piety ever entering into it.' There then follows a crucial sentence: 'At least I've now firmly made up my mind about Saint Elizabeth' (letter to Kietz of 10 September 1842).

It was not until the following April, by which time both *Rienzi* and *Der fliegende Holländer* had received their first performances and Wagner had been appointed Conductor to the Royal Court of Saxony, that he found occasion to complete the libretto. He returned to Teplitz (modern Teplice) for the summer break, where he began the composition sketch of Act I on 20 July but failed to make any real progress. He needed calm and composure in order to be able to work. Because of his exhausting professional commitments, it was not until the summer of 1844 that he found time to compose. He began the orchestral sketch of Act II at Loschwitz in September, finishing it on 15 October. The orchestral sketch of Act III was completed in Dresden on 29 December. The task of instrumentation occupied him during the months which followed and the full score was finished by 13 April 1845. Only after the whole work had been completed did Wagner alter the title to *Tannhäuser und der Sängerkrieg auf*

Court Theatre, Dresden,
19 October 1845
Costumes: Ferdinand Heine
Costume design for
Tannhäuser. This design also
served as a model for the first
performances in Paris in 1861.

Wartburg ('Tannhäuser and the Song Contest on the Wartburg'), since the original title [Der Venusberg = Mount of Venus = *mons Veneris*] had already given rise to ribald comments in Dresden.

'It was an all-consuming and voluptuous excitement,' Wagner wrote in *Eine Mittheilung an meine Freunde*, 'which kept my blood and nerves seething in a state of feverish agitation.' He was convinced that only a musician could deal adequately with such a subject. 'This work had better be good, otherwise I shall never be able to achieve anything good. I felt thoroughly spellbound by it; the first time I came into contact with the subject, and on each subsequent occasion, I trembled with warmth and ardour. Even after the lengthiest interruptions had kept me away from my work, it required only an instant to reimmerse myself in the unique aura which had intoxicated me the moment I had first conceived it,' he wrote to Karl Gaillard on 5 June 1845 on the occasion of his sending him a copy of the printed score.

The most important difference between Wagner's version and that of his predecessors concerns the central figure of Elisabeth, the polar opposite of Venus. Wolfram's mention of her name in Act I persuades Tannhäuser to return with the other minnesingers to the Wartburg. She protects him in Act II from the anger of the assembled company, following his song in praise of love which, for him, means love of Venus; and when Tannhäuser fails to find absolution of his sins in Rome and seeks to return to the Venusberg, it is Elisabeth's compassion and self-sacrifice which finally redeem him. Once again there is a tragic triangular relationship involving the hapless lovers Wolfram, Elisabeth and Tannhäuser. In the song contest, which is the pivotal point of Act II, we find Wagner writing very much as a music dramatist. Here music itself has become the theme of the opera. The task imposed upon the minnesingers is no longer to praise their respective suzerains but to fathom the nature of love. In its lay-out this scene is entirely the invention of Wagner himself in his new role as poet-composer; it is introduced in order to allow him to put forward his ideas about music drama. In his own words,

'It is obvious that only the poetic intention could and should predominate here, the more so since this scene has to precipitate the catastrophe. Having the singers trying to outdo each other by means of vocal expertise, embellishments and *cadenzas* might have been appropriate in a voice competition but not in a dramatic contest

involving thoughts and feelings. On the other hand, this contest of poets, in which each of the participants concerned lays bare his very soul, would have failed to achieve any dramatic impact at all without what I take to be the highest and most varied force of musical expression [...] I chose my own direction as a musician who, starting from a firm belief in the inexhaustible richness of music, desires to produce the highest work of art, namely drama. I say 'desires' in order at the same time to give an indication of my efforts in this direction. Whether I can indeed achieve that aim is something I am not in a position to judge (letter to Freiherr von Biedenfeld of 17 January 1849).

Whenever attempts are made to characterize Tannhäuser's dilemma, they are invariably couched in terms of such slogans as sacred and profane love and the antitheses of asceticism and eroticism. Wagner himself saw the issue as rather less straightforward. Right from the outset, in his *Mittheilung an meine Freunde,* he parallels Tannhäuser's fate to the facts of his own life. It is true that he gives only vague hints which biographers have either ignored or failed to decipher and yet,

Court Theatre, Dresden, 1847 Closing scene, taken from the *Leipziger Illustrirte Zeitung* of 1855, probably based on the 1847 Dresden production with the new ending. Tannhäuser sinks to his knees by Elisabeth's body.

Court Theatre, Hanover,
21 January 1855
Designer: Carl Wilhelm
Doepler
The Hall of Song in Act II, as
conceived for the first
production in Hanover. The
original design was the work of
Doepler and the present
drawing was probably prepared
for an inventory of the theatre
store. Clearly influenced by the
sketch in Wagner's scenario: A
Gothic hall viewed from an
angle.

in the context of Tannhäuser, they are an important clue to the latter's character. Tannhäuser/Wagner was disgusted not by sensuality *per se* but by its modern, frivolous and trivial variant and he longed for something pure, chaste and virginal as a 'means of satisfying a nobler but basically still sensual desire' which the present age was incapable of satisfying. From the 'sublime heights of purity and chastity' he felt a sense of ecstatic and blissful loneliness in a 'clear and sanctified element of ether'. But, having reached those heights, he longed to return to the depths, 'from the sunlit radiance of the most chaste purity to the familiar shadow of the most human and loving embrace.' From these heights, moreover, his glance perceived 'woman: [...] the woman who, like some celestial star, directed Tannhäuser heavenwards from the Venusberg's caves of wanton delight.' Elsewhere in the same essay Wagner repeats this train of thought and comes to the conclusion that such a yearning seems to be none other than the desire 'to perish in an element of infinite love such as does not exist on earth and which is attainable only through death' but which is at the same time a desire for 'that love which has sprung from the ground of the most uncompromising sensuality.'

One can sense here an inner bond which links together all the works from *Der fliegende Holländer* through to *Tristan und Isolde.* At all events, Wagner defended himself vigorously against 'those critics whose intelligence had been shaped by modern debauchery' and who attempted to read into *Tannhäuser* 'a specifically Christian, impotently idolizing tendency'.

Wagner was concerned not with questions of faith but with a human situation. Tannhäuser interested him as a human being. Venus imagines him as a 'god' as he lies in her embrace: earlier he suffered, now he knows only joy. Tannhäuser, however, counters with the argument that he is not a god, since the gods can only enjoy themselves and never feel pain; rather is he a man, who is subject to change; he is not a god but slave to Venus and for that reason he longs for his 'freedom', for 'pain' and even for 'death'; in a word, he wishes to become human again and suffer both joy and anguish. This longing to become human leads him back to womankind in the person of Elisabeth who now suffers with him. Out of compassion for her and in order to 'sweeten her tears' he agrees that, by way of atonement, he will take upon himself the pilgrimage to Rome. He seeks salvation not for the sake of his own spiritual well-being, as is the case with the other pilgrims, but for the sake of Elisabeth. Since his contrition is so great, his disgust must be equally profound when, having reached what he believes to be the goal of his journey of salvation, he is met only by 'lies and heartlessness'. Not only is Tannhäuser himself denied salvation; so, too, is Elisabeth; hence his anger against a world 'which, because of the utter sincerity of his feelings, denies him the right to exist.' If he longs to return to the Venusberg, it is not out of delight or desire but out of hatred towards a world which he can only despise now that he has proved to himself his inability to sweeten the tears of his 'angel', Elisabeth. Only the love of Elisabeth can achieve what 'the whole moralistic world had failed to achieve', for, in spite of the world, she includes her lover in her prayers; and that is why she can offer Tannhäuser the possibility of redemption, whatever the world and the institution of the Church may say ('Über die Aufführung des "Tannhäuser"' ['On Performing *Tannhäuser*']).

The action of the opera, which on a superficial level is simple and straightforward, more obviously develops out of its own inner motifs than was the case with the earlier works. In the conflict in Act II concerning the nature of love, what forces the decision is 'no other power than that of the most hidden reaches of the soul' (letter to Hector Berlioz of February 1860). Basically what we find in *Tannhäuser* is Wagner already carrying out his own maxims for the reform of opera: the demand for appropriateness of action and the drama inherent in it, a drama which must develop out of the situation or the mental disposition of the characters concerned and which must not appear wilful or imposed from outside. Unmotivated scenes or passages which are introduced simply to create an effect should be avoided. The work should make obvious intellectual demands. The music should be concerned with characterization and not with pictorialism or pure effect. And, last but by no means least, the nationalistic element was also important for Wagner, who hoped that an independent German opera might emerge to rival the claims of Italian and French opera and thus bequeath to posterity the inheritance of Carl Maria von Weber. For that reason he now limited himself to composing operas on themes from German literature. His oft-quoted remark to Karl Gaillard, 'Tannhäuser, as he lives and breathes: a German from head to toe,' can be taken in the first place to mean that the original folk poem and the figure of Tannhäuser himself are German. The depiction of figures from the national past as models for the present and the formulation of a national consciousness were part of a general appeal made to all artists at this time. For Wagner the solution of Tannhäuser's dilemma in favour of what one might call the 'Elisabethan' principle was more than simply a means of distancing himself from the Young German ideal of free love; he believed he was dealing here with a specifically German theme and that he could appeal in his own defence to a number of important literary models ranging from Goethe's *Faust* to the Romantic poets. The conflict between sensuality and metaphysics appeared to Wagner to be a fundamental characteristic of what we are now used to calling national character or national consciousness.

Tannhäuser additionally provides an example of the sureness with which Wagner had in the meantime learned to handle the apparatus of grand opera and to make that apparatus serve his own particular demands. The Venusberg, admittedly, is a magic stage effect, but it is also dramaturgically justified. The entry of the guests into the Hall of Song is an operatic set piece and the scenery for it was ordered from Edouard-Désiré-Joseph Despléchin, one of the several designers who also provided the sets for the Paris Opéra in 1861; but both these elements are once again bound up in the total dramaturgical context. There has not been a singing festival for a number of years, with the result that the throng of people is now particularly great and the hall which has stood empty for so long is once again greeted with joy.

Wagner was concerned that the dialogue should not be simply traditional operatic melody. Instead, he hoped to give intensified musical expression to 'the emotions expressed in the spoken verse'. His attempts in this direction, however, were only intermittently successful, as he himself was the first to admit *(Eine Mittheilung an meine Freunde)*. In Tannhäuser's Rome Narration in Act III he has achieved a hitherto unprecedented congruity between words and music and many writers on Wagner consider that this passage marks the true beginnings of music drama.

Rehearsals began in September 1845 and proved unusually difficult. Josef Tichatschek, with his magnificent tenor voice, was admittedly a musical singer, but he had no acting ability whatsoever and was quite incapable of meeting the role's demands. Sympathy for Tannhäuser's fate as an outsider, on which Wagner knew the success of the work depended, was something which the 'joyfully

Théâtre Impérial de l'Opéra,
Paris, 13 March 1861
Costume design for male
member of the chorus. There is
a clear attempt to produce
costumes in the style and colour
of medieval miniatures.

Théâtre Impérial de l'Opéra,
Paris, 13 March 1861
Designer:
Edouard-Désiré-Joseph
Despléchin
Engraving of Act II, showing
the climax of the Song Contest.
The Hall of Song is seen here
from an angle, as prescribed by
Wagner's scenario. For the new
production in Munich in 1867,
Wagner similarly insisted that
Despléchin's design should be
followed; King Ludwig II was
unable to assert his own desire
for a Romanesque hall. This set
was particularly admired by
Munich audiences.

Court Theatre, Munich,
1 August 1867
Choreography: Lucile Grahn
Michael Echter's illustration of
the bacchanal, based on the
Munich production of 1867.
The bacchanal was staged
according to this model up to
the end of the nineteenth
century. It shows a grotto lit in
blue and pink, with
stalactite-lined passages leading
off it and decorated with
rose-coloured garlands of
flowers. To the left is Venus's
shell-shaped couch and in the
middle is the wild swirl of
Bacchantes. Cupids fly
overhead 'like a flock of birds'
and shoot down 'an incessant
hail of arrows on to the turmoil
in the depths below' (Richard
Wagner). They were
presumably played by children
who could be drawn up into the
flies on ropes.

trumpeting' tenor was unable to instil in the audience. Even Wilhelmine Schröder-Devrient, who had grown somewhat matronly in the intervening years, was for that very reason a less than ideal Venus and initially at least scarcely knew how to begin to tackle her part. Wagner's niece Johanna, the daughter of his brother Albert, sang the part of Elisabeth and with the help of her attractive soprano voice and her apparent youthful innocence (she had just turned nineteen), she was able to win over the Dresden public, but it was immediately evident to Wagner that she was not equal to the psychological dimensions of her demanding role, particularly in her prayer and death scene in Act III. The young baritone Anton Mitterwurzer was the only singer who understood Wagner's intentions and who was able to incorporate them in his interpretation of that part. It should be added that Wagner, who was his own producer, knew how to inspire his cast with a sense of enthusiasm but he lacked the practical experience necessary to realize his new style.

Since von Lüttichau believed the new opera would rival the success of *Rienzi* (and after all it had more to offer in the way of scenery than the parsimonious *Dutchman*), he ordered completely new sets to be built. If we may believe the press reports of the time, the outlay and costs must have been phenomenally high. The costumes were designed by Ferdinand Heine, in consultation with Wagner himself,

and were medieval in style. The sets, as already mentioned, were designed by Despléchin and built in Paris. Whereas the valley of the Wartburg was an outstanding success, the Venusberg caused Wagner endless trouble. The set-painter had been instructed to produce something which would be both awe-inspiring and seductive, a request which he interpreted as a licence to import into the wild mountain cave of the Venusberg statues and groves from the gardens of Versailles. Everything had to be painted over. Wagner's biggest problem, however, was the set for the Hall of Song. Lüttichau had initially thought that the hall from the opera *Oberon* would be a suitable substitute; it was a romantic imperial hall and had only recently been bought. It cost Wagner considerable effort to persuade his superior that he needed a particular set which accorded with his own ideas on the subject. Agreement was finally given for the new hall to be commissioned, but the finished set never arrived. Every day Wagner would hurry away in desperation to the station, rummaging through bales and crates, but the Hall of Song was not among them. In the end the *Oberon* hall had to be used after all and the Dresden first-night audience, anxious to behold new scenic wonders, was naturally disappointed when the curtain went up on the familiar set.

A letter written by Wilhelmine Schröder-Devrient on the evening of the first performance bears witness to the expectant atmosphere which gripped the town; in it she reports that all the tickets had already been sold at the theatre 'in which the supporters of the past and of the future intend assembling for a grand battle in the course of which the ashes of Gluck, Mozart and others may well be scattered to the four winds.' The first performance took place on 19 October 1845 and was conducted by the composer. In spite of the ticket prices having been raised, the house was packed to the rafters.

The Venusberg scene passed virtually unnoticed, a fact for which Wagner blamed not so much Schröder-Devrient as his own sketchy and immature writing of the part. In Act II Tichatschek was completely overwhelmed by the other singers, but what was worse was his inability to gain the audience's sympathy at the extremely crucial and decisive point, 'Erbarm' dich mein' ('Have pity on me'), as a result of which Wagner reluctantly had to cut the passage at all later performances. What most distressed Wagner, however, was the fact that the key scene of the whole opera, the Song Contest in Act II, was turned into a recital of arias. The audience, moreover, was unable to understand the ending of the opera, since Venus's reappearance was conceived simply as a vision in Tannhäuser's delirious imagination and indicated by a reddish shimmering glow in the Hörselberg; and Elisabeth's death was merely reported by Wolfram while the Wartburg was lit by torches. When the curtain finally fell, it was 'less the attitude of the audience, who were still friendly and favourably disposed,' than his own 'inner experience which convinced him that, as a result of immaturity and the unsuitability of the means at his disposal, the performance had been a failure.' His arms and legs 'felt like lead'. That same night he considered what alterations, cuts and improvements he might make to the score in time for the second performance.

Because of Tichatschek's hoarseness this second performance had to be postponed for a week. But the press was by no means as convinced of the work's lack of success as Wagner imagined it to be. As always, the supporters of his new school of thought were enthusiastic in their following, while the conservatives were equally clearly against him; the only difference between them was that the latter were the more numerous and often excessively spiteful. They described the work as tedious and frightfully lascivious, as devoid of any melody, an abomination, dramatically wishy-washy, an operatic bedlam, coffee-mill and tea-pot music. Wolfram's

Ode to the Evening Star was a cats' chorus and Wagner himself was dubbed Walther von der Pfingstweide. The most considered and intelligent review was written, albeit six months later, by Eduard Hanslick, who was subsequently to become Wagner's bitterest critic. By now Tichatschek had decided that he no longer wished to sing the part and Lüttichau was beginning to wonder whether he should cancel the set he had ordered from Paris, which had still not arrived. The second performance was admittedly poorly attended but the audience showed a greater understanding of the work than had previously been the case. By the third performance there were 'sold out' notices outside and both composer and singers were enthusiastically called out in front of the curtain after each act. At Wolfram's words, 'Heinrich, du bist erlöst' ('Heinrich, you are redeemed'), a great cry of jubilation rang out. The fourth performance was a similar success; the eighth took place on 25 January 1846 and was the last of the opening series.

There was little likelihood that any other theatre would take up the opera: it was considered to be too extravagant and costly and its success deemed questionable. But Wagner

Basil Crage, costume design for a siren in the bacchanal, before 1896
This sketch was one of those on offer by the Baruch Studios in Berlin and was used *inter alia* in the 1896 London production. Crage, who also designed sets for revues, was inspired by the fashions of the day. The dancers for the *Tannhäuser* bacchanal and the flowermaidens in *Parsifal* were very often fashionably attired at this time.

was dependent upon performances away from home if he were not merely to stand on his reputation as one of Dresden's local celebrities, just another routine conductor who occasionally turned his hand to writing operas. There were already enough men like that around. In addition, he needed the money. He had had the full score privately printed and was now having difficulty making ends meet. In December he travelled to Berlin to open negotiations with Karl Theodor von Küstner, general intendant of the Court Opera. Küstner thought the work was too epic. Wagner then begged permission to dedicate *Tannhäuser* to the king, in the hope of interesting him in a production. Count Redern answered that the king only accepted works which were already familiar to him and suggested that Wagner might have a selection of numbers from the opera arranged for wind band. Although Wagner agreed to this humiliating condition, which was intended to put the upstart composer back where he belonged, His Majesty declined to consider the matter.

From the very first performance Baron von Lüttichau had been critical of 'the opera's tragic *dénouement*' and had drawn the undiscerning composer's attention to the fact that Weber's operas had always ended on a 'satisfactory' note. Wagner, of course, could not alter the tragic ending, but the reappearance of Venus and the death of Elisabeth had to be made easier for the audience to understand. The first performance of the revised *Tannhäuser*, with its new ending, was given on 1 August 1847. When Tannhäuser calls upon her by name, Venus appears with her corybantic retinue in the reddishly shimmering Hörselberg; Elisabeth is then carried in on a bier, having been brought down from the Wartburg to the valley below, and Tannhäuser sinks down lifeless beside her corpse. It is this version with its revised ending that is nowadays known as the 'Dresden Version' to distinguish it from the 'Paris Version' which dates from the Paris production of 1861. None of Wagner's works was revised and altered as often as *Tannhäuser;* and even at the very end of his life, he admitted to Cosima that he still owed *Tannhäuser* to the world. This may be taken partly to mean that he still hoped to mount a model production of the work in Bayreuth; but it also indicates his desire to revise further the score and the libretto for these performances. Dramatically he considered the work had succeeded, but each time he was involved in a new production of the opera, he took the opportunity to alter details of the musical design.

Not even the revised ending met with universal approval since it was regarded as too straightforward and too concerned to create an effect. People preferred the old solution, where they felt that the opera as a whole did not so much end as fade from view. These are convincing arguments and are indicative of the way discussions about Wagner's new ideas were conducted not only by the press but, to an important degree, by an interested audience which seriously wanted to come to terms with each new work from the pen of the young composer. Wagner had found supporters, although they did not yet call themselves 'Wagnerians', and it was with justifiable pride that he was able to write in his autobiography that people attended performances of his operas 'who would normally never have gone to the theatre and least of all to the opera.'

The first theatre outside Dresden with the courage to stage *Tannhäuser* was Weimar, where it was rehearsed and conducted by Liszt. The first performance took place on 16 February 1849. Weimar supported one of the smaller court theatres and was in no position to afford lavish sets; indeed, with the exception of a new Venusberg, all the scenery came from what was already available in the theatre store. And yet the work enjoyed an immense success with the general public, tunes from *Tannhäuser* being whistled in the street. Liszt helped the opera achieve its decisive breakthrough. Wagner himself did not see the production until 13 May, when he attended a rehearsal for a revival of the opera. It was no longer in his capacity as Conductor to the Royal Court of Saxony that he was there, but as a political refugee. In Liszt's contribution he recognized, as it were, his *alter ego,* an experience which led to a deepening of their already long-standing acquaintanceship; from now on the two men were to be lifelong friends.

The supraregional interest aroused by the Weimar production, backed as it was by Liszt's authority, suddenly made *Tannhäuser* attractive to other theatres as well. Schwerin staged the work on 26 January 1852, followed by Breslau (modern Wrocław) on 6 October of the same year and Wiesbaden on 13 November. The Wiesbaden production was rehearsed by Louis Schindelmeisser, an old friend of Wagner's, and caused quite a sensation, and the Munich intendant Franz von Dingelstedt sent a representative to observe the production.

Tannhäuser was the first of Wagner's operas to be produced in his own birth-place of Leipzig, where it opened on 31 January 1853. But the townspeople evidently thought very

little of their spiritual offspring since, even by
the date of the second performance, the theatre was virtually empty. In Cassel, Ludwig
Spohr, one of the few contemporary composers to have recognized Wagner's importance
at this early date in spite of his own commitment to a completely different school of musical thought, followed the production of *Der
fliegende Holländer* with one of *Tannhäuser* in
the town's court theatre. The first performance took place on 15 May 1853 under
Spohr's baton. Poznań followed on 22 May
and Hanover on 21 January 1855, when Albert Niemann sang the title-role for the first
time. The first performance in Karlsruhe followed a week later, on 28 January 1855, in a
production by Eduard Devrient. From 1859
onwards the title-role in this production was
sung by Ludwig Schnorr von Carolsfeld.
Wagner attended a performance in March
1862 and was appalled to see Devrient's idea
of having the ladies and gentlemen of the
chorus line up to the right and to the left of

the stage, along the walls of the Hall of Song
in Act II, before 'executing the regular *chassé
croisé* of a quadrille and thus changing their
relative positions' *(Mein Leben)*.

Wagner was most concerned that *Tannhäuser* should not be performed in medium-
sized theatres in the traditional operatic style
but in the form in which he himself intended
it to be produced, as a music drama. Clearly it
was beyond his strength to involve himself in
each individual production of the work and
so in 1852 he drafted the essay 'Über die
Aufführung des "Tannhäuser". Eine Mittheilung an die Dirigenten und Darsteller dieser
Oper' ('On Performing *Tannhäuser*: a Communication to the Conductors and Performers of this Opera'), which on the one hand is a
manual of theatre practice and on the other
an outline of Wagner's own ideal stage performance. He begins by demanding a new
and closer relationship between the music and
the stage. What is new in the libretto and in
the music must be depicted in a way which it-

Teatro alla Scala, Milan,
29 December 1891
Giulio Ricordi had large
hand-coloured photographs of
the 1891 Bayreuth sets sent to
him. The Hall of Song was
copied by Giovanni Zuccarelli
from the original Bayreuth
designs.

self is new. The earlier division into separate
areas of responsibility, which gave the conductor an exclusive say in musical matters and
which limited the producer to what took
place on stage, had to be abandoned: the two
of them should work together in intensive
co-operation, since the potential effectiveness
of Wagner's own particular kind of theatre
rested precisely on a perfect congruity between stage and pit. Not only the conductor,
but the producer, too, should attend all the
rehearsals for the principal singers. Wagner
was not interested in the argument that all
that people expected of a singer was that he
should be able to sing beautifully and that his
ability to act was of no importance; anyone
who held this view, he went on, would never
manage to understand what *Tannhäuser* was
all about. Wagner wanted singers 'whose participation in the performance would be the result of their understanding and sympathizing
with the work and that such a sense of involvement would be based ultimately upon
their own inner convictions'; in other words,
he wanted what we should nowadays call a
'singing actor'. What was important was a
dramatically appropriate form of expression
and not simply beautiful singing. In *Tannhäuser*, he argued, there was no difference
between so-called declamation and sung
phrases: 'declamation is at the same time singing and singing declamation.' There was no
attempt to draw the usual distinction between
recitative and aria.

The work's effectiveness, Wagner continued, was entirely dependent upon the ability of the interpreter of the title-role to sing
the phrase 'Erbarm' dich mein' ('Have mercy

on me'), which is repeated eleven times in the
second act, in such a way as to instil in the listener a feeling of the most profound sympathy for Tannhäuser's fate. This passage
was 'the nerve centre of Tannhäuser's entire
subsequent existence'; it was the pivotal point
of the whole drama. It had to sound like 'a
cry for redemption' and demanded a 'penetrating accent' if Tannhäuser were not to
appear a pitiful irresolute weakling. The fact
that Wagner had to cut this passage in Dresden in no way alters its significance: he was
forced to do so simply because of the total in-
competence of the leading singer, who 'stared
straight out into the footlights with an expression of sheep-like affability on his face and,
in the most delicate of accents, sang the
eighth line of a vocal octet.' The first scene in
the Venusberg, Wagner insisted, was not one
of the usual ballets but more of a mime, 'a seductive, wild and enthralling chaos of figures
moving and regrouping, a chaos of emotions
ranging from the tenderest contentment, lan-
guishing and yearning to the most drunken
impetuousness of exultant abandon.' The
rosy clouds in the cave should be indicated by
lightly painted gauzes, which could be raised
quickly at the end of the scene. On no account did he want a complicated and noisy
change of scene. The transformation of the
Venusberg into a spring landscape should be
instantaneous, since it was precisely this
abruptness which constituted the element of
surprise and the atmospheric effectiveness of
the scene. The entry of the guests into the
Hall of Song required particular skill on the
part of the producer; on no account was it to
be staged 'in the manner usually reserved for

marches', whereby 'the chorus and extras march on in pairs, proceed in a crocodile across the stage and then, with military precision, line up in two rows on either side of the stage, in anticipation of further operatic development.' During the entry and formal welcome of the guests, there should be an attempt 'to imitate real life in its freest and most noble forms'. Groups should emerge in an entirely natural and informal way, with older and younger princes, knights and ladies coming together according to their social rank and the degree of their mutual familiarity. These differences should be clearly marked in their costumes as well.

Two further essays, 'Die Scenirung der Oper Tannhäuser' ('Staging the Opera *Tannhäuser*') and 'Die Kostümbeschreibung' ('Costume Description'), were intended to serve the same purpose of making the performances in question as stylistically pure as possible. Both essays exist in manuscript copies prepared after the first performances in Dresden and intended as compulsory reading for the scene-painter and costume designer. They give a clear picture of Wagner's production ideas. Truthfulness and dramatic expressiveness in interpretation were demanded and all those vacuous operatic gestures whose sole purpose was to impress were proscribed. The ideal was to recreate a picture of life. We should not worry unduly if these ideas resulted in stage directions which modern sensibilities would regard as implausible; Wagner's contemporaries saw things differently and we must assume that they were motivated by a different kind of willingness to yield to theatrical illusion. The approach of the pilgrims in Act I, for instance, was staged in such a way that a group of between

Stadsschouwburg, Amsterdam,
22 March 1913
Producer: Anton Fuchs.
Designer: Hermann Burghart.
Conductor: Henri Viotta
Set for Acts I and III by
Burghart of Vienna. Typical
example of a studio-produced
design. The layout is
traditional: the way-side shrine
is on the right and the steps
leading to the Wartburg in the
back on the left; in the middle
is an open space for the chorus
scenes; the Wartburg is painted
on the backcloth and the whole
scene is framed by trees. The
bottoms of the flats rest directly
on the stage floor, which
destroys any sense of illusion. It
should be added, however, that
photographs such as this were
not taken under conditions of
stage lighting, which was much
softer and therefore allowed the
contrasts to become softened.

twenty-six and twenty-eight children wearing beards and dressed like the older pilgrims entered in the distance, upstage right, at the very top of the hill-side path; they then disappeared into the wings behind the fifth row of flats, at which point the real pilgrims entered further downstage from behind the third row of flats. Similarly, in Act III, when Elisabeth has ended her prayer and, singled out by death, dragged herself up the slope towards the Wartburg, she was supposed to be replaced at the very summit of the hill by a small girl dressed in identical clothes, in order to give a greater impression of perspective.

Wagner liked such forms of realism. He also insisted on having the horses in the hunting scene bridled in the medieval fashion; sheep bells were to be heard ringing before the shepherd's song and church bells after the departure of the pilgrims, while for Elisabeth's death he asked that the sound of her death knell be heard tolling from the direction of the Wartburg. The entry of the guests was to be staged with great ceremonial formality: field-marshals were to enter, followed by trumpeters and pages who were to escort the guests to their seats. The landgrave's greeting was to cover the whole range of emotions from respect to cordiality and intimacy. Following Tannhäuser's song in praise of Venus, the minnesingers and nobles were to crowd in on him with their swords, while Elisabeth threw herself in their path. This was how Götz Friedrich staged the scene in his 1972 production at Bayreuth, an interpretation condemned by certain sections of the

audience who argued that such an act of violent aggression ran counter to the spirit of the work. In the final act, the valley of the Wartburg was to be bathed in subdued autumnal colours, so as to form a contrast with Act I. Stars were to be seen twinkling in the night sky during Wolfram's Ode to the Evening Star, and the evening star itself was to be positioned directly above the Wartburg. At the end of the opera, the sun was to rise over the valley. The costumes were to be 'medieval in style', apart from Venus who was to wear a 'Grecian' three-layered tunic. The Bacchantes were to be similarly dressed in short white tunics, with tiger skins draped over their shoulders; also stipulated were flesh-coloured tights, 'gold-laced' sandals, tambourines and thyrsi.

Tannhäuser had already been staged in forty other theatres before the larger opera-houses of Munich, Berlin and Vienna made up their minds to perform it. Franz von Dingelstedt, the Munich intendant, began a series of correspondence with Wagner and asked that the Court Theatre be granted performing rights, in return for which he promised an 'exemplary' staging of the work. Wagner had grave doubts about the conductor, Franz Lachner, the local *kapellmeister* who himself had written operas, including *Catarina Cornaro* which had enjoyed a considerable success in both Munich and Berlin. Dingelstedt was able to calm Wagner's doubts. Wagner, however, insisted that the conductor, producer and cast should read his published instruc-

Court Theatre, Cassel, 1894
Designer: Oertel
The Hall of the Wartburg:
Design for Act II. The design is
an exact copy of the Bayreuth
model of 1891.

Opera House, Düsseldorf, 1928
Designer: Harry Breuer
The Hall of the Wartburg:
Design for Act II. There is
nothing medieval about either
the architecture or the
colouring. Only the traditional
arches with their panoramic
vista have been retained.

tions on performing the opera. Even while rehearsals were still in progress, the Munich press had begun to inveigh against 'this Orpheus who has built barricades in Dresden,' 'this refugee criminal' and this 'prisoner'. 'He belongs in the prison at Waldheim, not in the Munich opera-house.' This was ten years before his summons to Munich by King Ludwig II. The sets were built to the Dresden designs of Simon and Angelo Quaglio and Heinrich Döll. The costumes were by Franz Seitz and the producer was August Kindermann, who also sang the part of Wolfram, an achievement which was by no means unusual at that time. The 'bacchanal in Frau Holda's (Venus's) rocky *salon*' was arranged by the celebrated ballerina Lucile Grahn. In his letter to the king of 8 August 1855, there was an air of self-importance about Dingelstedt's claim that the production 'will mark the beginning of a new era from both a musical and scenic point of view'. There was an enormous rush to buy seats, even at the over-inflated prices which audiences were asked to pay if they wished to get hold of a ticket at all. It was after all the first performance of any of Wagner's operas in Munich. The première took place on 12 August 1855. Venus's magically lit grotto was particularly loudly applauded and the 'magnificent set' in Act II was similarly acknowledged.

We doubt whether we have ever witnessed a scene more pleasingly arranged than the arrival of the guests, who included knights and their ladies, patricians and the like. The producer has avoided the traditional method of having the singers march on like marionettes; instead they appeared to enter as if by chance, depending on the speed with which their horses had brought them there. Having been welcomed by the landgrave, they then went to look for their seats and, thanks to the characteristic verisimilitude of the costumes and surroundings, we felt ourselves transported, as it were, into the reality of a world which had once existed centuries ago (*Augsburger Allgemeine*).

The costumes, too, were much admired; they 'leave nothing to be desired in the way of picturesque beauty; not only the courtly hunting costumes and ceremonial robes worn by the minstrels, but all the accessories such as belts, hats and pouches were all differently marked to suit the style and character of the period' (ibid.). There was applause for Lachner and the orchestra at the end of the overture, and after both the first and second acts all the performers were called out in front of the curtain. Dingelstedt reports in his *Münchner Bilderbogen* of 1879, 'The air that evening was heavy with the heat of battle and with that same unholy and infernal din which has been the order of the day during the whole of the last fifteen years whenever some new manifestation of the Music of the Future has seen the light of day.' However controversial the music may have been, *Tannhäuser* was a success in Munich as it had been elsewhere largely on account of the way in which it was staged. The Venusberg ballet was always applauded, even though the subject-matter itself may have been found somewhat *risqué,* and the picture of medieval

Deutsche Oper, Berlin-Charlottenburg, 31 October 1928
Producer: Ernst Lert. Designer: Ernst Stern. Conductor: Bruno Walter
The Hall of the Wartburg: Stern's set-design for Act II. Stern was Max Reinhardt's designer and, like the latter, knew how to group large choruses. The chorus could spread out over flights of steps and ramps at various levels, thus creating a remarkable tonal effect by being positioned so as to face the audience. The triple arch, the classical motif of the Wartburg sets, is repeated here many times, thus providing a vertical contrast to the horizontal elements formed by the galleries.

splendour evoked by Act II must have exactly coincided with what contemporary audiences liked, since even Wagner's opponents expressed their enthusiasm for this act.

The Weimar production was seen by Botho von Hülsen, the new intendant of the Berlin Opera, and he immediately sounded Wagner on the possibility of a production in Berlin. Negotiations became protracted and were twice broken off. The fee was no problem, but Wagner refused to forego his demand that overall control of the production could only be entrusted to his *alter ego,* Franz Liszt. He himself was prevented from making the journey to Berlin. Hülsen felt this to be humiliating for his own staff and once again refused; the score was returned to the composer without so much as an accompanying letter. Wagner's difficult financial position in exile, where he had no fixed income, forced him in the end to accept Hülsen's terms unconditionally, and the first performance finally took place on 7 January 1856. The conductor was Wagner's former colleague from Riga, Heinrich Dorn, while the producer was the intendant himself, Botho von Hülsen. He followed Wagner's instructions in lavishing great care and attention on the entry of the guests into the Hall of Song. 'I can still see him now, rushing at the speed of lightning from one side of the stage to the other, in order to show most of the ladies of the chorus and ballet how deeply to bow, so that they might learn to regulate their entry and behav-

iour in accordance with the ceremonial of the time,' Helene von Hülsen reported of the rehearsals. Liszt attended the final rehearsals, albeit in a private capacity. The new sets were designed by Carl Wilhelm Gropius, the Hall of Song being, at the king's request, 'a photographically reproduced' copy of the historical Hall of Song on the Wartburg. The castle had been restored in 1838 in a style which was considered faithful to the spirit of the Middle Ages. Liszt claimed never to have seen anything more magnificent. Johanna Wagner, who in the meantime had become one of the stars of the Berlin Court Opera, sang the part of Elisabeth, a role with which her name has since become associated. Once again the performances were more successful visually than musically. Helene von Hülsen voiced the prevailing opinion when she wrote in her memoirs, 'I can still see the brilliant procession entering [...] the hall of the Wartburg and the majestic figure of Johanna Wagner, the sky-blue garland on her noble brow, enveloped in a white cloak over her white dress, welcoming her guests and receiving their oaths of allegiance. Yes, it was quite an event, this first performance of *Tannhäuser* in Berlin, a far-reaching event for Richard Wagner, for the intendant and the audience, and nobody who was there, whatever he may think of the music, would dispute this.'

It was at one of Vienna's theatres, the Thalia Theatre in Neulerchenfeld, a large wooden structure reputed to seat 3,000 people used in the summer only, that Wagner made his theatrical début in the Austrian capital. His musical personality was no longer a stranger to the Viennese public since the Waltz-king Johann Strauss had regularly included excerpts from Wagner's latest works in the programmes of his popular concerts. The financial demands which Wagner made of the theatre manager, Johann Hoffmann, were by no means inconsiderable, but Wagner had no intention of allowing a wretched first performance in some suburban theatre to ruin his chances of gaining entrée to the Vienna Court Opera. Hoffmann agreed to the sum demanded without hesitation and was able to present the first performance of *Tannhäuser* in Vienna to a packed house on 28 August 1857. The production was such a success that eight further performances followed immediately afterwards and there were almost thirty in all during the remainder of the winter season at the Josefstadt Theatre. One indication of the popularity of *Tannhäuser* in Vienna is Johann Nestroy's parody, *Tannhäuser und die Keilerei auf Wartburg. Zukunftsposse mit vergangener Musik und gegenwärtigen Gruppierungen* ('Tannhäuser and the Punch-up on the Wartburg. Futuristic Farce with Music that is Past It and Groupings that are from the Present'), first performed at the Carl Theatre on 31 October; it was one of Nestroy's greatest theatrical successes and has remained in the repertory ever since. Wagner himself attended a performance on the occasion of one of his subsequent visits to Vienna. Nestroy himself played the part of Landgrave Purzel, the typical anti-Wagnerian, while contemporary 'modern' Wagnerian singers were parodied in the figure of Tannhäuser.

It was not until 19 November 1859 that *Tannhäuser* was first performed at the Vienna Court Opera, which at that date was still housed in the Kärntnerthor Theatre. The first American performance had taken place in New York at the Stadt Theater six months previously, on 4 April 1859. In Zurich, meanwhile, there had been two performances of *Tannhäuser* in February 1855, conducted by Wagner himself. The orchestra was reinforced 'by kind co-operation of several amateur musicians from the area'; the sets were by a Herr Erber and the 'new and brilliant costumes' were designed by Herr Krasser.

With the exception of the two productions already mentioned, which took place within the modest framework of the local theatre, Wagner's years of exile in Zurich were marked by a steadfast refusal to involve himself actively in the theatre. He had to try to

make ends meet by means of concert tours, which, as he told Otto Wesendonck in a letter of 21 March 1855, made him feel like some 'travelling salesman' going from country to country with his 'wretched samples'. His works belonged in the theatre, not in the concert hall. It is true that during the 1850s Wagner's music was played a great deal and that he himself witnessed a real breakthrough, but he had to limit his own participation to voluminous correspondence and printed instructions, in his constant concern to be properly understood.

On completion of the composition of *Tristan und Isolde*, Wagner travelled to Paris in September 1859, where he began by arranging concerts at the Théâtre Italien, and then turned to the idea of staging model performances of his works, in particular *Tristan und Isolde*. Nothing came of this plan. Indeed,

State Opera, Berlin,
12 February 1933
Producer: Jürgen Fehling.
Designer: Oskar Strnad.
Conductor: Otto Klemperer.
Elisabeth: Franzi von Dobay.
Tannhäuser: Sigismund Pilinsky
Scene between Elisabeth and Tannhäuser in Act II. This is no brightly coloured picture of the Middle Ages but a harsh and stone-bound world. Elisabeth portrayed as a nun. To the left are the stairs which were pivoted for the entry of the guests.

New Theatre, Leipzig, 1936
Producers: Wolfram
Humperdinck and Max Elten.
Conductor: Paul Schmitz
Scene from Act II. Realistic sets
again came to predominate in
Germany during the 1930s. On
the walls are panels copied from
the Manesse Codex, a popular
motif at the time. The beamed
roof is in the style of the local
architecture.

events turned out quite differently. His pro-
tectress, the Princess Pauline Metternich, was
able to persuade the Emperor Napoleon III to
order a production of *Tannhäuser* at the Opéra, this being the only work by Wagner
which was known about in France at the time.
Wagner's lifelong dream seemed about to be
realized, but his dream was to become the
most notorious theatrical scandal of his day.
In the course of his first meeting with
Wagner, the director of the Opéra, Alphonse
Royer, stated the most important precondition for a successful production – a large-
scale ballet in the second act, an idea which
struck the composer as nonsensical, although
he was prepared to write an elaborate ballet
scene for the Venusberg in Act I, since he
himself felt the Dresden version of this scene
to be inept. Royer rejected this suggestion out
of hand: a ballet in Act II was imperative. The
aristocratic members of the Jockey Club, all
of whom were season-ticket holders and
therefore immensely influential, were not in
the habit of attending the opera until after
they had dined and it was precisely at that
moment, in the second act, that they expected
a ballet. But Wagner remained deaf even to a
direct appeal from the minister of state. He
was already half-inclined to abandon the
whole undertaking but was torn at the same
time by the idea of working in a theatre in
which he appeared to have been given every
possibility of mounting an ideal production.
In Germany he could never hope to find conditions which were even as remotely favourable as those in Paris. His old enthusiasm
reasserted itself and, as he wrote to his sister
Cäcilie, 'The whole of the vast institution of

the Opéra has been placed at my disposal; I
am master here; I have only to ask for something and my wish is granted. The advantage
I shall gain from this, I believe, is that, if nothing else, at least the production will be the
best ever to have been mounted of the work.'
A similar sentiment was expressed in his letter
to Liszt: 'I have never in all my life been
granted such total and unconditional control
over all the material that is necessary for an
outstanding production.'

As was the case with all his other works,
Wagner began by sketching a prose draft of
the Paris bacchanal, in which the Venusberg
scene, which in the Dresden version had
served simply as an exposition, was expanded
in such a way as to become a worthy antithesis to the world of the Wartburg. This bacchanal is Wagner's 'Classical Walpurgis
Night', with Goethe as the implicit model. In
it Wagner's vision of what Hans Mayer has
called a *'paradis artificiel'* has taken on a fantastic form and become an allegory of ram-
pant sexuality and the palliative force of
eroticism. At the front of the stage, 'Venus is
seen lying on an opulent couch' and in front
of her, his head in her lap, is Tannhäuser,
with his harp. At the back of the stage are nai-
ads bathing in a lake, while sirens recline on
the shore. The Three Graces can be seen,
'their bodies charmingly intertwined'. Little
cupids encircle Venus and Tannhäuser,
'forming a tangled knot, like children who,
exhausted by their fighting, have fallen
asleep.' Youths with goblets in their hands
recline on rocky ledges; nymphs entice them
into dancing around the waterfall, 'the couples come together and mingle, animating the

dance with their searching, fleeing and delightful teasing.' A procession of Bacchantes storms in, 'inviting the others the join their wanton revelries'. The dancing grows more abandoned, satyrs and fauns appear from the crevasses and chase after the nymphs; 'the general frenzy gives way to maenadic fury.' It is at this moment, when the fury is at its height, that the Three Graces rise to their feet in dismay and wake the sleeping cupids, who fly up like a flock of birds and aim their darts into the midst of the tumult. The dancers break off and, moving apart, all sink down in exhaustion. The Graces approach Venus and 'report as it were the victories which they have won over the dissolute passions of the subjects of her realm.' *Tableaux vivants* appear as visions at the back of the stage, depicting amorous scenes from Greek mythology, including Europa's abduction by the bull, and Leda and the swan.

In his so-called 'ballet-master letter' to Mathilde Wesendonck of 10 April 1860, in which Wagner describes the whole course of the bacchanal, there is also mention of the murdered Orpheus, carried on by an exultant troupe of maenads, a black ram which is sacrificed, and the Norse *strömkarl*, or water-sprite. Wagner was quite correct when he told Mathilde that 'What is certain, however, is that only dance can be performed here and have any effect: but what a dance! People will be astonished at all that I've hatched up here!' He completed scoring the bacchanal on 28 January 1861, convinced that it was only now that he had written Isolde's Transfiguration that he could have captured in music the horror of the Venusberg. Otto Wesendonck, who was present at one of the rehearsals, is reported to have remarked to Wagner, 'Those are such sensual sound.' Wagner subsequently commented to Cosima, 'I expect he was afraid I might have danced like that in front of his wife.'

Rehearsals had already begun on 24 September 1860 and were to achieve the previously unheard-of total of 164 sessions. Wagner was impressed by the exemplary sense of commitment on the part of everyone involved and the meticulous precision of all the run-throughs. Once again Despléchin was responsible for the Hall of Song set, basing his design on the one he created for the Dresden première; (the other sets were designed by Charles-Antoine Cambon, Joseph François Désiré Thierry and Auguste-Alfred Rubé); the original costume designs were also recalled from Dresden. Since the ensemble of the Paris Opéra did not include a suitable tenor for the title-role, Albert Niemann was engaged from Hanover. His début in Paris was heralded in large letters on the playbill and his fee was the incredible sum of 6,000 francs a month. Elisabeth was sung by the young and pretty soprano Marie Sax and Wagner heard the third-act prayer sung for the first time as he had intended it; his niece, he felt, had never succeeded in performing it properly. The Italian mezzo Fortunata Tedesco, a somewhat voluptuous but attractive singer, was Venus and the part of Wolfram was sung by another Italian, Signor Morelli.

It was not until orchestral rehearsals began in the theatre itself (the Salle le Peletier) that Wagner realized with a sense of dismay 'that the standard was no better than that of a routine operatic performance.' There were problems with the conductor, Pierre-Louis Philippe Dietsch. Hans von Bülow, in his usual direct manner, called him 'a mangy ass who has gone through the treadmill of the rehearsals and shown himself utterly incapable of ever learning anything.' Wagner hoped to persuade the management to agree to his conducting the opening performances himself but he came up against the most embittered opposition on the part of Royer and the orchestra. He demanded of the famous ballet-master and choreographer, Lucien Petipa, something in the style of classical reliefs showing maenads and Bacchantes; he was thoroughly dissatisfied with the 'wretchedly executed little steps of Petipa's maenads and Bacchantes'. The answer he received was to the effect that, 'In that case I should have required only first subjects; if I were to tell my people a single word of all this and indicate what your feelings towards them really are, we should immediately have them performing a cancan and then we'd really be in trouble' *(Mein Leben)*.

Scarcely a day passed throughout the whole of this period without reports appearing in the Paris newspapers about the rehearsals and preparations for the first night. The première took place on 13 March 1861 in the presence of the court and several ambassadors and was a major event in the social calendar. Encouraged by the Jockey Club, whose members still felt deprived of their ballet, the anti-Wagnerians among the audience greeted the performance, in spite of the emperor's presence, with shouts, shrill whistles and laughter. Princess Metternich was forced to leave her box at the end of the second act, in order to avoid further public humiliation. Wagner pinned all his hopes on Act III which, dramatically, was the high point of the evening. The atmospheric set, Marie Sax's affecting performance of the prayer, Morelli's Ode

Municipal Stages, Frankfurt am Main, 1934
Designer: Caspar Neher
Design for Act III. The sets here reflect the dramaturgy of the work. Almost monochromatic, a mood of forlornness and grief, no leafy trees, but only withered branches. The scene is dominated by the pathway which passes over the width of the entire stage, representing Tannhäuser's journey through life and his *via dolorosa*. On the left is Tannhäuser, returning from Rome without having found absolution; Wolfram von Eschenbach is on the right.

Opera House, Cologne, 1930s
Producer: Alexander Spring.
Designer: Alf Björn
Scene from Act I. Entry of the hunting party, with horses, dogs and a large body of retainers. Such crowd scenes were very popular with audiences at the time and every large theatre which could afford to stage the scene in this way made it a point of honour to do so. In the Bayreuth performances of *Tannhäuser* in 1930 a pack of hounds was brought on in this scene and there were also hunting dogs in Herbert von Karajan's Vienna production of 1963.

Opera House, Kiel, 1941
Designer: Nina Tokumbet
Set-design for Acts I and III. Her speciality was projections. Different atmospheric colours and effects, cloud formations and so on could be projected onto the vast expanse of sky. In this way the set became dynamic, and dramaturgical intent could be translated into visual images.

Maggio Musicale, Florence, 1953/1954
Producer: Frank de Quell.
Designer: Cajo Kühnly.
Conductor: Artur Rodzinski.
Elisabeth: Herta Wilfert.
Landgrave: Arnold van Mill
Unit set with the classical
Wartburg motif of a triple arch.
Stage centre are the thrones for
the Landgrave and Elisabeth.

to the Evening Star, which he sang 'with perfect, elegiac tenderness', Niemann's Rome Narration, which was 'the best part of his performance': but nothing could stem the tide of tumult. The second performance was similarly interrupted by the most incredible scenes. Actually, it wasn't just the ballet but the noblemen of the Jockey Club were also part of a group that objected to the pro-Austrian clique that incensed Napoleon (headed by Princess Metternich). So the protest was really political. The Jockeys had handed out silver whistles inscribed with the words 'Pour siffler Tannhäuser'. They were afraid that if the opera scored a lasting success they would have to forego their balletic pleasures for some time to come. Some of the other members of the audience, who refused to be terrorized any longer, responded by shouting *A la porte les Jockeys* ('Kick the Jockeys out the door'). Niemann was so incensed by all the howling and whistling that, during the Rome Narration, he took off his pilgrim's hat and hurled it across the footlights into the auditorium. In spite of everything, there was spirited applause and Wagner spoke admiringly of the Paris audiences who had not allowed themselves to be intimidated by one particular faction. He was of the opinion that 'only the inviolable social standing of Their Honours, the Disturbers of the Peace' had prevented them from being assaulted.

In the final analysis, however, Wagner could not continue to allow his artists to be subjected to such a strain and after the third performance he withdrew his score. The management was appalled, since several of the performances which had been announced to follow were already sold out and *Tannhäuser* promised to turn out to be a sensational success. Wagner, however, saw that in such a fraught situation there could be no question of the right conditions prevailing for a proper understanding of the opera, if audiences were prevented from listening calmly and concentratedly to it. In addition, he believed that, for all its magnificence, the production had scarcely scratched the surface of the work in a number of crucial areas and that it had therefore communicated very little of his own stylistic intention ('Bericht über die Aufführung des "Tannhäuser" in Paris' ['Report on the Production of *Tannhäuser* in Paris']). 'To sum up: the idea is on the move, the breach has been made: this is what matters most. More than one French composer will wish to reap the benefits of the salutary thoughts which Wagner has put forward. Brief though the period may have been since the work appeared before the public, the imperial command to which we owe those performances has nevertheless had a beneficial influence upon the French mind.' This was the conclusion drawn from the *Tannhäuser* affair by Charles Baudelaire in an important essay which he published after the first performance. Wagner's concerts in Paris and the three performances of *Tannhäuser* at the Opéra marked the first stages in a history of fascinated involvement with the Wagnerian phenomenon to which many French minds succumbed and which has come to be known as *wagnérisme*. Soon after the first-night scandal, a letter of protest had already begun to circulate in Paris, signed by painters, writers and musicians. Wagner only ever heard one Tannhäuser who was capable of realizing the ideal of his own artistic intentions and that was Ludwig

Metropolitan Opera, New
York, 26 December 1953
Producer: Herbert Graf.
Designer: Rolf Gérard.
Conductor: George Szell.
Elisabeth: Margaret Harshaw.
Landgrave: Jerome Hines
Lavish, historicist costumes,
operatic in style. The
architecture disposed over the
vast stage in the Hall of Song is
neutral and has no particular
message.

Metropolitan Opera, New
York, 26 December 1953
Producer: Herbert Graf.
Designer: Rolf Gérard.
Conductor: George Szell.
Elisabeth: Margaret Harshaw.
Wolfram: George London
Scene from Act III, following
Elisabeth's Prayer. Wartburg,
Valley of the Wartburg and
wayside shrine as usual. The
vast expanse of sky offered
possibilities for projection
techniques.

Schnorr von Carolsfeld, his first Tristan in Munich. Schnorr sang the role of Tannhäuser in a single performance of the opera at the National Theatre in Munich in 1865. The crucial passage in the finale of Act II, the words 'Erbarm' dich mein' ('Have mercy on me'), which Wagner had had to cut both for Tichatschek and also for Niemann in Paris, 'was performed for the first and only time by Schnorr in a shattering and hence deeply moving manner which suddenly turned the hero from an object of loathing into the incarnation of a man deserving of sympathy.' 'The demonic element in his joy and anguish was never lost for a moment.' At the end of Act III, 'in these final ravings of despair', Schnorr was 'truly awe-inspiring'. Instructive even for Wagner himself was the impact which his performance made on the audience, which showed more astonishment and amazement, and even displeasure, than genuine understanding. Wagner found a number of his more understanding friends telling him that he really had no right to ask Tannhäuser to play the part that way since, as far as the general public was concerned, they preferred the usual, 'more easy-going and insipid interpretation', which Wagner himself found 'inadequate' *(Mein Leben).* This experience must have come as quite a shock to a composer who was always striving to achieve performances which should be as perfect as possible, if not ideal.

Wagner himself produced *Tannhäuser* at the Vienna Court Opera in November 1875. It was a commitment he agreed to in view of the first Bayreuth Festival which was to be held the following summer and for which he was dependent upon the support of the Viennese management, since Amalie Materna, his intended Bayreuth Brünnhilde, needed to be released from her engagements in Vienna for the rehearsals and performances in Bayreuth. She sang the part of Elisabeth in the Vienna *Tannhäuser.* The conductor was Hans Richter and the part of the Landgrave was taken by Emil Scaria, who was to sing Gurnemanz at Bayreuth in 1882. Angelo Neumann, who later became impresario of the touring Wagner Theatre company but who in 1875 was still a singer at the Vienna Opera, has left us a vivid account of Wagner's work as a producer:

How superbly he showed us Tannhäuser finding himself once more in the wooded Thuringian valley after the spell of the Venusberg had been broken. He stood there with his arms raised, almost as if turned to stone; when the pilgrims entered he began to tremble with increasing violence until, profoundly convulsed, he sank

to his knees and burst out with the cry, 'Ach wie drückt mich der Sünden Last' ('Ah, how the weight of my sins oppresses me'). What nobility of movement and courtly ardour he brought to the part during Wolfram's aria; the way he interpreted the big scene at the end of Act I; the way he moved and inspired all the others and indicated moves and gestures to the Landgrave and the other knights and minstrels up to the moment when the hunting party enter with their horses and dogs – each one of these moments was indelibly imprinted upon the memory of everyone present. His staging of the entry of the guests left its mark on all later productions. It was *his* directive that the Landgrave and Elisabeth should welcome their guests with their backs to the audience and that the pages should busy themselves announcing each visitor in turn. In earlier productions the royal couple had remained seated on their respective thrones throughout the entire scene and the pages had only once, summarily, announced the entry of the guests. It is true that it was already traditional for a widow and her two daughters to appear at the end of this scene, but it required Wagner to show us all how Elisabeth, following the official reception of the other guests, should take the two young girls by the hand and present them, on this, their first visit to the court, to the assembled company, before leading them back to their mother and only then accompanying the Landgrave to their thrones. In the Song Contest, at the words 'O Wolfram, der du also sangest' ('O Wolfram, you who sang thus'), Wagner expressly forbade the singer playing Tannhäuser from making the by then traditional but unsubtle gesture of thrusting his clenched fist in Wolfram's face. In the finale he showed us how Tannhäuser had to sink down, utterly broken, with the cry, 'Weh mir Unglücksel'gen!' ('Woe betide me, wretch that I am!') and in doing so he offered us a masterly example of dramatic art. And then he showed us Elisabeth mounting the steps to the throne in devout humility and there folding her hands in prayer, her eyes raised towards heaven, a position which she maintained without moving until the curtain fell: it had a quite indescribable effect on us. But the culmination of his performance was Tannhäuser's Rome Narration. The words, 'Hör an, Wolfram, hör an!' ('Listen, Wolfram, listen!'), were already instilled with the deepest emotion and his excommunication sounded utterly shattering [...] In all

Royal Theatre, Stockholm, 1953
Elisabeth: Birgit Nilsson.
Tannhäuser: Conny Söderström
At the beginning of her international career, Nilsson, one of the very great Brünnhildes and Isoldes, also sang Wagner's young dramatic female roles. She is seen here in a studio photograph with Söderström. The first roles which Birgit Nilsson sang in Bayreuth were Elsa, in Wolfgang Wagner's 1954 production of *Lohengrin,* and Ortlinde, one of the Valkyries.

these scenes it was a truly great actor who stood before us.

Wagner, we can see, was concerned to achieve a style of acting which was true to life and deeply felt, something which we should nowadays call realism in acting.

The first performances of *Tannhäuser* in Bayreuth were given during the 1891 Festival, in a production which presented Cosima with 'the supreme Bayreuth challenge'; for her, it was 'a life-and-death struggle between opera and drama'. In the intervening years *Tannhäuser* had overtaken even *Lohengrin* in popularity and headed the repertories of all the major opera-houses. But the 'melodic variety of the work' had 'so overshadowed its poetic content that there was need for a dramatic re-working of the piece, in which the music, for all its melodic variety, should create its effect not simply as music but as the expression of certain characters and situations,' Cosima explained to George Davidsohn (a Berlin journalist and editor as well as a member of the Berlin Wagner Society) in a letter dated 11 September 1891. Cosima's acceptance of this youthful work into the Bayreuth repertory was not at all popular with those whom her son Siegfried called the 'hyper-Wagnerians', since it was their view that *Tannhäuser* could not be made to stand beside *Tristan, Parsifal* and the *Ring.* Cosima's missionary zeal was

intended to prove that *Tannhäuser* pointed the way forward and that it was a true music drama; such an attitude on her part is typical of the way she saw her task.

This was the first time that Cosima did not have recourse to earlier model productions, as had been the case with *Tristan und Isolde* and *Die Meistersinger von Nürnberg.* Instead she had to attempt to assemble all the evidence she could relating to the earlier performances in Dresden in 1845, Paris in 1861 and Vienna in 1875, three productions she considered 'authentic'. She wanted to know exactly where Venus had stood in Act III, whether the entry of the guests had continued past the first choral entry, whether Tannhäuser had sat on the right or the left of the stage in Act III, where the trumpeters had been located in the Paris production, and so on. Interestingly enough, she could make very little use of Heine's costume designs. The meticulous nature of her preparatory work was quite astonishing. She even consulted the archaeologist Reinhard Kekulé von Stradonitz, asked about illustrated portfolios on Pompeii or Greek vases, and developed an interest in the Hellenes and Greek costume. Max Brückner, who designed the sets in close consultation with Cosima, was encouraged to be guided by the original Dresden and Paris stage sets. She herself wrote, 'I am destined in fact to a life of laborious industriousness, since it has not been granted to me to take lightly even the tiniest detail. And when I see how much others rely on spontaneity and inspiration, I cannot help feeling that I am quite inartistic and philistine by nature.' She was not concerned with any independent artistic achievement but merely with carrying out what she considered to be the Master's wishes and with realizing those plans which Wagner himself had not lived to complete.

It is interesting to recall that on a number of occasions during preparations for *Tannhäuser* there was talk of a possible collaboration with Adolphe Appia. Appia had attended the 1888 Festival in the company of Houston Stewart Chamberlain, who was later to become Cosima's son-in-law. Appia must at least have submitted costume designs, since Cosima is known to have replied that he still had much to learn, that she had never yet encountered 'genius without industry' and that what Appia lacked was level-headedness. White as the colour of Venus's costume, as Appia seems to have suggested, struck her as being quite impossible, since white was the colour of coldness and innocence; and what colour would then be left for Elisabeth to wear, she asked Chamberlain in a letter of 28

March 1889. In spite of this, she wondered whether a good costume designer might not be able to make something of the sketches and suggested that Appia might perhaps be appointed 'costume designer and lighting consultant for Bayreuth' (23 October 1888). However, the proposed collaboration came to nothing.

Once again, a great deal of attention was paid to individualizing the chorus by means of costumes and movement. In order to distinguish them more readily and to give the singers a characteristic repertory of gestures, the various chorus members were provided with historical names. There were, for example, the Count of Hirschberg and his wife, the Counts of Lauterberg and Hohenstein, a Count Poppo of Henneberg, young girls of 'aristocratic' and 'more lowly' descent, and so on. A numerous retinue and pages completed the picture of a colourful and magnificent medievalism. According to Wolfgang Golther, Professor of German Literature, the costumes were based on a thirteenth-century Thuringian book on heraldry. 'In the opening scene we have to create something awesomely classical and in the second half evoke the very soul of the Middle Ages, a period which produced both Saint Francis and Saint Elizabeth,' Cosima wrote to Felix Mottl, who had taken over as conductor. In the Venusberg scene, in particular, the choreographer, Virginia Zucchi from Milan, must have achieved something quite new and striking. 'Thanks to the appearance of a number of leading prima

ballerinas and to the use of classical models, the dance became a true bacchanal, whereas all that theatres had previously offered at this point was simply the usual ballet,' according to Golther. A series of studio photographs have survived showing the dancers; and even if these photographs do not show the costumes under the original stage-lighting conditions, and even if the attitudes are consciously posed, what remains seems to us to show a certain lack of conviction; or is this simply because we see things differently nowadays?

A point which was widely argued and a source of some dissension was Cosima's idea of casting in the leading role of Elisabeth young and inexperienced singers rather than established operatic divas. Eliza Wiborg, a young, blonde Swedish singer, and Pauline de Ahna, who was later to marry Richard Strauss, corresponded exactly to Cosima's ideas of what Elisabeth should look like. 'What I wanted to show, on the basis of the drama, was above all a virginal, childlike character, whom the first terrible experience she suffers marks out as a saint, by dealing her a mortal blow,' Cosima wrote on 11 September 1891. Venus, on the other hand, played by Rosa Sucher, was a first cousin to Kundry, 'the fullest blossoming of womankind in her most demonic and enchanting power.' In order to emphasize the idea of 'drama', great stress was placed upon the singers' clear articulation. 'We have broken away from opera and are committed to demonstrating this break in the clearest possible

Bayreuth Festival, 1961
Producer and designer: Wieland Wagner. Conductor: Wolfgang Sawallisch. Tannhäuser: Wolfgang Windgassen. Shepherd boy: Elsa-Margrete Gardelli
Tannhäuser as a drama of ideas and the stage area a symbolic space. There is no longer any Wartburg nor any forest. The pilgrims make their way to Rome in front of the golden backdrop which creates what Wieland Wagner called 'the transcendency around man'. At the front of the stage, on the circular platform, lies Tannhäuser; further upstage, in the centre, is the shepherd boy.

Théâtre National de l'Opéra,
Paris, 21 June 1963
Designer: Leonor Fini
Set-design for the Venusberg.
Whereas Fini's sets for Acts II
and III were very plain, clearly
defined areas, the twinkling and
glittering grotto seemed to go
on into infinity. During this
period it was traditional to
choreograph the bacchanal as a
wild and aggressive dance. Fini,
however, conceived the
Dionysiac element as being
entirely within the
romanticizing style of the
nineteenth century, although
the artistic means she employed
were modern.

way in all that we do [...] The direction which our art is to take sets out from drama, and the primary vehicle for this drama is language. To concede this point would be tantamount to denying all that Bayreuth stands for,' Cosima had written to Felix Mottl in 1884. The advocates of a purely melodic vocal art spoke dismissively of the 'Bayreuth bark.' According to Richard Strauss, the secret behind the creation of this particular *Tannhäuser* consisted in the fact that 'what was seen to take place on stage was so bound up with the music' that there emerged 'from both a perfectly united whole' (letter from Bayreuth, 1891). Cosima's solution to the final scene must have been particularly impressive, for, as she wrote to Davidsohn on 11 September 1891, 'We must thank the *chorus* for the fact that the normally anticlimactic ending of the work became what it should really be, a preaching of the doctrine of salva-

tion and an enthusiastic profession of the belief that under God's holy guidance mankind feels spiritually uplifted beyond the tragedy of life.' As in Dresden, the sun rose behind the Wartburg and flooded the whole valley with its radiant light.

The 1894 Bayreuth performances were conducted by Richard Strauss and in the 1904 revival Isadora Duncan appeared as one of the Graces in the bacchanal wearing a Greek tunic, which was considered both sensational and scandalous.

As a direct result of Cosima's own production, the general public now began to clamour for performances of the opera in other theatres besides Bayreuth. Theatre managers were additionally goaded on by their ambition to rival Bayreuth and the Festival's international audiences wanted to have productions at home which were modelled on Bayreuth. For a time there was a marked fashion and, indeed, a real pressure on all those in the world of the theatre to acquire the Bayreuth imprimatur. This of course was linked to the fact that Cosima's work in Bayreuth laid claim to being regarded as authentic. Nevertheless, not all productions which claimed to model themselves on Bayreuth could be judged by Bayreuth's standards. Managements often went no further than ordering the Bayreuth sets from Max Brückner's studios in Coburg, where they were mass-produced. There was certainly plenty of talk of 'music drama,' but the results of course can no longer be verified and the suspicion remains that what was involved here was often no more than the mindless repetition of fashionable words, or else simply unrealizable dreams. An average theatre with its full programme of performances was quite incapable of providing conditions which would allow the singers an intensive study of their parts, and which would permit an exact balance to be achieved between chorus, orchestra and stage action, such as was worked out at Bayreuth over a long period of rehearsals. It is nevertheless to Bayreuth's credit that the thought ever entered anyone's mind that contemporary operatic practice was in need of urgent reform.

The first performance of *Tannhäuser* at La Scala, Milan, on 29 December 1891, was directly influenced by the Bayreuth model. The sets by Zuccarelli were exact copies of the ones used in Bayreuth, large, hand-coloured photographs of Brückner's sets being sent from the Festspielhaus to Milan. As in Bayreuth, Virginia Zucchi was engaged to choreograph the bacchanal. To judge from a surviving drawing, only the fauns had classical costumes, with their skins and goats' hooves; the Bacchantes and the Three Graces wore their usual tutus. Zucchi was also choreographer for the new production in Paris which had its first performance on 13 May 1895, thirty-four years after the scandal of the first production there. She herself danced in this production and her performance was praised as *une radieuse vision de l'antique* ('a shining vision from Antiquity'). The sets were designed by Amable (the Venusberg), Jambon (the two Wartburg valleys) and Carpezat (the Hall of Song), all of whom based their work principally on the Bayreuth sets. If the two Wartburg valley sets turned out to be somewhat conventional, Amable and Carpezat in particular decked out their basic scenic forms in a highly individual manner. The arches in Carpezat's hall were almost like something out of Moorish Spain, whereas the roof beams had a Teutonic look, with massive

Scandinavian carvings. The general impression was of something bizarre and contrived. Theodor Herzl, Paris correspondent for the Vienna *Neue Freie Presse*, attended several performances of this production, at a time when he was working on his famous book *Der Judenstaat* ('The Jewish State'). He confided to his diary that only Wagner's operas had the ability to fire his imagination and that it was only on those evenings when he was able to see a Wagnerian performance that he was not assailed by doubts as to the validity of his ideas. In his imaginary Jewish state he dreamed of festive audiences like those at the Paris Opéra, an elegant public and 'sublime processional marches'. Tannhäuser in this production was sung by the famous Belgian tenor Ernest van Dyck; Elisabeth was sung by Rose Caron and Venus by Lucienne Bréval. In later revivals, the part of Tannhäuser was sung by Albert Alvarez, Elisabeth by Aino Ackté and Venus by Louise Grandjean, Felia Litvinne and Lola Beeth.

The first performance of *Tannhäuser* at the Metropolitan Opera, New York, was given on 17 November 1884 in the old Dresden Version. It was not until 1889 that the conductor Anton Seidl, who had been a *répétiteur* at the first Bayreuth Festival of 1876, introduced the Paris Version. The part of Venus was sung by Lilli Lehmann, who had sung Woglinde and Ortlinde at the first Bayreuth Festival and who was one of the first Wagnerian singers to make an international reputation for herself. In the two decades leading up to the outbreak of the First World War, a period which writers like to describe as 'the Golden Age of Opera', there were entire seasons at the Metropolitan Opera that offered almost exclusively German operas, although the works themselves were not always sung in German. (It was not unusual for the same work to be sung in Italian and French, as happened for example in a performance of *Tannhäuser* in 1896.) The work remained in the repertory until 1914, during which time the cast lists included such famous names as Ernest van Dyck (1898), Leo Slezak, Milka Ternina as Elisabeth (1903), Olive Fremsted (1903), Aino Ackté, Berta Morena and Nellie Melba. This brief list may serve to correct the mistaken belief that itinerant opera-singers are an invention of the jet age. Even before the turn of the century, there were much sought-after international singing stars who gave guest performances of their most famous roles in all the world's major opera-houses and who were regarded as the definitive Tannhäuser or Elisabeth. The world's major operatic stages could not survive with-

State Opera, Vienna, 8 January 1963
Producer and conductor: Herbert von Karajan. Designer: Heinrich Wendel. Elisabeth: Gré Brouwenstijn. Landgrave: Gottlob Frick
Against the shimmering gold background of the lofty walls, which seem to emerge solemnly out of the darkness, there stands out the brilliantly colourful ceremonial society of the Wartburg, reminiscent of a medieval painting with its background of gold. Elisabeth's throne is at right, that of the Landgrave on the left; the minnesingers are lined up centre stage.

Municipal Stages, Frankfurt am Main, 22 December 1965
Producer: Joachim Herz
Designer: Rudolf Heinrich.
Conductor: Lovro von Matacic.
Elisabeth: Claire Watson.
Tannhäuser: Hans Hopf.
Landgrave: Franz Crass
The producer staged *Tannhäuser* as the drama of an artist caught in a bourgeois society. The designer made dramatic use of the classic arch motif: the narrow arches form both a kind of cage for the self-righteous and prejudiced Wartburg society and a prison for Tannhäuser.

out the attraction of famous names. During the First World War German operas were dropped from the repertory of the Metropolitan Opera and it was not until 1923 that *Tannhäuser* was reinstated. The new sets were provided by Kautsky's studios. Maria Jeritza sang Elisabeth, followed by Elisabeth Rethberg (1925), then Maria Müller, Lotte Lehmann and Kirsten Flagstad (1934). Lauritz Melchior made his Metropolitan début in the part of Tannhäuser on 17 February 1926; the role was also sung by Max Lorenz in 1931. Wolfram was sung by Friedrich Schorr; the Landgrave by Alexander Kipnis, Ivar Andrésen, Ezio Pinza and Emmanuel List, and Venus by Maria Olczewska. Whereas in Europe the main emphasis in fostering Wagner's music lay in production techniques and new stylistic tendencies in set-design, questions of staging remained of secondary importance in New York, as well as in Paris, the primary object of interest being the performances of the top-class singers.

It was in about 1910 that traditional ideas about the set-designs for *Tannhäuser* began to be called into question. As had been the case previously, it was the Hall of Song which first benefited from these new ideas, as a brief but necessary digression will indicate. It was remarkable that the 1861 Paris Version of the Hall of Song, which was ultimately based on that used in the original Dresden production of 1845 and which Wagner himself had al-

ways singled out as the ideal realization of his intentions, had had so minimal an influence elsewhere. It was a high-ceilinged room, featuring Gothic arches and tracery windows with stained glass, its timber-work reminiscent of the neo-Gothic period of English architecture. During preparations for the Munich revival of 1867, King Ludwig II had initially insisted on having a copy of the original Hall of Song from the Wartburg. He had undertaken an expedition on his own to Eisenach and the Wartburg in order to familiarize himself with the locations in which *Tannhäuser* was set. He insisted on historical accuracy in all matters relating not only to set construction but to architectural design in general. Wagner objected that in preparing the Paris production he had consulted Gropius's sketches in Berlin, which 'were a faithful copy of the restorations carried out on the Wartburg itself', but that he had found them 'unattractive' and 'totally unsuited' to his purpose. In seeking 'the ideal expression' of what he was looking for, he had used 'all the stylistic characteristics which had stood out in the faithful copy which I consulted [. . .] in order at the same time to give the ideal space a faithful air of period authenticity' (letter to the king's secretary, Lorenz von Düfflipp, of 17 May 1867). Wagner finally had his own way in spite of Ludwig, who gained his revenge by including a copy of the Wartburg banqueting hall, with its 'Singers' Arcade', in

Bayreuth Festival, 1972
Producer: Götz Friedrich.
Designer: Jürgen Rose.
Conductor: Colin Davis.
Elisabeth: Gwyneth Jones.
Landgrave: Hans Sotin.
Wolfram: Bernd Weikl.
Tannhäuser: Hermin Esser
Having offended their taboos, Tannhäuser is driven out by the society of the Wartburg. Above, at the left are the menfolk, massed like a black and threatening wall, bristling with arms; on the right, beneath them, stands the outcast Tannhäuser. Between these two elements, is Elisabeth, 'this white dove', as Götz Friedrich called her, no longer able to find a place, either above or below. Production photo from the 1977 revival.

San Francisco Opera,
6 October 1973
Producer: Paul Hager.
Designer: Wolfram Skalicki.
Conductor: Otmar Suitner.
Elisabeth: Leonie Rysanek.
Landgrave: Clifford Grant.
Wolfram: Thomas Stewart
A few pointed Gothic arches
forming cupolas sufficed to
suggest the style of the Middle
Ages in this production.

his castle at Neuschwanstein. Wagner himself visited the Wartburg in 1862 but the efforts at restoration left him 'completely cold'. He was not concerned with historical details but with an 'ideal' picture and the 'atmosphere' of the period. It is surprising that, for her own production in Bayreuth, Cosima used a copy of the Wartburg banqueting hall, and not the Hall of Song. The former was a wide, architecturally impressive hall, richly decorated in the magnificent historicist style. Contrary to Wagner's own intentions, Cosima's attempt to achieve authenticity took recourse in historicism and in precise topographical detail. She apparently lacked the artistic inspiration necessary for the 'ideal'. However that may be, it is ultimately to Cosima's influence and

that of her imitators that we owe the historicism of both costume and set-design which was characteristic of all productions of *Tannhäuser* around the turn of the century. A remark made by Marie Schmole, who had attended both the first Dresden production of 1845 and the later new production there in 1890, when the original design for the hall was again used, may be regarded as typical: everything about the 1890 production, she said, was historically faithful, but in the earlier production the style had been simpler and 'more ideal'.

The new trend was to reproduce not the banqueting hall but the actual Hall of Song at the Wartburg, or at least to make use of certain architectural features of the hall. The

Hall of Song is a plain, low-ceilinged room, its flat wooden-beamed ceiling supported on two stone columns in the centre of the room and its walls painted with ornamental Romanesque designs, with one wall decorated with Moritz von Schwind's fresco *Der Sängerkrieg* ('The Song Contest'). The only exceptional feature of this Hall of Song is the triple-arched arcade of the *Sängerlaube* or 'Singers' Arcade'. In its simplicity this hall corresponded rather to what the new generation of set-designers imagined the Middle Ages had looked like. The two columns in particular were frequently used as elements to divide the stage area and almost every set included the arcade as an architectural quotation. Any attempts to introduce changes generally began selectively with individual artists and medium-sized theatres, and only gradually achieved any widespread impact. That these attempts were accompanied by efforts to create interpretative sets is shown by a sketch dating from 1909/1910 by Rochus Gliese for the Baruch Theatre Studios in Berlin. His Hall of Song was a forbidding, stone-grey structure whose unequivocal message was 'law and order'; it was the expression of a fixed, intolerant society which was bound to reject Tannhäuser as an anarchist following his song in praise of Venus.

It was precisely the medium-sized theatres which had difficulty in freeing themselves from the Bayreuth model on which their audiences insisted for reasons of prestige, as the example of a new production in Mannheim in 1913 will indicate. The conductor was Arthur Bodanzky and the sets were designed by Ottomar Starke. The Venusberg was a kind of hell, with Venus as a medieval she-devil. The Hall of Song was a simple Romanesque hall whose walls were covered with stylized early Romanesque murals on a deep blue background. There were no large gateways or archways, merely simple wooden doors. On her entrance Elisabeth did not rush into the hall with outstretched arms, but entered with an air of modesty and awe. The trees in the sets for the valley of the Wartburg were stylized and impressionistic. Venus no longer appeared in Act III. In general there was an evident attempt to break away from the historicism of Romantic medievalism and put forward an authentic view of the period. The production was rejected by the majority of those present, who found it too modern. One worthy citizen of Mannheim even went so far as to have a pamphlet printed at his own expense, lamenting the loss of 'that splendid woman, Venus', 'the sultry fragrances' and 'dancing nymphs', instead of

which there was a black Venusberg with red lighting which looked like 'Vesuvius erupting'. Not even the valley of the Wartburg looked in the least familiar, but had become a mountain ridge with a few fir-trees scattered about in front of the cyclorama, a stage picture which was cold and unatmospheric.

The stylizing tendencies of the younger generation of set-designers who were striving to escape from the nineteenth-century system of painted flats and backdrops and who made use instead of the cyclorama, electric lighting and semi-representational blocks of scenery, did so because of the allegiance which they felt towards *art nouveau* and the newly emerging expressionist style; but the only reaction they found was one of opposition and incomprehension. The new tendencies in set-design were related to and dependent on stylistic movements in contemporary art. Two examples may serve to illustrate this point. In their colouring and precious formalism, Heinrich Lefler's costume sketches for the Vienna Volksoper production of *Tannhäuser* in 1907 and Alfred Roller's costume designs for the Vienna State Opera's production in the same year are quite clearly a product of the Vienna Secession. Equally, one might mention abstract solutions to the problem of staging the Hall of Song, solutions such as those offered by Emil Pirchan in Prague or Lothar Schenck von Trapp in Darmstadt in 1930.

It was not until 1930 that Siegfried Wagner was able to fulfil his greatest ambition as a producer and restage *Tannhäuser* in Bayreuth. The aftermath of the First World War had prevented the Festival Theatre from reopening its doors until 1924, and even after that date the theatre continued to be beset by financial difficulties caused by the conditions of the time. Funds for the new production were given to Siegfried as a present on the occasion of his sixtieth birthday. The sets were designed by Kurt Söhnlein, working in collaboration with Siegfried. (The general public, however, was rather more interested in the Bayreuth conducting début of Arturo Toscanini.) Siegfried conceived *Tannhäuser* entirely from the standpoint of art. In a radio talk he characterized the Venusberg as being 'in the voluptuous style of Rubens', the opposite of 'the severe style of Holbein' which typified the world of the Wartburg. The Venusburg was modelled on the *Feengrotten* ('fairy grottoes') at Saalfeld – a system of caves which seems to extend endlessly – in shades of reddish brown and ochre.

As was always the case in Bayreuth, particular attention was paid to the staging of the bacchanal. The choreographer was Rudolf

Metropolitan Opera, New
York, 22 December 1977
Producer: Otto Schenk.
Designer: Günther
Schneider-Siemssen. Conductor:
James Levine. Venus: Grace
Bumbry. Tannhäuser: James
McCracken
Venus's grotto, following
Wagner's own stage directions,
with lake, waterfall and
picturesquely reclining couples.
Venus and Tannhäuser are at
the front of the stage.
Nineteenth-century illusion is
achieved by modern technical
means. Critical opinions ranged
widely from 'perfect' to
'questionable'; but the
favourable reviews far
outnumbered the negative ones.

von Laban, assisted by Kurt Joos. Laban was one of the great innovators of twentieth-century ballet and an advocate of modern dance, who freed ballet from the ornamentalism of its classical style and gave it new possibilities of expression. What was characteristic about Laban's style was his new way of controlling space, something which he must have been particularly successful at achieving in Bayreuth with the Dance Theatre of the Essen Folkwangschule. He had earlier choreographed the bacchanal at the National Theatre in Mannheim in 1921 and on that occasion had based his ideas on 'the pantomimic interpretation of the music which Wagner put forward in his letter to Mathilde Wesendonck,' in other words, the so-called 'ballet-master letter'. For the Bayreuth performances he based himself on 'the Master's choreographic sketches for the Paris production', by which he can have meant only the prose sketch which, in contrast to the description in the published libretto, is less polished, wilder and more Dionysian. Laban felt that Wagner's ideas could probably be better realized 'with the techniques of modern theatrical dance than by means of the old ballet'. As in the case of Maurice Béjart in 1961, Laban was criticized for the fact that his choreography involved more gymnastics than actual dancing. Daniela Thode designed the cos-

tumes, 'which were modelled on F. Weege's fine book on classical Greek dance.' Venus's costume was based on the peplos worn by the caryatid figures on the Erechtheum. Daniela described Laban's choreography for the Three Graces as 'archaic'.

The change of scene to the valley of the Wartburg did not take place suddenly but was gradually introduced by means of a change of lighting. The scene was divided by a large, practicable ramp and bridge that extended the width of the stage, which created additional acting areas. Siegfried had had in mind a picture such as may be seen in Hans Thoma's severely beautiful landscape paintings. In the final tableau of Act I a vast hunting party, complete with horses and dogs, crowded on to the stage. In contrast to the 1891 production, the Hall of Song was a wide but simply fashioned and symmetrical hall with Romanesque designs painted on the high, gold-coloured walls. In the centre at the back there was a single, huge Romanesque arched doorway which commanded a view of the Thuringian mountains and through which the guests entered. The Manesse Codex served as a model for the costumes. The general impression made by the starkly coloured hall with its claret-red carpet and the golden background of its walls was that of a medieval painting. Elisabeth and the Landgrave received their

guests from the front of the stage, their backs to the audience; it was a picture of 'ancient courtly and princely magnificence'. The individual handling of the chorus members and a subtly differentiated lighting plot were the chief characteristics of Siegfried's production style. At Tannhäuser's song in praise of Venus, the whole stage faded into darkness, leaving only Tannhäuser lit by the 'Venus spot' of Act I, an iridescent play of colour. Similarly during Tannhäuser's Rome Narration in Act III, only he and Wolfram were picked out by bright spotlights. As in earlier productions, the ending of the opera was transfigured by the early morning light of the rising sun.

Maria Müller, who sang the part of Elisabeth, was praised as the epitome of a singing actress, a young woman touching in her child-like innocence who was able to make plausible the change in Elisabeth's character from radiantly jubilant lover to intercessor and broken-hearted saint. The Tannhäuser of Sigismund Pilinsky, on the other hand, failed to fulfil the hopes which had been placed in him. The Landgrave was sung by Ivar Andrésen, Wolfram by Herbert Janssen and the tiny part of the shepherd was taken by the young Erna Berger. Toscanini received a rapturous reception from the audience, although his interpretation divided critical opinion; he was nevertheless the sensation of these particular performances. The technical director, Friedrich Kranich, reports that dozens of those who had been unable to obtain tickets crept both backstage and into the orchestra pit, getting in the way of the technicians as they went about their work.

Siegfried Wagner was a cautious, rather than a radical, innovator. He understood his role as that of continuing a living tradition. One merit of his production was that it was sufficiently lucid to provide important questions for discussion. Behind the attractive exterior of a fairy-tale, topical problems could be discerned. The 'morality play' in medieval costume could be taken as a topical 'human drama'. Writing in 1930, the Wagner commentator Bernhard Diebold suggested that:

We should never forget that 'virtue' is the enzyme and *social bond* of the whole of feudal courtly society. If virtue were to be abolished here, society would fear for its cultural survival. Every age needs its own kind of 'virtue'. Our twentieth-century virtue, for example, is trust in capital. If in the midst of a bastion of finance and industry, someone were to call out at the top of his voice, 'Down with capitalism!' – in the midst of the General Assembly – he would

be treated in exactly the same way as Tannhäuser on the Wartburg. There is no difference between them [...] What once caused panic as the Venusberg is nowadays called Moscow or such like. And so this Tannhäuser is a highly dangerous character for our Wartburg Christian. His error, admittedly, is human. (Even a Muscovite may be 'humanly pardoned' by certain circles.) But what exists to justify humanity is not the *law* of the bourgeoisie but divine *grace.* In cursing Tannhäuser the pope in Rome has no inkling of grace [...] Grace only appears in the figure of the individual who loves mankind through God. This is the saint, who in this case is Elisabeth. None of this needs to be interpreted in a specifically Catholic sense. Grace will be transfigured in a love which pays no sociological regard to bourgeois existence as a whole; it is through this love that 'mankind' will reveal itself. *Ecce homo.* Wagner grants neither the league of virtue nor Venus poetic justice. Only the saint receives her supreme justification.

The Berlin State Opera marked the fiftieth anniversary of Wagner's death with a production of *Tannhäuser* by Jürgen Fehling, designed by Oskar Strnad and conducted by Otto Klemperer. It was an apparent attempt on the part of Heinz Tietjen, the general intendant, to take over at the point where the Kroll Opera had left off, when it had closed two years previously in 1931. The first performance on 12 February 1933 received considerable attention but only three more performances could be given before firm pressure from the Nazi *Kampfbund* ('Battle League') forced it to be replaced by the old 1929 production of Franz Ludwig Hörth, which had been conducted by Leo Blech and designed by Panos Aravantinos. Fehling's production was scarcely able to influence contemporary theatre practice, although its significance was immediately recognized. Indeed, it was not until the New Bayreuth productions of Wieland Wagner and Götz Friedrich that Fehling's ideas about the work were developed any further. Both Wieland and Friedrich took the Berlin production as their starting-point and their intentions had much in common with those of Fehling, Strnad and Klemperer. A point which they all shared was their questioning of the audience's traditional way of seeing things. Although the avant-garde's skirmishes with Wagner had often proved profitable in the past, it was precisely in the case of Wagner that anything new and radically thought out had always had difficulty in asserting itself in the face of a familiarity and traditionalism which liked to pass itself off as 'faithfulness to the original'. Any form of debate leaves the spectator feeling uncomfortable, since it makes demands and disturbs his simple, bland enjoyment. In the Berlin production there was the additional complication involving a situation which involved both the history of the theatre and politics. The opera was not staged in an illusionistic style, since *Tannhäuser* was by that time a well-known, popular piece which had not simply been handed down and preserved in a traditional style of production. There was no longer any question of merely replacing an old solution by a new and better one. Instead the work was analysed and one particular aspect of it brought out in performance, so as to make the opera seem relevant; this aspect was the situation of the artist who exposes himself to the two spheres of experience provided by the Apollonian and Dionysian principles, who carries this attitude over into society and who comes to grief as a result.

State Opera, Dresden, 10 December 1978
Producer: Harry Kupfer. Sets and costumes: Peter Sykora. Conductor: Siegfried Kurz. Venus: Ingeborg Zobel. Tannhäuser: Reiner Goldberg
The classical ideal of Venus is no longer valid. The goddess is depicted as a ruined statue, whose lap forms the couch for a dishevelled, seedy deity. Not even this alternative, which Tannhäuser has sought for himself, can be made to work—this according to the producer in defence of his production.

The Venusberg could be seen through two large circular openings, one behind the other. The set was hung with black gauzes and films were projected on the backdrop. The dancers, wearing flesh-coloured tights, began by remaining inside the area limited by the circles. There were just two huge symbolic props at the front of the stage, a harp on the left and a tiger skin on the right, indicative of the Apollonian and Dionysian principles (the Wartburg and Venus) and of the 'two souls' in Tannhäuser's breast. The Dresden version was performed, without the extended bacchanal. A few key phrases from reports on the production will not, it is true, allow us to form any real impression of what the stage actually looked like, but they will serve to confirm that the Venusberg in question was a place of terror rather than a pleasance lit with roseate hues: 'a bare robbers' cave'; 'a gloomy mountain hole'; 'the indecent exposure of an ecstatically lascivious nudist colony'; 'like a Last Judgement by Rubens'. The second scene was no longer the familiar cleft in the valley of the Wartburg, but a green, spring-like meadow situated high on a mountainside and dotted with individual trees. The hunting party entered the pasture over steps at the back of the stage. There were no hounds, falcons or horses. Children with fronds of greenery greeted the returning Tannhäuser. In Act II there were two sets, an arrangement which was dramatically justified. The scenes with Elisabeth, the Landgrave and Tannhäuser demand an intimate setting and so Fehling's production had the scenes before the entry of the guests played in front of a steep flight of steps. The steps were then turned on their axes and two large platforms for the chorus were brought in to form an arena for the song contest. A single large harp stood on a pedestal in the centre of the stage, and banners were unfurled from the flies. The ladies of the court and the knights sat apart. The chorus and the minnesingers were all identically dressed in white and purple. Gone was the charming evocation of a Middle Ages brought to life again, and in its place was a quite specific society with specific ideas about the role of the artist. The world of the Wartburg was seen in a critical light. Following Tannhäuser's song in praise of Venus, turmoil broke out, the women fleeing in horror from the hall and the knights attacking Tannhäuser with their swords; their strict rules had been broken and anarchy reigned. The third-act set similarly departed from the traditional model. It showed the wall surrounding the Wartburg pierced by a huge gateway, with drawbridge and portcullis leading into the castle. A withered tree grew beside the wall. Everything was a subdued brown in colour. The realm of Venus appeared in the same gateway through which Elisabeth passed to die, thus bringing the two opposing worlds together in a single image. Tannhäuser, no longer a part of either, died outside the walls. At the end the young pilgrims were reported to have carried a 'huge Whitsuntide bush' rather than the usual green staff.

Tannhäuser was the first Wagnerian opera to be designed by Caspar Neher for a production in Frankfurt am Main in 1934. Neher was Bertolt Brecht's set-designer and described by him as 'the greatest set-builder of our day'. His designs are dramaturgically well thought out, intelligent and – in their sparing, almost monochromatic use of colour – of a profound, poetic and artistic appeal. On the Venusberg scrim he painted a playful and allusive variation on the theme of Antoine Watteau's *L'Embarquement pour Cythère* ('Embarkation for the Island of Cythera'). For the Venusberg itself he designed a collage of quotations from classical architecture. His Hall of Song was a high-ceilinged and obliquely angled room. The chorus entered through an open door diagonally to the right, which led out into a gallery, and the canopy above the Landgrave's throne served as a balcony for the trumpeters. Here, too, we find the use of a narrow pillar to accentuate the shape of the hall. Its walls were painted in pale shades of grey, which gave them the appearance of rough-cast. Neher's costume designs similarly gave an almost monochromatic impression, with delicate tones of brown, russet and muted beige. In appearance the costumes approached the style of those worn at the late medieval Burgundian court, the women having the loose-fitting sleeves characteristic of the period. A gala performance of *Tannhäuser* was produced by Rudolf Hartmann at the Munich National Theatre in 1939 to celebrate the 'Day of German Art'. To mark the occasion, the Vienna State Opera chorus travelled to Munich to give a guest performance alongside the Munich State Opera's own chorus. The conductor was Clemens Krauss. Hartmann recalls in his memoirs that 'not even in New Bayreuth, with all the sexual orgies that went on there,' had he witnessed 'a choreographic staging of the Venusberg which was so artistically superb and so much in accord with the spirit of classical eroticism.' This was reputedly the first time that totally naked girls had appeared on the stage of the National Theatre in a *tableau vivant*. It must be said that the set-designs of Ludwig

Sievert were somewhat less convincing. Since his Freiburg productions of the *Ring* and *Parsifal* in 1912/1913, Sievert had emerged as arguably the leading reformer in matters of stage-design, and at the same time he had made his own brilliant use of the ideas of Adolphe Appia. That such an artist as Sievert, when provided with unlimited funds, could come so perilously close to the official state naturalism of the period, is something which is at least worthy of note.

Wieland Wagner produced *Tannhäuser* at Bayreuth in 1954 and 1961 and in both productions retained the same basic conception of the work. For him, the impulse which had driven Richard Wagner to create all the works from *Der fliegende Holländer* through to *Parsifal* had been to fathom 'der Liebe wahrstes Wesen' ('The truest essence of love'). As he wrote in his essay, 'Zur Tannhäuser-Tragödie' ('On the tragedy of Tannhäuser'), in 1955, 'The true essence of love is a responsible, trusting and selfless devotion to the lover's self. In *Tannhäuser*, accordingly, man's typical self-absorption appears as the "evil principle" which must be eradicated and which is opposed to woman's readiness for sacrifice and unquestioning devotion; it is not, as is usually claimed, the phenomenon of Eros itself.' For Wieland, Tannhäuser's tragedy is 'that of man in general in a Christian age who, conscious of the split in his inner life between mind and impulse, seeks the way back to his original, divinely human oneness. The "cross" which he has to bear is the mistaken belief that salvation can be achieved by means of a total realization of one or other of the two poles of human existence, namely "ecstasy" or "asceticism".' He finds salvation first of all in the love which Elisabeth bears him in spite of the grief he has caused her. On the basis of the final lines of the work, 'Heil, der Gnade Wunder Heil! / Erlösung ward der Welt zutheil' ('Hail! Hail to the miracle of grace! / The world has been granted redemption'), Wieland saw Tannhäuser's private tragedy within the overall context of 'the meaning of man's fate in general'. 'From his state of self-absorption, the individual must find his own way to an understanding of "the truest essence of love" and that understanding can only be acquired through guilt. This insight stands at the beginning of the human soul's Via Dolorosa and is a prerequisite for the efficacy of divine grace, which alone makes it possible for the "sinner" to return to the eternal order' (ibid). This is how Wieland saw the central problem of *Tannhäuser*, a problem obscured in the course of the stage history of the work by its wealth of external action, which had always tended to determine its success with the general public.

As long as the theatre retained an illusionistic style of staging, such an interpretation of *Tannhäuser* as a 'drama of ideas' was bound to be less than obvious. Traditional productions had seen their efforts to achieve authenticity confirmed precisely by their exact imitation of the topography of the Thuringian setting. For Wieland this could only be a distraction from the real issues, which was why he eliminated all forms of realism from his two productions of the work, thereby exposing himself to the charge of skeletonizing the drama and introducing an abstract, untheatrical, 'oratorio style'. (It is worth mentioning in passing that on the occasion of the very first production in Dresden, Wagner himself had been rebuked for staging an oratorio in Act II.) Wieland's interpretation had no need of the Teutonic forests, the Wartburg, the blossoming staff or Elisabeth's corpse; for Wieland who, as in all his productions, was his own designer, the Middle Ages were 'an imaginary space', symbolically realized in the permanent gold background against which the action of the work enfolded in a strict formalistic style. As he himself wrote in 1961, 'The gold background created the transcendency around man.' The stage was a space for symbols, not for illusion.

The two opposing worlds were present from the very outset. The Venusberg presented a broad, slanted golden form of light, coiled into a spiral ellipse. Tannhäuser (Ramon Vinay) lay downstage at right at the foot of a cross which was almost as high as the proscenium. The wild procession of Bacchantes (choreographed by Gertrud Wagner and Ehrengard von Dessauer) issued from the ellipse and moved downstage; in their midst, untouched by the goings-on around them, was a single, radiant couple, charming and tender, an allegory of sexuality and eroticism. In the second scene, the chorus of pilgrims to Rome was a black, heavy mass of Barlach-type figures who passed diagonally across the stage. Nature was indicated in this scene simply by a ground cloth covered in geometrically ordered floral designs. Equally block-like was the entry of the chorus in Act II, divided according to sex, the embodiment of orderly thought and a picture of stark solemnity. It was certainly not because of any overreaction to the realism of the traditional Bayreuth style of producing this scene that persuaded Wieland to attempt a stylized interpretation; rather was it because such an interpretation was dramaturgically justified. What one saw here was not an opera chorus

ostensibly made up of historical characters but a chorus upon which devolved the function which it had once performed in classical drama. Its movements were ordered along stylized and clearly choreographed lines. The Hall of Song consisted simply of a number of arches in front of the gold backcloth, reminiscent of Paul Klee's *Revolution des Viaduktes* ('Revolution of the Viaduct'). Wieland had originally studied to become an artist and he liked his work in the theatre to include references to modern art. Only in the positioning of Elisabeth and the Landgrave, with their backs to the audience, and in the entry of the chorus from the back of the stage, was there any reference to the traditional way of staging this scene. The chorus was positioned on seats on either side of the stage, Elisabeth presiding over the women, the Landgrave over the men. The whole of the central stage area was geometrically laid out to form a battle arena for the Song Contest, with the minstrels resembling figures on a chessboard. Only Tannhäuser broke free from this strict sense of order. The criticism of Wartburg society, which was to become a general feature of all later productions, was already implicit here in Wieland's first staging of the work. After Tannhäuser had been packed off to Rome to atone for his sins, the chorus and soloists bowed down before Elisabeth in an act of obeisance to the idea of high courtly love. In his 1961 production Wieland altered this scene so that Elisabeth now sank down to the ground in a dead faint; she no longer belonged to the world of courtly love but was as much an outcast and as much condemned to suffer as Tannhäuser himself. The ending of the opera, too, showed a sublimation of the Middle Ages: the chorus formed a towering, irregular triangle of halos, a distant vision on the cyclorama, like Giotto's depiction of the Last Judgement in the Arena Chapel at Padua; they sang 'Der Gnade Heil' ('The salvation of grace') over the dead Tannhäuser, who lay at the foot of the huge cross as he had at the beginning of the work.

The new production of 1961 showed a deepening and a crystallization of the original concept, a point particularly well illustrated by the polar opposites of Venus and Elisabeth. Grace Bumbry's engagement as 'Bayreuth's first black Venus' caused a sensation at the time and Wieland received a lot of criticism as a result. She was only twenty-four. Wieland was able to use her dramatic abilities to present Venus as a powerful goddess, a bronze, archaic idol, an Asiatic Astarte rather than the usual Hellenic Venus. The antithesis of this world found its perfect embodiment in the small, delicate and madonna-like Elisabeth of Victoria de los Angeles. Two idols confronted each other in their struggle for Tannhäuser, and both lost. The bacchanal was choreographed by Maurice Béjart and his Ballet of the Twentieth Century. In wild frenzy the dancers encircled the immovable idol of Venus, 'a mixture of Wagner, rue Pigalle and Henry Miller', the music critic of *The Times* wrote. Béjart's choreography was considered very daring for the time, which was before the so-called sexual revolution.

When Götz Friedrich produced *Tannhäuser* in Bayreuth in 1972, he sparked off one of the greatest scandals in the entire history of the Festival. He believes, however, that he did not set out with the conscious intention of breaking with all that had gone before, but rather that he approached the piece from the same basically analytical standpoint as that which had been characteristic of Wieland's work in the theatre. He had 'learned from Felsenstein how to handle people on stage' and Wieland's productions had shown him 'how to operate on an uncluttered stage'; what he now sought was 'a link between these two strands, between hyper-activity and hyper-stylization [...] but certainly neither as an exorcist nor as an angry young man of Bayreuth.' 'The traditional antitheses of "earthly" and "spiritual" love, Venus and Elisabeth, Venusberg and the Wartburg world's seemed to Friedrich to be no longer adequate in bringing out the 'complexity and diversity of the phenomena with which Tannhäuser has to come to terms in his search for the true nature of his existence and of his activity as an artist.' Tannhäuser's fate is the 'journey of an artist through inner and outer worlds, in search of himself, as depicted in the theatre'. Friedrich was not concerned simply with the position of the artist inside and outside society – an interpretation to which the work has frequently been reduced – but rather with the position of the artist inside and outside his own dreams, in other words what he imagines art to be about. For Friedrich, *Tannhäuser* is the tragedy of a German artist in the tradition of Goethe's *Tasso,* or Heinrich von Kleist, an example of artistic genius which is defined by its being set against certain social requirements.

It is no longer possible to adopt an 'idealistically uncritical' view of the Wartburg community, which 'sets itself up' not simply as a judge in artistic matters but as 'a moral gauge of events'. On the other hand, no interpretation can limit itself exclusively to the question of social criticism, since this is merely one narrative level among many in the work. It is in any case impossible to take a wholly objective view of Tannhäuser himself, if he is not to be glorified as a martyr to the cause of some anarchical concept of freedom. 'The historical and, at the same time, the topical greatness of Tannhäuser grows [...] from his struggle to understand that the artist [...] can only realize himself through communicating with society.' Rebellion against society can only prove to be 'creatively revolutionary' if it achieves 'an awareness of religion and commitment, even though it be a new commitment or an as yet unknown religion.' Tannhäuser's struggle to achieve this awareness is what constitutes his greatness and his tragedy. Tannhäuser is a seeker, like Faust, who prefers knowledge to faith. His attempt at self-realization is just as unsuccessful 'in the "artificial paradise" of the Venusberg' as it is 'at the heart of the regime, on the Wartburg'.

The overture was acted out on the open stage, with Tannhäuser fleeing from reality and bursting into the artist's ivory tower of art for art's sake, where he creates for himself his artificial paradise. This paradise was visibly created by theatrical means and shaped within his own head. The Venusberg had no basis in reality, unlike the Wartburg; it was a dream-world, or trauma, conjured by Tannhäuser's own imagination. The roles of Venus and Elisabeth were performed by the same singer (Gwyneth Jones). Tannhäuser's dream-world, however, turned to hell. The 'images of a youthfully naïve love and the vision of the possibility of fulfilment offered by the love between man and woman become increasingly frenzied and turn suddenly into a destructive orgasm [...] Ecstasy is transformed into barbarity and brutality,' into blood and death. The choreographer was John Neumeier. Long, red ribbons hanging from the flies were stretched taut around Tannhäuser like the bars of a prison; or else they formed an enormous, fantastic harp on which he accompanied his songs to Venus. The alternative reality of the feudal world of the Wartburg was made visible in a concrete image on its very first entry: the hunting party was carried in on chairs.

The setting for all three acts was the same simple wooden floor, the basic form of all European stages from time immemorial. Every reminiscence of a particular style or of historical forms of architecture was avoided. In Act II the platform of planks was raised to form a great rostrum. Fourteen steps led up to what might have been a pyramid or a hill on to which the chorus stepped and greeted each other in the name of art. Banners were then unfurled, revealing an ironic parallel with the

Festival Theatre itself. But it was more than simple irony and more than the mere effect of recognition. A fictitious and a real situation were seen to coincide here, for the same question was being asked both on stage and in the stalls: a holy place occupied by society, or an intellectual 'workshop'; empty solemnity and social elegance, or analysis, disquiet and a contribution to thought. Wartburg society sang of art and peace, but as soon as Tannhäuser's false notes rang out, there was no longer any question of the peace which is a precondition for art; swords were drawn instead. In acting as he does, Tannhäuser has no wish to provoke the others or to boast of his experiences with Venus; he simply wishes to support beliefs which he sees to be true; in Friedrich's words, he is a 'truth-fanatic'.

Following this confrontation, all that remains in Act III is a number of lost, lonely and distraught individuals, a Beckett-like emptiness and despair. Elisabeth wanders in hope and fear through the stream of returning pilgrims who, intoxicated and enraptured at their having been pardoned, drag after them a huge cross hung with devotional objects; they are oblivious to her anguish. She tries to recognize Tannhäuser among their number, until the realization finally dawns that he is not going to return. Friedrich has called this 'an image of eternity' in a world marked by wars and catastrophes.

By Act III Elisabeth herself has become an outsider, no longer the Wartburg princess but an old, broken, grey-haired woman who has taken the sins of another upon herself and who suffers with him. She represents an early Christian attitude which involves 'real humanity', compassion and understanding. Following a blackout on stage, the annunciation of divine mercy at the end of the work was sung by the chorus in radiant brightness; they were fully visible on stage, first of all in neutral clothing, but then in a mixture of various costumes intended to characterize them as 'humanity in general', a group which 'is not part of the establishment but which challenges the establishment by calling for tolerance'. Friedrich interpreted the final chorus not as a confirmation of what had gone before but as a demand that a man like Tannhäuser who had chosen for himself not comfort and conformity but the anguish of wanting to increase his knowledge and experience, should not be allowed to perish mercilessly. To quote Friedrich again, 'Those who survive [...] tell the others: understand this fate as a call addressed to us all, a call for humane tolerance. And this humane tolerance might actually be the greatest mercy of all.'

All subsequent productions of *Tannhäuser* have been to a greater or lesser degree realistic in their basic concept, with the exception of the new production at the Metropolitan Opera in New York, first seen on 22 December 1977. With its elaborate sets and tableau effects borrowed from the nineteenth century, it seemed to be a protest against modern European attempts to interpret the work; and it effectively restored *Tannhäuser* to the status of grand opera.

This chapter has largely been concerned with Bayreuth productions since, ever since its first production, *Tannhäuser* has represented a supreme challenge to Bayreuth. The examples discussed have shown, moreover, how different generations in the same theatre have each come to terms with the work by rediscovering and reinterpreting it in a way which affords it contemporary relevance. If the word 'scandal' has been mentioned so often in this account of previous productions, it is not for the sake of sensationalism but because such scandals are typical of the critical reaction which has greeted this one work in particular, a work which continues to exhibit its unique ability to arouse both consternation and indignation.

Hof=Theater.

Weimar, Mittwoch den 28. August 1850

Zur Goethe=Feier:

Prolog

von Franz Dingelstedt, gesprochen von Herrn Jaffé.

Hierauf:

Zum Erstenmale:

Lohengrin.

Romantische Oper in drei Akten.

(letzter Akt in zwei Abtheilungen)

von Richard Wagner

Heinrich der Finkler, deutscher König,	Herr Höfer
Lohengrin,	Herr Beck
Elsa von Brabant,	Fräulein Agthe
Herzog Gottfried, ihr Bruder,	Frau Hettstedt
Friedrich von Telramund, brabantischer Graf,	Herr Milde
Ortrud, seine Gemahlin,	Fräulein Fastlinger
Der Heerrufer des Königs,	Herr Bätsch

Sächsische und Thüringische Grafen und Edle
Brabantische Grafen und Edle
Edelfrauen.
Edelknaben.
Mannen. Frauen. Knechte.

Antwerpen: erste Hälfte des zehnten Jahrhunderts.

Die Textbücher sind an der Kasse für 5 Sgr zu haben.

Preise der Plätze:

Fremden=Loge	1 Thlr.	10 Sgr.	— Pf	Parterre=Loge	— Thlr.	20 Sgr.	— Pf
Balkon	1	—	—	Parterre	—	15	—
Sperrsitze	1	—	—	Gallerie=Loge	—	10	—
Parket	—	20	—	Gallerie	—	7	6

Anfang um 6 Uhr.   Ende gegen 10 Uhr.

Die Billets gelten nur am Tage der Vorstellung, wo sie gelöst worden.

Der Zutritt auf die Bühne, bei den Proben wie bei den Vorstellungen, ist nicht gestattet.

Das Theater wird halb 5 Uhr geöffnet.

Die freien Entréen sind ohne Ausnahme ungiltig.

Lohengrin

Wagner spent the evening of 28 August 1850 sitting with his wife Minna at the Swan, an inn in Lucerne, while the curtain went up in Weimar on the world première of *Lohengrin*. Wagner was a wanted man in Germany and hence was prevented from being present in person; instead he followed the performance on his watch, in a state of some excitement, timing it from the beginning to what he reckoned was the end of the performance. 'An immense longing has been kindled within me to see this work performed. I entrust this plea of mine to you. Produce *Lohengrin* for me! You are the only man to whom I would ever make this appeal: to no one but you can I entrust the task of producing this work,' he had written to Franz Liszt during the previous April, and Liszt had responded by successfully mounting the first performances of *Lohengrin*, in spite of Wagner's exile and in spite of the limited means at the disposal of the Weimar theatre.

Like so much else, Wagner's familiarity with the Lohengrin legend had begun in Paris. In the same monograph by Lucas which had provided him with the crucial pointer towards a conflation of the Tannhäuser legend with the Wartburg Song Contest, he had found what he described in *Mein Leben* as a 'critical paper' on the Lohengrin poem, with a detailed account of its contents. As a result, a new world of poetry was immediately opened up to him. Initially, Wagner was put off by the epic form of the poem, and the figure of Lohengrin aroused in him the same sense of revulsion and mistrust which he felt 'at the sight of carved and painted saints on main country roads, and in the churches of Catholic countries'. And yet the theme continued to obsess him. According to *Mein Leben*, it was only when he had got to know the Lohengrin myth in its simple outlines and in its 'profounder significance as a true folk poem' — a knowledge he acquired from more recent researches into the history of the legend — that the subject began to exercise a growing attraction for him. His intensive in-vestigations led him to study Joseph Görres' edition of the Lohengrin epic, published in 1813 and containing a vast introduction to the poem; he also read Jacob Grimm's *Deutsche Mythologie* ('German Mythology'), *Deutsche Rechtsalterthümer* ('German Legal Antiquities') and *Weisthümer* ('Lore'), the *Deutsche Sagen* ('German Legends') of Jacob and Wilhelm Grimm, and San Marte's edition of Wolfram von Eschenbach's *Parzival* (1836/1841). He even consulted such an out-of-the-way work as Warnkönig's *Flandrische Staats- und Rechtsgeschichte bis zum Jahr 1305* ('Constitutional and Legal History of Flanders up to 1305'). It may be remarked in passing that it was not until his period of appointment in Dresden that Wagner had the means whereby to build up his library to suit his own particular interests. He took greater care than had been the case with *Tannhäuser* to familiarize himself with the German Middle Ages. His method, it is true, lacked philological precision, but, as he said himself, he was 'serious', in spite of the fact that many of his friends in Dresden could not understand why he was wasting his time with such 'crudities'. And yet it was precisely to these studies that Wagner attributed the fact that *Lohengrin* later came admiringly to be credited with having so unique a physiognomy.

In June 1845 Wagner wrote to the critic Karl Gaillard, informing him that on completion of *Tannhäuser* he hoped to be able to devote a whole year to nothing else but studying the books in his library. Although he was keen to begin work on his new subject, he intended, he said, to force himself to stand back from it, since, in the first place, he wanted to learn a lot more about the subject and, in the second place, an original work of dramatic art was the product of a particular period in the artist's process of education, whereas the manufacture of insignificant products was undertaken as a means of making money. But things would be different in the future.

Bohemia was again the setting, on this occasion Marienbad (modern Mariánské

Court Theatre, Weimar,
28 August 1850
Playbill announcing the first performance.

101

Lázně), where Wagner had gone to take the waters. He took with him the two epics of *Parzival* and *Lohengrin* and buried himself in the forest where, stretched out on the banks of a stream, he passed his time in the company of these strange but somehow familiar tales. In order to distract himself from *Lohengrin*, which was beginning to take an obsessive hold of him, he sketched the first draft of *Die Meistersinger von Nürnberg*. But it was to no avail. His excitement grew to an alarming degree: Lohengrin 'suddenly stood before me, fully armed, the whole subject-matter dramatically formed right down to the very last detail' *(Mein Leben)*. It must have been at the end of July or early August, around midday, that Wagner literally leapt out of his bath and ran back to his rooms, like a madman, scarcely even bothering to dress properly, in his haste to commit *Lohengrin* to paper. The great prose draft was completed on 3 August 1845. As had been the case with *Rienzi* and *Der fliegende Holländer*, large sections of the text were already couched in dialogue form.

The libretto was written in Dresden that autumn, after the first performances of *Tannhäuser* were over. Wagner read the text of the opera to a fair-sized circle of friends at the 'Engelclub' in Dresden on 17 November. It was the first of his poetry readings, which were later to become famous; the audience included Robert Schumann, the architect Gottfried Semper, and the painters Julius Schnorr von Carolsfeld and Friedrich Pecht. Schumann declared that the text could never be set to music. It was the two painters who were most deeply impressed by what they had heard. After a few minor corrections the libretto was finally completed on 27 November 1845, but the composition sketch had to wait until the end of the current opera season before Wagner had time to devote himself to it. It was written in Gross-Graupa near Pillnitz between 15 May and 30 July 1846. He began the orchestral sketch in Dresden on 9 September, starting strangely enough with Act III, a procedure which he never again repeated. Wagner himself explained that he had been moved to do so by the fact that the musical *motifs* of the Grail Narration were the heart of the entire work. It was not until 5 March 1847 that he was able to complete the orchestral sketch of this act. He began the orchestral sketch of Act I on 12 May, that of Act II on 18 June and by 28 August had put the finishing touches to the work with the composition of the Prelude. There followed the process of instrumentation, and the full score was complete by 28 April 1848.

Wagner was relieved when Lüttichau offered to stage the first performances of his latest opera in Dresden. He hoped for a distraction from the excitement and confusion which the events of 1848, including the Paris Revolution, had brought him. Since he had taken rather too prominent a political stance in the intervening years, however, the mood at court was against him, with the result that the project had to be abandoned. There was no longer any possibility of a reconciliation with the Dresden Opera.

In spite of his fascination with the subject, Wagner had initially had difficulty in penetrating the vast and rambling epic with its thousands of lines and in sorting out the complicated strands of action; the problem was to distil from it the essence of the plot. He wrote to his brother Albert on 4 August 1845 that he had 'freed the almost indecipherable legend from the rubble and decay of the old poet's incompetent and prosaic treatment of it, and raised it up once again, by means of my own inventiveness and recreative ability, to the true level of its rich and highly poetic value'. He experienced similar difficulties with both *Tristan und Isolde* and *Parsifal* in shaping his own version from the old epic poems. He summarized the essence of the Lohengrin legend as follows: 'An archetypal characteristic, which is found in countless variants, can be traced throughout the legends of all nations who dwell by the sea or by rivers which flow into the sea: over the blue mirror of the waves there approached a stranger of supreme beauty and purest virtue, who drew all towards him and who won over every heart by means of his irresistible charms; he fulfilled the wishes of those who yearned and dreamed of happiness in that distant land across the waves they could never know. The stranger disappeared again, returning across the billowing sea as soon as he was asked what his true nature was. Once, the legend related, a blissful hero had arrived from the sea in the lands of the Scheldt, drawn in a bark by a swan: there he had freed persecuted innocence and become betrothed to a maiden; but when she had asked him who he was and whence he had come, he had to leave her and abandon everything' *(Eine Mittheilung an meine Freunde)*.

The plot of the opera is sketched here in outline. As in the epic, the time and place of action are localized in Antwerp during the first half of the tenth century, at a time when King Henry the Fowler was assembling troops for his wars against Hungary. *Lohengrin,* in Carl Dahlhaus's words, is 'the paradox of a tragic fairy-tale opera in the outer

Court Theatre, Weimar,
28 August 1850
Lohengrin's arrival in Act I in
the first production, taken from
the *Leipziger Illustrirte Zeitung.*
The scenery is laid out
according to Wagner's own
production instructions—the
oak-tree is on the left, with the
king's seat; in the centre are the
banks of the Scheldt for
Lohengrin to disembark; the
chorus is ranged along both
sides of the stage and Elsa is at
the front centre. This
arrangement was standard until
well into the twentieth century.

Imperial Theatre, St Petersburg,
16 October 1868
First Russian production, sung
in Russian. The windmill is an
evident topographical reference
to Brabant.

form of a historical drama. Opposites which appear to be mutually exclusive, such as myth and history, fairy tale and tragedy, are forced together, but without the joins being visible. Romantic opera, which reaches its culmination in *Lohengrin,* proves itself as "universal poetry"'. Wagner attempted an accurate restoration of the historical framework, at least as far as it was still possible to reconstruct it on the basis of surviving sources, including such details as the king's arrival, the court sitting and the ordeal. He felt that it was only through historical truthfulness that the naïve elements in such an extraordinary subject could be given convincing visual expression. Reality, in its social forms, was visually realizable, whereas the dimension of unreality and miracle had to be made credible through the appearance of Lohengrin alone and could only be depicted musically. The world of the grail, the counterpoint of reality, asserts a conspicuous musical presence in the Prelude and in Lohengrin's account of his origins. As a character, Lohengrin is infinitely more a celestial knight of the grail than he is a loving individual. His declaration of love, 'Elsa, ich liebe dich' ('Elsa, I love you'), even if such a sentence did not sound as trivial in Wagner's day as it does now, cannot compete, on a musical level, however deeply felt it may be, with the theme of the grail, which again and again transports Lohengrin to a distant realm of

transfiguration. As a result, Wagner has been reproached for turning Lohengrin into a cold, even hurtful character who, having descended from a glorious domain where suffering is unknown, laid down unfulfillable conditions and then withdrew once again from the world of men. Such an interpretation, however, shows a lack of understanding of the nature of Lohengrin's profound tragic conflict.

In *Eine Mittheilung an meine Freunde,* Wagner's great attempt at justifying and analysing all his works from *Der fliegende Holländer* through *Lohengrin,* Wagner has given an elaborate account of the tragic conflict in *Lohengrin,* the main outlines of which may usefully be summarized here: From the delights of solitude imposed by his own higher nature, Lohengrin longs to descend to be closer to the world of men; he longs for a woman who might love him. He wants to be loved for his own sake alone, without the need for explanations and justifications. For that reason he was forced to conceal his higher nature, since he did not wish to be an object of wonderment or admiration; what he desired was to satisfy his longing for love, his longing 'to be understood through love'. He wished to be freed from his loneliness. He is acutely conscious of his desire to become a sensitive human being, an essential human being. His tragedy, however, consists in the fact that

there still clings 'irremovably to him the tell-tale halo of his own higher nature'. He cannot do otherwise than appear miraculous to mankind and to cause astonishment and the inevitable concomitant of astonishment, which is envy; and it is this envy which is able to sow the seeds of doubt in the heart of the woman he loves. Lohengrin is forced to learn the painful lesson that he is not loved for what he is but worshipped as a marvel. He is obliged to confess his name and where he comes from and to return to his former loneliness.

In Elsa Wagner has discovered the nature of women's hearts. She is the longed-for opposite of Lohengrin, 'the *other part* of his own nature'. She is something unconscious and involuntary. Lohengrin's conscious nature seeks to be absorbed by Elsa. His desire, however, is 'something unconsciously necessary', and in this point he is related to Elsa. Wagner called this psychic condition 'conscious unconsciousness', realizing that Elsa was justified in asking Lohengrin the forbidden question and that only in that way can 'the purely human nature of love' be understood. For, as Wagner went on, what mankind constantly demands from love, even though that love be projected onto the divine, is the purely human; man longs for 'the enjoyment

of his own nature as the thing most worthy of being desired'. The essence of human nature is the '*necessity of love,* and the essence of this love, in its truest form of expression, is the *desire for total sensual realization*', for the enjoyment 'of an object which may be grasped with every one of our senses'. The relationship between the two figures is therefore of necessity tragic, their destruction inevitable. Elsa's greatness, however, lies in the fact that 'she plunges to her destruction in full knowledge of what she is doing, for the sake of the necessary nature of love.' Since she cannot fully embrace her lover as a human being, she prefers to perish. Only when she no longer worships Lohengrin but wants to know who he is, does she love him and reveal to Lohengrin through her downfall the nature of love. With that, Lohengrin was lost to Wagner as a character, as he himself expressed it, and yet he (Wagner) was certainly on the right course to discover 'the truly feminine', a discovery which was to be of consequence for his later works. Elsa, 'this most necessary and essential manifestation of the purest sensual instinctiveness' made a revolutionary out of Wagner. 'She was the spirit of the people for which I longed, so that as an artist, too, I might be redeemed.'

Eden-Théâtre, Paris, 30 April 1887
Designer: Joseph Flüggen.
Conductor: Charles Lamoureux
A scene from Act II (with insets depicting the hero's arrival in the swan boat and his duel with Telramund in Act I) from the first Paris production of the opera, which was staged in the French capital thanks to the initiative of Lamoureux. Cosima had serious reservations about the production. She advised Lamoureux to commission designs from Flüggen, so that at least the 'national costumes' should have more style to them.

Court Theatre, Munich, 1894
Lohengrin's arrival, based on a
performance at the Munich
Court Theatre in 1894. Ernst
von Possart had staged
Lohengrin with magnificent sets
and costumes in order to rival
those of the Bayreuth Festival.
His staging was more successful
than Cosima's own new
production of the same year.

In order to invest the epic with a dramatically effective plot and to create a psychological weight to counterbalance Elsa and Lohengrin, Wagner introduced the two antagonists Ortrud, 'the scion of Radbod, prince of Friesland', and Count Friedrich of Telramund. The latter was Elsa's accuser in the medieval epic, but Ortrud is Wagner's own creation. She shows him writing as an experienced operatic composer who knows how to create an effective role without recourse to what for him were obsolete stock operatic situations. Ortrud is not the traditional intrigante, but has been developed entirely from within the dramaturgical framework of the action.

Ortrud is a woman who does not know – love. This says all we need to know about her, though it is the most terrible thing one can ever say about another person. Her nature is politics [...] This woman does admit to one love, a love of the past and of long-dead nations, a frighteningly insane love of ancestral pride whose only form of expres-

sion is a hatred of all living things and of everything that really exists. In the case of a man, such a love as this would be ridiculous, but in a woman it becomes terrible because a woman [...] has to love *something* and in this way ancestral pride and a yearning for the past turn into a destructive fanaticism [...] What motivates Ortrud, therefore, is not the jealousy which she feels towards Elsa [...]: her all-consuming passion reveals itself only in the scene in Act II, following Elsa's withdrawal from the balcony, when she leaps up from the steps of the minster and invokes her ancient and long-lost gods. She is a reactionary, someone who is concerned only with the past and who is therefore hostile to all that is new; and she is this in the most rabid sense of the word. She would like to destroy the world and nature simply in order to breathe new life into her decaying gods. This is no idiosyncratic or sickly whim on Ortrud's part, but a passion which she espouses with all the violence of a woman's longing for love; and that is why she is so *magnificent* in her dreadfulness. The actress playing this part must never allow the least pettiness to enter her portrayal of the character: she should never appear simply malicious or annoyed: every expression of her contempt and of her spite must make it apparent that the violent force of her terrible madness can only be satisfied by the destruction of others or – by her own destruction.

This was how Wagner described his conception of the character of Ortrud in a letter to Franz Liszt of 30 January 1852.

Like her counterpart, Elsa, Ortrud is the exponent of an idea. She is a reactionary (figuratively realized as a Germanic heathen) in the sense of the *Vormärz*, the period in German history between 1815 and 1848; she is a supporter of antiquated customs, ancestral pride and of magic; and she is a personification of the struggle for power. Elsa, on the other hand, embodies the values which Wagner longed to see realized in the future, human love, the 'purest sensual instinctiveness', the 'spirit of the people', in short, all that had persuaded Wagner to 'become a revolutionary'. It is true that Ortrud can still triumph over Elsa and destroy her happiness, but Elsa's downfall is also her own: the conflict ends in tragedy for both of them. Elsa's dream, however, lives on as an idea and a utopian hope: Gottfried receives the sword, ring and horn from the grail. The clash between ancient paganism and early Christianity is one which operates only on the level of

Bayreuth Festival, 1908
Designer: Max Brückner
Sets for Act II, based on a
design by Siegfried Wagner and
realized by Brückner in Coburg.
The stage layout corresponds
exactly to Wagner's own
directions. Like his father,
Siegfried laid great emphasis on
the chorus scenes in this act.
The female chorus entered via
the balustraded loggia at the
upper left of the stage and
descended the steps down on to
the floor of the stage, before
crossing to the main door of
the minster at the right. The
male chorus entered upstage at
right. Siegfried's particular skill
at producing lay in his handling
of the chorus.

an historical veneer. 'Those for whom only the Christian-Romantic element appeared intelligible, understood no more than an accidental and superficial feature of the work, but certainly not its essence,' Wagner wrote in *Eine Mittheilung an meine Freunde.* In his opinion the Lohengrin epic had not sprung from any 'Christian point of view', but was 'archetypally human'. Christianity had never been 'primevally creative': 'none of the most significant and most stirring Christian myths owes its original derivation to the spirit of Christianity, such as we normally understand it; they have all been taken over from the purely human ideas of prehistory and adapted to suit its own particular nature.'

Wagner even went to the lengths of believing that such a folk poem must have been directed against the clergy, since the Christian moral of the tale would appear to be that, 'The good Lord would do better to spare us His revelations, since He cannot repeal the laws of nature: nature – in this case human nature – is bound to seek revenge and destroy the revelation' (letter to Hermann Franck of 30 May 1846). We can already find one element of the Lohengrin legend in the myths of ancient Greece and there is no doubt that these myths themselves preserve a comparatively late account of the legend: 'Who has not heard of Zeus and Semele? The god loves a mortal woman [Semele] and, out of his love for her, descends to earth in human form; Semele, however, discovers that she cannot know her lover as he really is and so, driven by the true zealousness of love, she demands that he should reveal his nature to her in a form which is fully perceptible. Zeus knows [...] that the actual sight of him will destroy her; he himself suffers from this knowledge and from the necessity of having to destroy her in order to meet his loved one's request. He tolls his own death knell as the fatal radiance of his manifest divinity consumes his beloved.' In this version, too, Wagner recognized 'the universal force of man's poetic instinct as it is revealed in popular myth' *(Eine Mittheilung an meine Freunde).*

Opera House, Graz, 1914
Designer: Karl Reithmeyer
Design for Act II, dated 1914.
Its clearly defined structures,
including the flights of steps,
and its bright and delicate
colours show the influence of
Alfred Roller's Viennese stage
designs.

The topicality of Lohengrin's tragedy was something to which Wagner repeatedly and emphatically drew attention. As he wrote to August Röckel on 25 January 1854, 'I remain convinced that, as I myself have conceived it, *Lohengrin* encapsulates the deepest tragedy of the present day, which is man's desire to descend from the most intellectual heights to the depths of love; it is man's yearning to be understood intuitively, a yearning which modern reality is not yet in a position to satisfy.' Lohengrin's personal tragedy seemed to him to be characteristic of the situation of the artist in the period between 1815 and 1848. For Wagner, the 'artist' is mankind in the fullest potential of his creative abilities, someone who has no desire to be critically analysed and questioned but who longs to be understood and loved intuitively. In its barren sterility, the world around him was not in a position to satisfy the artist's desire for love and his need for happiness. Wagner's inchoate awareness of contemporary issues is something which we find where we should

perhaps least expect it, namely in his elucidation of the Prelude to *Lohengrin*, that 'great symphony-like composition in the character of an idealized mysticism', as Franz Liszt had described it. It must be added that it was not until 1853 that Wagner formulated this particular account of the Prelude, which he saw not as a traditional exposition of the drama but as a narrative complete in itself: love no longer legislated in the community of men; the world was informed by hatred and discord and by a barren concern for profit and gain. But man's indestructible longing for love, which could never be satisfied in real life, desired to be consoled by a physical revelation of the metaphysical and hence created for itself, outside the world, a 'wondrous form which was soon deemed to be actually present, although unapproachably distant, and which was believed in, longed for and sought after under the name of the "Holy Grail"'. The 'sacred chalice' of the grail was wrested from men's unworthy gaze and transported to the heights above, before being brought back to earth once again by a host of angels who entrusted it to the care of 'solitary individuals burning for love'. These men are now the 'earthly champions of everlasting love'. The actual musical content of the Prelude is the grail's 'miracle-bestowing descent to earth in the company of an angelic host'.

Hans Mayer was the first writer to recognize 'that the drama of *Lohengrin* [...] operates within the framework of practical politics. King Henry the Fowler is mentioned in the sources. In the years between 1846 and 1848, however, King Henry's exhortations in the opera were understood by contemporaries to imply a defence of the German fatherland against tsarism. The question of Schleswig-Holstein and its affiliation to Germany also played a part during these years of intensified national life and consciousness.' Russia, which had quelled the Polish Revolution of 1831 (the reader will recall that Wagner's *Polonia* Overture was written at that time), was felt to be a threat to Germany's own attempts at democracy and to the liberal aspirations of the *Vormärz*. During recent years, writers on Wagner have stated that *Lohengrin* should be seen as a parable of political conditions in Germany during the *Vormärz* and, in particular, during the period around 1845. There is no doubt that Wagner saw illuminating parallels between the subject-matter of *Lohengrin* and the contemporary situation. This is certainly one narrative level, which stands out within the context of the work as a whole, but it is not an independent and autonomous level, overriding all other aspects of the work. It is dialectically bound up with what Wagner himself singled out as the actual thematic core of the work, the conflict between a reactionary attitude, on the one hand, and a utopian one, on the other, a conflict personified in Ortrud and Elsa/Lohengrin. It is the clash between the revolutionary utopian idea of human love as a constitutive element of life, and the reaction to this, which is concerned for power and possessions and which ignores the claims of love. It should not be forgotten, of course, that all Wagner's remarks on the subject were written down after the failure of the 1848 revolution. But Wagner's dissatisfaction with the present, which went hand in hand with his utopian hopes for a better future, is a constant factor in his thinking and is by no means limited exclusively to the period before 1848, nor specifically to *Lohengrin*. And this is only *one* of the drama's narrative levels. Wagner's way of looking at things was not as simplistic as this, but rather the outcome of what Nietzsche called his 'double perspective'.

Wagner himself explained that, in order to anticipate an arbitrary interpretation of his work and to communicate the character of Lohengrin according to the impression which it had made on him, he had proceeded with the greatest possible accuracy and care 'in depicting those historico-legendary elements which are the only means of allowing such an extraordinary subject to impinge upon our consciousness and of convincing us of their actual truth.' The precise dating to the year 933 and King Henry's call to arms are more than a stage backdrop: they are the concrete historical basis on which both the miracle and the utopia (with its tragic *dénouement*) can be played out.

Although it was objected that the world première of a modern opera was scarcely an appropriate way of celebrating either the 101st anniversary of Goethe's birth on 28 August 1850 or the dedication of the Herder memorial in Weimar, Liszt carried the day, an achievement which the general public admitted was as much to Liszt's own credit as it was

Teatro alla Scala, Milan, 3 December 1922
Designer: Vittorio Rota
Set-design for Act II. Antwerp Castle as a Roman citadel with a round tower reminiscent of the Castel Sant' Angelo, and a triumphal arch – in the style of the entrance to the Galleria in Milan – flanked by a pair of free-standing Corinthian columns.

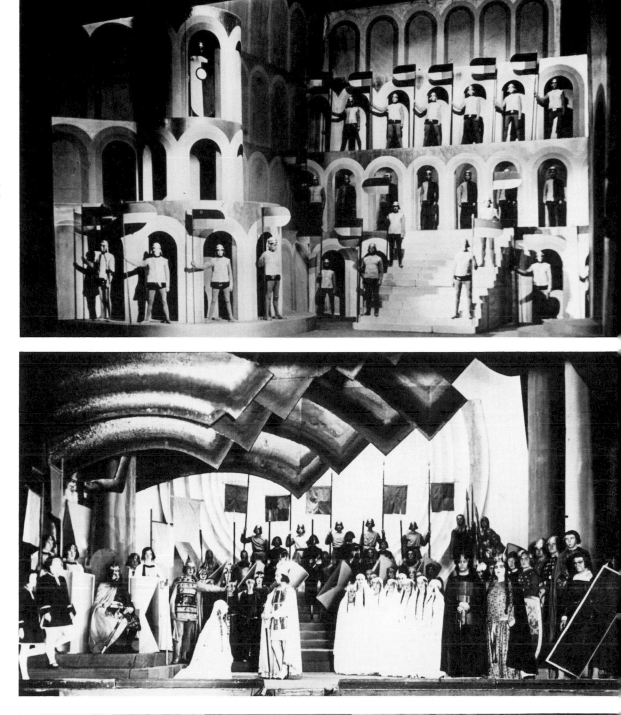

Regional Theatre, Darmstadt,
16 September 1928
Producer: Renato Mordo.
Designer: Lothar Schenck von
Trapp
The problem of where to place
the chorus in Act II has been
solved here in a somewhat
unusual way. The male chorus
members have been positioned
in horizontal rows, and stand in
'sentry boxes', so as to leave the
steps free for the entry of the
female chorus. The colours
were blue, white and silver.

Municipal Theatre,
Mönchengladbach-Rheydt,
1929/1930
Even in such an expressionist
interpretation as this one, the
traditional layout for Act I was
preserved.

German Theatre, Prague,
4 June 1933
Producer: Herbert Graf.
Designer: Emil Pirchan.
Conductor: George Szell
Entry of the herald in Act II.
Lohengrin as a deromanticized
opera. Influence of the Bauhaus
in the architecture.

Bayreuth Festival, 1936
Producer: Heinz Tietjen.
Designer: Emil Preetorius.
Conductor: Wilhelm
Furtwängler. Lohengrin: Franz
Völker. Elsa: Maria Müller.
King Henry: Josef von
Manowarda. Telramund: Jaro
Prohaska. Ortrud: Margarete
Klose. Herald: Herbert Janssen
End of Act I. Although
traditional, the sets are
stylistically superior to the
naturalism which predominated
throughout the 1930s. The
stage picture was further
enlivened by brilliantly coloured
costumes. The production was
given only for two seasons, in
1936 and 1937, and achieved a
legendary reputation on the
basis of its cast.

to the open-minded ducal court. As was customary at all gala performances throughout the nineteenth century, a prologue was written especially for the occasion, the author of this particular effusion being Franz Dingelstedt. Liszt presumably was guided as far as possible by Wagner's own wishes and instructions. He had written to the composer, asking for detailed information and Wagner had replied by submitting sketches of the sets and precise instructions for staging the opera, which were subsequently published in 1853 under the title of *Dekorative und kostümliche Scenirung zu Lohengrin* ('On sets and costume design for *Lohengrin*').

For the first-act set Wagner demanded an old oak-tree to the left of the stage, with a simple stone table against its trunk, where the king could convene the court. A group of trees lined the right-hand side of the stage. The grass was to rise slightly towards either side, in order to facilitate an advantageous grouping of the chorus. The grass led down in a gentle hollow at the back towards the banks of the Scheldt. The castle of Antwerp was visible in the distance. In order to give the impression of perspective, Lohengrin's approach was to be indicated first of all by means of a child appearing towards the back of the stage and then disappearing into the wings, whereupon the real Lohengrin would enter downstage right. For the four royal trumpeters, Wagner demanded 'trombone-like instruments of the simplest possible design, such as we see being blown by angels of

the Resurrection in church paintings.' The costumes, including that of the king, were to be solemn and plain, without any hint of magnificence. Wagner was worried about Götze, who was to sing the title-role and whose voice and appearance, he felt, were lacking in radiance. He expressed these doubts in a letter to Liszt of 2 July 1850, insisting, 'Just let him wear a costume skilfully made to look as dazzlingly bright as possible: people's eyes will be blinded as soon as they look on him.' But Wagner was under no illusions: as he admitted to Ferdinand Heine in a letter of 14 September 1850, 'The good Lord refuses to perform any private miracles for me, which is why He won't make the sort of performers I need grow on trees.'

The scenery for Act II was designed by Wagner in such a way as to provide different acting levels for the great choral processions. Elsa's balcony was downstage at left, with a passage leading from it to the ramp in front of the *palas,* which occupied the whole of the upstage area. Beside it was a practicable castle gate for the Brabantines to enter, and downstage at right was the portal of the minster, through which the procession would pass at the end of the act. In its architectural style, the castle was to be 'extremely ancient', its 'masonry dating back to the time of the Romans'. The walls should grow out of the living rock. Ferdinand Heine had the task of preparing an engraving for the *Lohengrin* article and Wagner wrote to him on 31 October 1853, saying that in Act II he did not want any great 'ceremonial', but rather the 'noble, naïve simplicity of that time. Henry the Fowler knew nothing of marshals and such like in the sense in which they were later to appear [...] It was not until the reign of his son that Frankish-Byzantine court customs were introduced [...] It is an ancient Germanic kingdom which we should see before us, in its finest and most ideal form, and which should constitute the local colour of *Lohengrin* [...] Here is no tyrannical splendour, with its "bodyguards forcing the crowd back" to form "a guard of honour" for their royal majesties. Let my *Lohengrin* be beautiful but not ostentatious and – stupid.'

The bridal chamber of Act III is dominated by the bridal bed enclosed by 'magnificent curtains'. Downstage right is a 'tower-bay

with an oriel window' and an upholstered bench running round it for the duet between Lohengrin and Elsa. The open windows afford a view 'onto a beautiful summer's night and tall flowering shrubs'. Before Lohengrin's line, 'Das süsse Lied verhallt' ('The sweet song's echo fades'), the area upstage of the tower-bay was closed off by means of a curtain. This not only produced a greater intimacy for the scene in question, but it also allowed the set for scene 2 to be built behind it. This set was the same as that used in Act I. Wagner insisted, tenaciously, on the need for having horses accompany the entrance of the armed warriors, a stage direction to which he repeatedly returned.

It is no longer possible to tell whether the theatre in Weimar was in fact able to realize all the composer's wishes right down to the very last detail. There seems little doubt that the theatre warehouse must have come to the rescue for more than one item of scenery. Wagner thought the Act II set a total disaster, although, in forming this impression, he was forced to rely on the accounts of various friends. This fact may also explain why his reactions to the event are so inconsistent. But what was never in doubt was the contribution of Liszt himself, 'the real hero of the performance'. According to Franz von Dingelstedt, the audience remained silent, not knowing what was going on. Liszt reported to Wagner in a letter of 2 September 1850, 'As far as the vast majority of the audience is concerned, they will no doubt feel themselves honoured to find the work beautiful and to applaud something which they do not understand.'

As he wrote to Hector Berlioz in February 1860, Wagner was afraid that in the meantime he had become the only German never to have seen *Lohengrin*, since, unlike his earlier works, *Lohengrin* had been taken up by other theatres very soon after its first production in Weimar. Up until 1860 there were productions in Wiesbaden in 1853; Frankfurt, Leipzig, Stettin and Darmstadt in 1854; Hamburg, Hanover, Cologne and Riga in 1855; Karlsruhe, Prague, Mainz and Würzburg in 1856; Munich, Sondershausen and Vienna in 1858; Berlin (finally!), Dresden (where Minna Wagner saw the work for the first time) and Mannheim in 1859; and Danzig and Königsberg in 1860.

The first performance in Munich on 28 February 1858, under Franz Lachner, did not meet with the same spectacular success which *Tannhäuser* had previously enjoyed in the city, although King Maximilian was so impressed that he attended no fewer than

State Opera, Vienna, at the
Theater an der Wien,
30 April 1948
Producer: Stephan Beinl. Sets
and costumes: Robert Kautsky.
Conductor: Hans
Knappertsbusch. Elsa: Maria
Reining. Lohengrin: Julius
Patzak
Following the war-time
destruction of the auditorium of
the Vienna State Opera, the
company performed at the
Theater an der Wien until the
reopening of the new house in
1955. Shortage of materials
meant that all post-war
productions had to make do
with very simple scenery and
costumes; but the swan never
fell victim to the scenic
restrictions.

four performances in that year alone. On 2 February 1861 he allowed the fifteen-year-old Crown Prince Ludwig to attend a performance of the work; it was Ludwig's first visit to the opera, although the figure of the swan-knight had been familiar to him since his childhood at Hohenschwangau and all he ever dreamt about was the legends of German antiquity. To quote Gottfried von Böhms, Ludwig wept 'tears of ecstatic rapture' on the occasion. He learned the text by heart and he was also given Wagner's prose writings to read, in the belief that such difficult reading would dampen his effusive and youthful enthusiasm. The opposite proved to be the case. It must have been at this time that he conceived the desire of summoning the composer to his court following his future accession to the throne; this was indeed one of the first acts of the young king in 1864. Nine years later Ludwig wrote to Wagner, 'However bad [the performance] was, I was still able to recognize the essential nature of this divine work.' In June 1861 he saw the young Ludwig Schnorr von Carolsfeld as Lohengrin. The young crown prince's swooning enthusiasm for *Lohengrin* soon became a regular fashion in Munich. When Albert Niemann, who, from a purely physical point of view, was the finest Lohengrin of his day, gave a guest performance in Munich in 1864, all the society ladies appeared 'wearing the insignia of the Knight of the Holy Grail – with the white dove and the swan – in the form of silver jewellery in their hair and on their bosoms' (Sebastian Röckl).

Wagner himself saw *Lohengrin* for the first time the same year as did the future King Ludwig II. It was on the occasion of a rehearsal at the old Vienna Court Opera, which he watched in silence from a seat in the wings. 'For the first time in this artist's life of mine, with all its struggles and unhappiness, I felt a total sense of enjoyment which reconciled me to everything that had gone before,' he told Minna in a letter of 13 May 1861; what he felt on this occasion was 'joy, gratitude and emotion'. Twelve years had passed since the completion of the score and in the meantime he had written *Tristan und Isolde*. Indeed, Wagner was so impressed by the two protagonists in *Lohengrin*, Alois Ander and Luise Dustmann, that he made up his mind to stage the first performances of *Tristan und Isolde* with them. Having had to forego the pleasure of seeing a performance of his beloved *Lohengrin* for three years, Ludwig ordered a new production to be mounted in 1867, with Wagner himself assuming total artistic control. Wagner initially declined to become involved, since he hoped to be able to complete the composition of *Die Meistersinger von Nürnberg* in peace, but he was finally forced to yield to the king's insistent demands. Hans von Bülow was appointed conductor. Ludwig's determination to see his dream fulfilled led to a series of violent disagreements between himself and Wagner, since his own taste and sense of style ran directly counter to the composer's own ideas about the work. He exerted a considerable influence on the set-designs of Heinrich Döll and Angelo Quaglio and on the costumes of Franz Seitz.

Wagner was unable to persuade Ludwig to change his mind and refused to regard the production as providing a model perform-ance of the work. He considered the castle courtyard in Act II to be utterly wrong and impracticable, and when he lost his temper after one of the rehearsals and asked who 'had designed this completely unsuitable and downright silly costume', the answer which he received embarrassed him deeply, as he wrote to the king on 25 June 1867. All the scenery and costumes were designed to suit Ludwig's taste, which was for a lyrical, ro-manticizing style similar to that of Neu-schwanstein. Wagner, however, refused to give way over the question of who was to sing the leading role. Ludwig wanted Albert Nie-mann, but Wagner would have nothing to do with Niemann after what he had had to put up with during the Paris production of *Tann-häuser.* The king then insisted on having the young tenor Franz Nachbaur in the part. But for Wagner there was only one singer who could seriously be considered for the part and that was Josef Tichatschek, his Dresden Ri-

enzi and Tannhäuser, now sixty years old. The 'king's poetic nature [...] recoils before the destruction of an ideal', the Court Secre-tary Lorenz von Düfflipp wrote to Wagner, but the latter was not impressed. The dress re-hearsal, as a result, led to a major row.

Wagner had warned the king not to use his opera-glasses; but in vain. Ludwig was aghast to see the aging Tichatschek standing in the bark and leaning on a pole specially designed for the purpose: the king's dream was shat-tered. In a peremptory manner, which took Wagner by surprise and which brooked no re-fusal, Ludwig gave instructions that he wished never again to see this 'knight of the doleful aspect'. Ortrud, too, who had rushed around the stage like a fury, was to disappear and not return. In a mixture of hurt pride and recalcitrance, Wagner reproached the king for this 'marionette show' and his 'worthless theatrical company'. The letter was dated 25 June 1867 – scarcely two years after the ideal first performances of *Tristan und Isolde.* The king packed his bags and left, followed by Tichatschek, and then by Wagner himself. Heinrich Vogl had to learn the title-role at very short notice, in time for the opening night. Elsa was sung by the young Mathilde Mallinger, Telramund by Franz Betz, Bay-reuth's first Wotan. The king also got his way

Royal Opera House, Copenhagen
Lohengrin as a Romantic fairy-tale opera. The silver-clad knight is centre stage. This is how generations of opera-goers saw *Lohengrin* and learned to love it.

Théâtre de la Monnaie,
Brussels, May 1949
The bridal chamber in Act III
designed in a mixture of styles,
incorporating elements of naïve
art, Russian icon painting,
folk art and Belgian *art nouveau.*
Exoticism as a visual attraction
of the fairy-tale play.

Finnish National Opera,
Helsinki, 1952
Designer: Max Bignens. Elsa:
Irja Aholainen. Lohengrin:
Alfons Almi
The bridal chamber constructed
of draperies and veils. During
the post-war decade many
theatres had to content
themselves with simple
solutions, like the one shown
here. The results, however,
often revealed a great deal of
intimacy and charm.

over the question of Franz Nachbaur, who sang in the performance on 29 September; and even the horses, on which Wagner had insisted so firmly, were dismissed on Ludwig's orders after the first performance, since they destroyed the audience's mood of artistic enjoyment and introduced a note of 'circus humour' into the performance. Wagner immediately cut the music for this scene. Wagner at least gained satisfaction over one point, inasmuch as, for the first and only time in his life, he heard the musical side of his work performed 'in perfect accord with my intentions', so that his astonishment was all the greater when it appeared to be a matter of total indifference to the audience 'whether they had *Lohengrin* performed this way or any other: when the opera later slipped back into its old routine, the impression still remained the same,' as he wrote to an Italian friend on 7 November 1871. All this, of course, left the theatre manager feeling somewhat smug, since he had always regarded Wagner's involvement as a disruption to the smooth running of the theatre. Wagner, on the other hand, increasingly lost interest in the audience. What he needed was his own theatre with its own committed and well-informed audience.

The production at the Teatro Comunale in Bologna on 1 November 1871 was an important event, not least because it was the first performance of any of Wagner's operas in Italy. The stage manager, set-designer and costume designer undertook a fact-finding mission to Munich and a German producer, Ernst Frank, was engaged to ensure as authentic a production as possible. The conductor was Angelo Mariani, the title-role was sung by Italo Campanini, Elsa by Bianca Blume and Ortrud by Maria Destin-Löwe. The organizers found it necessary to issue a press statement, explaining that the production was not intended as an affront to Italian composers or to Italian opera in general. The audience was aware of the uniqueness of the occasion and the packed auditorium buzzed like a hornets' nest. Shouts of 'Viva Verdi' and 'Viva Rossini' descended from the gallery. The performance began at eight o'clock. On the whole the first two acts were favourably received, although the long scene between Ortrud and Telramund did not go down well with the audience. On the other hand, the Prelude to Act III was encored. The ensuing scene in the bridal chamber witnessed a renewed waning of interest, since it was felt to be too philosophical for an Italian audience, however good the music itself was considered to be. By contrast, they enjoyed the ending of the opera. Applause and whistles greeted the final curtain, but on the whole Wagner had scored a considerable triumph, even though the music aroused more admiration than emotion and more surprise than enjoyment. The following year, 1872, Wagner was granted the freedom of the city of Bologna.

The performance on 19 November was notable for the presence in the audience of a particularly distinguished visitor, who sat at the back of box 23, trying in vain to remain undetected; his name was Giuseppe Verdi. The audience broke into a chant of 'Viva Verdi'. He followed the performance with the aid of a score, making notes on the music and on the staging, comments which on the whole were rather more negative than positive. The singers and orchestra are reported to have been thrown into confusion by the presence of so famous a composer, with the result that they gave a mediocre performance. Verdi liked the Prelude, although he thought the constant high *tessitura* of the violins to be tiring on the ear; but the second act was banal and excruciatingly boring, and he had expected rather more of the bridal chorus; the grail narration, on the other hand, struck him as pleasing and interesting, but on the whole he felt repelled by what he described as 'all this fuss about the Bologna *Lohengrin*'.

The opera was first performed at La Scala, Milan, on 20 March 1873, when the title-role was again sung by Campanini. When the doors of the opera-house were opened, the throng of people was so great that one of the

Teatro alla Scala, Milan, 10 January 1953
Producer and conductor: Herbert von Karajan. Designer: Emil Preetorius. Elsa: Elisabeth Schwarzkopf. Lohengrin: Wolfgang Windgassen
With minor alterations, Preetorius used this basic design for the bridal chamber in all his productions of *Lohengrin*, including Bayreuth in 1936 and Munich in 1938. In Preetorius's view, Wagner's early operas demanded 'historical specificity' and 'more individualization of design'.

Bavarian State Opera, Munich,
21 December 1954
Producer: Rudolf Hartmann.
Designer: Helmut Jürgens.
Conductor: Hans
Knappertsbusch. Ortrud:
Marianne Schech. Telramund:
Hermann Uhde
Scene between Ortrud and
Telramund at the beginning of
Act II. Almost the entire stage
area is taken up by a flight of
steps like those first used by
Leopold Jessner in his theatrical
productions in Berlin during the
1920s.

huge marble slabs in the foyer was shattered. The performance, too, was spoiled by constant bursts of applause alternating with audible expressions of disapproval: it was impossible to achieve the calm and concentration which were necessary if the audience was to get to know the new work properly. Whereas in Bologna the opera had found increasing favour with each passing performance, the very second performance in Milan was already a virtual fiasco, with shouts of 'basta' interrupting the second act. The third performance was heavily cut and put on together with the ballet *Le due Gemelle* ('The Two Twins') in an attempt to appease the audience. There seems little doubt that the powerful Milanese publisher Ricordi had used his influence to mould public opinion and that he had employed whatever means he could against his old rival, Giovanna Lucca, who was Wagner's agent in Italy.

Wagner lived to see Lohengrin and his swan landing in almost all the major cities of Europe, as well as abroad. The first performance in Hungarian was given in Budapest in 1866; in 1870 it was performed in Danish in Copenhagen and the same year in Brussels there began an illustrious series of first performances in French. Stockholm followed in 1874 with a Swedish translation, when the audience was so moved that it apparently forgot to applaud. Dublin and London added their names the following year, first in Italian and then in English in 1880. The first production in Switzerland was given in Basle in 1876, and in 1877 it was performed in Lemberg (modern Lvov) in Polish. The opera was first seen in Rome in 1878, when it was con-

ducted by Amilcare Ponchielli, the composer of *La Gioconda* ('The Madonna'). Antwerp and Madrid followed in 1881, Barcelona in 1882 and Lisbon in 1883. The first Russian performance was given at the Imperial Theatre in St Petersburg in 1868 and in Moscow it received a gala first performance on New Year's Eve 1881. In New York the opera had been first performed in 1871, and from 1883 onwards was almost never out of the repertory of the Metropolitan Opera. There were also performances in Boston in 1875 and in New Orleans, San Francisco and Philadelphia in 1877. The first Australian production is believed to have taken place in Melbourne on 7 October 1877. In 1883, the year of Wagner's death, *Lohengrin* was produced in Buenos Aires and Rio de Janeiro; and there were also productions in Alexandria in 1897, in Malta in 1896, in Corfu in 1902 and in Johannesburg in 1905. In an age before films and television, touring opera companies reached the remotest regions of the globe and performed *Lohengrin* with a great deal of courage and improvisatory talent in what were often totally inadequate conditions.

It is impossible to estimate the number of knights in silver armour and silver helmets who have bewitched the public in the role of Lohengrin since the first performances in Weimar. A few names will suffice here, in addition to those already mentioned: Italo Campanini, who was the first Lohengrin not only in Italy but also at the Metropolitan Opera, New York, where the conductor Anton Seidl described him as the epitome of Italian opera, with his enormously long blue plume on his helmet and his resplendent cloak; Ernest van

Teatro alla Scala, Milan,
11 December 1957
Producer: Mario Frigerio.
Designer: Georges Wakhevitch.
Conductor: Antonino Votto.
Lohengrin: Mario del Monaco.
Elsa: Marcella Pobbe. King
Henry: Nicola Zaccaria
Scene from Act I.
Three-dimensional sets, but still
showing the traditional layout.
Typical of the style of
set-design which could be seen
at La Scala during the 1950s.

Teatro alla Scala, Milan,
11 December 1957
Producer: Mario Frigerio.
Designer: Georges Wakhevitch.
Conductor: Antonino Votto.
Elsa: Marcella Pobbe. Ortrude:
Elena Nicolai
Scene from Act II, showing not
Brabant but Italy. Somewhat
conventional style of Grand
Opera.

Dyck who for years was the leading Wagner tenor in Vienna, Brussels, Paris, London, Bayreuth and New York; Jean de Reszke, the 'divine Jean' of Paris audiences, who made his Wagnerian début in the part of Lohengrin during the 1891/1892 Metropolitan Opera season; Charles Dalmorès, the 1908 Bayreuth Lohengrin, a boyish swan-knight who insisted on being paid very high fees for his international guest appearances; then Jacques Urlus, Walter Kirchhoff, Heinrich Knote, Erik Schmedes and Leo Slezak, whose name has come to be identified with the part of Lohengrin; and, after the First World War, Lauritz Melchior, Franz Völker, Max Lorenz and Set Svanholm. Throughout the 1950s and 1960s the world's leading Lohengrin was Wolfgang Windgassen, followed, some distance behind, by Jess Thomas, Sándor Kónya and Jean Cox; in recent years the role has

come to be associated with the names of René Kollo, Peter Hofmann and Siegfried Jerusalem. In 1957 Mario del Monaco attempted his only excursion into the Wagnerian repertory when he sang the part of Lohengrin at La Scala; and in 1966 Nicolai Gedda sang the role in Stockholm.

Among the interpreters of the role of Elsa are to be found the names of Lilian Nordica, the first Bayreuth Elsa and for a number of years the leading performer of the part at the Metropolitan Opera; Nellie Melba, the *prima donna assoluta* of the turn of the century, who sang Elsa in Stockholm, London and at the Metropolitan Opera; Louise Grandjean, leading soprano at the Paris Opéra and Elsa there in 1896; Christine Nilsson, one of the vocal celebrities of her day and the first Elsa at the Metropolitan Opera; the great Czech soprano Emmy Destinn; Olive Fremstad, who bade farewell to the stage of the Metropolitan Opera on 23 April 1914 in a performance of *Lohengrin* and who received one of the most extraordinary displays of an audience's appreciation in the whole history of the house; Germaine Lubin, the Paris Elsa of 1922; Delia Reinhardt; Elisabeth Rethberg; Maria Jeritza, who appeared in a polyglot version at the Metropolitan Opera in 1922, when the principals sang in German, while the chorus sang in English; the young Kirsten Flagstad; Lotte Lehmann and Maria Müller, a girlish Elsa at Bayreuth in 1936, as well as in Paris and New York; Helen Traubel and Eleanor Steber in the 1940s and 1950s at the Metropolitan. Renata Tebaldi sang the part in a new production at La Scala in 1946 and Birgit Nilsson made her Bayreuth début in the part in 1954, in Wolfgang Wagner's production; other interpreters of the part in Wieland's production have included Elisabeth Grümmer and Leonie Rysanek. Mention should finally be made of Elisabeth Schwarzkopf, Ingrid Bjoner, Régine Crespin, who sang the part in Paris in 1959, and Hannelore Bode, who has sung Elsa in Bayreuth, Vienna and elsewhere.

Lohengrin had difficulty making headway in France, in spite of the fact that a number of leading French minds were fervent *wagnéristes*. The reason was Wagner's growing hostility towards the French, a hostility which found expression in his later prose writings and above all in his unspeakable satire *Eine Kapitulation. Lustspiel in antiker Manier* ('A Capitulation. Comedy in the ancient manner'), which, following the defeat of 1871, turned public opinion against him. The orchestral manager Charles Lamoureux, a pioneer of Wagner's music in Paris, succeeded in spite of violent opposition in presenting the first performance of *Lohengrin* in France at the Eden-Théâtre on 30 April 1887, although it required a guard of police bayonets to enable the performance to begin. Lamoureux himself conducted and the title-role was sung by Ernest van Dyck. Cosima, whom he had consulted beforehand, had warned him against going ahead with the enterprise. He put up a notice on 5 May, announcing that no further performances would take place. The new director of the Palais Garnier, the Opéra's former singer Pierre Gailhard, included a new production of *Lohengrin* in the 1891 season, not because he felt any particular affinity for Wagner's music but because he urgently needed a popular success. He, too, sought Cosima's advice on the scenery and sent her the sketches, which she calmly proceeded to correct.

The first night on 16 September was a political event, accompanied by what were probably the biggest demonstrations in the whole history of the European theatre. Patriots regarded the performance as an act of treason, and as Germany's revenge on the French. The newspapers were full of such political caricatures. Some 20,000 protesters are believed to have assembled in front of the Opéra on the evening of the first performance and there were up to a thousand arrests; a further 700 were arrested at the second performance. The police plan of action has survived: a squadron of cavalry from the Republican Guard was stationed around the building and in the Avenue de l'Opéra, while 112 members of the Infantry Guard were responsible for maintaining order within the opera-house itself. The theatre electricians had to vacate their room, which was then placed at the disposal of the police chiefs. The Opéra staff required special passes and were allowed to use only specially designated entrances. The conductor, it should be added, was again Lamoureux and the title-role was once more sung by Ernest van Dyck; the Elsa was Rose Caron. The new sets were designed by Lavastre and Carpezat (First and Third Acts) and Amable and Gardy (Second Act), and the costumes were by Charles Bianchini. In spite of the protest action, *Lohengrin* was an overwhelming success with the general public and by 1894 had already chalked up one hundred performances.

'Lohengrin must be rediscovered,' Cosima had written in her Festival programme in the autumn of 1883. Wagner had never lived to see an ideal production, having been dissatisfied both by the Munich production of 1867 and by the Vienna performances of 1875. In

Metropolitan Opera, New York, 1958
Designer: Charles Elson.
Conductor: Thomas Schippers.
Elsa: Lisa della Casa.
Lohengrin: Brian Sullivan. King Henry: Otto Edelmann
Lohengrin still entirely within the traditional style of a spectacular grand opera.

Bayreuth Festival, 1958
Producer and designer: Wieland
Wagner. Conductor: André
Cluytens. Elsa: Leonie Rysanek.
Lohengrin: Sándor Kónya. King
Henry: Kieth Engen. Ortrud:
Astrid Varnay. Telramund:
Ernest Blanc. Herald: Eberhard
Waechter. Chorus-master:
Wilhelm Pitz
Wieland Wagner's silver-blue
Lohengrin production. The
swan was an *objet d'art* designed
by Ewald Mataré. The chorus is
placed on stepped platforms
around the orchestra of the
classical Greek theatre,
witnessing and commenting on
the action as in Greek drama.

the latter case, it is true, he himself was the
producer, but he had had no influence on the
style of the sets and costumes. Basing herself
upon Wagner's own remarks on the subject
and upon her own ideas about what constituted fidelity to the original work, Cosima
decided to produce the opera in the style of
the tenth century, which was the period when
the Lohengrin fable was set, rather than the
by now traditional thirteenth century, or
High Middle Ages, when the epic had been
written down. Instead of 'all the heraldic
paraphernalia of double eagles and swans'
which 'have inflicted such a mark of "operaticality" on poor Lohengrin', she shifted the
main emphasis to what, in a letter to Hermann Levi of 12 December 1886, she called
the 'awe-struck religiosity' of the work. This

shift to the tenth century was also intended to
give a precise historical framework to the
conflict between Christianity and paganism
which Cosima considered to be central to the
plot. As before, her preparatory work was in-
tensively researched. On this occasion she
was assisted by the writer Wilhelm Hertz and
by the young Germanist Wolfgang Golther,
although very few records had survived from
the time in question. As with *Tannhäuser*
there was an attempt to find names for the
counts and nobles and 'insignia for the
shields and banners'. It was discovered that
Saxons and Brabantines had not used their
swords in the same way. Instead of the king's
having a banner with an eagle on it, they now
used the old flag of St Michael. The nobles
did not display any coats of arms since these

were not invented until the twelfth century; banners were carried alongside the king's standard only during the armies' departure for battle in Act III.

All the sets and costumes were to be as historically accurate as possible and in this way *Lohengrin* was to be distinguished from *Tannhäuser* by its greater simplicity and antiquity. For the first-act set Cosima demanded from the Brückner brothers a kind of pagan stone altar on the right-hand side of the stage, from where the king would address his Christian prayer. It was to be positioned facing the oak-tree, which was the traditional Germanic site for the discussion of legislative and parliamentary matters. In Act III Ortrud was to celebrate her triumph beneath the oak-tree, the royal judgement seat. For the first time in any production, there was no castle of Antwerp in the background, since Wagner had discovered on the occasion of his visit there in 1860 that the fortress occupied a totally different site from the one which he had indicated in his instructions for staging the work. The second act and the bridal chamber were similarly designed by the Brückners in a sombre and heavy Romanesque style.

As in Paris, Lohengrin was sung by Ernest van Dyck; for the part of Elsa, Cosima had engaged the young Lilian Nordica, who went on to make a name for herself in all the world's major opera-houses. George Bernard Shaw, who was an extremely critical visitor to the Festival, expressed himself favourably on the intelligence of a production which, he felt, exactly matched the music.

There were bitter exchanges between Bayreuth and the management of the Munich Court Opera, which had drawn up plans, in advance of the Festival's own arrangements, for a new production of *Lohengrin* during the 1894 season. It, too, was to have been in the style of the tenth century. Cosima responded by invoking the laws of copyright. Since the costume designer Joseph Flüggen, the producer Anton Fuchs and the Brückner brothers, who were also contracted to Munich, could obviously not be compelled to ignore Cosima's instructions, she asked that the Munich production be postponed until after the Festival or else produced in what until then had been the traditional style of the thirteenth century. Munich refused to negotiate and went ahead with its own first night in defiance of Bayreuth. Tenth-century sets and costumes, it may be observed, were by no means an exclusive novelty at this time. In the 1889 Budapest production, for example, the bridal chamber had been a simple, intimate Romanesque vaulted room.

Cosima's production of *Lohengrin* did not have the same reformative influence in matters of staging as her *Tannhäuser* had done. This was less a result of any lack of quality than of the enormous popularity which *Lohengrin* had come to enjoy during the intervening years in all the world's major opera-houses and which subjected all new productions to certain expectational constraints on the part of audiences, who resented the loss of the more immediately appealing picture of the High Middle Ages which had gained common currency ever since the Munich production of 1867. In Nietzsche's words, *Lohengrin* had become an opera for sentimental women: a silver-haloed dream prince was what they had come to see. No one bothered much about Wagner's own soul-searching reflections on the tragic conflict. The fact that the knight disappeared whence he had come and that the delightful fairy-tale did not end happily ever after was felt to add to its tragic charm; and tragedy soon turned into sentimentality.

This is no doubt one of the main reasons why Lohengrin and his swan, more than any other of Wagner's characters, became an object of kitsch and caricature. The swan became nothing short of proverbial: 'Mein lieber Schwan' ('My dear swan') was one of Bertolt Brecht's favourite quotations and Leo Slezak's joke about 'Wann geht der nächste Schwan?' ('What time does the next swan leave?') has passed into the common language. The swan's appearance was always the climax of the opera and a moment which the audience awaited with eager anticipation; if it misfired, as often happened, much to the chagrin of the stage crew, the scene could quite easily slip from the sublime to the ridiculous. At the same time, the swan became the favourite bird of *art nouveau* poets and painters, for whom the swan represented a beautiful, proud and solitary white bird. There is no doubt that it owed its popularity to *Lohengrin* and to the swan-cult of King Ludwig II. Ludwig's identification with the legendary swan-knight was so complete that, shortly before the outbreak of the Austro-Prussian War of 1866, he withdrew to the Roseninsel on Lake Starnberg where, inaccessible to his ministers and cut off from politics, he and his companions would dress themselves up as Barbarossa and Lohengrin and cavort beneath an artificial moon. The previous year he had invited Wagner to a midnight fête on Lake Alp near Hohenschwangau, at which Lohengrin, in the person of Prince Paul von Taxis, had been drawn across the lake in a swan-shaped boat. The boat itself

Bavarian State Opera, Munich, 17 July 1964
Producer: Hans Hartleb. Designer: Rudolf Heinrich. Conductor: Joseph Keilberth. Elsa: Ingrid Bjoner. Lohengrin: Jess Thomas
Heinrich's attempt—following a period when abstraction was in vogue—to evolve a fresh, historically more specific style for *Lohengrin,* based on the nineteenth century's view of the Middle Ages. Here is a world which does not bristle with arms but which is delicate and of a filigree lightness. Act II unfolded in front of the façade of a minster designed in a nineteenth-century romanticized Gothic style.

State Opera, Vienna, 15 May 1965
Producer and designer: Wieland Wagner. Conductor: Karl Böhm. Elsa: Claire Watson. Lohengrin: Jess Thomas. King Henry: Martti Talvela. Ortrud: Christa Ludwig. Telramund: Walter Berry
Act II of Wieland Wagner's *Lohengrin* as a mystery play set in front of a blue stained-glass window, on which a medieval representation of the Madonna was projected. The swan, too, was projected on this wall of leaded glass. The staging was based on the Bayreuth model of 1958.

Bayreuth Festival, 1968
Producer and designer: Wolfgang Wagner. Conductor: Alberto Erede. Elsa: Heather Harper. Lohengrin: James King. King Henry: Karl Ridderbusch. Ortrud: Ludmilla Dvorakova. Telramund: Donald McIntyre. Herald: Thomas Stewart
A new three-dimensionality in Bayreuth replacing the earlier abstractions. A few Romanesque architectural ornaments are visible on the tall, tightly constructed brick walls. The stage area in Act II is cut off from the non-worldly element embodied in the figure of Lohengrin, and is here reserved for human confrontations. The architectural elements have also been carried over to the costumes.

was a miracle of technology, the swan having an electrically illuminated crown on its head.

The note of rapt ecstasy which has come to characterize and influence the direction of all later reactions to the work was present from the very outset, Liszt being the first to describe *Lohengrin* as 'a unique and indivisible miracle'. The reader should compare Wagner's own account of the Prelude with Liszt's interpretation, with its talk of a radiant temple resplendent with 'opaline columns' and 'jewel-encrusted forecourts'. Countless writers have attempted to capture in words the miracle of *Lohengrin*'s music. Charles Baudelaire called it 'an ecstasy of sensuality and knowledge, hovering far above the world of nature'. Thomas Mann wrote to Emil Preetorius after the Second World War, long after he had placed a critical distance between himself and Wagner's works, assuring him that even now he 'still felt the deepest love for the silvery-blue beauty of *Lohengrin* [...] It is a youthful love which is genuine and lasting and which is renewed with each fresh contact with the work [...] Each time I heard the words, "In lichter Waffen Scheine – ein Ritter nahte da" ("In the gleam of bright weapons a knight drew near to me"), I felt a searing ecstasy as though I were eighteen once more – it's the epitome of Romanticism!'

Even more than any other work of Wagner's, *Lohengrin* had the ability to release the forces of inspirational creativity in a great number of later artists. When the young Vasiliy Kandinsky heard the work in 1889, it evoked in his mind the associations of Moscow at sunset: 'But Lohengrin seemed to me to be the perfect realization of this Moscow. The violins, the deep bass notes and, above all, the wind instruments embodied for me at that time the whole force of the hour before evening. I saw all my colours in my mind; they appeared before my very eyes. Wild and almost insane lines were sketched out in front of me. I hesitated to use the expression, "Wagner had painted 'my hour' in music," but it became quite clear to me that [...] painting could develop the very same forces which music already possesses' (*Rückblicke* ['Reminiscences'], 1913).

For entire generations of opera-goers, their first theatrical experience was a performance of *Lohengrin*, an experience which, as often as not, they set down in writing. The best-known of these accounts is the description of Hanno Buddenbrook's first visit to the opera in Thomas Mann's novel *Buddenbrooks:* 'And then good fortune

had become a reality. It had come over him
with its solemnities and delights, its secret
trembling and shaking, its sudden inward
sobbing, its all-consuming, effusive and in-
satiable drunken ecstasy [...] Admittedly,
the cheap fiddles in the orchestra had broken down occasionally during the Prelude,
and a fat, conceited man with a straw-
coloured beard had come floating in, rather

fitfully, in a bark [...] But the sweet and
transfigured splendour of what he was listening to had raised him above all this.'

It is only too easy to see why, after the
end of the First World War, all those who
were involved in theatre reform, particularly
in central Europe and the Soviet Union,
should have made such a determined effort
to abolish the opera's element of Romanti-

Opera, San Francisco, 1978
As in other productions, the
bridal chamber in Act III is
indicated simply by draperies.

cism. Their efforts certainly helped to rescue the work for the present generation, for
up until that time all productions had been
influenced by those of Munich or Bayreuth
and the sets which were provided by theatre
workshops had resulted in a total standardization in staging the work. Moreover, after
the pre-1914 excesses, Wagner was now out
of fashion among intellectuals. Bold and
constructivist shapes were the basis of Feodor Fedorovsky's designs for the Bolshoi
Theatre production in Moscow in 1923. The
sets were based on a system of steps and
sloping ramps which allowed the chorus to
be grouped in echelons. The production was
at its best in the great choral scenes, although it must be admitted that, as is so
often the case with reforms in the theatre, the
costumes turned out to be rather conven-

tional when compared with the scenery
(which was constructivist). Importance was
attached to the lighting in Fedorovsky's overall conception of the work, just as Adolphe
Appia had demanded it should. He attempted
to interpret the music of the overture and that
of the interludes and preludes by means of
lighting changes on stage.

Also worth mentioning are the harshly
stylized and rhythmically ordered images
created by Leo Pasetti for a new production
in Munich in 1929, by Emil Pirchan for the
German Theatre in Prague in 1933 and by
Lothar Schenck von Trapp for Darmstadt in
1928. Darmstadt was one of the centres of
the *art nouveau* movement and it was for the
theatre there that Kurt Kempin had provided one of the few set-designs to be produced in this style; this had been in 1913.

Italy and Spain adopted an alternative solution, particularly in their topographical location of the second-act set. For the La Scala production of 1921, Vittorio Rota created a castle courtyard in the style of a Roman citadel. For the Teatro Costanzi's production in Rome in 1928, Duilio Cambelletti provided a stylized landscape of tall, narrow, crenellated towers, like those at San Gimigniano; and for the Liceo in Barcelona, the great Catalan designer José Mestres Cabanes produced a castle courtyard with a rambling but airy and pastel-shaded architecture of arcades, columns and balustrades, with evoked memories of Moorish Lusitania.

Whereas the aesthetes, the sensitives and the decadents had thrilled to the 'silvery-blue beauty' of *Lohengrin*, the German nationalists of the Second Reich interpreted the work's historical level of action as a confirmation of their own sabre-rattling and jingoistic ideology. The longing felt by the generation of 1848 for German unity and for medieval imperial splendour, in which both regressive and progressive tendencies coincided, was now declared to be a reality. But the dreams of 1848 were not at all the same as the realities of 1871 and later. The earlier nationalist movement had been directed against princes and the aristocracy and inspired by the outstanding liberal minds of the age, who, more often than not, paid the price for their ideas with imprisonment or exile. Following the establishment of Kaiser Wilhelm's Second Reich however, the ruling class of Wilhelmine Germany passed itself off as the guarantor of nationalist thought. Nationalist ideas were now imposed upon the populace from above; all it had to do was to agree and shout 'hurrah' or 'heil' when told to do so. In his novel *Der Untertan* ('Man of Straw'), Heinrich Mann describes his conformist hero, Diederich Hessling, attending his first performance of *Lohengrin* with his fiancée. The satire shows clearly how Wilhelmine Germany interpreted *Lohengrin* for its own ends:

The king beneath the oak-tree [...] His entrance was not especially rousing [...], although what he had had to say was certainly to be welcomed from a nationalist point of view. 'Des Reiches Ehr' zu wahren, ob Ost, ob West' ('To safeguard the empire's honour, whether in the east or in the west'). Bravo! Whenever he sang the word 'German', he stretched out his hand and the music, for its part, underlined the gesture [...] What most struck Diede-

rich was the way in which one immediately felt at home in this opera. Shields and swords, a great deal of rattling steel, jingoism, 'ha' and 'heil' and banners held aloft, and the German oak: one would have liked to join in [...] for here, in the text and in the music, all nationalist demands seemed to him to have come to fruition. Indignation here was tantamount to a crime; all that was established and legitimate was celebrated with brilliant pomp; the greatest emphasis was laid on nobility and on the doctrine of divine right; and the people – a chorus constantly overtaken by events – willingly took up arms against the enemies of its masters. The substructure of war and the mystical climaxes were both observed [...] A thousand performances of an opera like that and there would have been no one who was not a nationalist.

For Diederich Hessling Lohengrin's swan-emblazoned helmet became the eagle-crowned helmet of the Kaiser, that other emissary from heaven. For his entry into Hamburg, for example, Wilhelm II was provided with a swan-drawn motor-boat. His identification with the swan-knight, which for King Ludwig had been no more than a harmless and romantic theatrical game, was here pressed into the service of official ideology. Kitsch was now being taken seriously. Hugo Dinger, in an essay written during the war, in 1915, and entitled 'Was ist uns Richard Wagner in dieser Zeit?' ('What does Richard Wagner mean to us nowadays?'), referred to *Lohengrin* in the same breath as Heinrich von Kleist's *Die Hermannsschlacht* ('Battle of Arminius') and *Prinz Friedrich von Homburg* ('The Prince of Homburg') as the drama of the age. The lines about the threat of enemy action were said to glow 'like a prophetic message written in letters of fire on the walls of Germany's frontiers'; and the German nation joins in with reverence and enthusiasm when its emperor and military commander addresses the words of the king's prayer to the 'disposer of battles'. The divinely appointed hero's prophecy that the eastern hordes would never be victorious in their advance on Germany was now so topical that it seemed as though it had been written with this very occasion in mind.

And the next divinely appointed hero was already waiting in the wings. Adolf Hitler had first seen *Lohengrin* when he was twelve and 'had immediately been riveted. My youthful enthusiasm for the Master of Bayreuth knew no bounds' *(Mein Kampf)*.

Bayreuth Festival, 1980
Producer: Götz Friedrich.
Designer: Günther Uecker.
Conductor: Woldemar Nelsson.
Elsa: Karan Armstrong.
Lohengrin: Peter Hofmann.
King Henry: Hans Sotin
Bridal chamber as a 'cathedral of love' (Uecker), constructed of 100 metal rods of varying length. In the centre is the bridal bed, an *objet d'art*, shaped like an enormous pair of swan's wings.

Teatro alla Scala, Milan, 7 December 1981
Producer: Giorgio Strehler.
Designer: Ezio Frigerio.
Conductor: Claudio Abbado.
Elsa: Anna Tomowa-Sintow.
Ortrud: Elizabeth Connell
Scene between Elsa and Ortrud in Act II. Elsa is standing in the column of light, high up in the centre, with Ortrud below her. The gleaming black pillars forming the set were moved around and remained on stage for all three acts.

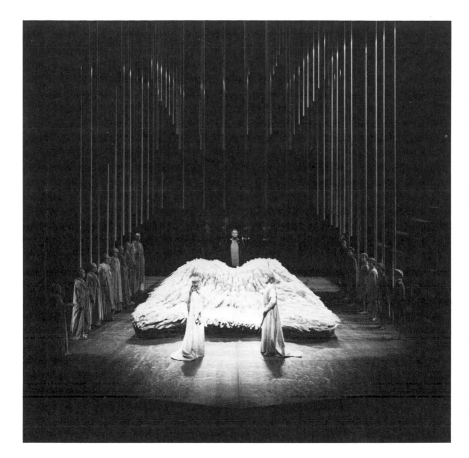

National Socialist propagandists wasted no time in identifying the 'leader of Brabant' with the leader of the Third Reich, an identification which quickly caught on with the masses. In writing *Lohengrin,* Wagner, we now learned from Karl Hermann Müller, had 'glorified the symbol of purest heroism, which exists not for the individual but for a good cause and in support of an idea.' The fact that it was during this period that it became common practice for Lohengrin to be raised aloft on the Brabantines' shoulders or on their shields at the end of Act I and to be carried across the stage in triumph (an idea which Oskar Fritz Schuh had suggested as early as 1922) is entirely in accord with contemporary thought.

The 1936 Bayreuth production has repeatedly been given a key position in this development, if for no other reason than the fact that it coincided with the sixtieth anniversary of the Bayreuth Festival, the one-thousandth anniversary of the death of King Henry the Fowler and, by no means least, the Olympic Games in Berlin. If one looks at this production not in isolation, but in comparison with what was the norm in Germany at the time, what is surprising is its stylistic originality and its basically lyrical and romantic mood, together with its noticeable lack of sabre-rattling and clash of arms. It may be objected that, in presenting a cultural image of itself to the world, the Third Reich may have felt that a certain reserve was necessary this year of all years, in view of the presence of what was still an international festival audience; and that in any case the identification was already firmly established and had no need of being demonstrated yet again in public. That may indeed be true, but what is undeniable is that there was no question of this production ever being a propagandist exercise organized by the Nazi party: those who exercised artistic control over the Festival knew how to preserve their own integrity, at least as far as that was possible in a totalitarian state. The following discussion is therefore consciously limited to the production itself and takes no account of the innumerable scribblings of the various reporters who toed the party line and whose reviews have been quoted sufficiently often in the past.

The scenery by Emil Preetorius was more soft-edged and rounded than the severe, harsh and (if one chooses so to describe them) defensive sets which he had designed for the Berlin Municipal Opera in 1928. One finds here no trace of those Germano-Romanesque stylistic features which were characteristic of artistic taste at this time and which one finds in Max Elten's sets for the 1937 Leipzig production; nor is there anything of the Third Reich's old German folkloristic style, such as inspired Wilhelm Reinking's 1933 Hamburg production; and still less was Preetorius indebted to the dubious solutions proposed by Alexander Spring in Cologne in 1934 or by Benno von Arent's sets and costumes for the Deutsche Oper in Berlin in 1935. Typical of their time were the massed processions: at times the on-stage chorus was upwards of 300 strong, with an additional 70 extras as squires. The costumes, of which there were more than 800 in all, were no longer accurate in historical detail, but made free use of various medieval stylistic features. Act II was dominated by white and silver. The overall artistic impression was what Dietrich Mack described as 'Romantic Heroic Drama', which had not been subjected to the topicality of current politics.

The annexation of Austria was celebrated by a gala performance of *Lohengrin* at the Vienna State Opera, at which the combined choruses of the Berlin and Vienna opera-houses both participated. On the occasion of the Munich gala performance, which was held to celebrate the 'Day of German Art' in 1938, Clemens Krauss had similarly engaged the Vienna Opera chorus to supplement his own Munich chorus. But the most lavish spectacle of all was the one mounted in the Foro Mussolini in Rome, on 3 and 8 May 1938, to celebrate the occasion of Hitler's visit to the city. It was the second half of Act II of *Lohengrin* which was performed. Above the stage, which was 130 yards wide, there towered a central keep 130 feet in height. The chorus alone numbered 10,000 and the total number of spectators is reported to have been around 100,000. The cast included such famous singers as Maria Caniglia and Ebe Stignani.

Might one therefore argue that the German Reich, which had come into the world in 1871 and which was destroyed and buried in 1945, was a child born of Wagner's spirit? After his initial enthusiasm of 1871, Wagner soon began to complain bitterly about the barrenness of Prussian state thinking; and he would never have accepted Hitler's idea of art as the servant of the state. Wagner was a part of the hopes for German national unity, just as he was a part of the tragedy of German nationalism. To quote Reinhold Brinkmann, 'If there is any one moment in Wagner's music dramas when one senses the beginnings of a threat to and a perversion of nationalistic thought, then that moment is in *Lohengrin*

[...] It contains what is probably Wagner's most unguarded statement of our national pathos.'

When Wieland Wagner produced *Lohengrin* at Bayreuth in 1958, it was as a highly stylized mystery play of a stern and ceremonial character. As in a Greek amphitheatre, gradually rising stepped platforms in tiers half surrounded a circular central area to form its basic architectural feature. A flight of stairs rose up in the centre at the back of the stage, and, in the second act, projected onto the cyclorama, were the gentle outlines of a medieval stained-glass window. Classical and medieval antiquity were intended merely as indicators to a correlation of meaning: they were not intended to set the scene, since 'miracles [...] cannot be localized; they are events of the mind.' They are realizable only through art. Lohengrin's swan was a sculpture by Ewald Mataré, an object of art. Wieland's production became famous for the stylized and hieratic movements of the soloists and chorus, which he himself described as 'a community of believers in miracles'. What could have become ossified into something coldly mechanical and stiffly geometrical was in fact imbued with a tangible radiance which was at once rational and tenderly dreamy and mystical. Wieland's later productions in Stuttgart (1960), Berlin (1961) and Vienna (1965) were indebted to the basic concept of his Bayreuth production; and Peter Lehmann, Wieland's assistant in Bayreuth, also based his work on this interpretation for the new production at the 1966/1967 Metropolitan Opera in New York, which he took over after Wieland's death.

In the two decades following the end of the Second World War, stylization was by and large the magic formula which all theatres invoked in staging new productions of *Lohengrin*'s romantic fairy-tale. For the appearance of the swan-knight, lighting effects were now used by preference, so that the question 'with or without a swan' came to have a fundamental significance.

A new beginning was marked by Joachim Herz's 1965 Leipzig production, with sets by Reinhart Zimmermann, although at the time it was criticized for being realistic and historicistic. Herz's production was influenced by Brecht and in particular by the latter's *Der gute Mensch von Sezuan* ('The Good Woman of Sezuan'): 'Before us glittered the golden legend; / In our hands it came to a bitter end.' Herz took as his starting-point the historical situation of the year 1933. For the first time the real world was shown to be harsh, unfriendly and not in the least like a dream. The historical element was necessary in order to give a physical dimension to the confrontation between the miracle and historical fact. Unfortunately, Brechtian parables and historicism did not go well together. The 1975 Vienna State Opera production, with sets by Rudolf Heinrich, gave Herz an opportunity to realize his ideas in more precise detail. The action developed on two levels of meaning: on the one hand, historical reality and, on the other, in the psyches of the characters concerned. Lohengrin was a figment of Elsa's imagination and the miracle a product of sordid reality. Mud-flats, fishcarts, fascines and the stonily expressive early Romanesque architecture of the minster and castle gave a precise indication of time and place. The crowd scattered in agitated confusion to reveal Lohengrin, a miracle and figure of terror at one and the same time. According to Herz, Elsa ends up by destroying 'her dream and sending Lohengrin back to his icy world, dreaming of him as an offensive upstart and would-be judge.'

Rudolf Heinrich had previously designed the sets and costumes for the 1964 Munich production, when he had based his designs on the style of nineteenth-century neo-Gothic, the period at which the opera had been written. The producer Hans Hartleb pleaded in favour of the work's 'pre-eminent operaticality, its unique theatrical glamour'. He admitted that 'the purification of abstraction' and 'the simplifying process of tracing the work back' to its essentials had been successful in making *Lohengrin* more accessible to a new and different generation; but he argued that this circle had now been broken.

In Bayreuth, the period of abstraction came to an end in 1967 when Wolfgang Wagner's production of *Lohengrin* opened up a new three-dimensionality in which concrete architectural forms, including Romanesque features from St Zeno in Verona and from the Baptistery in Pisa, indicated 'a human area of action'; it formed the acting area which, as an 'area of conflict for human confrontations', was clearly distinguished from the non-worldly sphere embodied in the figure of Lohengrin. The world of reality was confronted with a miracle. In his handling of the characters and in the corresponding visual allusions, Wolfgang's aim was to reveal the work's 'mythopoetic core'.

Götz Friedrich in his 1979 Bayreuth production and Giorgio Strehler for his 1981 production at La Scala, Milan, both interpreted *Lohengrin* as a pessimistic tale of a love which could not be realized in a cold, black, war-torn world. Günther Uecker's Brabant in Bayreuth was built up on a sheet of lead, which covered the entire stage area. The universal cry of 'Weh' ('Woe') which goes up at the end of the opera, took on a terrible significance. With their sombre splendour, glittering armour and horses, Ezio Frigerio's lavish sets and costumes for La Scala turned *Lohengrin* into a grand opera in black. At the end Elsa was excluded and cut off. What survived was not the miracle but the world of men with its gleaming weaponry.

All these more recent productions have generally revealed a clear attempt to come to terms once again with what Wagner himself described as the real tragic conflict of *Lohengrin*.

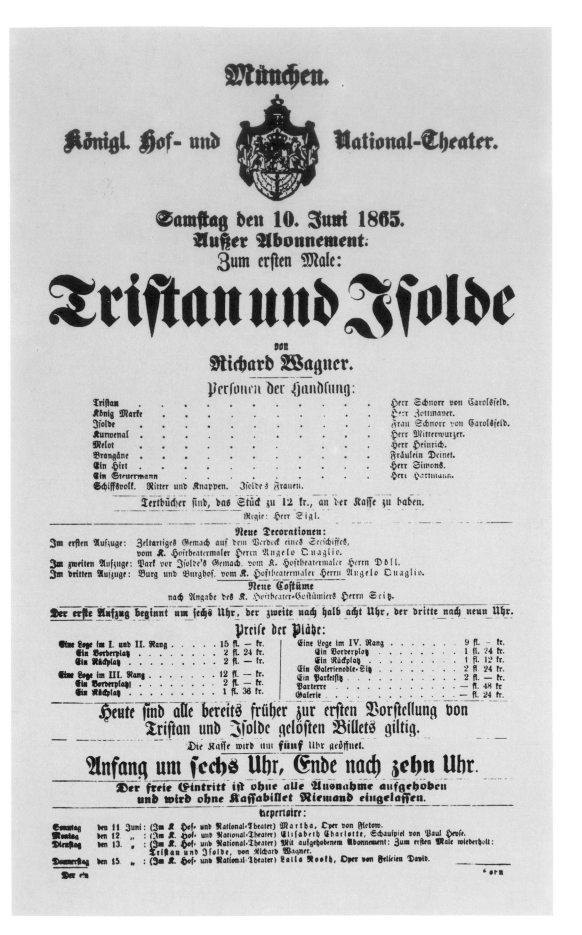

Tristan und Isolde

'But since I have never in my life enjoyed the true happiness of love, I want to erect a further monument to this most beautiful of dreams, in which, from beginning to end, this love will for once be properly sated: I have outlined in my mind the plan for a "Tristan and Isolde", the simplest but most full-blooded musical conception; I shall then shroud myself in the "black flag" which flutters at the end – in order to die.' When Wagner wrote these lines to Franz Liszt on 16 December 1854, he was in the middle of Act III of *Die Walküre*. The end of the *Ring* was nowhere in sight, so vast were the dimensions of the work. Nor could there be any question of the tetralogy ever being staged in an ordinary repertory theatre: it was already evident that, if a performance were ever to take place, a number of exceptional conditions would first have to be met. But a more pressing problem for the exiled composer was the question of his immediate day-to-day finances. His only source of income was from performances of his works. The obvious answer seemed to be for him to write a work which could be easily performed, with a small cast, and which would quickly be taken up by other theatres.

Wagner had already come across the Tristan story during his studies in Dresden. His library included an edition of Gottfried von Strassburg's *Tristan* in Hermann Kurtz's modern German translation of 1844, together with the Middle High German editions of Hans Ferdinand Massmann and Friedrich Heinrich von der Hagen, which also included the later continuations of Ulrich von Türheim and Heinrich von Freiberg. In order to be able to follow the original text, Wagner obtained Adolf Ziemann's large Middle High German dictionary, which included a grammatical introduction to the language. As far as foreign-language versions were concerned, Wagner also had access to the Old French Tristan romance, the Middle English poem *Sir Tristrem,* the Welsh *Trystan* (with a parallel English translation) and a volume, edited by von der Hagen, including extracts from all the various European versions of the Tristan story. Wagner could scarcely have prepared himself more thoroughly.

In his autobiography, Wagner gives three motives for his sudden interest in the subject. In the first place, he was again beset by the 'urge for poetic conception' which regularly assailed him whenever he had been involved in writing music for any length of time. Secondly, his mood of seriousness, which had resulted from his reading Schopenhauer, now demanded 'the ecstatic expression of its essential features'. In October 1854 Wagner had lapped up Schopenhauer's principal work, *Die Welt als Wille und Vorstellung* ('The World as Will and Imagination'). The third reason was of a somewhat more trivial nature. The young Karl Ritter had shown him his outline plan for a stage work on the subject of Tristan, in which the main emphasis was to have lain chiefly on the burlesque elements in the story. Wagner, on the other hand, felt drawn by the profound tragedy of the subject and wanted to change things, imagining the work instead without all those secondary details which he felt distracted from its basic message. Also decisive, no doubt, in determining Wagner's course of action at this time was the refusal in May 1854 of the publishing house of Breitkopf & Härtel to publish the *Ring*. All his friends to whom he confided his plan were sworn to the strictest secrecy. Was he afraid that his breaking off the *Ring* would be interpreted as failure on his part?

The first ideas were jotted down in October 1854: 'Returning home from a walk one day, I sketched the contents of all three acts into which the action was compressed, ready for reworking at a later date. Into the last act I wove an episode which, however, was not later developed – it was a visit to Tristan's sick-bed by Parzival in the course of his wanderings in search of the grail. Tristan, wasting away from the wound which he had received and unable to die, became identified in my mind with the figure of Amfortas in the grail romance. For the time being I was able to resist the temptation to abandon myself entirely to this new idea, so as to be able to continue undisturbed with my major musical task of the moment' *(Mein Leben)*. But at the same time as he was continuing the composition sketch of *Die Walküre*, his lively imagination was already getting to work on the new subject. Attacks of erysipelas interrupted his progress on *Die Walküre*, but it was during this 'time of suffering' that the poem of *Tristan und Isolde* began to take on increasingly clear outlines in his mind, as he himself noted. During the autumn of 1856, Liszt's mistress, Princess Caroline Sayn-Wittgenstein, paid a turbulent visit to Zurich and on one particular evening at Wagner's home, after the company had made music together, a 'group had formed' around Wagner, 'half sitting, half reclining, to create a picture which was by no means lacking in charm': it was to this gathering that Wagner now read out for the first time his 'newly conceived poetic subject'.

On 26 June 1857 he interrupted the composition of Act II of *Siegfried* at the point where Siegfried lies down beneath the lime-tree. He intended leaving him there for a year and in the meantime producing *Tristan und Isolde*. 'Tristan already decided on,' he noted on the title-page of the orchestral sketch of Act II of *Siegfried*. He suddenly felt 'a strange reluctance' to continue his work on the *Ring,* being overcome instead by a pressing desire to make an immediate start on *Tristan und Isolde*. His first priority, however, was to complete the composition sketch of Act II of *Siegfried.* The prose draft of *Tristan und Isolde* was begun on 20 August 1857 at the 'Asyl', Wagner's new home in Zurich which the Wesendoncks had placed at his disposal. The Wesendoncks themselves moved into their adjoining villa on 22 August. On 31 August Hans von Bülow arrived in Zurich on honeymoon with his wife, Cosima *née* Liszt; they were house guests of Wagner's. During the morning everybody had to remain quiet in the 'Asyl' since Wagner was busy working on the libretto of *Tristan und Isolde,* which he then read to his friends in the evenings, act by act. The libretto was completed on 18 September, when a small circle of friends was invited to attend a complete reading. Martin Gregor-Dellin has drawn attention to the particular configuration of those present in the audience on this occasion: they included Wagner's wife Minna, Mathilde Wesendonck and Cosima von Bülow. The reactions of all three women were highly revealing in their very different ways, as Wagner observed in *Mein Leben:* 'Since Frau Wesendonck appeared to be particularly moved by the last act, I said, by way of comforting her, that one could not be saddened by such a tale since in such a serious matter it would only end this way *at very best: Cosima* agreed with me on this point.' Minna thought the text 'disgusting, blazing with an almost indecent love'.

The following winter Wagner organized a further reading for the benefit of a rather larger circle. The Swiss writer Gottfried Keller was among those present and he expressed himself 'particularly pleased by the concision of the whole thing: the work in fact contained only three scenes developed at length.' The architect Gottfried Semper, on the other hand, was irritated and accused Wagner 'of taking everything too seriously: the pleasure afforded by the artistic reworking of such a subject,' Semper argued, 'should consist in the seriousness of its mood being interrupted from time to time, so that the listener is able to derive a sense of enjoyment from even its most profoundly moving passages [...]. Basically everybody shook his head' *(Mein Leben)*. It was just as the fictional Beethoven had predicted in the 1840 essay, 'Eine Pilgerfahrt zu Beethoven'.

Wagner's reworking of his medieval source material was even more radical in the case of *Tristan und Isolde* than it had been with *Tannhäuser* and *Lohengrin.* Whereas the two earlier works had owed much of their theatrical effectiveness and popular success to their colourful medievalism, there was no longer any need for such local colour in *Tristan und Isolde.* As in the libretti of the two previous operas, Wagner dispensed with the wealth of epic detail contained in his sources: he had no time for lively episodes of medieval chivalry, courtly intrigues, the obstacles placed in the lovers' path and the ruses which they employ to circumvent them. In their extreme concentration, the basic ideas and relationships have been reduced to the barest essentials: Tristan is sent to woo Isolde on behalf of his uncle, King Marke, and to bring her back to Cornwall; Isolde offers him what she takes to be a death potion as a means of atoning for the guilt which he incurred in slaying her betrothed lover, Morold; the potion, however, has been substituted by a love philtre by Isolde's companion, Brangäne. In Act II Tristan and Isolde meet in the castle gardens to celebrate their night of love. Tristan's friend, Melot, betrays them to King Marke. Swords are drawn and Tristan is fatally wounded. In Act III we see Tristan lying in the courtyard of his castle at Kareol, tormented by feverish

Court Theatre, Munich,
10 June 1865
The closing scene, Isolde's
'Liebestod': a painting by
Michael Echter based on the
first production.

imaginings and by his longing for Isolde. Her arrival is announced and he tears open his wound and dies.

And now Wagner's own account of the ending: 'What fate kept apart in life is now revived in death, in transfigured form: the gates of union are opened. Over Tristan's body, the dying Isolde perceives the most blissful fulfilment of her fervent longing to be joined together with Tristan for all eternity, in measureless space, without barriers or limitations, inseparable.' Wagner called *Tristan und Isolde* an 'action', which is a translation of the Greek word *drama* and also of the Spanish term *auto* as used by Calderón, who was the most important author read by Wagner at the time of *Tristan und Isolde.* As in Greek tragedy, the plot resides not in what we should nowadays call the stage action, but in the individual word; and, for Wagner, the word was the means of expressing the real action, which consists of inner processes. 'I immersed myself in complete confidence here in the depths of inner mental processes and unhesi-

tatingly gave external shape and form to this most intimate centre of the world.' The elaborate historical details which the poet requires to elucidate the external links in the action and which Wagner had been so concerned about in the case of *Lohengrin* were no longer of importance here. 'Life and death, the whole meaning and existence of the external world, depend here solely on inner emotions. With its ability to move us emotionally, the entire action rises to the surface only because our innermost soul wills it to do so; and it comes to light in the form which it had already assumed within us.' Thus Wagner's own explanation in his essay 'Zukunftsmusik' ('Music of the Future').

This relegation of the outward action to a position of secondary importance has exposed *Tristan und Isolde* to a charge which one occasionally still finds repeated today, namely that nothing really happens in the work. In his essay 'Über die Benennung "Musikdrama"' ('On the Term "Music Drama"'), Wagner used the example of Act II to show

133

Municipal Theatre, Leipzig, 1882
The discovery of the lovers in the castle garden (Act II): engraving after drawing by F. Waibler based on a performance at the Municipal Theatre in Leipzig. From left to right: King Marke, the treacherous Melot, Tristan, Isolde and Brangäne.

what would have corresponded to current expectations of an operatic plot: he was being criticized for having missed the opportunity 'of having a dazzling ball take place on stage, during which the unhappy lovers might have slipped opportunely away to hide in a bower where their discovery would then have given rise to a suitably scandalized reaction and all that that normally involves; instead of which virtually nothing happens in this act except for music [...], which is made worse by the fact that I have offered the spectator practically nothing to look at.' According to Wagner's own view of music drama, every element in the external action should develop logically and consistently from the psychology of the characters and from the latters' motives, which in turn should be revealed by the elements in question. A ball scene would have had only a superficial appeal. Wagner was fully justified in claiming, 'I am quite prepared to allow this work to be judged by the strictest standards such as follow from my theoretical assertions – not because I fashioned it to suit a particular system [...] but rather because I proceeded here with total freedom [...] vis-à-vis every theoretical consideration, with the result that it was only during the process of writing the work that I became aware of the extent to which I had outstripped by own system.' And that was only possible, Wagner concluded, because the task of producing the work had been preceded by a long period of reflection ('Zukunftsmusik'). *Tristan und Isolde* has been

called an epic drama. Melot, for example, whose act of betrayal in Act II precipitates the external catastrophe in the sense understood by classical dramaturgy, has a mere nine lines of text to sing. The greater part of this scene is given over to King Marke and his long and moving reproach. Day – night – day: even the indications of time for the three acts symbolize an 'inner mental process'. Tristan longs to escape from 'barren day' into the 'wondrous realm of night'. Day, for Tristan, is the world of chivalry with its medieval code of virtues including honour, reputation and loyalty – the world in which he was a 'hero'. As a result of what, in the eyes of the world, is his illicit love for Isolde, he abandons this system of values and yearns for night and for death, since only in death can his love exist 'eternally united'. 'Was träumte mir von Tristans Ehre?' ('What was it I dreamt of Tristan's honour?'), he sings, having drunk Isolde's draught of love and death. Only under cover of night can the lovers give themselves up totally to each other. Melot's act of betrayal in Act II drives away the wondrous realm of night: 'Tags-Gespenster! / Morgen-Träume – / täuschend und wüst – / entschwebt, entweicht!' ('Ghosts of day! / Dreams of morning – / deceptive and desolate – / Avaunt! Away!'). In Act III the fatally wounded Tristan is forced to reemerge from night and return once again to the accursed light of day, since Isolde is still 'in the realm of the sun', having called him 'out of night'. Mistaken for a death potion, the love philtre, it is true, had allowed the

Bayreuth Festival, 1886
Costumes: Joseph Flüggen
Costume sketch for Isolde. On Cosima's instructions, the artist adhered closely to Franz Seitz's designs for the first production, which Wagner himself had corrected.

lovers to confess their love for each other, but it had also driven them back once again towards the hateful light of day, preventing their deaths and ultimate union. That is why, in Act III, Tristan must curse the potion. The light of day blinds his consciousness.

The lovers' yearning for night gives the work its particular colouring. Thomas Mann drew attention to the parallels between *Tristan und Isolde*, Novalis's *Hymnen an die Nacht* ('Hymns to Night') and Schlegel's *Lucinde*. Night was one of the major themes of Romantic and sentimental poetry. Wagner certainly stood in this tradition, but he left it far behind him, just as he did with his free adaptation of the medieval epics. Wagner's night is no longer Eichendorff's 'moonlit night of magic', although he, too, uses the atmospheric devices of horn calls and a murmuring fountain. Wagner's night, again, is more than the night celebrated by Novalis in his Hymns. As in classical antiquity, it is the brother and gateway of death, the entrance to oblivion, to death, to Hades, to the final resolution and redemption of that love. That is why in Act II Isolde, a second angel of death, has no alternative but to extinguish the torch, in spite of Brangäne's opposition; and that is why, in Act III, Tristan cries out in his delirium, 'Ach Isolde [...]! Wann endlich, / Wann, ach wann? / löschest du die Zünde?' ('Ah, Isolde [...]! When, finally, / When, ah when / will you douse the light?'). Tristan has already been in this 'vast realm of the world's night'. What he has experienced verges on the inexpressible and defies retelling. He cannot explain it to either Marke or Kurwenal. And here Wagner has managed to produce perhaps the finest verses in the whole of *Tristan und Isolde*, which as a work of rhetoric is certainly his most significant achievement. Only the music can 'say' what Tristan cannot say. Wagner himself called it 'the profound art of resonant silence'. In a letter to Mathilde Wesendonck of 15 April 1859 he described the libretto as 'a poem destined entirely for music'; in the poem, he explained, the musical form had already been fully laid out in advance; the variety and inexhaustibility of the music were already totally implicit within it. That was why he thought it ill-considered to publish the libretto before he had finished writing the music, since a music drama was completely different from a stage play, not being complete until complemented by the music.

The influence of Schopenhauerian philosophy on *Tristan und Isolde* is a subject which has given rise to endless speculation and discussion. Current thinking tends towards the view that, in Martin Gregor-Dellin's words, 'Wagner's boldest work can quite easily be thought of independently of Schopenhauer's philosophical pessimism.' Wagner found in Schopenhauer a confirmation of much that corresponded to his own world of ideas and there is no doubt that he was stunned by this recognition. He had written to Liszt on 16 December 1854: 'His main idea, the ultimate denial of the will to live, is of terrible seriousness but is the only thing that can redeem us. The idea of course was not new to me and no one can possibly conceive it if it has not already lived within him.' Schopenhauer's philosophy of pessimism corresponded to Wagner's own mental state in 1854. But later on, when he was working on Act II in Venice, he wrote to Mathilde Wesendonck, informing her that Schopenhauer's system was in need of correction: he could not pronounce himself in agreement with the philosopher's 'metaphysics of sexual love', which had included love among those forms of desire which were to be extinguished and reduced it to the level of an instinct required to preserve the species. According to Wagner, Schopenhauer had failed to recognize 'the path of salvation which leads to a total pacification of the will through love, a love which is certainly not some abstract love of humanity but the actual love which is genuinely engendered on the basis of the attraction between men and women' (1 December 1858).

What Wagner did find in Schopenhauer, on the other hand, was a metaphysical approach to music. Sentences such as the following must have left a deep impression on him: 'Music, after all, reveals its power and superior capability in conveying the deepest and most arcane information about those sensations which are expressed in words or the actions depicted in opera, in expressing the true and actual nature of such sensations and actions and in teaching us to recognize the innermost soul of the events and occurrences whose empty shell and body the stage has to offer us [...] This music, however, having been written with the drama in mind, is, as it were, the soul of that drama inasmuch as, in its association with the events, characters and words of the drama, it comes to express their inner meaning and the final, secret necessity, which in turn is based on that meaning, of all those events.'

Wagner began the composition sketch of Act I on 1 October 1857 and in doing so produced the famous 'Tristan-chord' which is generally regarded as marking the beginnings of modernism in music. The composition sketch of this act was completed on 31 December, and the full score of Act I received its

Designer: Carlo Brioschi.
Set-design for Act I, undated.
The vessel as a bridal ship:
bright, festive and decorated
with floral garlands. In her
1886 Bayreuth production
Cosima used heavy, dark-red
draperies for Isolde's shipboard
pavilion. It was not until 1927
that Siegfried Wagner
introduced brighter colours into
this scene. Brioschi's studios
rendered the design reproduced
here on various occasions,
including the first performances
in Holland at the
Stadsschouwburg in Amsterdam
in 1896, organized by the
Dutch Wagner Society.

finishing touches on 3 April 1858. 'It is a remarkable piece of music,' he wrote to Liszt in
January 1858. He felt tired and overworked,
complaining, in *Mein Leben,* of the 'strain' on
his 'mental strength'. He had no idea what an
effort this work was still to cost him. 'Still at
the Asyl', he wrote in the composition sketch
of Act II, which he had begun on 4 May
1858. The previous day his new piano had arrived, a gift from Madame Erard. Only now
did he realize what a 'toneless instrument' the
'old conductor's piano' had been which he
had had to make do with until then. 'The new
piano flattered my musical sensitivity,' he recalled in *Mein Leben,* 'and it was almost as a
matter of course that, in the process of impro-
vising to myself, I came upon the tender night
sounds for the second act of *Tristan und
Isolde.'* The composition draft of Act II,

which Wagner described as being still somewhat sketchy, was completed on 1 July. The
idyll at the Asyl had come to an abrupt end, as
a result of Minna's jealousy of Mathilde and
the constant rows which ensued. The house-
hold was disbanded and Wagner once again
found himself homeless. In August he went to
Venice. He kept a diary to show to Mathilde
and in it he wrote on 3 September 1858, 'This
is where Tristan will be finished, in spite of
the world's ragings [...] Well now! Hero
Tristan, heroine Isolde! Help me! [...] This is
where you shall bleed to death; this is where
your wounds will be healed and where they
will close. From here the world will learn of
the sublime and noble distress of highest love,
the lamentations of the most anguished delight.' On 15 October he resumed work on
the orchestral sketch of Act II but failed to

Cologne Opera Festival, 1911
Producer and designer: Hans
Wildermann. Isolde: Edyth
Walker
Instead of the dimly lit park
prescribed by Wagner, which
had been a traditional feature
of all nineteenth-century
productions, the scene here
shows a vast, midnight-blue,
starry sky, indispensable in
meeting Adolphe Appia's
demands for the dramatically
valid use of light in Act II. Only
at the extreme sides of the stage
are there three-dimensional
units of scenery that provide a
framework for the action.
Isolde is centre stage, with what
Appia described as the
'irrefutable' torch dramatically
raised above her head.

make the expected progress. 'But – what sort of music will this turn into! I could spend my whole life just working on this music alone. Oh, it's turning into something deep and beautiful and the most sublime wonders accommodate themselves so easily to the senses. I have never before achieved anything like this,' he wrote on 8 December, again in the diary. And how right he was to be proved when he told Minna on 16 January 1859, 'Just have faith in me: whenever I compose anything, then the result is never anything commonplace.' He was sure in his own mind that the music of this second act would be the culmination of his art: it would turn out better than anything else he had ever written. The full score of Act II was completed on 18 March 1859.

The third act was written in Lucerne, in the Schweizerhof Hotel, beginning on 9 April. The very next day he wrote to Mathilde lines which have since become famous: 'This "Tristan" is turning into something *terrible!* This final act!!! – [...] I'm afraid the opera will be banned – unless the whole thing is parodied by a bad performance –: only mediocre performances can save me! Ones which are at all *good* will drive people insane – I can't imagine how it could be otherwise! This is how far I've had to come!! God! – [...] It's a monstrous tragedy! Overwhelming everything' (10 April 1859). Many of his letters from this period speak of the nervous tension and excitement and the physical exhaustion which he felt while working on the score. It was such a

strain that he was afraid he would no longer be able to complete the work. In an attempt to recover some of his strength, he went on a brief walking holiday on the Rigi. A servant woke him there in the morning with a tune on his *alpenhorn*, a tune which he could not get out of his head and which he used as the basis of the shepherd's merry tune that heralds the sighting of Isolde's ship. At half past four in the afternoon of 6 August 1859, he completed the full score of *Tristan und Isolde* at the Schweizerhof, 'bringing the whole of Romantic art to a divine conclusion with the most beautifully orchestrated B major chord in the entire history of music,' as Richard Strauss described it.

Even before a single line of the prose draft had been written down, Wagner was already thinking of a suitable venue for the first production. He firmly believed that the opera would be a success and a success in the theatre was something which he urgently needed. Since 1853 his earlier works had been taken up by other theatres in Germany, thanks to the support which Liszt had given them and to the latter's highly acclaimed Weimar productions. It seemed as though a new work might stand a good chance of becoming accepted.

Wagner's thoughts turned initially towards Strasbourg, possibly because the author of one of the Tristan versions, Gottfried von Strassburg, had come from there. Strasbourg, moreover, was close to Germany, a country which Wagner was still barred from entering.

Designer: Ernst Gutzeit
Set-design for Act III for a
production in London in 1916.
The most radical realization of
Appia's idea that Act III should
be dominated by a 'scorching
sun'. The visual image derives
from the psychology of the
character of Tristan in this act,
with his sense of having been
rejected by the night and cast
back into the burning light of
day, the torch which is never
extinguished, delirious fantasies
and the 'light' which he believes
he can 'hear'.

He thought of borrowing the orchestra from Karlsruhe and of casting Albert Niemann and Luise Dustmann in the leading roles. Everything else still seemed comparatively easy to deal with, since, incredible as it must seem today, Wagner was of the opinion that *Tristan und Isolde* would not present any particular difficulties for a reasonably equipped theatre. 'I believe I am justified in assuming that a thoroughly practicable work, such as Tristan will turn out to be, will quickly bring in a de-

cent income and keep me above water for some time to come,' he had written to Liszt on 28 June 1857, before starting work on the libretto. But even when the text had been finished, he was still convinced that 'the subject can be reduced to a very modest outer framework so that, given the fact that there should be virtually no problems with sets and chorus and given the fact that the work's only demand is for two good singers for the leading parts [...], the opera has every chance of re-

National Theatre, Prague,
18 December 1924
Producer: Ferdinand Pusman.
Designer: Vlastislav Hofman
Set for Act II in its traditional
layout: a forest, with the castle
door and the tower with its
torch on the left. The style,
however, is that of the New
Objectivity of the 1920s.

ceiving a perfectly good first performance and a prospect of quickly [...] being taken up by other theatres' (30 September 1857). These lines, it is true, were written to his publishers Breitkopf & Härtel, but there is no reason to interpret them simply as calculated optimism on Wagner's part, since he wrote in a similar vein on 29 October 1857 to his old friend Wilhelm Fischer, chorus-master at Dresden and someone whose opinion Wagner valued in practical matters connected with the theatre; here, too, he spoke of a task which was not difficult to carry out. And as late as January 1858 he was still hoping that the first performance would take place before the end of the year. How wrong he was once again to be proved.

One curious episode deserves to be mentioned here and that concerns the projected world première of *Tristan und Isolde* in Rio de Janeiro. In March 1857 the Brazilian consul, acting on behalf of Emperor Dom Pedro, offered to have Wagner's works performed in Rio in Italian. Wagner was 'agreeably taken' by the suggestion and thought it entirely conceivable, as he observed in *Mein Leben,* that 'a passionate musical poem could be produced which would prove quite admirable in Italian'. Initial contacts were made and the consul was presented with a number of expensively bound piano scores (only Minna retained her sense of realism and insisted that

what Wagner had paid the book-binder was money down the drain); whereupon the consul disappeared without trace.

Plans to stage the work in Karlsruhe took on a more concrete form. Eduard Devrient, manager of the town's court theatre, had visited Wagner in Zurich at the beginning of July 1857 and discussed terms with him. The Grand Duke and his wife were keen on music and especially admired Wagner's operas. Devrient's trump card, however, was the existence in the Karlsruhe ensemble of a talented tenor who would be suitable for casting in the title-role – Ludwig Schnorr von Carolsfeld. But when the score was complete and Wagner insisted on his being present at all the rehearsals, Devrient began to have second thoughts and finally abandoned the project. He was afraid that Wagner, with his ambitious artistic demands, would overtax his theatre's modest resources and reduce the place to a state of chaos. The official explanation, however, was that none of the women in the company dared take on the part of Isolde, and even Schnorr was said to have doubts 'about the feasibility of the final section of his role'. The work, in any case, was claimed to be unperformable.

In September 1859 Wagner went to Paris in an attempt to organize model productions of all his works, including the première of *Tristan und Isolde.* At a concert on 25 January

Designer: Adolphe Appia.
Set-design for Act III, dating
from 1896 and used in Milan in
1923
The castle courtyard at Kareol
as an interior bay, with the
outside world visible only
through a single opening, as in
paintings by old Dutch masters.

Munich, 1927
Designer: Leo Pasetti
Set-design for Act III. For all
its atmosphere of melancholy
and desolation, this design
differs from Appia's in being
more lyrical. Probably Pasetti's
most successful design. Emil
Preetorius designed Act III in a
similar style for the 1938
Bayreuth production, as well as
for a number of other
opera-houses.

1860, at the Théâtre Italien, the Prelude to *Tristan und Isolde* was heard for the first time in public, the audience on that occasion including Hector Berlioz, Giacomo Meyerbeer and François Auber. In May the second act was performed in front of a small circle of friends at the home of Pauline Viardot-Garcia; the famous mezzo-soprano sang the roles of Isolde and Brangäne, while Wagner himself took on the parts of Tristan and King Marke. A further run-through was given on the occasion of a soirée at the Prussian Embassy, when Princess Campo-Reale of Naples, accompanied at the piano by Camille Saint-Saëns, sang Isolde's 'Liebestod', astonishing Wagner by her accomplished performance. But the *Tannhäuser* scandal confounded all Wagner's hopes of staging the first performances of *Tristan und Isolde* in Paris.

Having been granted permission to re-enter Germany, Wagner travelled to Dresden in the autumn of 1862 to sound out the theatre there, but he was still regarded as a *persona non grata* by the Dresden administration. The general intendant in Berlin, Botho von Hülsen, refused even to see Wagner.

The outlook in Vienna seemed somewhat less bleak. When Wagner had visited the city in search of singers who might be released from their contracts to appear in the Karlsruhe production, the intendant Count Lanckoronski offered to have *Tristan und Isolde* produced at the Court Opera and had suggested 1 October 1861 as the date of the first performance. Wagner was initially highly enthusiastic about the idea, but disappointment was soon to follow. The tenor, Alois Ander, who was to sing the part of Tristan, lost his voice and so the date set for the first rehearsal had to be postponed. In addition, Wagner was forced to simplify the singer's task by cutting sections of the role and by 'revising the lower register'. Ander showed no sign of regaining his voice and rehearsals were called off in November. The following year they were somewhat surprisingly resumed, only to be abandoned definitively in April 1863; after seventy-seven rehearsals it was conceded that the undertaking had failed. *Tristan und Isolde* became stigmatized as unperformable. One Berlin newspaper rather sarcastically described the opera as the only art work of the future since it was unperformable in the present. Wagner's prophecy of August 1860 had come true: 'How dreadfully I shall one day have to atone for this work if I intend performing it complete: I can quite clearly see the most unspeakable suffering ahead of me, since, if I'm honest with myself, I have gone far beyond what lies within the realms of possibility as far as our present achievements go.' He was 'sick' of it all; *Tristan und Isolde* had become a 'fairy story' for him and by 1864 the work seemed to be over and done with (18 April 1865).

It was at that point that an event took place in his life which has often been described as a 'miracle' – the intervention of King Ludwig II. Ludwig wanted the première to be staged at his own court theatre in Munich and he gave Wagner complete authority to engage whatever forces were necessary for mounting an exemplary production of the work. He himself obtained permission from the King of Saxony for three singers from the Dresden Opera to be released for the performances; these three were Ludwig and Malwina Schnorr von Carolsfeld for the title-roles and Anton Mitterwurzer for the part of Kurwenal. Wagner was fully occupied with the task of producing the opera and therefore unable to take on the additional burden of conducting the performances, so that, at his suggestion, Hans von Bülow was entrusted with overall musical control. Rehearsals began on 5 April 1865. In spite of the intensity of the sessions, Wagner was relaxed and engaged in tomfoolery with the singers, evidently happy to be working in the theatre once more. His last première had taken place fifteen years earlier. In retrospect, too, Wagner was to look back on these weeks of rehearsals as among his happiest memories. But it seemed simply impossible for him to avoid controversy: the people of Munich were evidently of a highly inquisitive nature and rumour was rife in the town. 'I tell you, it's mad the way people are carrying on here, for and against Wagner,' Josephine von Kaulbach (wife of the painter) reported. 'Rumour has grown into a hundred-headed monster; the Wagner cult is quite nauseating; the young king is now rechristening everything around him with the names of Tristan and Isolde.' A thoughtless remark made by Bülow in the heat of the moment during the course of a particularly exhausting rehearsal was blown up into a sensational scandal, in spite of Bülow's issuing a public apology; there was an immediate outcry, demanding that the Prussian *junker* be made to leave the city.

The dress rehearsal finally took place on the morning of 11 May before an audience of 600 invited guests. Wagner was visibly moved and gave a speech, as did Bülow. Among other things, the composer told the audience: 'Difficulties of a nature never before encountered have been successfully overcome; the task has been resolved [...]. But our finest

Teatro alla Scala, Milan,
11 December 1930
Designer: Edoardo Marchioro
Act II was traditionally
designed in this style
throughout the nineteenth
century and later. Marchioro's
realistic sets replaced the
abstract designs of Adolphe
Appia which had first been seen
in 1923 and which Milan
audiences had found too
austere.

and ultimate achievement is that the artist may now be forgotten beside his work of art.' The first night was fixed for 15 May. 'Rapturous day! Tristan, – how eagerly I await the coming of evening! Would that it might soon be dark! "Wann weicht der Tag der Nacht?" ("When will the day yield to night?").' These lines from the king were handed to Wagner on the morning of the 15th. The international press had gathered in the city and so, too, of course, had Wagner's friends and supporters. 'The area around the Court Theatre had turned into a European market-place in which the tongues of all languages were to be heard,' according to Robert von Hornstein. 'The atmosphere in the cafés along the Maximilianstrasse was like that which you find at times of extreme political agitation.'

But the Fates, who had always looked unkindly on *Tristan und Isolde,* had not yet had their final say. On the very morning of the day fixed for the première, Wagner was handed a writ claiming the sum of 2,4000 florins which he allegedly owed from his time in Paris. Who was responsible for the writ was never discovered. Since Wagner could not pay, his furniture was provisionally seized by the bailiffs until the king's privy purse came to his rescue. The next bearer of bad

tidings was Schnorr: his wife had lost her voice and was therefore unable to appear that evening. News of the postponement of the premiere was not posted up until the afternoon, when it immediately set off the most fantastic rumours. Wagner's music of the future had ruined Malwina's voice; Bülow was refusing to conduct because students had threatened to pelt him with rotten eggs and because an attempt would apparently be made on his life; the orchestra was said to have gone on strike, and so on. The date for the first performance had to be postponed until 26 May, which provided the *Münchner Volksbote* with an opportunity to hold forth in the following terms: 'Next Friday "Adultery to the Accompaniment of Kettledrums and Trumpets", complete with Music of the Future, will be committed on the stage of the National Court Theatre. Many people, of course, have not hesitated to say that it is neither nationalistic nor courtly to celebrate the breaking of the Sixth Commandment with such pomp and circumstance' (23 May). A further postponement became necessary since Malwina had not recovered her voice. The première was now fixed for 10 June.

In the meantime, another first night had taken place, on schedule, at the Isar-Vor-

Salzburg Festival, 1933
Producer: Otto Ehrhardt.
Designer: Oskar Strnad.
Conductor: Bruno Walter.
Isolde: Dorothee Manski.
Tristan: Hans Grahl. Kurwenal:
Josef von Manowarda.
Brangäne: Gertrude Rünger
The problem of designing a
suitable set for Act I, with its
division into the intimate scenes
in Isolde's quarters and the
chorus scenes of the ship's
crew, had first been solved by
Alfred Roller in Vienna in 1903,
when he had used a two-tiered
deck. The scenes between
Isolde, Brangäne and Tristan
had taken place on the lower
deck, the chorus scenes on the
upper deck. It was based on this
same principle that Strnad
designed his sets for Act I in the
Salzburg production shown
here.

State Opera, Stuttgart, 1938
Designer: Felix Cziossek
A simpler and, at the same time,
more economical solution than
Roller's elaborate two-tier deck
was the use of a curtain to
separate Isolde's quarters from
the main deck of the ship. The
pattern of the material here is
similar to that used in Vsevolod
Meyerhold's 1909 St Petersburg
production.

stadt-Theater, where, on 29 May, the opening performance of 'the frequently postponed exclusive world première of *Tristanderl und Süssholde*' had been given. It was a parody of *Tristan und Isolde,* in which reference was made to all the events that had accompanied preparations for the first night and which had created such a stir throughout the city.

And so the performance began at six o'clock on the evening of 10 June. Officially it was sold out, but there were many empty seats in the stalls and in the gallery which were not occupied until the Prelude was well under way. Fearful of demonstrations against Bülow, the police considered that allowing late-comers to be seated was a necessary precaution. As a result it was impossible to hear the Prelude because of the noise of people taking their places. King Ludwig and the other members of the royal family, including King Ludwig I, who had abdicated in 1848, were in the audience but not even their august presence was able to contain the audience's applause and hissing. In Act III King Ludwig II was moved to tears. Wagner was beside himself with joy: 'One thing has been accomplished,' he wrote to Ludwig on 13 June 1865. 'Tristan has been completed. You know that all previous poets to have written about Tristan left their versions incomplete from Gottfried von Strassburg onwards. It almost seemed as though my own work would be dogged by a similar misfortune: for it was not completed until it appeared before us in the flesh, as a living drama, and spoke directly to

our hearts and senses; this has now been achieved.'

Wagner himself described the production as perfect: his ideal seemed to have been achieved. Sets, costumes and the performances of both the singers and the orchestra had all been an outstanding success. The sketches for the sets followed Wagner's instructions to the letter and were produced in consultation with him. Acts I and III were designed by Angelo Quaglio, Act II by Heinrich Döll, a specialist in landscape painting. Isolde's tent-like pavilion in Act I was formed by elaborately folded red draperies. The only genuinely theatrical effect was Brangäne's drawing back the curtains at Isolde's words, 'Luft! Luft! / Mir erstickt das Herz! / Öffne! Öffne dort weit!' ('Air! Air! / My heart is suffocating! / Throw open the curtains there!'), to reveal a view of the open deck ending in a high stern-post terminating in an animal's head. The crew were on deck, with Tristan at the helm. On the ship's arrival in Cornwall at the end of the act, the silhouette of a rocky coastline came into view, with Marke's castle in the distance. The architectural details of the sets for Acts II and III were early Romanesque in style: it was Wagner's wish that the impression they made should be archaic rather than medieval. The costume designs by Franz Seitz were corrected by Wagner; they, too, tended towards a hybrid style of Germanic and Romanesque elements.

In Ludwig Schnorr von Carolsfeld Wagner had at his disposal a singing actor such as he had never known before and such as he was never to find again. No other artist who ever worked with Wagner was the object of such unstinting admiration on Wagner's part as was Schnorr. Wagner had heard him for the first time in Karlsruhe in 1862, singing the part of Lohengrin. He had initially had grave reservations about him, since it had been reported that the young singer suffered from obesity. But when he saw him on stage, he was immediately rivetted by his phenomenal gifts as an actor: 'If the sight of the swan-knight landing in his tiny bark created what was initially a somewhat disconcerting impression of the appearance of a young Hercules, then the quite specific magic of the divinely ordained legendary hero immediately took hold of one from the very moment of his first appearance, so that we did not ask ourselves, "Is this our idea of the hero?" but told ourselves, rather, "This is our idea of the hero!"' *(Mein Leben).* His portrayal of Tristan's suffering and delirium in Act III must have been so overwhelming that Wagner was unable to express the way he felt. During the

Between 1935 and 1941 The legendary couple of Kirsten Flagstad and Lauritz Melchior typified the ideal Tristan and Isolde for American audiences.

fourth and final performance Wagner is reported by the present-day expert on Wagnerian staging, Michael Petzet, 'to have been seized at the moment when Tristan curses love by a sense of utter horror at the incredible performance of his friend Schnorr, a performance which bordered on the sinful.' When Schnorr died suddenly on 21 July, Wagner stated that he never wanted the work performed again: it was to remain Schnorr's memorial.

Public opinion gave the bold new music little chance for the future, quite apart from the fact that many listeners found even the very subject of the work immoral. When Josephine von Kaulbach wrote to her husband on 11 June 1865, after the first night, telling him that Tristan and Isolde would now no doubt have to resume their private lives once more, she was not alone in holding that view.

It was nine years before a second theatre was prepared to risk a production of the work, and once again it was the small opera-house at Weimar which took up the challenge. The Berlin intendant, Botho von Hülsen, continued to resist the idea of a production until an imperial decree finally forced him to accept the work for performance. Wagner himself travelled to Berlin for the rehearsals. Tristan was sung by Albert Niemann, Isolde by Vilma von Voggenhuber, Brangäne by Marianne Brandt and King Marke by Franz Betz. Prices were raised for the first performance on 20 March 1876, which was given before a packed house. Opinions varied as to the success of the production. Frau von Hülsen confessed that, in spite of the excellence of the production, she had never been able to sit through an entire performance, so unbearable was 'the nerve-racking instrumentation'. Her husband was quite convinced that in fifty years' time very few people would have heard of *Tristan und Isolde* and that the work would scarcely ever be performed.

Following Wagner's death in 1883, *Tristan und Isolde* was the first production to be mounted in Bayreuth under Cosima's independent control. That was on the occasion of the 1886 Festival, when the choice fell on *Tristan und Isolde* rather than on any other work because of the relatively low production costs involved. The performances, however, were poorly attended: for one performance only twelve tickets were sold. Cosima attempted to reproduce the opera's first production, one which, according to Wagner's own testimony, could lay claim to authenticity. The Brückner brothers created close copies of the Munich sets, although the cos-

tumes for the Bayreuth production were designed not by Franz Seitz but by Joseph Flüggen, who worked under Cosima's instructions. She insisted that the costumes were not to be in the style of Kleist's *Die Hermannsschlacht* or *Der Ring des Nibelungen*: 'Ireland, Cornwall and Brittany should not have an excessively wild, Nordic character,' she instructed Flüggen on 9/10 September 1885. The interpreters of the two leading roles, Heinrich Vogl and Rosa Sucher, were urged to be sparing in their movements and gestures and not to act out the raging passions which they felt. This was the result of Cosima's awareness of the enormous difficulties inherent in staging *Tristan und Isolde*, 'where the most intricate ramifications of the characters' inner lives are revealed by the music' and 'where facial gestures can scarcely do justice to the power of the musical sounds, without their seeming to be absurd.' A 'well intentioned realism' was 'least desirable of all' here, Cosima wrote to Hermann Levi on 8 September 1886, whereas 'the calm which appears, so to speak, to be the covering which veils the emotions indicated by the orchestra is at least innocuous, however inappropriate it may be.' The conductor Felix Mottl was encouraged to reduce the level of the orchestral sound so that the audience would be able to understand the text.

It was not until the 1880s that *Tristan und Isolde* began to gain general acceptance in other theatres, with local premières taking place in 21 cities, including London in 1882, where the conductor was Hans Richter, Vienna in 1883, Prague and New York in 1886, and Strasbourg and Rotterdam in 1890.

State Opera, Vienna, 1 January 1943
Designer: Alfred Roller. Conductor: Wilhelm Furtwängler. Tristan: Max Lorenz. Kurwenal: Georg Monthy
The new production of *Tristan und Isolde* which opened on 1 January 1943 marked the production début of the conductor Wilhelm Furtwängler. He insisted on using Roller's sets from 1903. In Act III the massive block-like structure of the castle gate formed a vertical contrast to the sea and broad horizon of the sky.

The history of all later reactions to the work has been called 'a history of fascination', with only a few critical minds speaking of the dangers of such a fascination. No other work of Wagner's has had such an influence on literature, art and music. Twentieth-century composers have described it as the only work by Wagner which is genuinely 'sacrosanct'.

Among the French intelligentsia around the turn of the century, one could speak not only of *wagnérisme* but of a quite particular *tristanisme.* Claude Debussy, Emmanuel Chabrier and the young composer Guillaume Lekeu, a pupil of César Franck's, attended the 1889 Bayreuth Festival production of *Tristan und Isolde.* Lekeu fainted during the Prelude and had to be carried out of the auditorium, while Chabrier broke down and wept. Odilon Redon and Henri Fantin-Latour painted Wagnerian subjects, as did Aubrey Beardsley in England. Paul Cézanne and Emile Zola were both members of the Wagner Society of Marseilles. There was a good deal of literature which was devoted exclusively to Wagner in Italy (Gabriele d'Annunzio), Germany (Thomas Mann) and in England. Since the larger theatres of the French capital remained closed to Wagner's works, audiences went instead to the Sunday concerts of Charles Lamoureux, Jules Pasdeloup and Edouard Colonne. These particular 'heroic Sundays' were a time for celebration. Stéphane Mallarmé took notes during the concerts and, back home, relived the works at a pitch of unattainable perfection. Wagner was the talking point of the *salons,* which were frequented by a class of people who set the tone in matters of society and art. Marcel Proust's Madame Cambremer was as much a Wagnerian as his Madame Verdurin, for whose sensitive nerves even 'a bit of *Liebestod'* was dangerous. It became fashionable to go to Bayreuth, and many of these audiences spoke of the Bayreuth Festival in the same breath as the exclusive spa theatres at Karlsbad (modern Karlovy Vary) or Marienbad (modern Mariánské Lázně). 'Bayreuth threatened to turn into a meeting-place for snobs,' Siegfried Wagner wrote. The First World War put an end to all that.

One of the visitors who attended the 1886 Festival was later to play a role of crucial significance in the stage history of the opera; his name was Adolphe Appia. He was bitterly disappointed by the staging. The traditional, illusionistic sets were made of flats painted to give the impression of perspective and these, together with the gas lighting, particularly that of the footlights, seemed to him to be inappropriate to the vision of space and light which the work's music had conjured up within him. His aim was to interpret this music visually, rather than to design yet more settings incorporating a greater or lesser degree of historical accuracy. Stylization and abstraction, two of the twentieth century's most important contributions to staging and set-design, can be traced back to Appia. A solidly built stage area with acting areas on various levels to create a space of action for the

State Opera, Berlin, 1947
Producer: Frida Leider.
Designer: Lothar Schenck von Trapp. Conductor: Wilhelm Furtwängler
The set for Act I also included a sail stretched out to extend the width of the whole stage, as do the curtains for Isolde's quarters, their appliqué work lending an archaic air to the scene. The producer on this occasion, was Leider, a world-famous Isolde of the 1930s.

Metropolitan Opera, New York, 23 February 1953 Designer: Joseph Urban. Conductor: Fritz Stiedry. King Marke: Hans Hotter. Tristan: Ramon Vinay. Isolde: Margaret Harshaw
Scene from Act II. The sets from this production dated from 1920, the first new production of the work at the Metropolitan Opera after the First World War. It was not at all unusual for opera-houses like the Metropolitan or the Paris Opéra to retain the same sets for several decades.

three-dimensional actor, and lighting changes as a visual interpretation of the events taking place in the music: these were Appia's basic demands. He regarded himself not as a scene-painter in the traditional sense, but rather as an architect who designed his solid structures for the actor on stage.

In the appendix to his most important work, *Die Musik und die Inszenierung* ('Music and Staging'), written in French between 1892 and 1897 and published in German in 1899, Appia expounded his ideas on staging *Tristan und Isolde,* supplementing the text with illustrations. It was necessary, he argued, to stage the 'inner action' of *Tristan und Isolde;* the guiding principle for both the producer and the designer must be 'to enable the audience to see things the way the heroes of the drama typically see them.' That was why the external world was of such minor importance, being merely an illusion for Tristan and Isolde. In Act I 'a few ropes of characteristic rigging' were to suffice; on no account should the stage be 'cluttered with maritime objects'. For the second-act set extreme simplicity was of the essence. As she waits for Tristan, Isolde does not feel 'the mild summer's night' but 'the terrible space which separates her from Tristan'. Everything should appear indistinct, only the torch remaining 'irrefutable, a sign which keeps the man she loves away from her.' In extinguishing the torch, she causes time to stand still. All that one should see now is their 'being to-

gether, [...] time, space, the sounds of nature, the threatening torch – all have faded away.' The spectator should 'abandon himself utterly to the inner action'. The third act was dominated by the 'scorching sun' – the 'cold-coloured' light of hateful day – which sinks slowly into the sea during Isolde's Transfiguration, casting its 'last rays on the united lovers, like a blood-red aureole of light'. If one compares Appia's description with the general reaction to *Tristan und Isolde* at this time, one cannot but be struck by the absence of any mention of intoxicated rapture, and by the frequent references to 'harshness'.

In 1899 the *Journal de Genève* appealed to the management of the Grand Théâtre to engage Appia for its new production of *Tristan und Isolde,* but in vain.

Cosima, too, had come to realize while planning her own production that *Tristan und Isolde* was basically a psychological drama, as she made clear in the passage from her letter to Hermann Levi quoted above. She found her own compromise solution by having the singers gesticulate as little as possible. On 11 April 1903 she wrote to Count Hermann Keyserling, who had recommended Appia to her, saying that, although she was interested in Appia's theories, there could be no question of their ever being accepted at Bayreuth. 'Isolde's pavilion, Tristan's Act III backdrop showing the sea, everything, in short, has to remain just as was indicated by the creator of

Teatro alla Scala, Milan,
28 March 1957
Producer: Rudolf Hartmann.
Designer: Nicola Benois.
Conductor: Hans
Knappertsbusch. Isolde: Astrid
Varnay. Tristan: Hans Beirer.
Brangäne: Ira Malaniuk
Tristan's ship in Act I as a
Viking long-boat viewed from
an unusual angle.

Teatro alla Scala, Milan,
28 March 1957
Producer: Rudolf Hartmann.
Designer: Nicola Benois.
Conductor: Hans
Knappertsbusch. Isolde: Astrid
Varnay. Tristan: Hans Beirer
Scene from Act III showing one
of the most striking Wagnerian
sets. The traditional visual
elements have been interpreted
in the style of *pittura metafisica;*
similar to the sets designed by
Orlando di Collalto for the
Maggio Musicale in Florence
the same year.

the drama.' A subjective interpretation for Cosima meant pure arbitrariness and hence, according to her lights, was a crime committed against the spirit of the work. She regarded herself as custodian of the Bayreuth inheritance; her task was the ideal realization of all that the *Meister* had not been able to carry out in his own theatre; hence the inviolability of his stage directions. Certainly, there was no inclination on her part to lead the way in matters of staging, in the sense of being 'modern'; rather was it her concern to be 'correct' in the sense the *Meister* himself would have understood; the former was something she left to ordinary theatres.

'There is nothing left for us here to invent, but only to perfect in detail.' To demand from Cosima a reform of scenic and production styles would have shown a complete failure to understand her intentions and would certainly have lain outside her artistic capabilities. Where Cosima did hope to pioneer new developments was in the care given to the musical preparation of the production, the intensive study of the singers' roles and the realization of the music drama. She wrote back to Keyserling, saying that she knew a splendid job for Appia which would allow him to make a lasting contribution to the theatre: he should produce Shakespeare and

Goethe, since they had not left any model performances behind them.

It was in 1903 that Appia, together with Mariano Fortuny, was first able to test out his new style in Paris at the private theatre of the Comtesse de Béarn. The year 1903 also saw the famous Vienna State Opera production of *Tristan und Isolde*, conducted by Gustav Mahler and designed by Alfred Roller, and given to mark the twentieth anniversary of Wagner's death. The Viennese opera-going public had grown up on the historicist magnificence of designs by Brioschi, Burghart and Kautsky, and they found Roller's sets in the style of the Vienna Secession difficult to take. Roller, a friend of Gustav Klimt's and President of the Secession, had a sovereign command of those subtleties of composition in colour and form which were typical of the secessionist style. For the open deck on board ship in Act I, Roller devised a kind of double deck which allowed a clear distinction to be drawn between the choral scenes on the one hand and the intimate scenes in Isolde's tent on the other. The ship was positioned at a slight angle, so that, for the first time, it was possible to see the light playing on the surface of the waves. The orange-yellow sail stood out from the other colours and dominated the set. The second-act set had similarly been re-thought, with a vast purple-blue starry sky instead of the usual dense forest of leaves. The smooth marble walls of the castle gleamed in the pale moonlight. Here, too, the torch occupied a central position. Act III was set on a rocky outcrop above the sea. The walls and massive gate of the castle, made of rough grey stone, and a lime-tree were all bathed in brilliant flat light, creating an atmosphere of desolation and solitude. Many writers commented on the particular effectiveness of the lighting plot for Act II: first the flame-red torch, then, during the love duet, a deep blue night tinged with purple and, following Melot's betrayal, the pale, sulphurous rays of dawn.

Gustav Mahler's conducting was passionate and tensely agitated. The leading roles were sung by Anna Bahr-Mildenburg, who had travelled to Bayreuth in 1900 especially to study the part with Cosima, and Erik Schmedes; Richard Mayr was King Marke. It was a production which, in Marcel Prawy's words, 'proved the truth of the theory that today's experiment is tomorrow's law.'

It may be added in passing that new developments in the area of stage technology, such as the cyclorama and the use of dimmer control units, for example, played a decisive role in the realization of Appia's ideas. It was with a production of *Tristan und Isolde* that Vsevolod Meyerhold made his début as an opera producer at the Mariynsky Theatre in St Petersburg in 1909. His basic observations, which were a preliminary study for his work on the production, are characteristic of the way in which Appia's ideas were being taken up and developed at this time. As a producer from the legitimate theatre, Meyerhold had first of all to sort out in his own mind the particular conditions which obtained in producing opera, conditions which were dictated by

Maggio Musicale, Teatro Communale, Florence, 21 May 1957
Producer: Frank de Quell. Designer: Orlando di Collalto. Conductor: Artur Rodzinski. Isolde: Birgit Nilsson. Tristan: Wolfgang Windgassen
The Act II love duet between Tristan and Isolde. A forest at night with no sign of a castle. Three-dimensional sets.

State Opera, Stuttgart,
4 May 1958
Conductor: Ferdinand Leitner.
Tristan: Wolfgang Windgassen.
Kurwenal: Gustav Neidlinger
Scene from Act III. This
production was a try-out for
Wieland Wagner's legendary
Bayreuth production of 1962.

the music. The only feasible course seemed to him to lie not in staging the libretto, but in 'immersing oneself in the emotional world of the music'. The acting style of opera singers should be neither naturalistic nor stylized; it had to follow 'the laws of the all-powerful rhythm'. 'The rhythm of opera has nothing in common with that of everyday life.' He quoted Anton Chekhov in support of this: 'Life, other than it is, other than it is supposed to be; a life such as it appears in dreams.' The singing actor must 'grasp the essence of the score' and convey 'all the orchestral nuances in the three-dimensional stage picture; [...] co-ordinated with the set and co-rhythmic with the music, man is transformed into a work of art.' It was in this way that Meyerhold interpreted Wagner's description of the music drama as 'acts of music which have become apparent', since it is only in performance that music can be carried over from time into space. In a concert performance the music projects an imaginary mental picture in time. In a stage performance, on the other

hand, what is imagined becomes reality, being realized in space.

Meyerhold conceived of *Tristan und Isolde* not as an 'historical subject' but as a myth, which was why he found the historical style sanctioned by Bayreuth to be a mistake. The historicism of 'metal helmets and shields gleaming like samovars', he argued, was a 'historicism without secrets', whose only purpose was to seduce the spectator into guessing in which century and in what country the action was taking place. Designers and producers had to strive 'to safeguard the fairy-tale elements of the piece, so that the spectator feels completely enclosed by this atmosphere'. Historical props were not enough 'to create an atmosphere; this atmosphere is far better reflected in the speech rhythms of poets and in the colours and lines of great painters [. . .]. Just as Giotto, Memling, Brueghel or Fouquet can transport us far more readily into the atmosphere of a particular age than any historian can, so the artist who designs costumes and props according to his own im-

agination creates a more convincing and credible stage picture than the set-designer who plunders museums for the costumes and props which he then proceeds to use on stage [...]. Designers and producers [...] will find the motifs which they need for their tableaux by listening to the orchestra.'

In Act I Meyerhold thought it sufficient to have 'a single sail [...] in order to allow a ship to be conjured up in the audience's imagination.' In Act II the orchestra evokes a picture of the castle gardens and the rustling of leaves and it would show 'an appalling lack of taste' to depict those leaves on stage as well. Meyerhold confined himself to huge castle walls which soared upwards, disappearing out of sight beyond the top of the proscenium, while 'the mystical torch burned in front of them, at the centre of the stage'. Act III simply showed a vast and dreary open sky and the bare cliffs of Brittany. The sets for Meyerhold's production were designed by Alexander Konstantinovich Chervachidze. In his observations on the style of the production, Meyerhold also drew attention to traditional *nō* drama and to Japanese art which, he noted, was able to express the whole of spring by means of a single blossoming tree-branch.

In 1923 Arturo Toscanini gave Appia the chance to produce *Tristan und Isolde* at La Scala. Unfortunately no photographic re-

cords have survived of these performances, but the basis for the sets is said to have been an even more simplified version of the designs shown in *Die Musik und die Inszenierung*, Appia at that time being already in his abstract phase. The Milanese called him a relentless Calvinist and the La Scala audiences, who judged everything according to the standards of picturesque craftsmanship displayed by the great scenographers of Milan, found Appia's evocative but anti-illusionistic sets deeply disconcerting. The garden in Act II, they objected, looked more like a prison yard on which the cold white light fell like snow, and the two solitary cypresses were insufficient for a park. The lime-tree in Act III looked as though it were sick or dying, which made it 'right' when regarded from Appia's point of view, but 'wrong' from that of the audience, who saw it simply as a tree. In spite of the opposition, Toscanini remained loyal to the production. Isolde was sung by the young Scandinavian soprano Nanny Larsén-Todsen and King Marke by Ezio Pinza. Appia's production remained an isolated episode in the history of La Scala. His importance lay with his principal observations, which have acted as a stimulus to later designers and producers and changed the theatre in that way, rather than with his own stage productions which, at least as far as Wagner was

State Opera, Vienna,
17 December 1967
Producer: August Everding.
Designer: Günther
Schneider-Siemssen. Isolde:
Birgit Nilsson
Everding defined the stage here
as cosmic space. Isolde's
Transfiguration was realized as
her absorption into the
universe.

worth recalling, by way of comparison, that the first performances of the work in Buenos Aires (under Toscanini) and Cairo had taken place three years previously and that the first performance in São Paolo had been given as early as 1886, the same year as Bayreuth; here, it must be admitted, the work met with no success whatsoever, local audiences preferring the more immediately accessible Italian and French operas. In Berlin the work had already achieved a total of one hundred performances by 1907, whereas in Paris it was 1938 before a similar figure was reached. The sets by Jambon and Bailly remained in use until 1958 and it was only in 1936 that the production was overhauled. Paris had to wait until 1966 for its first completely new production, which was based upon Wieland Wagner's 1962 Bayreuth designs.

At the Metropolitan Opera in New York, on the other hand, *Tristan und Isolde* was performed almost every season from 1886 to 1917, the year of America's involvement in the First World War, when German opera was banned. In 1909, for example, both Gustav Mahler and Arturo Toscanini conducted the work there. And when the ban on German operas was lifted in 1920, *Tristan und Isolde* reappeared in the programme of each of the subsequent seasons until 1941. During the 1880s and 1890s, in particular, the Metropolitan was a stronghold of Wagnerian opera and the years in question have been described as 'Wagner decades'. Even though the Metropolitan suffered as much as other houses from the management's reliance on famous guest artists, including those from Bayreuth, and from the fact that some Wagner performances were sung in Italian or an improvised mixture of various languages, the engagement of Anton Seidl as conductor at least ensured a significant improvement in musical standards. Seidl had been musical assistant at the first Bayreuth Festival of 1876 and had conducted *Parsifal* there in 1897. All the major theatres were concerned to acquire the Bayreuth imprimatur and to engage singers and conductors who had worked at the Festival. One need think only of the first London performances of *Tristan und Isolde* at the Drury Lane Theatre, when the conductor was Hans Richter, Tristan was sung by Hermann Winkelmann, Isolde by Rosa Sucher, Brangäne by Marianne Brandt and King Marke by Eugen Gura. One should not underestimate Bayreuth's achievement in producing artists from whom other singers might have something to learn and who in that way established criteria by which general musical standards could be judged.

concerned, had surprisingly little influence. The next production of *Tristan und Isolde* to be staged at La Scala in 1930, which was designed by Edoardo Marchioro, marked a return to realistic scenery.

It was thirty-nine years after the Prelude to *Tristan und Isolde* had first been heard in Paris that the opera itself was finally performed there, on 28 October 1899. It was Charles Lamoureux who took the initiative, hiring the Nouveau Théâtre and engaging Felia Litvinne as Isolde and Marie Brema as Brangäne, a part she had also sung at Bayreuth. It was unfortunate that the auditorium lay right next to a café, because it meant that snatches of café music mingled with the strains of *Tristan und Isolde* throughout each performance. It was the Paris snobs who stood out most noticeably from the audiences who attended the work's ten performances. The pianist Alfred Cortot conducted a series of performances of the work in 1902, at the Théâtre du Château-d'Eau, when Isolde was again sung by Felia Litvinne and the Tristan was Charles Dalmorès. It was not until 1904 that the work entered the repertory of the Palais Garnier, when Louise Grandjean and Albert Alvarez sang the title-roles. It is

Royal Opera House, Covent Garden, London, 14 June 1971
Producer: Peter Hall. Designer: John Bury. Conducter: Georg Solti. Tristan: Jess Thomas. Kurwenal: Donald McIntyre. Shepherd: John Lanigan
Tristan's couch in Act III, not lost in the vast expanses of the stage but hidden away within a circular structure.

Bayreuth Festival, 1974
Producer: August Everding. Designer: Josef Svoboda. Conductor: Carlos Kleiber. Isolde: Catarina Ligendza. Melot: Heribert Steinbach. Tristan: Helge Brilioth. King Marke: Kurt Moll. Kurwenal: Donald McIntyre
Scene from Act II. Green foliage was projected onto myriad tautly strung plastic cords which looked like glass. During the love duet the colours turned to dark blue. In the shadow one can see the tower for Brangäne's dawn-song. The plastic cords confined the action but also invested the scene with a glass-like translucency and effects of distance. Unlike a cyclorama, which has a flat surface, these cords had the advantage of making the projections appear three-dimensional.

155

State Opera, Dresden,
12 October 1975
Producer: Harry Kupfer.
Designer: Peter Sykora.
Conductor: Marek Janowski.
Isolde: Ingeborg Zobel. Tristan:
Spas Wenkoff. King Marke:
Theo Adam
Isolde's quarters in Act I as a
boudoir in the late
nineteenth-century style of
Wahnfried, with potted plants
and ornamental palms; the area
was closed off by a rose-pink
curtain fixed to the mast, which
was raised at the end of the act.
In this production King Marke
entered at the end of Act I. His
gaze is directed beyond the
recumbent figure of Isolde and
fixed on Tristan.

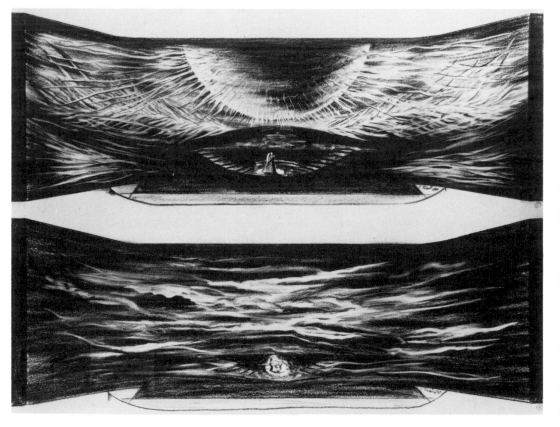

Wagner Festival, Seattle,
26 July 1981
Designer: Siegwulf Turek
Turek's design for Act II.
Above: Entrance of Tristan.
The acting area of this wide
stage is a sheltering hollow
formed out of steps. The design
is dominated by a huge 'sun of
passion'. Below: The duet 'O
sink hernieder, Nacht der
Liebe' ('Descend, o night of
love'). The previous image has
dissolved into constantly
shifting movements of light
which fill the entire stage. The
external world has been
internalized. Panoramic
projection techniques enable the
stage picture to follow the flow
of the music.

State Opera, Stuttgart,
21 March 1981
Producer: Götz Friedrich.
Designer: Günther Uecker.
Conductor: Dennis Russell
Davies. Tristan: Manfred Jung.
King Marke: Peter Meven.
Melot: Jörn W. Wilsing
King Marke's lament in Act II
performed as an interrogation
beneath watch-towers with
searchlights and in a forest
which seemed to be made of
barbed wire. A high, prison-like
wall surrounds the scene.

State Opera, Stuttgart,
21 March 1981
Producer: Götz Friedrich.
Designer: Günther Uecker.
Conductor: Dennis Russell
Davies. Tristan: Manfred Jung.
Kurwenal: Raymond Wolansky
Tristan's death scene in Act III.
The scene of action as a cipher
for coldness, harshness and
pitiless suffering. Tristan's
couch is a slab of reinforced
concrete.

Bayreuth Festival, 1981
Producer and designer:
Jean-Pierre Ponnelle.
Conductor: Daniel Barenboim.
Isolde: Johanna Meier. Tristan:
René Kollo
The Act II love duet, set beside
a spring in which Tristan and
Isolde narcissistically gaze at
their own reflections. A huge
tree arched over the whole
stage; at the beginning it was lit
with flaming red by Isolde's
torch; it then shimmered in
gentle shades of gold until, with
Marke's entrance, the tree lost
its magic in the pale grey
morning light of hateful day.

On 18 August 1931 the first live world-wide broadcast of *Tristan und Isolde* was relayed from the Bayreuth Festspielhaus, an event which belongs in the annals of radio rather than in a stage history of the work. The conductor was Wilhelm Furtwängler and the cast included Lauritz Melchior as Tristan and Nanny Larsén-Todsen as Isolde. Four microphones were used, two on stage and two in the pit, and a total of 200 radio stations in Europe, America and North Africa were linked up for the broadcast.

Many great singers have been associated with the roles of the two lovers, the names standing out like monuments in the performing history of the work and traditionally invoked in tones of reverential awe, rather like a litany. Indeed, no account of *Tristan und Isolde* would be complete without a list of the names of Lilli Lehmann, who first won international acceptance for the part of Isolde, Amelia Pinto, Toscanini's Isolde, Ada Adini, the first Isolde at the Liceo in Barcelona, Felia Litvinne, who knew the part in five languages, Olive Fremstad, Lilian Nordica, Milka Ternina, Nanny Larsén-Todsen, Gertrude Kappel, Elisabeth Ohms, Frida Leider, Anny Konetzni at the Salzburg Festival, Kirsten Flagstad, who for many people is the 'Isolde of the century', Germaine Lubin, Helen Traubel, Astrid Varnay and Martha Mödl, who gave legendary performances not only in

Bayreuth but all over the world, Birgit Nilsson, who sang the part 208 times in the course of her career, thereby establishing an unbeatable record, Catarina Ligendza, Hildegard Behrens and others. Birgit Nilsson was also one of the few opera-singers ever to make headlines in the *New York Times,* whose front page is traditionally given over to political events; the occasion was a performance of *Tristan und Isolde* at the Metropolitan Opera in 1961 when she was obliged to sing opposite three different Tristans, one for each act. Interpreters of the role of Tristan who deserve to be mentioned here include Ernest van Dyck, Jean de Reszke, Charles Dalmorès, Giuseppe Borgatti at La Scala, Carl Burrian, Jacques Urlus, Gotthelf Pistor, Gunnar Graarud, Lauritz Melchior, Max Lorenz, Set Svanholm, Ludwig Suthaus, Ramon Vinay, Wolfgang Windgassen, Hans Beirer, Jon Vickers, Jess Thomas, Jean Cox and Spas Wenkoff.

In the course of its performing history, *Tristan und Isolde* has increasingly become a vehicle not only for great Isoldes but also for great conductors, since of all Wagner's works it is *Tristan und Isolde,* together with the *Ring* and *Parsifal,* which offers the conductor the most significant opportunities for an individual interpretation. The names of Hans von Bülow, Felix Mottl, Gustav Mahler and Arturo Toscanini have already been mentioned and others which deserve at least to be listed here include Sir Thomas Beecham, Bruno Walter, Fritz Busch, Fritz Reiner, Erich Kleiber and, more recently, his son Carlos, Clemens Krauss, Wilhelm Furtwängler, Herbert von Karajan, Hans Knappertsbusch, Wolfgang Sawallisch and Karl Böhm. During the 1968 Munich Festival the conductor Joseph Keilberth collapsed during a performance of *Tristan und Isolde* at the point in Act II where the lovers sing, 'So starben wir, um ungetrennt' ('Thus we died, undivided'); Keilberth died the same night, thereby fulfilling his wish to die during a performance of the work.

Early attempts to produce *Tristan und Isolde* in the spirit of the music should not mislead one into thinking that the old style of traditional painted flats had been replaced by any general reform in matters of staging the

opera. In 1903, the same year as Alfred Roller's designs for Vienna, Eugen Quaglio designed new sets for the Berlin Court Opera which were wholly within the pictorialist tradition of the nineteenth century. Nevertheless, Roller's style and Appia's suggestions for staging the work had a signal influence on the younger generation of set-designers whose *art nouveau* aestheticism was also a feature of their work in the theatre. Darmstadt again comes to mind in this context, with Kurt Kempin's designs for the 1913 production and those of Ernst Gutzeit in 1923; other designs in this style were by Heinrich Lefler for the 1914 Vienna Volksoper production, Hans Wildermann for the Cologne production of 1911 and Johannes Schröder for the 1924 Hanover production. Even the picturesque sets by Panos Aravantinos for the 1920 Berlin State Opera production, although clearly bearing the marks of his own very personal style, point in the same general direction.

In the final analysis, none of these artists could bring himself to accept the stark severity of Appia's style, which was felt to be too unpoetical for such a Romantic work as *Tristan und Isolde,* with its basic mood of tenderness and lyricism. That was why their sets for Act II were always dominated by a vast starry sky, cut off at the extreme left of the stage by a corner of the tower and on the extreme right by a scattering of tall trees. Even that *artiste manqué,* Adolf Hitler, has left behind in one of his surviving sketch-books a rough drawing for Act II in this same style, clearly copied from the designs by Alfred Roller. For the third act the designers took as their starting-point the melancholy mood of the shepherd's sad lament: a rocky outcrop, commanding a vast sweep of sky and sea, was accented by a single tree, beneath which Tristan lay; there was neither castle gate nor walls to be seen. The stage was completely open, apart from a cyclorama at the back and this, together with a sophisticated lighting plot, was far better suited to creating a visual image on stage of the music's freely vibrant, endless melody than the old system of flies and parallel flats had been. This insight, which goes back to Appia, continues to influence today's producers and designers in their concern to realize *Tristan und Isolde* on stage.

In a number of leading opera-houses, the same production of *Tristan und Isolde* often survived for decades in the same sets. Wilhelm Furtwängler, for example, insisted that Alfred Roller's old sets should be used for the revival of the work at the Vienna State Opera in May 1943, which he both produced and conducted.

It was Emil Preetorius – and later Wieland and Wolfgang Wagner in their Bayreuth productions of 1952 and 1957 and elsewhere – who gave new impetus to the tradition. Preetorius designed the sets and costumes for no fewer than seven productions of the work, in Paris at the Théâtre des Champs-Elysées in 1936, at Bayreuth in 1938, Florence in 1941, Rome in 1943, Amsterdam in 1948, Munich in 1958 and Vienna in 1959. His three-dimensionally conceived sets were based upon Wagner's own precise instructions for each act, but incorporated a moderate degree of stylization so as to produce large, restful forms. The forest of leaves in Act II remained a feature of several of his productions; and the Act I set, with its broadly curving sail, and that of the third act, a rocky outcrop with a broad horizon, also retained their basic structure. Preetorius's international commitments resulted in a kind of standardization in set-designs for the work. His sets were persuasive and tasteful. The Wagnerian designs of Günther Schneider-Siemssen, such as those which he designed for Herbert von Karajan's production of *Tristan und Isolde* at the 1972 Salzburg Easter Festival, and Roberto Oswald's designs for productions in Buenos Aires and Chicago in 1979 are currently in the best traditions of Preetorius's work.

In Wieland and Wolfgang Wagner's first Bayreuth productions of the work, the Festival's limited financial resources during the first seasons coincided with the artistic desire for a simple, clear and inexpensive form of expression. They took as their starting-point the basic image of stage area and the cyclorama onto which lighting effects were projected. Both Wieland and Wolfgang designed the opening act as a tent-like interior without any sign of a sail or any other maritime object. Its intimacy formed a conscious contrast with the vast openness of the second and third acts. In Wolfgang's production, the second act was dominated by a night sky in which Tristan and Isolde, sung for the first time by the 'ideal couple' of Wolfgang Windgassen and Birgit Nilsson, appeared to hover in space like two lovers in a painting by Chagall. Wieland's third-act set was a picture of loneliness and forlorn desolation, such as one finds in Beckett's later plays. This 'uncluttered' style had come into being as a result of reinterpreting the work and its rendition, and was entirely in accord with the spirit of the age. Moreover, the basic system of stage area and cyclorama was practicable in smaller theatres as well, which were able to mount productions of the work without involving themselves in vast expense.

At the same time, designers continued to produce sets involving solid architectural details and landscapes, such as those designed by Nicola Benois for the 1957 production at La Scala, Milan, and by Teo Otto for the Metropolitan Opera in New York, where his ruined castle for Act III deserves particular mention. Wieland's 1962 Bayreuth production remained in the Festival repertory until 1970 and was one of the most influential interpretations of the work ever to have been seen. Wieland turned the tragic love-story into a mystery play about the power of *eros thanatos,* the destructive force of love. For Wieland, *Tristan und Isolde* was also a mythical work: 'Myth is always topical; and this is true whether it deals with an obsolete morality and the ordered world of chivalry or with our modern, allegedly emancipated society. Every passion is a threat to the order which has been achieved and represents a fatal danger to society [...] In its most hidden recesses, it was no more and no less than the will to die and the passion for night which dictated every decision taken by both Tristan and Isolde.'

Once again Wieland was his own designer. Each of the three acts was dominated by a huge three-dimensional symbol, a magical symbol of, so to speak, totemic power. The fascination of these images derived precisely from the mysterious ambiguity of the symbols, which eluded specific interpretation. They were matched by a complex and subtle lighting plot in intense shades of green, blue and red, which was perfectly timed to what was happening on stage and in the pit. The first scene was dominated by the suggestion of a vast and towering ship's prow, behind which shone a greenish yellow light. Universal night had already set in on this opening act. Wieland interpreted the lovers' journey from Ireland to Cornwall as their crossing the underworld river of oblivion in their search for the kingdom of the dead. Tristan's ship was also the boat of Charon, the ferryman of Hades.

The second act was dominated by a huge stela, a Celtic monolith, Brangäne's watchtower, Tristan's gravestone and a phallic symbol all in one. It was modelled on the standing stone at Fowey in Cornwall with its inscription 'Here lies Tristan, Marke's son,' a sentence which preoccupied and moved Wieland deeply. The death-marked lovers stood at the foot of this monolith, fading into the infinite blue of universal night. They remained standing for their duet, which was less a love scene in the traditional sense than an 'annunciation'. Only in death is Tristan vouchsafed a 'mystical vision of "eternal woman", [...] the ecstatic expression of cosmogonic love.' And Isolde, standing alone on the stage, with her arms outstretched, achieves at the moment of her transfiguration 'a mystical union with Tristan's soul [...] The fulfilment of passion in death: this mystical element reveals the profound significance of the Tristan myth,' according to Wieland. With its seamless unity of interpretation in matters of staging and musical realization, this production of *Tristan und Isolde* held Bayreuth audiences enthralled for seven successive Festivals, with the same conductor (Karl Böhm), Tristan (Wolfgang Windgassen) and Isolde (Birgit Nilsson).

In the wake of Wieland, the cosmic romantics came into fashion, covering the cyclorama with entire galaxies of stars during the love duet and Isolde's final transfiguration. August Everding, who has produced *Tristan und Isolde* a record number of five times in all (Vienna in 1967 and 1971, the Metropolitan Opera in New York in 1971, Bayreuth in 1974 and Munich in 1980) defined the stage as 'a space for the cosmos' on the occasion of his New York production, on which he collaborated with the designer Günther Schneider-Siemssen. The first moon-landing had taken place two years previously. During the Act II love duet, the two lovers soared upwards, lost to the world and shining like two stars in the firmament, as Everding described them; and Isolde's *Liebestod* was a similar sort of ascension into the starry vault. These years in particular witnessed a variety of experimental attempts to solve the problems of the ending of the work: producers were clearly tired of merely allowing Isolde to fade away into darkness during her transfiguration. Instead, they went to the other extreme of having her dying in gleaming brightness.

It was the Felsenstein school which again provided the encouragement for a new realistic interpretation of *Tristan und Isolde*. Götz Friedrich produced the work in Amsterdam in 1974, with designs by Heinrich Wendel, in Berlin in 1980, when the designer was Günther Schneider-Siemssen and finally in Stuttgart in 1981, in a production designed by Günther Uecker. Friedrich sees Isolde's bridal journey as a 'luxurious deportation' and, in Stuttgart, asked the question, 'Can Cornwall mean the same as Auschwitz to Isolde?' In all three productions the discovery of the lovers in Act II was like an interrogation, with batteries of searchlights stationed on watch-towers blinding the accused couple. Brambles in the Berlin production and barbed-wire-like lianas in Stuttgart evoked mental images of prisons and instruments of torture. For his 1976 Dresden production Harry Kupfer set the opera in the period during which it had been written, seeing in it details of Wagner's own life at the time.

Recent productions have, generally speaking, tended away from a mythological interpretation towards the direction of stage realism. Wolfgang Wagner's 1978 Milan production on the occasion of the bicentenary of La Scala was notable for its total absence of symbolism. The stage area and stage action were held in equilibrium by what Wolfgang called 'the tension between reality and transcendence'. In his 1980 production in Zurich Claus Helmut Drese gave the work's Romantic elements their rightful due. The Act II bower with its marble columns recalled Gottfried von Strassburg's cave of lovers. For his 1981 Bayreuth Festival production Jean-Pierre Ponnelle conjured up a miracle of light for the stage picture in Act II and staged the ending of the work as Tristan's vision.

The stage history of *Tristan und Isolde* has been rather more free, but at the same time more unified than that of Wagner's other works, veering basically between the two interpretative extremes of Romanticism and austere abstraction. If the Romantic interpretation has found greater favour with the general public, it is because audiences have always regarded *Tristan und Isolde* first and foremost as an emotional experience.

München.

Königl. Hof- und National-Theater.

Sonntag den 21. Juni 1868.

Mit aufgehobenem Abonnement.

Zum ersten Male:

Die

Meistersinger von Nürnberg.

Oper in drei Aufzügen von Richard Wagner.

Regie: Herr Dr. Hallwachs.

Personen:

Hans Sachs, Schuster	Herr Betz.
Veit Pogner, Goldschmied	Herr Bausewein.
Kunz Vogelgesang, Kürschner	Herr Heinrich.
Konrad Nachtigall, Spängler	Herr Sigl.
Sixtus Beckmesser, Schreiber	Herr Hölzel.
Fritz Kothner, Bäcker	Herr Fischer.
Balthasar Zorn, Zinngießer	Herr Weixlstorfer.
Ulrich Eißlinger, Würzkrämer	Herr Hoppe.
Augustin Moser, Schneider	Herr Pöppl.
Hermann Ortel, Seifensieder	Herr Thoms.
Hans Schwarz, Strumpfwirker	Herr Grasset.
Hans Folz, Kupferschmied	Herr Hayn.
Walther von Stolzing, ein junger Ritter aus Franken	Herr Nachbaur.
David, Sachsen's Lehrbube	Herr Schlosser.
Eva, Pogner's Tochter	Fräulein Mallinger.
Magdalene, Eva's Amme	Frau Diez.
Ein Nachtwächter	Herr Ferdinand Lang.

Meistersinger

Bürger und Frauen aller Zünfte. Gesellen. Lehrbuben. Mädchen. Volk.

Nürnberg.

Um die Mitte des 16. Jahrhunderts.

Textbücher sind zu 18 kr. an der Kasse zu haben.

Neue Decorationen:

Im ersten Aufzuge: Das Innere der Katharinenkirche in Nürnberg,   von den K. Hoftheatermalern Herrn
Im zweiten Aufzuge: Straße in Nürnberg,   Angelo Quaglio und Christian Jank.
Im dritten Aufzuge: Erste Decoration: Werkstätte des Hans Sachs,   Zweite Decoration: Freier Wiesenplan bei Nürnberg, vom K. Hoftheatermaler Herrn Heinrich Döll.

Neue Costüme

nach Angabe des k. technischen Direktors Herrn Franz Seitz.

Preise der Plätze:

Eine Loge im I. und II. Rang für 7 Personen	21 fl. — kr.	Ein Galerienoble-Sitz	3 fl. 30 kr.
Ein Logenplatz	3 fl. — kr.	Ein Parketsitz	3 fl. — kr.
Eine Loge im III. Rang für 7 Personen	17 fl. 30 kr.	Parterre	1 fl. — kr.
Ein Logenplatz	2 fl. 30 kr.	Galerie	— fl. 30 kr.
Eine Loge im IV. Rang für 7 Personen	14 fl. — kr.		
Ein Logenplatz	2 fl. — kr.		

Die Kasse wird um fünf Uhr geöffnet.

Anfang um 6 Uhr, Ende um halb elf Uhr.

Der freie Eintritt ist ohne alle Ausnahme aufgehoben
und wird ohne Kassenbillet Niemand eingelassen.

Auf die gefälligen Bestellungen der verehrlichen Abonnenten wird bis **Sonntag den 21. Juni**
Vormittags 10 Uhr gewartet, dann aber über die nicht beibehaltenen Logen und Plätze anderweitig verfügt.

Beurlaubt: Frau Possart.

Repertoire:

Montag den 22. Juni: (Im K. Hof- und National-Theater) **Minister und Seidenhändler**, Lustspiel von Scribe,
übersetzt von Heinrich Marr. (Graf von Ranzau — Herr Marr, Oberregisseur des Thaliatheaters
in Hamburg, als letzte Gastrolle.)
Dienstag den 23. „ : (Im K. Residenz-Theater) **Minna von Barnhelm**, Lustspiel von Lessing.
Mittwoch den 24. „ : (Im K. Hof- und National-Theater) Zum ersten Male wiederholt: **Die Meistersinger**,
Oper von Richard Wagner.
Donnerstag den 25. „ : (Im K. Hof- und National-Theater) Neu einstudirt: **Die Einfalt vom Lande**, Lustspiel von Töpfer.
Freitag den 26. „ : (Im K. Hof- und National-Theater) **König Heinrich IV.**, zweiter Theil, Schauspiel von Shakspeare.
Sonntag den 28. „ : (Im K. Hof- und National-Theater) **Die Meistersinger**, Oper von Richard Wagner.

Der einzelne Zettel kostet 2 kr.   Kgl. Hofbuchdruckerei von Dr. C. Wolf & Sohn.

Die Meistersinger von Nürnberg

Like so much else, the conception of *Die Meistersinger von Nürnberg* dates back to that crucial summer of 1845 in Marienbad. Wagner had intended that his next work should be a comic opera and in this resolve he was encouraged not least by the advice of his friends, who thought that, after *Der fliegende Holländer* and *Tannhäuser,* an opera 'of a lighter genre' stood a greater chance of achieving a popular success, which was something he now desperately needed. With the single exception of Dresden, *Rienzi* had been performed up until now only in Hamburg and Königsberg, and *Der fliegende Holländer* in Riga, Cassel and Berlin.

Georg Gottfried Gervinus's *Geschichte der poetischen National-Literatur der Deutschen* ('History of the National Poetic Literature of the Germans'), which Wagner had taken with him to Marienbad, contained a chapter on the 'Decline of the courtly romance and the transition to folk poetry', including a section on the poetry of the mastersingers and on Hans Sachs. What is curious is that Wagner felt immediately attracted by the name and function of the 'marker', although Gervinus mentions the poet himself only in passing. Even without knowing a single work by Hans Sachs or by any of his contemporaries, Wagner invented in the course of one of his walks a scene 'in which the cobbler, as a craftsman-poet of the people, hammers away on his last in order to teach a lesson to the marker, who has no choice but to sing on and who suffers a humiliating defeat for the pedantic outrages he committed earlier. Everything was concentrated in my mind's eye into two images, on the one hand the marker's holding out the board covered in chalk marks and, on the other, Hans Sachs's holding up the pair of shoes which had been made with the marks of the other's office.' Wagner additionally visualized a narrow, crooked alley as the scene of a street riot such as he himself had witnessed in Nuremberg in 1835. At this time he was still thinking of *Die Meistersinger von Nürnberg* as a 'satyr play full of refer-

ences' to his 'Song Contest on the Wartburg'. In this first prose draft he conceived of Sachs as 'the last embodiment of the artistically productive national spirit', setting him up in contrast to the 'typically middle-class mastersingers', to whose 'thoroughly comical *tabulatur*-poetical pedantry' he gave 'peculiarly personal expression' in the figure of the marker. The original inspiration behind *Die Meistersinger von Nürnberg* was therefore a parody of the role of the marker.

Wagner put the draft to one side and paid it no further attention until 1851, when he was working on *Eine Mittheilung an meine Freunde*. The scenario for *Die Meistersinger von Nürnberg* which he published in this essay already contains all the most important features of the plot, as it appeared in the final libretto:

The oldest member of the guild offered the hand of his young daughter to whichever Master won the prize at a public singing contest which was about to take place. The marker, who is already courting the girl, finds that he has a rival in the person of a young nobleman who, inspired by his reading of the *Heldenbuch* ('Book of Heroes') and the works of the old minnesingers, has left his impoverished and dilapidated ancestral castle in order to learn the art of the mastersingers in Nuremberg. He applies for membership of the guild, being motivated to do so chiefly by the fact that he has fallen passionately in love with the girl who has been offered as prize, one 'whom only a master of the guild shall win'. Required to perform a test piece, he sings an enthusiastic song in praise of women, to which, however, the marker takes such violent exception that the would-be mastersinger has already failed even before his song is half over. Sachs, who likes the young man, acts in the latter's best interests when he now foils a desperate attempt on the young man's part to elope with the girl; and at the same time he finds an opportunity to annoy the marker intensely. The latter, it should be added, has previously criticized Sachs in no uncertain terms, with the intention of humiliating him, for his having as yet not completed a pair of shoes he had ordered from him. The marker appears at night below the girl's window in order to test out, in the form of a serenade, the song by which he hopes to win her, since he is anxious to make certain of her vote, which will be decisive when the prize is announced. Sachs, whose cobbler's shop lies opposite the girl's house, strikes up a song at the same time as the marker begins his: the latter is beside himself with rage but, as Sachs explains, it is only by singing that he is able to remain awake so late in order to work; and the fact that the work is urgent is something which no one knows better than the marker himself, who has had to remind him so often in the past about his shoes. Sachs finally agrees with the poor fellow to stop singing, on condition that he be allowed to point out any mistakes which he feels the marker's song contains and to indicate them after his own fashion as a cobbler, namely by hammering the shoe which is on the last. The marker starts to sing; Sachs strikes the last time and again. The marker leaps up angrily: the former asks him calmly whether he has finished his song? 'Far from it,' the latter screams back. Laughing, Sachs holds the shoes out through the open window, adding by way of explanation that they have just been completed with 'the marks of the other's office'.

The marker finishes his song but fails miserably to make any impression on the woman sitting at the window, vigorously shaking her head. Disconsolate, he returns the next morning to demand a new song from Sachs to aid him in his courtship; the latter hands over a poem written by the young knight, claiming not to know where he has acquired it; he simply warns him to be especially careful about finding a suitable 'melody' to go with it. The conceited marker feels totally sure of himself in the matter and goes on to sing the poem, in the presence of the whole tribunal of mastersingers and common people, to a thoroughly unsuitable and disfiguring tune; the result is that he fails once again, this time decisively. Furiously he reproaches Sachs for foisting a quite disgraceful song on him and accuses him of deceit; the latter explains that the poem is perfectly acceptable but that it needs to be sung to the correct tune. It is agreed that whoever knows the right tune shall be awarded the prize. The

young knight accomplishes the deed and wins the bride; but he is scornfully dismissive of the mastersingers' offer to admit him to their guild. Sachs then good-humouredly defends their ideals and institution, ending with the lines:

Zerging' das heil'ge römische Reich in Dunst,

Uns bliebe doch die heil'ge deutsche Kunst.

('Though the Holy Roman Empire were to fade into mist,

There would still remain for us holy German art.')

Why did Wagner not carry out this plan immediately, but allow it to remain untouched for a further ten years? One reason for his hesitancy, which he mentions in *Eine Mittheilung an meine Freunde,* is that the mood of cheerful serenity necessary for such a subject had expressed itself up until now only in the form of irony, which related to the formal artistry of his tendencies and of his basic nature, rather than to their essence, which was rooted in life itself. At that time irony, for Wagner, was the only form of humour which was intelligible to the mass of humanity. It attacks, on a formal level, whatever is unnatural in public conditions, since this form, being something susceptible of rational explanation, is the only thing which is intelligible. That is why we are forced to express ourselves in precisely that form which we ridicule by means of irony. Cheerful serenity, accordingly, cannot find its true, radiant expression as a real force in life. In order to re-establish such cheerful serenity as a force of life, that element in life must first be opposed which inhibits the unadulterated declaration of such a mood. But this opposition can only declare itself nowadays as a form of yearning and, in the final analysis, of rebellion; hence its tragic features. Wagner's nature reacted against the 'imperfect attempt to divest myself' by means of irony 'of the force of the urge for serenity' and he was compelled to dismiss this attempt as 'the ultimate expression of a self-indulgent desire [...] which sought to become reconciled with the triviality all around.' According to Wagner's understanding, the 'truly and uniquely cheerful element of future life and art', in their highest potentiality, is the 'total unity of intellect and sensuality'.

But neither in the prose draft of 1861 nor in the final libretto did Wagner manage to achieve the desired radiant, sovereign, unadulterated 'Apollonian' serenity which, throughout his whole life, he admired in Mozart. *Die Meistersinger von Nürnberg* turned

Court Theatre, Munich, 21 June 1868
Producers: Richard Wagner and Reinhard Hallwachs. Designers: Angelo Quaglio, Heinrich Döll and Christian Jank. Costumes: Franz Seitz. Conductor: Hans von Bülow. Hans Sachs: Franz Betz. Walther: Franz Nachbaur. Beckmesser: Georg Hölzel
Animated scene from Act I: painting by Michael Echter based on the sets of the first performance. The young aristocrat, Walther von Stolzing, has failed the Mastersingers' test. The marker, Sixtus Beckmesser, holds the board and points out all the chalk marks to the masters, the said marks indicating the number of mistakes Beckmesser found in Walther's song. The apprentices dance round Sachs and Walther. This illustration clearly reveals why the first performance was so highly praised – the life-like acting, the interaction of the movements on the stage which were polished right down to the finest detail and the stylistic unity of sets and costumes.

Court Opera, Vienna, 27 February 1870
Designer: Carlo Brioschi
Design for the Festival Meadow (Act III, scene 2). Ever since the time of the first Munich production this arrangement enjoyed canonical status and remained a standard model until well into the twentieth century.

out to be neither a satyr play nor a comedy. The cheerful mood of the work was wrested by force from obstructive elements: it openly proclaims the effort involved and shows the scars of its injuries. On the first page of the orchestral sketch to Act II Wagner noted, 'On the edge of the abyss – as usual' (8 June 1866). In the various prose drafts he still described the work as a 'comic opera', but that was no longer the case with the final version of the text. But it is precisely the work's elusiveness, its refusal to be tied down by a particular terminology and the nuances of its basic mood which, to our modern way of thinking, give *Die Meistersinger von Nürnberg* its unique status and which assure it our lasting interest.

It was not until that disaster-filled year of 1861 that Wagner again took up his plans for the opera. He had visited Nuremberg during the previous summer and had found 'a great many pretty sights' there, as he wrote to Mathilde Wesendonck on 21 December 1861. Back in Vienna, he wrote to his wife Minna on 19 October 1861, 'With my new works I keep coming up against almost insuperable obstacles [...]. Nobody asks after me [...]. If things continue like this, I shall soon reach the end.' And once again there arose within him the desire for a less demanding work which he hoped soon to be able to complete and which might rescue him from his present predicament. He wrote to his publisher Schott on 30 October, informing him, 'I have already drawn up [...] a complete draft. The opera is called "Die Meistersinger von Nürnberg" and the – jovially poetic – main character is "Hans Sachs" [...] The style of the piece, both words and music, should be thoroughly accessible and popular and I can in fact guarantee that it will be quickly taken up by other theatres since on this occasion I need neither a so-called first tenor nor a great tragic soprano' (as had been the case with *Tristan und Isolde*).

In Venice, in November 1861, Titian's *Assunta* left upon him what he described in *Mein Leben* as 'an impression of the most sublime kind' and from this moment of 'conception' onwards, he felt his 'old strength reanimated with the most sudden speed'. Back in Vienna he immediately began to look round for suitable material and to draw up a full-length prose draft. He borrowed from the Imperial Court Library a copy of Johann Christoph Wagenseil's Nuremberg Chronicle which included an appendix 'Von der Meistersinger Holdseligen Kunst' ('On the Fair Art of the Mastersingers'), on which Gervinus had previously drawn for his own history of literature. Wagner's hand-written extracts run to

four complete sides; they are principally concerned with technical information such as the rules of the mastersingers' poetry, the names of the Masters and of their melodies, the way in which the singing school functioned, and so on. He was also familiar with Jacob Grimm's monograph *Ueber den altdeutschen Meistergesang* ('On the Old German Poetry of the Mastersingers') and Friedrich Furchau's account of the life of Hans Sachs; both these volumes were in his library in Dresden.

At the beginning of December Wagner retired to the seclusion of a small hotel room on the Quai Voltaire in Paris (he had not had his own place to live since his departure from the Asyl), in order to draft the libretto. It had 'a quite comical appeal' for him, knowing that he was locked up in Paris, of all places, with the Mastersingers, that 'sharp-witted and uncouth folk', those 'genuinely German but somewhat eccentric types', as he described them in letters to Mathilde Wesendonck of 21 December 1861 and to Betty Schott of 10 December 1861. There were times when he had to 'rub his eyes' whenever he became conscious of the 'comical contrast' between his plan on the one hand and 'the scene of its execution', on the other, as he wrote to Peter Cornelius on 11 December 1861. And he was often forced to smile when he looked up from his work and saw before him the Tuileries and the Louvre, the busy traffic on the quays and the bridges; and he reflected on 'how Hans Sachs looks in Paris' (ibid). The only pleasure and sense of contentment which he found in his seclusion came from his work. On his way to the Taverne Anglaise, where he generally dined in the evening, he was one day struck by the theme of the 'Wach auf' chorus, as he was passing through the arcades of the Palais Royal. He had written to his publisher Franz Schott, asking him to send him a book on old chorales, especially those from the time of the Reformation, together with a collection of German folk songs. In Paris he did not have access to the correct background reading for his subject. This German Protestant work was written in Paris, amongst other things, as a protest against 'Catholicism and the Latin temperament', to use Hans Mayer's expression. The desire, nine months after the *Tannhäuser* scandal, to write something specifically German as a reaction against the Romance world is something else which one senses in this work, together with a longing and a kind of nostalgia for a unity of homeland, nation and art.

The libretto was completed on 25 January 1862 but this initial version was subjected to repeated revisions in the course of the follow-

Bayreuth Festival, 1888
Designers: Max and Gotthold
Brückner
Set-design for the Nuremberg
street in Act II. On Cosima's
instructions, the Brückner
brothers copied the sets from
the first Munich production.
For decades this design
remained the model for all
other productions of the opera.

ing years when Wagner was working on the score. On 5 February he read out the whole of the text from beginning to end to a large gathering of friends at the home of Franz and Betty Schott in Mainz; and at the beginning of March he repeated the performance for the benefit of the Grand Duke and Duchess of Baden in Karlsruhe. From the outset of his resumption of interest in the work, Wagner had been convinced that *Die Meistersinger von Nürnberg* would be his most inspired creation and his most popular success. When he wrote to Mathilde Wesendonck that she should not be so misguided as to think that, with the exception of the 'Wach auf' chorus, which was a quotation from Hans Sachs's hymn to Martin Luther, there was anything in the new work which was not entirely his own invention, one cannot but agree with him; for little is gained in the case of *Die Meistersinger von Nürnberg* by drawing attention to the various literary reworkings of the theme which were familiar to Wagner, the framework of whose plots one occasionally glimpses in his own adaptation. From the wealth of literary versions which

deal with the character of Hans Sachs, two examples at least deserve to be mentioned in passing, Johann Ludwig Deinhardstein's play *Hans Sachs* of 1827 and Albert Lortzing's comic opera *Hans Sachs,* first performed in Leipzig in 1840; both works were popular and frequently performed. Most later versions were based on Deinhardstein's model, in which the young Hans Sachs woos the daughter of a rich goldsmith. His rival is a foppish councillor; misunderstandings and conflicts ensue, the issue being resolved by the Emperor Maximilian I. The subsequent festivities culminate in Hans Sachs's being crowned with the poet's laurel wreath. Lortzing's opera runs along similar lines. The significance of Wagner's own version, however, lies not in the points which he shares in common with his predecessors, but in those that set him apart from them.

In the libretto, the marker is no longer the central figure, as he was in the first draft; the main emphasis of the action has shifted to Sachs and Walther. In creating the character of Hans Sachs, Wagner has succeeded in producing one of his finest and most complex figures, and the image which we have in our minds of the historical cobbler-poet of Nuremberg remains to this day fundamentally influenced by the hero of Wagner's opera. His literary sources provided a number of important motifs with which Wagner fleshed out his own character of Sachs: *bonhomie*, doughtiness, honesty, his sentimental and emotional temperament, and, at the same time, his mischievous, roguish nature. But Wagner's Sachs is first and foremost an artist. Sachs's art of poetry and song corresponds to what Wagner himself demanded from art: it finds expression 'in a particular place, at a particular time and under particular conditions', which is why it is 'of the liveliest effectiveness'. Its theme, according to *Eine Mittheilung an meine Freunde,* is 'universal humanity': it is rooted in life, just as is the poetry of the ancient Greeks and of Shakespeare.

In this respect it is the opposite of what Wagner defined and rejected as absolute art or rather the art of the monumental. The type of true art for which Wagner strove and which he embodied in the figure of Hans Sachs can find expression only in life itself, and, indeed, in 'the most real and most sensuous life' *(Eine Mittheilung an meine Freunde).* This art stands in the same relationship to monumental art as a living person does to a Greek statue (by way of example Wagner mentions Greek drama which two thousand years previously had really been written with Athenian democracy in mind, and which was nowadays performed before the Prussian court at Potsdam). As Beckmesser scornfully remarks, Sachs writes popular melodies, histories, plays and farces for the people of Nuremberg. He asks that once a year the common people be allowed to judge the Mastersingers' artistic achievements and decide whether, 'in the rut of dull routine', they might not have lost their 'force and life'; he wants 'both common people and art to flourish and grow together'. His achievement consists in his not rejecting Walther's song in Act I which, though having no rules to it, has sprung from genuine feeling; Sachs attempts to understand it and takes on the young singer as an apprentice in his cobbler's shop in order to teach him the rules and make a Master of him. According to Sachs's view of art, rules and genius must work together. Rules devoid of genius, as embodied by Beckmesser, are uncreative and philistine, whereas genius without rules seeps away since it has no form to contain it; it is arbitrary and random. True art shows the two combined. That is the meaning of Sachs's lesson.

It was an inspired idea on Wagner's part to introduce the fertile and dramatically effective motif of tender feelings of love between Sachs and Eva. Sachs's renunciation of Eva is not undertaken in a spirit of gentle, smiling resignation, as it tends to be portrayed on stage, but is an act of prudence and insight ('Hans Sachs war klug, und wollte / nichts von Herrn Marke's Glück' ['Hans Sachs is wise and wants / nothing of Sir Marke's fate']). He refuses to delude himself into thinking that he can arrogate to himself by force a destiny other than the one allotted to him by fate. He achieves this insight not with any sense of ease and serenity but only after a great deal of suffering and rebellion. His cobbling songs in Act II, with their allusions to Eve and her corrupting influence in Paradise, speak very clearly of this fact. Sachs, too, it must be admitted, is a victim of delusion, but he is aware of the fact and knows how to 'steer it delicately', in order 'to do a more noble task'.

Beckmesser's antagonist is not his rival Stolzing, as would have been the case if the work had been a traditional comedy; rather is it Hans Sachs. Only on a superficial level are we concerned with the question of who gets the girl. The real conflict between Sachs and Beckmesser concerns their differing views of art. Beckmesser's art is textbook art and lacks inspiration. It is as though the position of marker had been created especially with him in mind. His art does not correspond to any personal experience or feeling; it is, to use Wagner's own term, 'reflection', and is the result of calculation. Beckmesser, the only one of the Mastersingers who is not a craftsman, goes about his business as a Mastersinger as a part of his career, a career which in his view includes a socially acceptable marriage. We are not concerned here with 'love affairs' but with 'matrimonial matters', to borrow a phrase from Johann Nestroy. He pursues a specific aim in singing his wooing song, which is most emphatically not a love song. He is bound to fail with Walther's stolen song, since this song is inspired by genuine feeling and is suitable only for Walther. Beckmesser can have no idea of what it truly means and is bound to garble the text. That he attempts to sing it in spite of everything betrays his view of art. He, too, is given a lesson in art by Sachs, this time in Act II, but, unlike Walther, he remains stubborn and pigheaded.

The parody of the function of the marker, which had been Wagner's basic inspiration in 1845, remains central to the work in the final

National Theatre, Prague, 1926
Sets for Act I, the interior of St
Katharine's Church. The
National Theatre in Prague was
famous throughout the 1920s
for a series of extremely
modern productions influenced
by contemporary art.

State Opera, Berlin, 1932 ▷
Producer: Heinz Tietjen.
Designer: Otto Pankok.
Conductor: Wilhelm
Furtwängler
The riot scene in Act II.
Pankok's Nuremberg included
the mere suggestion of
half-timbered houses;
otherwise, the façades were
rough-cast. Thus the shapes of
the windows and the
smoothness of the walls were
closer in spirit to the Bauhaus
than to the sixteenth century.

version as well. Sachs does not ridicule the rules in principle but criticizes only the mechanical, lifeless application of those rules. Beckmesser for his part undertakes his serenade since he is unable to talk Pogner out of giving his daughter the casting vote at the following day's singing contest. He wants to be sure of himself, since he is used to planning and ordering things and not leaving anything to chance. The serenade is his dress rehearsal for the singing contest. If Eva likes his song, he will have won; and that is an issue which can be resolved that very night. He does not doubt for a moment that the Masters will be on the side of their marker and, as far as the common people are concerned, they simply do not count. He does not realize that the serenade is bound to fail to make any impression on the girl, given the situation in which he finds himself, with his supposed rival Sachs looking on as witness. He agrees to his serenade's being turned into an artistic contest with Sachs. He continues to sing compulsively because he cannot allow himself to be proved wrong: but the issue is no longer his wooing of Eva but his view of art. The malicious pleasure and mockery which are showered on Beckmesser may strike our modern sensibilities as somewhat crude and heartless rather than comical but they are none the less well-established and legitimate means of achieving a comic effect. Fools are taken for a ride; unreasonableness and self-importance

deserve to be punished. That was a recurrent comic motif in Hans Sachs's Shrovetide plays.

In the Vienna prose draft Sixtus Beckmesser was still called Hanslich, an all too obvious allusion to the influential and much feared Viennese critic Eduard Hanslick. When Wagner recited the libretto of *Die Meistersinger von Nürnberg* before an invited gathering in Vienna on 23 November 1862, Hanslick stormed out of the room in disgust. There is no doubt that in his depiction of the character of Beckmesser Wagner was thinking of a 'malicious critic' (cf. his letter of 25 October 1872 to the singer Rudolf Freny). The character is also an expression of Wagner's own sense of personal injury: at the cost of great effort and in spite of the opposition of critics, he had created works of art which did not adhere to traditional rules: the fact that he now poured scorn on a character who was a fanatical supporter of rules and who dismissed everything which did not conform to his own particular set of rules was certainly not a sovereign and composed reaction on Wagner's part but there is no doubt that it was an entirely understandable one.

In the riot scene in Act II Wagner reworked an episode which he himself had experienced in Nuremberg in 1835: a brawl which had taken place one night outside an inn, which had broken out for no apparent reason and which had then subsided, fading away once again like a phantom. Wagner was never able

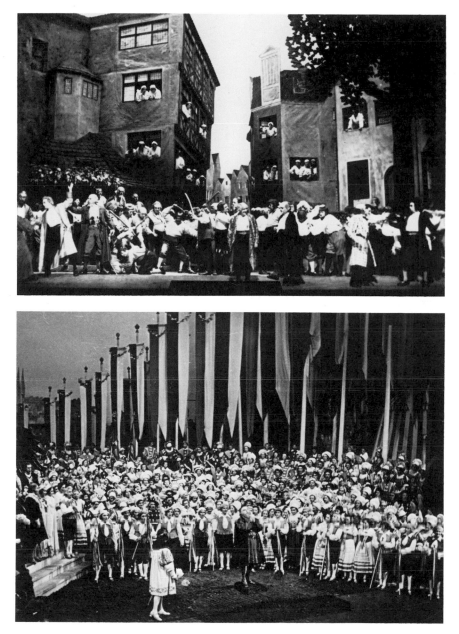

German Opera House, Berlin,
17 November 1935
Designer: Benno von Arent.
Costumes: Benno von Arent
The Festival Meadow in Act III
as a Nazi party rally with the
characteristic array of banners.
The sets and costumes were the
work of the Reich's official
set-designer and were
authorized by Hitler himself.

persecution were rife among the guilds, causing middle-class society to become distorted. Throughout all this, the Mastersingers exercised a moderating influence by means of their art and restored the 'dignity of custom'. But what Wagner also recognized in the riot scene was something which Nietzsche was later to describe as 'an echo of those secret and uncanny midnights of the soul when cause and effect seem to be out of joint and at any moment something can rise up "out of oblivion".' 'And,' to quote Wieland Wagner, 'when has a "new melody" ever been created without "a great deal of noise in the alley way", without utter confusion on the part of level-headed men and women, without a night-time riot of active and passive "midwives" – in a word, without that "madness" to which the fifty-year-old philosopher of art now attributed in the wisdom of his maturity a highly substantial part in the creation of a work of art?' To have shown all this by means of the riot scene is something which we have nowadays come to regard as Wagner's most perceptive achievement.

The settings for the opera, St Katharine's Church, a narrow Nuremberg street, the cobbler's workshop and the festival meadow, have played a by no means insignificant part in the later success of the opera. From the time of Goethe's *Faust* onwards, old German décor had come to be associated with an atmosphere of intimacy and cosiness. The inhabitants of modern towns, with their disassociated, industrial world of work, felt that in the midst of such cheerlessness they could still rediscover something of their own native home, a world of children's books such as had never existed in reality but which was all the more urgently yearned for, in the form of a dream about a world which may have been limited in outlook but which was whole, a world which continued to live on in the idea of the good old days and which the Germans in particular have so earnestly yearned for. The young Romantics discovered in Nuremberg the ideal embodiment of German character and art and the whole of the following century agreed with their assessment. In the case of Wagner, too, Nuremberg outgrew the idyll to become something of significance: he saw in the town a synthesis of German art and German life, something resplendent which he celebrated in his music. As Bernhard Diebold has remarked, 'Wagner saw in art an "aesthetic education" for the common people and the state: his work was to be political in the very highest sense, forming the *politeia*'. Wagner was of the opinion that, in presenting them with *Die Meistersinger von Nürnberg*, he

to find a rational explanation for this outbreak of mass hysteria. It appears in *Die Meistersinger von Nürnberg* at the end of Act II, in other words, at the point at which, according to the rules of classical dramaturgy, the catastrophe should have occurred. Wagner, one should add, has put forward the harmonious model of an ideal and closely knit community, as a unified whole, but at the same time he has called into question its load-bearing capacity. The state of harmony is fragile and under attack. Nuremberg is admittedly 'of peacefully loyal customs', but that is no safeguard against an elemental outbreak of hysteria. Back in the 1840s, when reading Gervinus, Wagner had discovered that in the sixteenth century feelings ran high among the lower classes, that resentment, hostility and

Théâtre National de l'Opéra, Paris, June 1948
Designer: Amable. Conductor: Louis Fourestier. Walther: René Verdière
Production photograph showing the sets dating from the first Paris production of 10 November 1897. They represent a good example of the profound skill of Amable's decorative style. He was one of the leading stage designers towards the end of the last century and continued the tradition of the Paris Opéra's spectacular style of production.

State Opera, Vienna, at the Theater an der Wien, 30 November 1949
Producer: Rudolf Hartmann. Designer: Robert Kautsky. Hans Sachs: Paul Schöffler. Beckmesser: Erich Kunz. Veit Pogner: Ludwig Weber. Eva: Trude Eipperle. Magdalene: Rosette Anday. David: Anton Dermota
The classic setting for the Festival Meadow, showing a view of Nuremberg in the background. Such backcloths were usually copied from various original sixteenth-century views of the town, a practice that enabled even smaller theatres to stage the Festival Meadow scene without incurring unnecessary expense.

had provided German audiences with 'a reflection of their own true nature'.

What it was that Wagner felt to be characteristically German is best shown by his depiction of Pastor Riemann at a meeting of a student society in Leipzig in 1865. Wagner described the occasion in *Das Braune Buch* ('The Brown Book'): 'That is German idealism. Little movement: none of your limp-wristed Hungarians, Poles or Frenchmen;

something heavy and lacking in daintiness; but what a contemplative mind the German has! The naïve glance, the strange belief which it expresses, the rapturous enthusiasm! [...] There is only the narrowest of dividing lines between this and the ridiculous: and now – there are calm, almost philistine people – who believe in it! And we may not mock them.' In the same way, Wagner's Hans Sachs, at the end of the opera, demands re-

New York City Opera, New York, 14 March 1951
Producer: Otto Erhardt.
Designer: H. A. Condell.
Conductor: Joseph Rosenstock.
David: David Lloyd.
Magdalene: Margery Mayer.
Hans Sachs: James Pease. Eva: Frances Yeed
The cobbler's workshop (Act III, scene 1), as it appeared in countless productions throughout the 1930s and 1940s: a low-ceilinged room with beams running across it and a small arched window. Ever since the time of Benno von Arent's designs in the 1930s, the tiled stove had come to be regarded as an indispensable feature of traditional German domesticity.

Teatro dell'Opera, Rome, 1956
Producer and designer: Wolfgang Wagner. Conductor: Rudolf Moralt. Walther: Sebastian Feiersinger. Hans Sachs: Gustav Neidlinger. Beckmesser: Erich Kunz
The Mastersingers' assembly in Act I in Wolfgang Wagner's production and stage-set. An intimate, bright, whitewashed room separated from the nave of the church, which is accessible through the three Gothic arches. The atmosphere is private rather than semi-official.

spect for the eccentric and limited Mastersingers, insisting that what is worth smiling at is also worth taking seriously. His figure of Sachs embodies 'the German type, as depicted in Sachs, rather crude if you like, but something distinct from the Latin type' (Cosima Wagner's Diary, 21 March 1881). 'This is the form [...] with a popular poet, [...] an enthusiastic youth [...] and a respectable pedant' that he 'visualized the Germans in their true character, their best light [...] This is their level in life; everything else, elegance, for instance, is affectation; but their feelings are of the highest pathos' (Cosima's Diary, 16 March 1873). In spite of all these reservations, what this image also contains is a resonant sense of love and pride: Wagner was firmly convinced that Germany would 'acclaim' his most popular work (Cosima's Diary, 15 February 1881).

Only on the most superficial level does the opera follow the traditional lines laid down for comedies: the lovers meet, a rival appears, forcing the two of them apart and yet all turns out right in the end. In the case of *Die Meistersinger von Nürnberg* everything is decided from the very outset. 'Euch oder keinen' ('You or no one') Eva assures Walther von Stolzing in the church scene in Act I. In the course of the subsequent action it becomes clear, on the one hand, what difficulties the two lovers must face to bring their relationship to a satisfactory conclusion (which is the cruel and painful aspect of the work, one which borders on tragedy) and, on the other hand, the elaborate and mad-cap attempts on the part of others to alter the course of events (which is the comic side of the opera). In the field of tension created by these two extremes Wagner has attempted to capture what he repeatedly called 'the most real, sensual life' – life which is not neatly divided between comedy and tragedy but which is governed by delusion. As he wrote to King Ludwig on 22 November 1866: 'The theme of Act III is "Wahn! Wahn! überall Wahn!" ("Delusion, delusion! Everywhere delusion!"), which I have allowed to penetrate everywhere [...] It is the theme which governs my own life and that of all who are noble: would we be forced to struggle, to suffer and to renounce, if "delusion" did not control the world?' And, following the dress rehearsal, he again wrote to the king on 20 June 1868, 'It is impossible for you not to have felt and clearly recognized beneath the wondrous layers of popular humour a deep sense of nostalgia, a cry of grief, poetry's cry for help as it lies bound in chains, its reincarnation, its rebirth and the irresistible force of its magic which it owes to its having overcome baseness.' *Die Meistersinger von Nürnberg* has nothing whatever to do with that 'gushy and insidious cosiness which selfishly turns away at the sight of human suffering around it in order to rent a plot of private heaven in the blue mists of nature's vague generality. These smugly good-natured people are quite happy to see and hear everything except the true undistorted man, who stands as a warning at the end of their dreams. But it is precisely this figure whom we must now place in the foreground' (*Das Kunstwerk der Zukunft* ['The Art work of the Future']). This, then, is what Wagner wanted to portray: the undistorted individual, the suffering and delusion of life and the salvation which art can offer.

Hans Sachs's closing words were the first lines which Wagner added in the margin of the 1845 prose draft. In the final version they have been expanded to form the great closing monologue. According to the rules of comedy, the curtain could fall once the lovers have been united. Sachs's address is first of all a rebuke directed at Stolzing for his refusal to accept membership of the Mastersingers' guild. He has written his Prize Song in order to win Eva, not in order to become a Mastersinger. In the second place, the address puts the record straight as far as the Mastersingers' historical achievements are concerned. They preserved German art even at its darkest hour, albeit 'grad recht nach ihrer Art' ('straight and proper in accord with their nature'): this art will survive both politics and empire.

The lines beginning 'Habt Acht!' ('Beware!'), however, fall outside the framework of the action, being an appeal to the public and a defence of a nationalist component in art, which was not necessary at this moment in the stage action. Wagner was aware of the danger of being misunderstood. Cosima reported to the king at the beginning of February 1867 that she had spent the whole day discussing with Wagner the ending of the opera and especially the lines beginning 'Habt Acht!' Wagner wanted to omit the closing address, believing that 'Sachs's great speech does not belong here: it is rather more an address directed by the poet towards the audience; he felt he would do better to leave it out entirely.' Cosima was firmly opposed to the idea and Wagner left the lines as they were. The reason for his doing so must indeed have been their essentially political appeal. *Die Meistersinger von Nürnberg* was initially intended to be performed in Nuremberg. Bavaria fought in the Austro-Prussian War on the losing side. Following the civil war, hopes of German unity had once again been dashed. Wagner was as dismayed by current political conditions as he had been after 1848 and he was tormented by what he described in a letter to Ludwig II of 14 July 1866 as 'the most violent concern for our betrayed and irreparably ruined fatherland'. The day of the first performance of *Die Meistersinger von Nürnberg* would be 'a bitter day for Bismarck and the North German League', he wrote to Ludwig on 25 October 1866. Wagner conceived of these lines as an expression of his concern for contemporary German politics, as had previously been the case with *Lohengrin*. Perhaps it seemed to him that the warning contained in these lines fulfilled the demands which he had made elsewhere of art, namely that it should find expression in a particular place, at a particular time and under particular conditions and hence develop the liveliest

Bayreuth Festival, 1956
Designer: Wieland Wagner.
Conductor: André Cluytens.
Hans Sachs: Hans Hotter
Wieland Wagner's most famous
set, described by Walter Erich
Schäfer as 'an unreal nocturne,
impishly phantasmal but with
the shadow of delusion cast
over it'. Two ball-shaped elder
clusters hover in the deep-blue
night sky. The acting area is
the much maligned 'kidney', a
modern shape typical of the age
of kidney-shaped tables.
Schäfer called the set 'the
solution of the century,
wonderfully secure in the
fragrant "sweetness" of its
atmosphere, inescapable in its
ability to concentrate the
audience's attention entirely on
the action.'

effectiveness. It is precisely the closing address which, more than any other operatic
text, has given rise to misunderstanding and
misuse. Even Wagner himself was unable entirely to prevent that from happening.

'How anyone can set to music an object
like the thing that Wagner calls a comic opera
is a puzzle to us all; all we can do is sit back
and wait to see what solution the composer
proposes,' the *kapellmeister* Heinrich Esser
wrote to Franz Schott following Wagner's
read-through of the libretto in Vienna on
23 November 1861. Wagner wanted to begin
work on the score as soon as the libretto had
been completed. His new publisher, Franz
Schott of Mainz, was instructed to have the
separate fascicles of the manuscript score en-
graved the moment they reached him, so that
the work's eventual first performance should
not be unnecessarily delayed. In February

1862 he settled down in Biebrich, with a view
over the Rhine and over Mainz, had his Erard
grand piano brought from Paris and resolved
not to move from where he was until he had
finished the whole score.

The history of the genesis of *Die Meistersinger von Nürnberg* is a reflection of the crisis
in Wagner's life and creativity in which he
had become caught up in this, the fiftieth year
of his life, following the completion of *Tristan und Isolde.* The beginning of the orchestral sketch of the Prelude bears the date
'Biebrich, 13 April 1862' and at the end has
been written the date, 'First day of Easter',
which was 20 April. Wagner was still quite
optimistic and hoped that the first performance of his new work could be given during
the 1862/1863 opera season. He did not
make a note of the date on which he began
the composition sketch of Act I. The fact that

he made little progress was due, he claimed, to adverse circumstances, notably illness and Schott's delay in granting him further advances on the unfinished project. By September, he was still working on Act I. He now set himself the goal and indeed swore an oath that he would complete the work by his fiftieth birthday on 22 May 1863. It was with extreme effort that he forced himself to go on with the work. In October he wrote an embittered letter to Schott, 'Do you think that, if worry prevents me from sleeping at night, I shall feel sufficiently cheerful and inspired during the day to continue with my work?' Schott's famous reply was dated 21 October and for Wagner it meant a temporary end to his continuing work on the opera: 'There is no music publisher in the world who can meet your needs; this is something which only an enormously wealthy banker can do, or else a *prince* who has millions at his disposal. If the latter cannot be found, an appeal would have to be made to the *German people.*' The Prelude was first performed at a concert in the Leipzig Gewandhaus on 1 November 1862 and it turned out to be a fiasco. This was the first time that Wagner had appeared in Saxony since his flight from Dresden. The concert hall was half empty and when Wagner walked to the conductor's desk, he was greeted by total silence. It is true that the Prelude was encored, but Wagner's most popular work got off to a start that was anything but popular.

When rehearsals for *Tristan und Isolde* were resumed in Vienna, Wagner moved back to the Austrian capital in November 1862. He suggested to the Court Opera that *Die Meistersinger von Nürnberg* should be written with the ensemble of the Vienna Opera in mind, and rehearsed under his direction; but the suggestion was turned down. In order to make ends meet, Wagner then set out on a series of lengthy concert tours which took him as far as Moscow. In May or June 1863 he wrote to Countess Pourtalès that his Erard grand piano had arrived at his new flat in Penzing, near Vienna, and that *Die Meistersinger von Nürnberg* lay open on his desk. The full score of Act I, scene 1 includes the date 'Penzing, 8 June 1863'. He now began the process of instrumenting the first act, even before he had completed the orchestral sketch, no doubt because instrumentation for Wagner was a mechanical task which required no particular inspiration on his part nor that he should be in the right mood. On 10 July he wrote to Wendelin Weissheimer: 'Things have reached an impasse! [...] I've no longer any desire to continue [...]. The ex-

Municipal Theatre, Leipzig, 8 October 1960
Producer: Joachim Herz.
Designer: Rudolf Heinrich
Opening production in the new opera-house. The Festival Meadow in Act III. *Die Meistersinger* without the 'Nuremberg ideology' of the nineteenth century, but played instead as a 'Renaissance comedy' of the sixteenth century. The scaffolding of the Hans Sachs stage was anti-illusionistic, but offered possibilities for acting; it was an appeal to the imagination. The production was highly controversial.

pression "being sick of life" sums up precisely the way I feel [...]. Up to now I've been working on the instrumentation of *Die Meistersinger*, but it's a slow process: I confess that the abundant spring of good humour and the courage to face life [...] has now dried up inside me.' He added that if *Tristan und Isolde* were ever to receive its first performance, he might once again derive some pleasure from his work.

This frame of mind does not appear to have been a momentary depression, since similar turns of phrase can be found in all the letters which he wrote during these months. What was particularly crucial was the fact that, having reached his fiftieth birthday, he could see no prospect ahead of him for himself or for his work. It was not until January 1864 that he could report that his work on the opera was giving him any sense of pleasure. In February he again set himself a clear deadline: the work would be finished by the coming winter. On 23 March he fled from Vienna in order to avoid being imprisoned for debt and found refuge with his friends François and Eliza Wille in Mariafeld near Zurich, intending to continue working undisturbed until the end of the summer. 'I really have to force myself to work,' he wrote to Mathilde Maier on 29 March 1864; 'whether

the Mastersingers will ever see the light of day depends entirely on whether I can now manage to arrange my own affairs satisfactorily – because, if I put the work to one side now, there'll never again be any possibility of my completing it.' Then, on 12 April, he wrote to Joseph Standhartner, begging him, 'Don't remind me of the Mastersingers! Ever!' It was no doubt simply in order to reassure Schott and put him in a suitable frame of mind to agree to a further advance that he wrote on 25 April of his having reached a definite agreement with the Vienna Opera for a production in January 1865; he went on, 'I swear by my word of honour that I shall not waver from this task, which is now the most important thing in my life, and that I shall deliver the work to you, completely finished and ready for performance before the year is out.' In the plans which he drew up for performances of his operas in Munich, following his summons there by King Ludwig II, the first performances of *Die Meistersinger von Nürnberg* were scheduled to take place first of all in 1865 and then in 1869, following the completion of *Der Ring des Nibelungen*. After he had been driven out of Munich, too, Wagner resumed work on Act I in Geneva, and on Wednesday, 21 February 1866, he was finally able to put the finishing touches to the orchestral sketch of this act, the full score being completed on 23 March. It was not until he settled down at Tribschen, where he took up residence on 15 April, that Wagner found the right conditions for uninterrupted work. He began work on the composition sketch of Act II on 15 May and this, together with the orchestral sketch, were completed by 23 September. It bears a note in the margin, 'I have actually written the music for this second act during the summer of 1866 (see biography).' Cosima in the meantime had separated from Hans von Bülow, with all that that involved in the way of disturbances. He began the third act on 8 October, completing the orchestral sketch on 5 March 1867. He then turned to the instrumentation of Acts II and III. On 24 October he sent a telegram to Hans von Bülow, 'This evening at the stroke of 8 the final C will be written into the score. Please mark the occasion with a moment's silence. Sachs.' Almost twenty-two years had elapsed since his first conception of the work in Marienbad in the summer of 1845.

Die Meistersinger von Nürnberg contains no reworkings of any musical elements from the time of Hans Sachs, although the historical nature of the material might have tempted Wagner into doing so. But, as Egon Voss has indicated, the music of the opera alludes to 'an older age, and the purpose behind these allusions is self-evident: the aim is to create a sort of local colour of Old Nuremberg and an atmosphere redolent in general of the German Renaissance. The listener does not, of course, associate the music he hears with the age of Dürer and Hans Sachs, but rather with the age of Bach with its figurate themes, its ornaments and its cadenzas.' What is important, Voss goes on, is that Wagner has had recourse 'to the Protestant chorale and, above all, the folk song, both of which are specifically German forms.' In his characterization of the Prelude to *Die Meistersinger von Nürnberg* in *Jenseits von Gut und Böse* ('Beyond Good and Evil'), Nietzsche described the piece as 'magnificent, heavy and mature art which is proud enough to presuppose for its understanding that two centuries of music are still alive.' It contained 'something German in the best and worst sense of the word; something which, in its typically German way, is manifold, informal and inexhaustible; a certain German powerfulness and excessive soulfulness which is not afraid to masquerade beneath the refinements of decay.' This music, Nietzsche continued, best expressed what he thought about the Germans: 'They are of the day before yesterday and the day after tomorrow – they do not have a today.'

It was on 23 December 1865 that Wagner first suggested to Hans von Bülow the idea of giving the first performances of *Die Meistersinger von Nürnberg* not in Munich but in its original setting of Nuremberg. The king, too, having visited Nuremberg in 1866 during his tour of inspection of the German troops and having imagined himself as Hans Sachs, in his Gothic room in the castle, considered Nuremberg as the only proper venue. But since the Nuremberg theatre chose to honour the king's visit with, of all works, Meyerbeer's *L'Africaine* and Verdi's *Il trovatore*, Wagner began to have serious doubts about whether his plans for a model production of the opera could be realized in such a theatre as this one. The king commissioned Hans von Bülow to travel to Nuremberg and to contact the leading townspeople and patricians in order to sound them out on the possibility of staging the opera outside the normal repertory. The plan was not pursued, however, since, following the king's engagement to the Duchess Sophie of Bavaria, the première of *Die Meistersinger von Nürnberg* was now scheduled as an official celebration to mark the wedding. The date had already been fixed for 12 October 1867 in spite of Bülow's reservations about the suitability of the new opera for the occasion. When Ludwig broke off the engagement, nothing came of this plan either. A date was finally agreed for the spring of 1868.

The set-designers Angelo Quaglio and Heinrich Döll were sent off to Nuremberg in June 1867 to prepare architectural studies for Acts I and II. Wagner, who was miles away at Tribschen, was furious, convinced as he was that decisions would be taken over his head and that his wishes would be ignored. In November/December the set-designers together with the costume designer, Franz Seitz, travelled to Tribschen in order to submit their sketches to Wagner, who noted down various corrections, so that everything was carried out exactly according to his own ideas. In Act II, for example, he demanded practicable houses rather than ones which were simply painted on to flats; and he also wanted the architectural features of the church in Act I to be similarly practicable.

Difficulties arose with the new intendant, Karl Freiherr von Perfall, over the engagement of outside singers, since Wagner refused to have the opera cast from the local ensemble. He violently reproached the administration for its bad management; the intendant, on the other hand, replied by pointing out the high fees involved and the discontentment which the engagement of expensive guest artists would provoke within his

Bayreuth Festival, 1963
Producer: Wieland Wagner.
Conductor: Thomas Schippers.
Chorus-master: Wilhelm Pitz
Opening chorale in Act I.
Wieland Wagner's production on a Shakespearean stage, which served as a unit set. The chorus sang with its back to the audience. The triptych is a copy of Lucas Cranach's altar-piece in Neustadt an der Orla.

Bavarian State Opera, Munich,
21 November 1963
Producer: Rudolf Hartmann.
Designer: Helmut Jürgens.
Conductor: Joseph Keilberth.
Eva: Claire Watson. Magdalene:
Lilian Benningsen. Walther: Jess
Thomas
Opening production at the
rebuilt National Theatre. Scene
from Act I. Characteristic of
many productions during the
1950s and 1960s are the tall,
bright stained-glass windows in
the nave of the church.

Bayreuth Festival, 1969
Producer and designer:
Wolfgang Wagner. Conductor:
Berislav Klobucar.
Chorus-master: Wilhelm Pitz
This production was new in
1968 and marked the centenary
of the first performances in
Munich. Riot scene in Act II.
The walls of the houses were
half-timbered and symbolized
order and proportion. During
the *Fliedermonolog* they became
transparent, like brightly
coloured stained-glass windows,
but they became opaque again
for the rough and brutal riot
scene.

own company. Wagner, however, was finally given a cast which he felt able to describe as ideal: Hans Sachs was sung by Franz Betz from Berlin, Stolzing by Franz Nachbaur from Darmstadt, Beckmesser by Georg Hölzel from Vienna, David by Max Schlosser from Augsburg and Eva by Mathilde Mallinger, a young soprano of the up-and-coming generation, who belonged to the Munich ensemble. The conductor was Hans von Bülow. Dr Reinhard Hallwachs from Stuttgart was engaged as producer, although Wagner himself took charge of the rehearsals, dismissing Hallwachs's engagement as an unnecessary expense on von Perfall's part.

The rehearsals were certainly exhausting, even for Wagner, but he soon gained the impression that all concerned had it in their power to achieve something exceptional and exemplary. Even the dress rehearsal, which took place in the presence of the king, was a notable event, being attended by a large number of theatre managers, *kapellmeisters,* producers and singers. They were all of the same mind: an important event had taken place.

The official first night on 21 June was largely reserved for visitors from abroad, some of whom had travelled considerable distances. The local residents were prepared to pay several times the face value of the tickets in their attempts to gain admission. The king entered his box at six o'clock and the performance began. Ludwig invited the composer to sit beside him in the royal box and from there Wagner was able to bow to the audience after the second and third acts. No other composer had ever been so honoured

previously and the *Kemptener Zeitung* reported the incident as follows:

The impression made upon the general public here by this show of royal favour was quite overwhelming: everyone fell silent and looked up at the magnificent ceiling of the vast house to see whether it was not showing signs of falling in at such an unparalleled mark of favour. Wagner, who had once been denounced and exiled [...] has been rehabilitated in the most incredible way [...] It is scarcely to be wondered if a number of young ladies of the highest nobility pinched themselves to see whether it was indeed really they who were present at such a unique event.

For Wagner it was his greatest ever triumph in the theatre. Press reactions, it is true, were mixed, but there was only praise for the quality of the performance itself. The sets and costumes must have been overwhelming in their magnificence. The audience felt itself transported back in time to the real world of the sixteenth century. A Gothic church or an old German street scene were admittedly nothing particularly new but what was striking about the Munich sets was their faithfulness in matters of stylistic detail and their practicability.

'The sets and costumes which have been lavished on the Mastersingers are quite fantastic,' a preliminary report in the *Neue Berliner Musikzeitung* announced:

Things never before seen on stage will be achieved here in matters of scenic design. For the act which takes place in the streets of Nuremberg, the traditional flats have

Salzburg Festival, 1974
Producer and conductor: Herbert von Karajan. Designer: Günther Schneider-Siemssen. Costumes: Georges Wakhevitch. Hans Sachs: Karl Ridderbusch
Sachs's *Fliedermonolog* in Act II. A complete reconstruction of the old town of Nuremberg on the stage of the Grosses Festspielhaus, with shingle roofs, half timbering, towers, oriels and illuminated windows. The Nuremberg alley had to be widened to a major road junction in order to fill the vast stage of the Festspielhaus.

disappeared in order to make way for the very embodiment of the town of Nuremberg with its houses, gables and overhangs. What one sees here are not painted houses but complete cardboard buildings, copied from real life, and streets, squares and perspectives so life-like as to deceive one into thinking them real.

There was praise, too, for the stage direction: 'There was a life, an interacting and a degree of truth about the acting such as we have never before witnessed [...]; only the most profound understanding of art, the most complete devotion on the part of all concerned, enormous effort and unshakable determination could achieve such an overall result' *(Signale für die musikalische Welt)*.

Wagner was unreservedly satisfied and pleased with everything and everyone, the single exception being Georg Hölzel of Vienna, who had turned Beckmesser into a caricature and had made a 'Viennese buffoon' out of him. For Wagner, Beckmesser was 'not a comic figure: he is just as serious as all the other Masters. Only his position and the situations in which he finds himself make him appear ridiculous,' Wagner wrote to Heinrich Esser on 18 July 1868. But Hölzel laid the foundations for an ineradicable tradition as far as playing the role of Beckmesser was concerned – ineradicable because this comic caricature met with popular acclaim from the very outset, which is why it has been repeatedly imitated ever since.

Once again it was the medium-sized theatres which first had the courage to take up the challenge of the new opera. The following year (1869) it entered the repertory in Dessau, Karlsruhe, Dresden, Mannheim and Weimar. The great court opera-houses of Vienna and Berlin did not follow until 1870. The first performances in Vienna were given in a heavily cut version, the total running-time being 3 1/2 hours, which annoyed Wagner intensely. It had by now become accepted practice to make extensive cuts in the scene with David in Act I and, later on, in Sachs's workshop. It was reported to Wagner that no one had been able to understand a single word; a trombone had had to do duty for the nightwatchman's horn and a guitar for Beckmesser's lute. 'R. is very despondent,' Cosima noted in her diary on 20 March 1870. During the serenade in Act II, the uproar in the audience had been so great that Johannes Beck, who was singing the part of Hans Sachs, had lost his concentration, so that the conductor, Johann Herbeck, had been forced to shout out his cues to him. Daniel Spitzer informed the readership of his *Wiener Spa-*

ziergänge that the latest product of the music of the future sounded to his ear 'like the swan-song of common sense'. Particular scorn was poured on the idea of having glove-makers, tailors and soap-boilers as operatic heroes, in other words, Wagner's much loved folk. The fact that a few notables managed to make themselves heard above the noise of the 'rabble' was only marginally reassuring.

In Berlin and Mannheim as well the serenade and the riot scene were both condemned as some of the worst excesses of modern music and provoked uproar in the auditorium. In Mannheim, Franz Bittong, who later became theatre manager in Hamburg, beat the protesters about the head with his score, which was completely destroyed in the process, so that the publisher Franz Schott, who happened to be present, promised to send him a new one. Marianne Brandt, who sang the part of Magdalene in the Berlin production, formed the impression that during the riot scene 'the punch-up in the audience' was worse than that on stage and that at the end of the act it seemed as though the theatre would erupt, 'so great was the noise of the howling, hissing, shouting, laughing, foot-stamping and Beckmesser-calling crowd.' Not even the third act could avert the catastrophe. Once again there was unqualified praise for the excellence of the performance and the achievements of the singers, particularly those of Franz Betz and Mathilde Mallinger, as had been the case in Munich, together with Albert Niemann, who sang the part of Stolzing. The critics were devastating: their aggressive tone must strike us as quite incredible today. A few examples will suffice: 'Chaos, hullabaloo', 'an opera for cobblers' apprentices', 'a mountain of stupidity and insipidity', 'no more appalling a cats' chorus could ever have been devised [...] even if all the organ grinders of Berlin had been herded together into the Renz Circus and if each of them had played a different waltz', 'a musical changeling', 'ear-splitting confusion', 'if music could stink, you'd be forced to hold your nose at this "abattoir of notes".'

In spite of all the protests, *Die Meistersinger von Nürnberg* slowly but surely found more and more supporters until by the 1880s it was being taken up by international opera-houses throughout the world. A correspondent to one of Berlin's newspapers accurately prophesied, 'Just as epidemics spread uncontrollably from place to place, so we shall have to suffer in silence while *Die Meistersinger* gradually makes the rounds of the various theatres.' The opera was performed for the first

Royal Theatre, Stockholm, 1 October 1977 Producer: Götz Friedrich. Designer: Günther Schneider-Siemssen. Conductor: Berislav Klobucar. Hans Sachs: Leif Roar. Beckmesser: Erik Saedén. Walther: Sven-Olof Eliasson. David: Gösta Winbergh. Eva: Helena Döse Friedrich's Festival Meadow scene began somewhat turbulently as the people of Nuremberg entered the Meadow, they were accompanied by mimes wearing medieval death's-head masks. Thus the cheerful, superficial façade of Nuremberg is threatened – 'No one, after all, is ever safe – neither in a town, nor in any prototype, nor in any Utopia', according to Friedrich. The open ending raised the question: 'In his totally unmythological *Meistersinger* Wagner was none the less struggling to find a kind of myth – the integration of art and the people, culture and democracy. A Utopia?'

time, in German, in Prague in 1871, in London in 1882 and in Amsterdam in 1883. The American first performance was given at the Metropolitan Opera, New York, on 4 January 1886 under Anton Seidl, and was also given in German. The Copenhagen première in 1872 was performed in Danish, the first performance in Budapest in 1883 was given in Hungarian and for the first performance at La Scala in 1889 an Italian translation was used. A particularly brilliant occasion was the first performance in French, given in Brussels in 1885 in the presence of Queen Marie Henriette of Belgium; the whole of Parisian society travelled to Brussels for the performances, since political conditions prevented the work from entering the repertory of the Palais Garnier until 1897, when the opera was finally performed for the first time in the city which had given it birth.

Die Meistersinger von Nürnberg first entered the Bayreuth repertory, at Cosima's instigation, in 1888. She had the sets and costumes copied from those which had been used at the Munich première. Only the set for Act I was altered so as to produce a plainly decorated, low-ceilinged and rather gloomy civic church. For the first time since it had been founded, the Festival was sold out.

The type of scenery sanctioned by Munich and Bayreuth was retained elsewhere and remained essentially unchanged for decades. Even as late as the 1920s the opera was treated as a realistic work and consciously excluded from all contemporary attempts at stylization. What is striking, however, is the way in which, especially from the 1880s onwards, many set-designers included in their work specific references to Nuremberg's architecture, attempting an even greater degree of historical realism than had been the case in Munich and Bayreuth; they showed the well-known round towers of the city wall and had a particular predilection for the double spires of Saint Sebald or Saint Lorenz looming up at the end of the narrow street.

As a musical festival and a festive celebration of music, *Die Meistersinger von Nürnberg* has established itself in the repertory as the festival opera *par excellence,* at least in German opera-houses. Particularly during the early years of the young empire after 1871, the large number of commemorative occasions, foundation-stone layings and national celebrations gave rise to an urgent need for patriotic festival dramas, which were enthusiastically churned out by overzealous poets. But for more august occasions, it was always *Die Meistersinger von Nürnberg* which was first choice, even if only in the form of excerpts, including the Prelude, perhaps, the festival meadow scene or the closing address. And for the official openings of the numerous new theatres which sprang up during the period leading up to the First World War, and even later, *Die Meistersinger von Nürnberg* was the obligatory choice to mark the occasion, often coupled with Beethoven's overture 'The Consecration of the House' or Goethe's 'Prologue in the theatre' from *Faust.* At the opening of the new opera-house in Cologne, for example, the architect and theatre manager were called on stage at Hans Sachs's lines 'Ehrt eure deutschen Meister' ('Honour your German masters'). For the official unveiling of the Wagner memorial in Berlin in 1903, *Die Meistersinger von Nürnberg* was again the inevitable choice. The part of Hans Sachs was sung by Theodor Bertram, Eva by Emmy Destinn and Stolzing by Ernst Kraus. There was also a popular tradition whereby profits from gala performances of the opera were donated to the fund set up for the Berlin memorial.

For those Wagnerians who were strict observers of the faith and whose orthodoxy was confined exclusively to mythology, *Die Meistersinger von Nürnberg* was a healthy, secular work, whose ending instead of being tragic was embarrassing. They paid little heed to the piece and were happy to hand it over to those who were sufficiently undemanding as to be satisfied with realism, cosiness and patriotic sentiment. Producers and designers regarded the work as unproblematical, an opera which effectively ran itself. Appia wasted very little

time on it. Ambitious designers capitulated to the opera's demands for realism, as well as to the expectations of audiences who wanted to see their familiar image of Nuremberg repeated here, on stage. Bad production habits soon began to emerge as a result. Beckmesser increasingly turned into a caricature, in spite of all Cosima's efforts to the contrary. The most important consideration, as far as the singers were concerned, was to make sure that they had the audience laughing with them rather than at them. And bass-baritones, who were pleased to have a 'philosophical' role in their repertory, turned Hans Sachs into a reflective, solemn and portentous old man. To those of a pre-national-socialist mentality, who were developing their ideology during these decades, the growing popularity of the opera was particularly welcome and they made decisive use of it in forming those ideals. The closing monologue and especially the lines beginning 'Habt Acht!' served as a confirmation of their provocative belief in Pan-German superiority and as a call to be vigilant in the face of a common foe.

When celebrations were held in 1898 to mark the tenth anniversary of the opening of the New German Theatre in Prague, two acts of *Die Meistersinger von Nürnberg* were included in the evening's programme, together with a festival play specially written for the occasion. What gave this production particular significance as a manifestation of Germanness were the bitter exchanges between the Czech and German inhabitants of the city which had culminated in street violence some few weeks previously. Infantry guards with fixed bayonets stood sentry outside the theatre and search parties raided the quarter of the city known as Královské Vinohrady, which was where the nationally minded Czech citizens lived. Inside the opera-house the doors were guarded by members of the armed forces; as Rudolf Fürst commented, the theatre resembled a 'military camp'. The glass panels in the main entrance doors had been shattered and replaced in makeshift fashion by cardboard, since 'hordes of Slav proles' had 'chosen' the theatre 'as their first object of assault' during 'the execrable November days of 1897'. Fürst ended his report, first published in *Bühne und Welt* ('Stage and World') in 1899, with the lines: 'Though almost all the political desires and aspirations of the Germans in Prague might fade into mist, one thing would still remain for us – German art.'

One of Wagner's own aims in writing *Die Meistersinger von Nürnberg* was his attempt to offer some basis for a national identity as a precondition for national unity. The proto-national socialists, on the other hand, set them-

Smetana Theatre, National
Theatre, Prague, 2 November
1978
Producer: Václav Kašlik.
Designer: Josef Svoboda.
Costumes: Jarmila Konečna.
Conductor: Milos Konvalinka
Act I. The timber framework
remained on stage throughout
all three acts. St Katharine's
Church was indicated by the
wooden rose-window. Wood
was employed to express the
work's sense of craftmanship
and a plain and austere view of
the late Middle Ages. The
costumes were similarly lacking
in opulence and magnificence
but were made out of simple,
coarse fabrics in broken shades
of white, beige and brown.

selves up as the sole guarantors and saviours of
national identity and took control of the opera,
including all its ambiguous passages. And nobody offered them any resistance, not even in
Bayreuth and the latter's publicity organs.
Quite the contrary. The seeds of discord were
already being sown by those writers and jour-
nalists who described themselves as 'the Bayreuth circle' or, in the case of the inner sanctum,
as 'the Wahnfried group'; it was they who prepared the ideological battle ground and set in
motion the politicization of Bayreuth. The
process had begun even before the First World
War. In the *Bayreuther Blätter* the Festspielhaus
had been given the title of 'Aryan citadel' as
early as 1896, and Hans von Wolzogen, Wahnfried's writer in residence, demanded that 'the
great issue' of Richard Wagner should be made
'a national issue'. After 1933 it could be noted
with satisfaction that this goal had been
achieved. The ideas attached to the names
'Bayreuth' and 'Wahnfried' no longer stood
for the Festival and its artistic aims but for a limited ideology of Germanness which was
national-conservative and anti-democratic.
The *Bayreuther Blätter* increasingly became
the journalistic mouthpiece of the ideologues
of Aryanism.

As early as 1914 the well-known and influential journalist, Maximilian Harden, had
warned, 'Abandon your attempts to falsify
[Bayreuth] by turning it into Mount Zion, a
stronghold, a heaven-reaching sanctuary of
German nationalism, a citadel from whose

battlements the Master himself speaks.' And
critic and musicologist Paul Bekker wrote in
his *Kritsche Zeitbilder* ('Critical Pictures of an
Age') in 1921:

What has turned out to be fatal and, in many
respects, nothing short of catastrophic for
the intellectual attitude of the Germans in
particular is the profoundly untruthful ethical and nationalistic presentation which, by
means of an increase in emphasis upon non-
artistic factors, transformed Bayreuth from
its original function as a centre of art to a
place of worship [...] dedicated to a misunderstood Germanness [...] Not only an aesthetic but a political reaction, as well, with its
second-rate Teutonism, false piety, racial
hatred and limited nationalism find support
here and believe, like Chamberlain, for example, that, starting from here, they are entitled to arrogate to their own ends the impressive phenomenon of the great artist
that Wagner was, in order to derive their
own justification from him.

Houston Stewart Chamberlain, who combined
a learned, all-round dilettantism with the
authorship of *Die Grundlagen des* 19. *Jahrhunderts* ('Fundamental Principles of the 19th Century'), had begun to correspond with Cosima
Wagner in 1888 and then, from 1901 onwards,
with the Emperor Wilhelm II, to whose crusad-
ing ideal he lent active support during the First
World War. He married Cosima's daughter
Eva in 1908 and in 1923 brought Wahnfried for

Bayreuth Festival, 1981
Producer: Wolfgang Wagner.
Conductor: Mark Elder.
Costumes: Reinhard Heinrich.
Chorus-master: Norbert
Balatsch
The Festival Meadow in Act III.
The town band plays and the
people of Nuremberg perform a
traditional Franconian dance
around the lime-tree. The
Festival Meadow scene as a
popular, improvised summer
festival, which only attains an
official schedule and a sense of
organization with the
commencement of the song
contest. But both schedule and
organization are constantly
interrupted by the people. The
lime-tree is at once a piece of
scenery and the Tree of Life
and *palma Christi* which
Walther addresses in his Prize
Song.

the first time into direct contact with Adolf Hitler. These dates indicate not only the stages of Bayreuth's drifting off into the camp of reactionary politics but also, in a more general sense, the course taken by German history in its march towards catastrophe. When the Bayreuth Festival reopened in 1924, after a ten-year interval brought about by the First World War, Adolf Rapp, in his article 'Wagner as a guide to the German character', published in the Festival programme, had no difficulty in claiming, 'We may say today that, on a political level as well, Bayreuth's patrons are gathered together in the camp in which everyone who wishes emphatically to be German increasingly finds himself.' Ludendorff even attended the rehearsals. At the opening performance of *Die Meistersinger von Nürnberg*, conducted by Fritz Busch, the audience rose to its feet during the closing address and at the end of the performance all joined together in singing the national anthem; isolated shouts of 'Heil' are also reported to have been heard.

According to Franz Stassen, Siegfried Wagner, who was in charge of the Festival, 'turned pale and indignant', remarking that 'I expect that after *Götterdämmerung* they'll sing the "Watch on the Rhine"'. But on the roof of the Festspielhaus Siegfried had the black, white and red imperial flag hoisted beside the Bavarian flag, which indicated a profession of faith. Similar excesses took place in 1925, forcing Siegfried to put up a notice: 'We request the audience to refrain from singing [patriotic songs], however well-intentioned their motives may be; our concern here is for art!' In 1921 Siegfried had categorically refused to give in to August Püringer's demands that Jews should be boycotted by the Festival; he regarded such a request as an attack on tolerance and in 1925 he wrote, 'For my own part I have done everything I can to ensure that the Bayreuth season should remain free from all political involvement and everyone, no matter what his faith and racial origin, will be welcome in Bayreuth if he comes in search of edification and experience. No one need be afraid that any incidents of an unpleasant nature might take place' (*Berliner 8 Uhr-Abendblatt* for 9 March 1925).

But it was too late. It was no longer possible to want one thing and prevent the other. Bernhard Diebold, who had attended the 1928 Festival, asked:

Where are the liberal minds for the liberal work of art? What has happened to the common people of *Die Meistersinger*? Where are those sensitive creatures with the soul of Tristan? Are we nowadays too sophisticated for the music of yesterday? Are we so inordinately astute in political matters that we can throw out the Wagnerian baby with Chamberlain's dirty bath-water? What has happened? [...] Instead of proclaiming *Die Meistersinger* as a democratic festival opera, the party spirit ingenuously handed over the whole of Wagner to the national socialists without so much as a struggle [...] Nationalist distortions should be confronted with the liberalism of Wagner's work.

Komische Oper, East Berlin,
3 October 1981
Producer: Harry Kupfer.
Designer: Wilfried Wertz.
Conductor: Rolf Reuter
Scene on the Festival Meadow.
A tree forms the unit set: in Act
I it serves for St Katharine's
Church, like a wood-carving by
the sixteenth-century German
sculptor Tilman Riemenschneider;
in Act II – Midsummer Eve – it
is festooned with blossoms; in
Act III – the Festival Meadow –
it is decorated like a festal tree.
Identified by their characteristic
props, the guild march around
the tree, which itself revolves.
The scene suggests
unsophisticated merry-making
with elements of a medieval
dance of death.

But voices such as Diebold's could no longer make themselves heard. 'The Germans have set up for themselves an image of Wagner which they can venerate; they have never been good psychologists: they are thankful for their misunderstanding.' Nietzsche's remark gained a new immediacy. Wahnfried suffered from enemy action during the war and was reopened as a museum in 1976, when Wolfgang Wagner was quite right to remark in the course of an official speech to mark the occasion 'I believe that the bomb had to fall.' Only when Wahnfried had ceased to exist as an institution was it possible for our generation to rediscover Wagner.

It was only to be expected that 'Potsdam Day' on 22 March 1933 should be celebrated with a performance of *Die Meistersinger von Nürnberg* at the State Opera Unter den Linden in Berlin, and that the work should then have been elevated (or rather debased) to become the festival opera of the Nuremberg Nazi rally. Hans Sachs's lines from the 'Wittemberg Nightingale', written during the Reformation and inserted by Wagner in the 'Wach auf' chorus at the end of the work, were described by Joseph Goebbels in a speech which he made on the occasion of a 1933 radio broadcast of the opera from the Festspielhaus as 'the outcry of a nation' (whatever would the chorus-master have said to that?) and as 'a tangible symbol of the reawakening of the German nation from its deep political and spiritual anaesthesia of November 1918.'

It was at the 'Party Rally for Freedom' that *Die Meistersinger von Nürnberg* was first per-

formed with new sets and costumes by the Reich's official set-designer Benno von Arent. Hitler commissioned the designs himself and personally approved the sketches before they were realized. Von Arent turned Sachs's workshop from a respectable burgher's parlour into a craftsman's place of work which, as he himself noted, was intended to convey the message, 'Honour work; respect the workers.' The only scene which fell outside this framework of old German historicity was the festival meadow which, with its parallel row of flags, resembled the site of the party rally; it really had become 'a national issue' after all. Benno von Arent provided the same sets and costumes as those authorized by Hitler for the reopening of the Berlin Opera on 17 November 1935, for the Reich's theatre festival week in Munich in 1936, for Danzig in 1938, for the 'Festival of German Youth' at the National Theatre in Weimar in 1939 and for the new production at the theatre in Linz in 1941, which Hitler subsidized out of his own private income. Paraphrasing one of the slogans of the time, one could speak of 'One nation, one Reich, one set-design.' It is characteristic of the cultural policies of all totalitarian regimes that attempts are always made to condition their loyal subjects' individual feelings so as to produce a unity of thought and experience. Another feature of these productions which was typical of the period was the massed crowd scenes which were mustered on stage particularly for the scene on the festival meadow. This had been a striking aspect of the new production at the Berlin City

Opera as early as May 1933, as well as at the Bayreuth Festival production that same year. At the gala performance held to mark the 1939 party congress and conducted by Wilhelm Furtwängler, the chorus was made up of the combined choruses from Nuremberg and Vienna.

This view of a lofty and sacred German art was put to practical use and recast as a rejection of all that was foreign and as a duty to prevent German art from being besmirched by the 'taints' of non-Aryan artistic influences. It was only a short step from this to the suppression and rejection of anything foreign and from a state of terror and barbarism perpetrated in the name of art. The Israel Philharmonic Orchestra, which had been founded in 1936 and which as late as April 1938 had performed the Preludes to Acts I and III of *Lohengrin* under the baton of Arturo Toscanini, dropped the Prelude to *Die Meistersinger von Nürnberg* from its programme following the Crystal night pogrom of 9/10 November 1938. Ever since then Wagner's music has been outlawed in Israel, notably with the orchestra in question, although no official ban was ever imposed. In the autumn of 1981 Zubin Mehta attempted to lift this ban at a concert in Tel Aviv.

Die Meistersinger von Nürnberg was the only work to be performed in 1943 and 1944 during the so-called War-time Festivals, which were organized by the Nazi group 'Strength through Joy'. Tickets were given away to soldiers, the war wounded, workers in the armaments industry and hospital workers as a token of recognition for their contribution to the war effort. While the towns of Germany were being reduced to rubble, the dream of a glorious past, when German culture had flourished in those very same towns, was once again being evoked in the Festspielhaus. Was it still possible for these audiences to hope that, if nothing else, then at least German art might survive the wholesale destruction which was reducing the Reich to rubble?

In his 1939 lecture, 'Die Wurzeln des Nazismus' ('The Roots of Nazism'), Ernst Bloch criticized the fact that it was 'now almost only in a Nazi context' that the name of Wagner came to the lips of 'educated anti-Fascists'; he went on, 'The music of the Nazis is not the Prelude to *Die Meistersinger* but "Die Fahne hoch" ("Hoist the flag"); they have no other claim to honour and no other claim can or should be given them.'

But the generation of those who survived the war was bound to see this misappropriated work in particular in the light of their own experiences. For the musicologist and philosopher, Theodor Wiesengrund Adorno, Beckmesser was the protagonist in 'The Jew Among Thorns' – one of the nastier of Grimms' fairy tales – and the riot scene was interpreted as a pogrom. 'Can you still put up with Hans Sachs's theatricality and that stupid girl, dear little Eva?' Thomas Mann wrote Emil Preetorius in 1949. In spite of all this, the opera remained viable. As Hans Mayer remarked, the work did not sink down to the same depths as those plumbed by the plays of Otto Ludwig who, like Wagner, was also born in 1813, any more than it sank to the same level of insignificance as that which has greeted the artistic achievements of the Third Reich, for the latter are totally different creations. As Mayer goes on to point out, 'This of course has something to do with the tremendous musician that Wagner was; but not just with Wagner. Surprisingly even the intellectual contradictions prove to be fertile.' All those productions of *Die Meistersinger von Nürnberg* which have been staged during the last thirty years and which have not attempted to deny this fact have been able to develop their own independent existence far more than was ever possible throughout the preceding decades.

Many theatres, on the other hand, acted as if nothing had changed and if the theatres' warehouses survived the war intact, the opera continued to be performed with the old sets and costumes. Outside Germany the work was treated in a surprisingly uninhibited way, with the controversial passages simply being cut. The opera was performed in Paris in 1948, 1949 and 1952, and in Copenhagen in 1951. The new production at La Scala, Milan, opened two days after the end of the war, on 10 May 1945, in the temporary surroundings of the Teatro Lirico, the Scala itself having suffered considerable damage in an air raid in 1943; a second new production followed soon afterwards in 1947 in the reopened house. In 1945 Guido Marussig designed marvellously clear, bright sets reflecting an agreeable sobriety of style and devoid of any sense of local Nuremberg colour. Otto Klemperer conducted a new production of the work, uncut, in Budapest in 1949; the first night was given in the presence of the Hungarian head of state, who decorated Klemperer with a medal.

The impoverished makeshift theatres of the immediate post-war period generally reopened their doors with works which were uncomplicatedly classical, such as Goethe's *Iphigenie auf Tauris*, Lessing's *Nathan der Weise* ('Nathan the Wise') or Beethoven's *Fidelio,* in other words with works which appealed to the whole of humanity and among which it was no longer (or at least not yet again) possible to include *Die* first time in the history of the Festspielhaus audiences loudly booed the performances): he opera-houses which sprang up all over Germany throughout the 1950s and 1960s once more required something rather more festive. *Die Meistersinger von Nürnberg* again became the most popular opera for such official occasions, whether at the Lindenoper in Berlin in 1955, at Mönchengladbach in 1959, at the National Theatre in Munich in 1963, at Würzburg in 1966 or at Wiesbaden in 1978.

What was striking about the first-act sets during these years were the tall, bright naves with huge windows admitting floods of light. Much the same was true of the rebuilding work carried out at this time on Gothic churches, where white or clear glass was preferred to brightly coloured stained glass. Looking back at this now, we may perhaps see here an attempt at enlightenment after a period of comparative gloom. For the second act, however, and particularly for the sets for the festival meadow, in the third act, Nuremberg was rebuilt as it had been before the war, with its old familiar skyline. The process of rebuilding the country was carried over onto the stage, as well, together with something else which was typical of the period, namely the suppression of the most recent past.

Wieland Wagner's 1956 Bayreuth production, coming as it did in the mood evoked by the early years of the economic miracle, was bound to cause offence, since it expressed the painful truth that the Nuremberg of *Die Meistersinger von Nürnberg* no longer existed: 'the symbol went up in flames,' to quote Hans Mayer. 'The Mastersingers without Nuremberg' was the way one critic described Wieland's production. Experience had taught this generation that the name of Nuremberg stood for party rallies, the Nuremberg Laws, the Nuremberg Trials and total destruction. Wieland was convinced that the last thing *Die Meistersinger von Nürnberg* could be described as was a 'milieu comedy'. He offered local colour only in a referential way, only inasmuch as what shone through it was 'something general, symbolic and divorced from local colour', since 'Wagner had never created a more humane work.'

His stage was a 'singers' stage', a 'small artificial theatre'. He himself wondered whether this 'Spitzweg* atmosphere', which Adorno had described as being 'functional in the matter', was really 'an essential element in the piece'; and he came to the conclusion that the dominant mood of Act II was 'the romantic irony of a Shakespearean summer's night'. Wieland also knew precisely the reason for the enormous sense of hostility which this new in-

terpretation provoked in the audience (for the first time in the history of the Festspielhaus audiences loudly booed the performances): he had stripped away the traditional 'sentimental cosiness' which, like his grandfather, he refused to accept as part of the work. For Wieland, *Die Meistersinger von Nürnberg* was 'a work of music's great past and its great post-Wagnerian future, standing somewhere between Bach and Debussy, as well as between *Figaro* and *Der Rosenkavalier.*'.

It was as a satyr play, in the original sense intended by Wagner, that Wieland designed his second Bayreuth production in 1963. The action enfolded 'on the wooden framework of the theatre of Shakespeare and Hans Sachs [...], a theatre within a theatre', since the comedy 'does not need the conventions of the illusionistic operatic stage'. 'I would ask you to think along somewhat Brechtian lines,' Wieland wrote to the costume designer Curt Palm on 18 September 1962. It was 'an amusing game played by craftsmen, cobblers, bakers, soap-boilers, goldsmiths, apprentices, cooks, teenage girls, knights and nightwatchmen.' Wieland justified his view of the opera by pointing out that true masterpieces are 'capable of the most varied interpretation' and that they are a challenge 'to constant experimentation'. This production provoked a debate about the possibilities and limitations of interpreting Wagner's works in such a way as to make them relevant for contemporary audiences. Whereas Hans Mayer spoke out in favour of the view that in this interpretation Nuremberg made an impact not as 'part of the background' but as 'the very substance of the opera', Marcel Reich-Ranicki insisted that Hans Sachs should be denazified and that the 'prestigious festival opera' had been turned into a 'harlequinade'. He demanded that any new production of the opera should take as its starting-point the Nuremberg not of the sixteenth century but of the period during which the work was written, a suggestion which was subsequently taken up by a handful of later producers and designers.

In the same way, Joachim Herz staged the opera as a comedy about art when he produced *Die Meistersinger von Nürnberg* on the occasion of the reopening of the Leipzig Opera in 1960. The sets by Rudolf Heinrich consisted of an anti-illusionistic framework of scaffolding such as would have been used in Hans Sachs's own time, with wooden galleries on both sides of the stage, separated

---

* Carl Spitzweg: German painter and illustrator (1808–1885)

from the River Pegnitz which was labelled in the Brechtian manner. Central to the interpretation of both Herz and Heinrich was 'the discussion about art', a discussion which was enacted in 'the cultural setting of a late medieval town'. They wanted to show 'a reflection of reality, readable and realizable', a popular play rather than a festival opera. Their production of the work was set during the German Renaissance, when a new period of history dawned with the Reformation. The tragicomedy of Beckmesser who for Herz was 'the most German character in this German opera' consisted in the fact that, as Herz himself said, 'he upheld tradition without knowing how to preserve it properly, as a result of which he stood in the way of reform.' The song which Beckmesser sang on the festival meadow was not to the garbled text of the Prize Song but to the original words which Sachs had written down in his workshop: these words were sung to the tune of Beckmesser's serenade, transposed into a minor key. In this way, words and music failed to match, which underlined the point about the work's being 'a comedy about art'. It is true that Beckmesser was ridiculed and sent packing but during Walther's performance of the Prize Song he returned to join the crowd once again and listened to the proper way in which the song should have been sung. The possibility of placing the chorus on wooden galleries, rather like those found in the theatre of Sachs's own day, and thereby improving their aural impact, had been exploited by Robert Kautsky in Vienna as early as 1955 and was used subsequently by Günther Schneider-Siemssen for the 1977 Stockholm production of the work. The reopening of the National Theatre in Munich in 1963 provided Rudolf Hartmann with a chance, in his sunlit set for the festival meadow, to show off the enormous new stage to an astonished audience. The guilds entered in a loose formation from the back of the stage. The designer, Helmut Jürgens, dispensed with the usual backdrop showing the town in the distance; instead, the three-dimensional insignia of the various guilds, with their architectonic motifs, made up an outline of the town. One idea which was later imitated elsewhere was that of framing the foreground with a high tented roof. Jürgen Rose used the idea in Vienna in 1977, and in Munich in 1979 he went on to build an actual beer tent in which the people of Nuremberg romped around in Franconian national costume. As early as 1936, in his production for the Salzburg Festival, Robert Kautsky had used tents on the festival meadow as a means of structuring the scene. The

other alternative, which had been in use since the 1920s, was to have the action unfold in front of the city wall, an idea which was still to be found in San Francisco in 1951 and in Stockholm in 1956. The traditional backdrop with a view of the town continued in use, although the simplest solution, which was adopted by smaller theatres, was still an empty stage decorated by flags, standards and garlands. Attempts were also made, particularly during the 1960s, to perform the opera on a unit set, or else to escape from the realism of Old Nuremberg by using a collage technique or by including referential details of late medieval craftsmanship.

It says much for the continuity of attempts to come to terms with Wagner's work in New Bayreuth that, on the occasion of his production to mark the one-hundredth anniversary of the first performance of the opera, Wolfgang Wagner started out from Wieland's basic insights and brought them into a new focus with the help of his own stylistic means. What was characteristic of this production was the state of suspense between worldliness and transparency. The motto for the basic structure of the sets was order and proportion: the scenic elements were composed of woodcut-like contours, reminiscent of Tudor beams, the coloured, transparent surfaces between the contours were lit from behind by xenon-light projections, thus breaking up the space into light. On a second layer of meaning, this also helped to convey optically the basic conflict of the opera between, on the one hand, legitimate form, committed to particular rules, and, on the other, creative imagination. The festival meadow was a tract of open countryside, an uncluttered space for cheerful, festive merry-making, with the coarsely comical entry of the guilds and with municipal bandsmen, mimes and acrobats.

In a conversation with Walter Jens in 1973, Wolfgang Wagner developed an idea which had earlier been hinted at by Joachim Herz and which fitted well into the conciliatory and tolerant atmosphere of this particular festival meadow scene. This idea, which he incorporated into his production that same summer, was to have Beckmesser remain on stage after his disastrous failure, rather than his being hounded out of office and deprived of his rank: rules and genius require a mutual corrective. The same idea was then taken up by Götz Friedrich in Stockholm in 1977 and by Michael Hampe in Cologne in 1980.

In his second Bayreuth production, Wolfgang showed an even greater concern for the psychological insights which his grandfather had achieved in this particular work, as well as an unemotional appeal for humanity and tolerance, an appeal which he recognized as the most important element in the work. A youthful Sachs, a romantically sensitive knight Stolzing, who dreamt about *minnesang,* and a self-conscious, elegant town clerk, Beckmesser, who, in Wolfgang's words, 'had failed to obtain the chair in Altdorf' but who single-mindedly exploited his position of power in order to further his career: these were the three individuals orbiting around the central figure of Eva, whose mind was already made up from the outset. They were all victims of the delusion which rules the lives of men. The fact that *Die Meistersinger von Nürnberg* is able to convey such insights into the weaknesses and contradictions in human nature and that it can do so in a way that is not hurtful or condemnatory but which shows a hard-won, sceptical sense of humour which is based upon the conviction *homo sum, humani nil a me alienum puto* ('I am a man and deem nothing human alien to me') and which can smile in a calm and understanding manner: all this is what distinguishes the work for us and proclaims it as a true masterpiece.

Der Ring des Nibelungen

Der Ring des Nibelungen. Ein Bühnenfestspiel aufzuführen in drei Tagen und einem Vorabend ('The Ring of the Nibelung. A stage festival play to be performed over three days and a preliminary evening'). Richard Wagner's *magnum opus,* is made up of four individual works: *Das Rheingold* (Preliminary Evening), *Die Walküre* (First Day), *Siegfried* (Second Day) and *Götterdämmerung* ('Twilight of the Gods')–(Third Day). Between the first prose draft of 1848 and the final completion of the score in 1874, a period of twenty-six years elapsed. If one subtracts the twelve-year interval following the completion of Act II of *Siegfried,* Wagner still required fourteen years to complete the tetralogy, his 'world poem' which, as he told Franz Liszt in a letter of 11 February 1853, contained 'the world's beginning and its destruction'.

A plan such as this was far in advance of anything that the European operatic stage had previously managed to attain, even taking into account its boldest achievements. Wagner's claim, that in conceiving the work he had never seriously considered the possibility of a performance, sounds almost self-defensive; and it was only hesitantly and confidentially that he initially informed even his friends of the full extent of his plans. It followed logically from this that in carrying out that plan he disregarded the limitations of traditional opera-houses and that the idea increasingly took shape in his mind of creating his own theatre in which to stage such an extraordinary work. The 'common-sense' reaction to such an undertaking as that of staging the creation and destruction of the world in four operas was to dismiss the whole scheme as pure megalomania.

The story of how *Der Ring des Nibelungen* came into being is told in *Eine Mittheilung an meine Freunde.* Following his return from Paris, Wagner's favourite reading was works dealing with German antiquity. His longing for home could not be satisfied by 'present reality' and its hateful coldness. He felt the urge to explore that 'archetypally native el-ement' which confronts us in the poetic works of the past. 'It is by means of images of the past that we attempt to give recognizable physical form to all those wishes and burning impulses which in truth carry us over into the *future.*' In his scientific curiosity he proceeded 'step by step into the depths of antiquity [...] through the poetry of the Middle Ages and down to the bottommost level of ancient archetypally German myth.' And here he came upon 'the youthfully beautiful *human being* in the most exuberant freshness of his essential vigour.' It was no longer 'the historically conventional figure whose outward garb was bound to be of greater interest than his actual form; but actual, naked man in which I was able to observe every rush of blood, every twitch of his powerful muscles in unhampered and total freedom of movement: *true man* himself.' Only now did it occur to Wagner that this true man of the Nibelung myth, Siegfried, could be the hero of a drama, a thought which would never have occured to him during his reading of the medieval *Nibelungenlied.*

The result of his deliberations was the essay *Die Wibelungen. Weltgeschichte aus der Sage* ('The Wibelungs. World history from legend'), written in the late summer of 1848. Here Wagner developed his philosophy of history in an extremely bold and highly personal view of the history of mankind and, in particular, the history of the Franks. History books which concerned themselves solely with 'the history of sovereigns and princes' instead of with the 'history of the people' remained close to the 'pragmatic surface of events'. Religion and legend provided information about men's motives: they represented the view which the common people had formed 'of the essential nature of things and of mankind [...] In their thoughts and creative activities the common people are invar-

Bayreuth Festival, 1876
Das Rheingold
Costumes: Carl Emil Doepler
Costume design for Wotan.
One can see why Cosima spoke
of 'Red Indian Chiefs'. The
blue cloak on which Wagner
had insisted remained a
characteristic feature of
Wotan's costume for decades.

Théâtre National de l'Opéra,
Paris, 14 November 1909
Das Rheingold
Costumes: Joseph Porphyre
Pinchon. Wotan: Jean-François
Delmas
Costume design for Wotan for
the first Paris production.
There is still the same
knee-length, tunic-like costume
and cloak, but the only
ornamental accessory is now a
wide belt. As a Germanic deity
Wotan wears a garland of
oak-leaves. The costume was
made for the singer
Jean-François Delmas.

Metropolitan Opera, New York, 1912 season
Das Rheingold
Conductor: Alfred Hertz.
Donner: William Hinshaw.
Wotan: Hermann Weil. Fasolt: Putnam Griswold. Fafner: Basil Ruysdael
Donner raises his hammer against the giants Fasolt and Fafner, while Wotan intervenes. Typical of the pre-1914 style of acting, a style which gave rise to the cliché of Wagner's 'bearskin-clad Teutons'.

iably highly gifted and truthful, whereas the learned historian [...] is pedantically untruthful.' These lines were written in 1848, the same year as the score of *Lohengrin* was completed. Whereas in *Lohengrin* Wagner required history as a material background for the myth, the historical element had ceased to play a part in his present deliberations, which were to lead him back to the source of myth. He abandoned his plans to write an opera about Frederick Barbarossa.

In order to understand the conceptual background of the tetralogy, the reader will find it useful briefly to review those ideas mentioned in the *Wibelungen* essay which have bearing on the *Ring* since, in writing the essay, Wagner was attempting to clarify his own thoughts on the Nibelung myth and to interpret the course of world history as a natural process of cyclical change, which preserves the world through death. Wotan, Siegfried's fight with the dragon and the Nibelung treasure are interpreted as symbols of power and domination. According to early man's way of thinking, light and day were regarded as the basis of existence, as the generative principle, the father-figure and the god; darkness and night were what was inimical and terrifying. As a common, fundamental principle of the religions of all nations there developed a moral awareness which, in the antitheses of night and day, elaborated the dichotomy between the beneficial and the

harmful, the friendly and the hostile, and between good and evil.

The legend of the Nibelungs is the tribal legend of the Franks. In the 'religious mythology of the Scandinavians', the black elves, or Nibelungs, are the opposite of the light elves who dwelt in heaven. The black elves are subterranean beings, 'children begotten by the night and by death', burrowing through the earth in search of metals which they melt and forge into jewellery and weapons for themselves, and into the Nibelung hoard. In its natural state the hoard consists of the 'metallic entrails of the earth, [...] it is the earth itself in all its splendour which, at break of day, as the sun casts forth its brightest rays, we recognize and enjoy as our property, now that night has been dispelled which, in eerie terribleness, had held its dark dragon's wings stretched out over the world's opulent treasure.' The Nibelungs set to work in their forges and convert the hoard into 'weapons, a ruler's coronet and treasures of gold'; it becomes the embodiment of all worldly power, since it incorporates 'the means by which to win and retain power, as well as being the emblem of that power itself.' Siegfried, 'the individualized light- and sun-god', wins the treasure by slaying the dragon which guarded it. But his acquisition of the hoard is also the cause of his death, since the dragon's heirs strive to recover what it had once possessed. The battle between light and darkness

National Theatre, Prague,
13 March 1915
Das Rheingold
Producer: Robert Polak.
Wotan: Otakar Chmel. Loge:
Antonín Lebeda
An early attempt at
three-dimensional scenery, with
solid elements in the
foreground. After all the
various earlier experiments, the
citadel of the gods had now
become a tower-like structure
surmounted by a dome and was
to remain so for a number of
years.

continues. The victory over 'the monster of the primeval night of chaos' is the original meaning of Siegfried's fight with the dragon, 'a fight such as that which Apollo fought with the dragon Python.' But just as nature dictates that day should yield to night, the dragon-slayer is thus himself brought down: the god becomes human and mortal, something which symbolizes the struggle of the human race, 'which progresses from life to death, from victory to defeat and from joy to sorrow, and thus through constant rejuvenation actively becomes conscious of the eternal element in man and nature.' The 'embodiment of this eternal movement, in other words of life itself' is Wotan (Zeus), the supreme deity, whose existence derived from 'man's more recent, more sublime awareness of himself', as a result of which he is 'more abstract' than the old nature-gods.

The striving after the Nibelung hoard is the striving for total domination. The image of the hoard contains within it the ambivalence of the concepts of power and domination: on the one hand, there is the domination which

finds expression as the natural moral responsibility of the individual towards those who have been entrusted to his care and which is found in a historical context in the progenitor, who is both king and priest, or *pontifex maximus;* on the other hand, there is domination as an egoistic and animal passion in man, involving the suppression and subjugation of other nations. The legend of an original town or citadel built by the Cyclopes (as was the case with Troy), as a symbol of power and a sanctuary, as the dwelling of the priest-king, can be found among all nations. The Greeks called it Olympus, while the Scandinavian name was Asgard. The Capitol of the Romans may originally have been something similar.

In their later development these towns gained control over other, less important towns, often by means of 'violent despotism' and repression, resulting in insurrection and the destruction of the original citadel. 'This may have been the first universal struggle for the Nibelung hoard.' In the course of history, the Nibelung hoard 'sought refuge in the realm of poetry and ideas: only one form of

Das Rheingold, 1924
Designer: Adolphe Appia
Design for scene 1. In the
depths of the Rhine. Absence of
any naturalistic means of
stylistic expression: the bed of
the Rhine is structured with
steps and platforms. The rocky
ledge in the centre has been
replaced by a sort of altar on
which the gold rests. Clear
emphasis on the 'hieratic'
element which Appia considered
indispensable to the work. This
design was used in Basle in
1924. In December 1976 the
set-designer Karl-Ernst
Hermann included a similar
block-like structure in his
designs for Peter Stein's
production at the Paris Opéra.

Municipal Stages, Frankfurt am
Main, 1925
Das Rheingold
Designer: Ludwig Sievert
Design for Erda's scene. A huge
representation of the goddess
Erda rises up out of the
ground. This effect was
technically quite simple: a wide
piece of fabric was raised up,
containing the large face mask.
The concept, however, was
better in theory than in practice,
since the singer had to be
positioned at the side of the set
and the visible figure of the
goddess remained silent,
effectively destroying the
illusion.

Municipal Stages, Duisburg,
1922/1923
Das Rheingold
Producer: Saladin Schmitt.
Designer: Johannes Schröder
A sketch for the closing scene
by Schröder. The effect is not
of a stage-set for the theatre
but a vision, with a projection
of Valhalla seen as a cristalline
structure. There is no
practicable rainbow bridge but a
rainbow which arches over the
whole stage. Schröder was not
afraid of monumentalism: his
sets were intended to create an
impression of 'powerful
grandeur, like the music'.

earth deposit had remained behind as sediment: *real estate.'* In the Nibelung myth one could recognize men's views 'on the nature of property and possessions'. Whereas the hoard, as it appeared in the oldest religious concepts about it, was still 'the splendour of the earth which the light of day revealed to everyone,' and whereas it later became 'the hero's power-giving booty, wrested by him as a reward [...] from his vanquished foe,' it is now interpreted as property and as a material possession and, as such, it is defended and fought for: 'And so we see blood, passion, love and hatred, in short what, from a material and intellectual point of view, are purely human determining and motivating factors, actively striving to acquire the hoard; and we see man, restless and suffering, and doomed to a death which he himself foresees as a result of his deed, of his victory and, above all, of his having possessed the hoard; it is this that stands at the head of all ideas about the primal relationship of the acquisition of property.' Value was transferred from the individual to the thing he possessed. It was not the virtue of the person concerned which was of importance, but 'the constantly increasing value placed on property'. Human nobility

came to be esteemed far less than actual possessions. 'Property now gave men the right which man had previously transferred to property of his own accord [...] Anyone who had had a share in property and who knew how to acquire it was regarded – *but only from this point onwards* – as the natural mainstay of public power.' And what did 'the poor people' do, without possessions and hence excluded from power? They sang, wrote and read the lays of the Nibelungs, since these latter were 'the only share of the hoard's inheritance that had been left to them'.

Immediately after the *Wibelungen* essay Wagner wrote *Die Nibelungensage (Mythus)* ('The Nibelung Legend [Myth]'), which he later published under the title of *Der Nibelungen-Mythus. Als Entwurf zu einem Drama* ('The Nibelung Myth. As draft for a drama'). In it he retold the entire course of the tetralogy's action, although at this time he was still only interested in dramatizing the final part, *Siegfried's Tod* ('Siegfried's Death').

The race of Nibelungs, sprung from the womb of night and death, lives in clefts beneath the earth, mining and forging metals. The Nibelung Alberich steals the Rhinegold and forges from it a ring which gives him su-

Bayreuth Festival, 1951
Das Rheingold
Designer: Wieland Wagner
Design for scenes 2 and 4, an
open space on a mountain top.
Consistent application of
Appia's ideas. Valhalla is a vast,
monolithic structure, rising up
into the flies, lacking any real
sense of architectural coherence
and independent of any
particular style. Between it and
the circular acting area are the
depths of the Rhine, from
which mists arise.

State Opera, Vienna,
23 December 1958
Das Rheingold
Producer: Herbert von Karajan.
Designer: Emil Preetorius
Preetorius's final series of
designs for *Der Ring des
Nibelungen* were for von
Karajan's new production in
Vienna. Preetorius had
previously provided designs for
Bayreuth in 1933, the Berlin
State Opera in 1936, La Scala in
1938 and Rome in 1953/1954.
His style remained basically
unchanged throughout the
whole of this period, although
the Vienna production was
much simplified. For decades
the arrangement of this scene
was the same: the acting area at
the front, beyond it a space
indicating a deep valley through
which the Rhine is presumed to
flow, and, projected onto the
backcloth, the castle of
Valhalla, formed of piled-up
blocks. This arrangement
basically derives from Appia's
designs.

preme power over the Nibelungs. He amasses
the Nibelung hoard, whose greatest jewel is
the *tarnhelm* which enables the wearer to assume whatever shape he pleases. His brother
Mime has forged it for him. The race of
giants is threatened by Alberich's lust for
power. 'This conflict is exploited by the race
of gods in their progress towards world domination.' Wotan engages the giants to build a
castle for the gods 'from which they will be
able to order and rule the world securely'. By
way of payment the giants demand the Nibelung treasure. 'It is thanks to their extreme
cleverness that the gods succeed in capturing
Alberich; he is forced to ransom his life by

handing over the hoard to them.' He asks to
retain only the ring. The gods, who are aware
of the power of the ring, wrest it from Alberich, who then places a curse upon it: 'It shall
be the destruction of all who possess it.'
Through their obstinacy the giants gain the
ring from Wotan, who yields when the three
Norns warn him of the downfall of the gods;
the giants then prevail upon a monstrous
dragon to guard the hoard. The Nibelungs
are subjugated and Alberich 'broods cease-
lessly on how to regain the ring'. The giants,
however, 'do not know how to use their
power': the dragon 'has lain on the hoard
since time immemorial, inertly terrible'. The

Bayreuth Festival, 1965
Das Rheingold
Designer: Wieland Wagner.
Conductor: Karl Böhm. Wotan:
Theo Adam. Loge: Wolfgang
Windgassen. Fasolt: Martti
Talvela. Fafner: Kurt Böhme
The giants are given the
Nibelung hoard as a ransom for
Freia. In most stagings the gold
was in bars or blocks, but in
this production Wieland
Wagner designed it to look like
a female idol, the goddess in
surrogate form. African
fetishes, prehistoric fertility
images and the famous
Willendorf Venus were the
models for this archetype.

Lyric Opera, Chicago,
13 November 1971
Das Rheingold
Conductor: Ferdinand Leitner.
Wotan: Hubert Hofmann.
Loge: Richard Holm. Freia:
Jeannine Altmeyer. Fafner:
Hans Sotin. Fasolt: Bengt
Rundgren. Donner: Gerd
Nienstedt. Fricka: Grace
Hoffman. Froh: Frank Little.
In Peter Lehmann's production,
these sets by Ekkehard Grübler
are predominantly abstract and
stylized in design. The stage
area in scene 4 is made up of
angular platforms and steps of
varying height, which are placed
against each other.

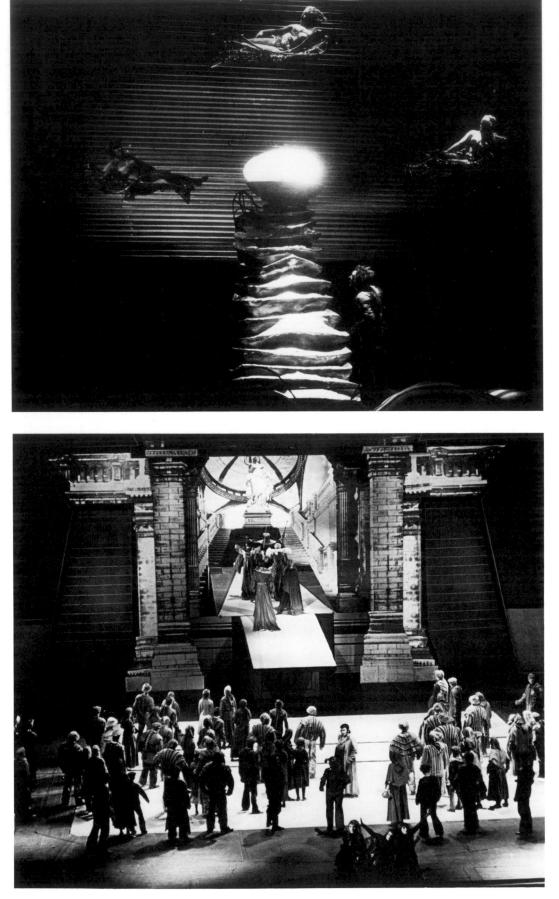

Municipal Theatre, Leipzig,
7 April 1973
Das Rheingold
Producer: Joachim Herz.
Designer: Rudolf Heinrich.
Conductor: Gert Bahner
Suspended in the hammocks,
the Rhinemaidens hover around
the glittering gold. The
swimming baskets in use around
the turn of the century looked
much the same.

Municipal Theatre, Leipzig,
7 April 1973
Das Rheingold
Producer: Joachim Herz. Sets
and costumes: Rudolf Heinrich.
Conductor: Gert Bahner
The closing scene, the entry of
the gods into Valhalla, as an act
of self-congratulation. 'Valhalla
– this castle won with plundered
gold – radiates a glorious light
for the benefit of the race of
Wotan. The light-elves enter it,
flaunting their magnificent
splendour, and pour scorn on
the Rhinemaidens'
lamentations. Loge, the roving
god, knows what is happening:
the light-elves are hastening to
their own destruction' (Joachim
Herz). The gang of
construction workers who
erected Valhalla watch as the
spectacle unfolds. Socio-critical
element in the confrontation
between the ruling and the
working class.

Royal Opera House, Covent
Garden, London, 30 September
1974
Das Rheingold
Producer: Götz Friedrich.
Designer: Josef Svoboda.
Costumes: Ingrid Rosell.
Conductor: Colin Davis
The closing scene, the entry of
the gods into Valhalla. *Der
Ring des Nibelungen* neither
interpreted as a timeless
document nor restricted to the
nineteenth century. Mythology
as alienation and identification
at one and the same time. The
fable of the *Ring* as a
permanent search for a principle
which might bring an end to the
divisions between power,
revolution and love. The stage
picture in *Das Rheingold*
structures the world
hierarchically: the gods at the
top, the Rhine in the middle
and the Nibelungs below. A
similar concept was found in
medieval mystery plays and
early Soviet revolutionary
drama. The scene of action is
not the circle of Greek tragedy
but the square of a theatre of
mime, suitable for a *comédie
humaine.*

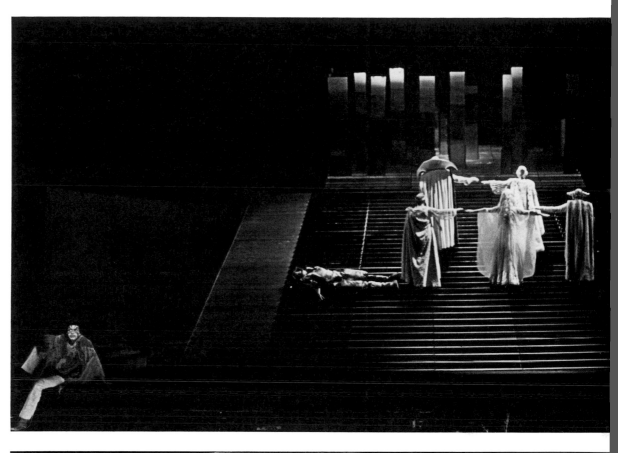

Grand Théâtre, Geneva,
16 January 1975
Das Rheingold
Producer: Jean-Claude Riber.
Designer: Joseph Svoboda
Svoboda's metallically glinting
abstract set. Structural forms
involving an aesthetic handling
of space and light, and intended
to convey the message that
music, speech and stage form a
synaesthetic whole. As in
Wagner's *Wibelungen* essay, the
starting-point is the solar myth.
The producer asked the
question, 'Myth from a
test-tube?' and answered it by
reference to his desire not to
stage any particular historical
situation, nor any political
programme or ideology, but to
show those conditions which,
although corresponding to our
own experience of reality, are
beyond human powers. It is not
a concrete, historical
interpretation, but an
imaginative one.

Bayreuth Festival, 1976
Das Rheingold
Designer: Richard Peduzzi.
Costumes: Jacques Schmidt.
Conductor: Pierre Boulez
The bed of the Rhine in the new production to mark the Festival's centenary, with Peduzzi's famous and infamous hydro-electric dam. According to Patrice Chéreau's interpretation, the dam is a 'threatening structure', a 'piece of theatrical machinery' by which the element of water can be represented, as well as an allegory of energy. The producer attempted to create a 'mythological presence' by presenting mythology in the emblematic images of our own day.

gods rule in new-found splendour. They restore order to the world, unite the elements through wise decrees and devote themselves to caring for the human race. 'But the peace on the basis of which they came to power does not rest upon appeasement; it has been achieved by force and cunning.' Moral awareness is the purpose behind their higher world order, but the injustice which the gods pursue clings to them. Wotan cannot eradicate that injustice without committing a new one: 'Only an act of free will on the part of an individual who himself is independent of the gods and who is capable of taking their guilt upon himself and atoning for it, can break the magic spell, and in man the gods see the possibility of such a free will.' They transfer their divinity to man, who thus no longer needs divine protection and who lives according to the dictates of free will. The aim of the gods, which is to educate man to eradicate their own guilt, could be achieved if they 'were to annihilate themselves in the creation of mankind'.

'The redeeming hero' must arise from the race of the Volsungs: 'he will achieve full awareness of his independent power and thus become capable of freely calling his boldest deed his own, in full sight of the knowledge that he must atone for that deed with his own death'. The Volsung twins Siegmund and Sieglinde fall in love with each other and produce a son. Hunding, Sieglinde's husband, sets out to avenge their double crime of incest and adultery. Wotan is forced to decree Sieg-

mund's destruction. The Valkyrie maiden, Brünnhilde, Wotan's daughter, protects Siegmund in the ensuing combat, in spite of her father's orders. Wotan holds out his spear and shatters the sword which he had once given to Siegmund. As a punishment for her disobedience, Brünnhilde is driven from the company of Valkyries and banished to a rock on which Wotan places her in a deep sleep: she shall belong to the first man who awakens her. Brünnhilde 'begs that, out of mercy, Wotan should surround the rock with the terrors of fire so that only the bravest of heroes shall be able to win her'.

Sieglinde flees into the wilderness, where she gives birth to Siegfried, 'who shall bring peace ['Friede'] through victory ['Sieg']'; she then dies. Alberich's brother Mime brings up the child and, once the boy has reached manhood, gives him the fragments of his father's shattered sword, which Siegfried forges into a new weapon. Mime lures him into slaying the dragon which guards the Nibelung treasure. After Siegfried has killed the beast 'his fingers are burnt by the dragon's blood and when he places them in his mouth to soothe them, he involuntarily tastes the blood and thus suddenly understands the language of the woodbirds who are singing all around him.' They direct him to the Nibelung hoard and warn him of Mime, who is plotting to murder him in order to gain the hoard for himself. Siegfried kills Mime and takes the ring and *tarnhelm* from the hoard. The woodbirds advise him to win Brünnhilde, the most

San Francisco Opera, 1977
Das Rheingold
Producer: Paul Heger.
Designer: Wolfram Skalicki
Modern projection techniques make it possible to create the illusion of flowing water. The Rhinemaidens, however, did not swim, but danced round their rocky ledge.

glorious of women. Siegfried sets off, reaches the rock, passes through the flames and awakens Brünnhilde. 'He marries her with Alberich's ring which he places on her finger.' But then Siegfried succumbs to the urge to ride forth to seek new adventures; Brünnhilde confides in him 'her secret wisdom enshrined in lofty precepts, and she warns him against the dangers of deception and faithlessness.'

The race of the Gibichungs can similarly trace its ancestry back to the gods. The mother of Gunther and Gudrun 'was once ravished by Alberich, to whom she bore an illegitimate son, Hagen.' Just as the desires and hopes of the gods rest with Siegfried, so Alberich pins all his hopes of regaining the ring on Hagen. It is the latter who shall bring about Siegfried's downfall. Siegfried arrives at the Gibichung court on the Rhine. Hagen has Gudrun offer him drugged a cup of welcome, 'the effect of which is that it causes Siegfried to forget his experiences with Brünnhilde, including his betrothal to her.' Siegfried desires Gudrun as his wife, and Gunther promises her to him on the condition that Siegfried help him to win Brünnhilde. 'They agree to become blood brothers and swear oaths to that effect.' 'For the first and only time', Siegfried uses 'his power as lord of the Nibelungs' in order to change himself into Gunther's shape with the help of the *tarnhelm* and thus to woo Brünnhilde for him. In the process he tears the ring from her finger. Gunther and Brünnhilde arrive at the Gibichung castle

where they are welcomed by Siegfried and Gudrun. Brünnhilde is beside herself when she sees Siegfried as Gudrun's husband. She recognizes her ring on his finger and 'cries out at the deception which has been perpetrated against her; she is filled with the most terrible thirst to be avenged on Siegfried.' Hagen offers to avenge her honour. Together with Gunther they decide on Siegfried's death. The following day, while out hunting by the Rhine, Siegfried comes upon three mermaids, 'prophetic daughters of the watery depths from which Alberich once snatched the bright Rhinegold in order to forge from it the powerful and baleful ring.' They demand the ring from Siegfried since its curse will be nullified if it is returned to the waters of the Rhine 'and thus dissolved once again in its original element.' Siegfried refuses to give them the ring. 'Guiltless, he has taken upon himself the guilt of the gods; he himself atones for their injustice by virtue of his defiance and independence.' The Rhinemaidens predict disaster for him, but Siegfried answers, 'That is why I laugh at your threats: the ring remains mine and this is how I cast my life away.' (He picks up a lump of earth and tosses it back over his shoulder.)

The hunting party led by Gunther and Hagen gathers around Siegfried. He 'sings to them of his youth: his adventures with Mime, the slaying of the dragon and how it came about that he can now understand the song of the woodbirds'. Memories of Brünnhilde come flooding back. Hagen thrusts his spear between Siegfried's shoulder-blades. Only now does Gunther realize 'the connection between all these incomprehensible events and Brünnhilde'. Siegfried utters the words, 'Brünnhild! Brünnhild! I greet you!' and then dies. His body is placed outside the Gibichung hall. Hagen demands the ring as his

Bayreuth Festival, 1976
Das Rheingold
Producer: Patrice Chéreau.
Costumes: Jacques Schmidt.
Conductor: Pierre Boulez.
Alberich: Zoltan Kelemen
One of the dramatic climaxes in Chéreau's production: Alberich curses the ring which Wotan has stolen from him. Alberich is played here by the late Zoltan Kelemen, who was one of the leading interpreters of this important role.

State Opera, Hamburg,
12 November 1980
Das Rheingold
Producer: Götz Friedrich.
Designer: Jürgen Rose.
Conductor: Christoph von Dohnanyi
The beginning of the 'world poem', starting not with the very first stirrings of the world, but in 'Atlantis', on the ruins of a previous civilization.

The Pacific Northwest Wagner Festival, Seattle, 9 July 1978
Das Rheingold
Producer: Lincoln Clark.
Designer: John T. Naccarato.
Conductor: Henry Holt.
Donner: Herbert Eckhoff.
Froh: Dennis Bailey. Wotan: Rudolf Holtenau. Loge: Emile Belcourt.
A Wagner Festival has been held every year in Seattle since 1975. Unique to this festival is the idea of two complete cycles of the *Ring*, the first of which is sung in German and the second in English. The final scene of *Das Rheingold* illustrated here shows Wotan greeting the citadel of the gods; it is a colourful scene with projections of Valhalla and the rainbow bridge. Wotan is not only carrying a spear but also brandishing a sword. In a diary entry for 30 May 1876 Cosima reports that Wagner was considering whether, at the line 'So grüss ich die Burg' ('Thus I greet the castle'), he should have Wotan pick up a sword from the Nibelung treasure, which would later become Siegmund's and Siegfried's sword Nothung.

Bayreuth Festival, 1876
Die Walküre
Designer: Joseph Hoffmann
Set-design for Act I, Hunding's hut.

Bayreuth Festival, 1876
Die Walküre
Designer: Joseph Hoffmann
Set-design for Act II, showing
the Annunciation-of-Death
scene. In the centre is a natural
rock bridge on which the fight
between Siegmund and
Hunding takes place.

rightful prize and strikes down Gunther, who had also laid claim to the ring. 'Brünnhilde then solemnly intervenes: "Silence your grief [...]. There stands before you a woman whom you all betrayed!"' She bids the vassals raise a funeral pyre on the banks of the river, 'in order to cremate Siegfried's body [...]; in his honour she desires to sacrifice her own body to the gods'. The ring, cleansed by the fire, shall be restored to the Rhinemaidens; never again shall it reduce others to bondage. Alberich, too, is free, like the gods. But 'One alone shall rule: All-father, glorious god that you are!' As the flames of the funeral pyre die down, the Rhine bursts its banks and the Rhinemaidens seize hold of the ring and *tarnhelm.* Hagen plunges after them 'as one insane' and is drawn down by them into the depths of the Rhine.

In the final section, which Wagner versified that same November as the drama *Siegfried's Tod,* a number of passages are already sketched out in dialogue form, as had been the case with the earlier prose drafts. In July 1850, Franz Liszt wrote to Wagner, who was by now living in exile in Zurich, informing him that the Weimar administration was keen to follow up its production of *Lohengrin* with the first performances of the Grand Heroic Opera *Siegfried's Tod;* and he offered him a contract. Wagner accepted the offer, 'but only for yourself and for Weimar' (July 1850). In August 1850 Wagner began the mu-

sical composition of the work and sketched the Norns' scene and the beginning of Siegfried's farewell to Brünnhilde, but soon 'all courage failed' him, since he felt obliged to ask himself the question 'where, during the next twelve months', he would find 'the soprano capable of breathing life into this heroic female?' *(Mein Leben).* He had no alternative but to break off composition. His attempt, however, failed not only because of the lack of a suitable singer for Brünnhilde but also because of his worry that his poetic intent would not be clear to an audience if he were to portray on stage only *one* of the many important incidents of the myth.

It was in order to sort out in his own mind the course of his own artistic development that Wagner wrote his main theoretical work *Oper und Drama* ('Opera and Drama') in 1850/1851. The work deals with Wagner's central concern, music drama, together with the relationship between words and music; and a number of chapters such as those on the function of myth in drama, on alliterative verse and the language of the orchestra seem to have been written with the specific purpose of clearing up the problems raised by the libretto and composition of the *Ring.* It was almost by way of an apology that he explained to Liszt that he now had 'a great deal of material to think about, [...] unfortunately to think about!' But he had to 'think it through to the end' before he could revert to being 'an in-

Bayreuth Festival, 1876
Die Walküre
Costumes: Carl Emil Doepler
The costume designer painted
the Valkyries on horseback on
sheets of glass, which were then
projected onto the backdrop by
a magic-lantern. The
effectiveness of these
projections was considerably
reduced by the fact that the
images were very difficult to
make out from a distance.

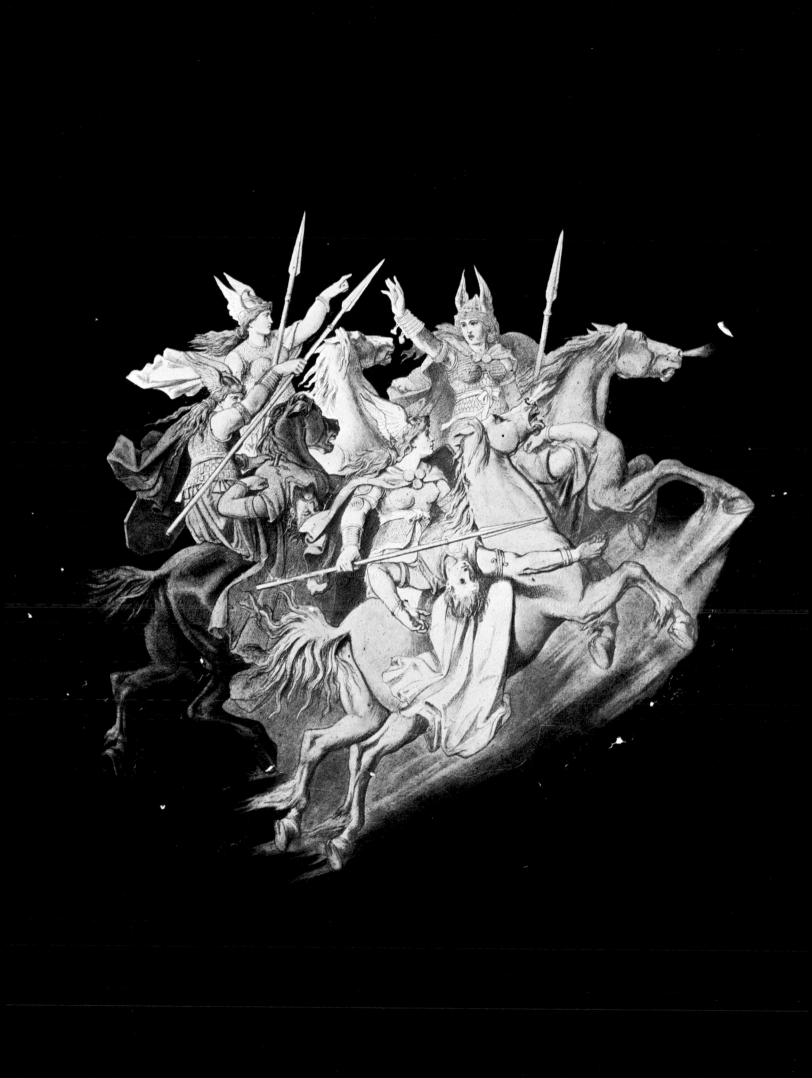

genuous and totally self-confident artist'; his work on the heroic opera for Weimar was not progressing (2 October 1850). During the whole of the following winter he was plagued by the idea of prefacing *Siegfried's Tod* with a separate work, *Der junge Siegfried* ('Young Siegfried'), in order to recount the preliminary stages of the story which were necessary for an understanding of the whole. In May 1851 he drafted the first prose sketch and then the full-length prose draft. The libretto was written the following month. But, as with his study on *Der Nibelungen-Mythus,* he had to return to the very beginning in order to explain the overall context of the complex tale.

In October 1851 Wagner conceived the subject as a four-part work. On 20 November he wrote to Liszt, informing him that nothing would now come of the new heroic opera for Weimar. On a note of solemnity he went on to disclose, 'Let me herewith reveal to you, in accord with the strictest truth, the history behind the artistic plan in which I have been involved for some considerable time and the course which this project must now necessarily take. My plan [...] has become clear to me in the whole of its logical consistency. Listen!' He then reported in detail how he had arrived at the decision to set out from *Siegfried's Tod* and to trace the myth back to its origins, so as to produce 'a complete unit' made up of three dramas and a prelude. He estimated that at least three years would be necessary for its completion. 'No matter how bold, unusual and perhaps even fantastic my plan may strike you, you may none the less be convinced [...] that it has imposed itself upon me as the inevitable consequence of the nature and content of the material in question.' In the same letter he gave Liszt an initial, still somewhat hesitant, indication of his idea for a special theatre festival: 'The performance of my Nibelung dramas must take place at some great festival which may perhaps have to be organized for the sole purpose of mounting this production [...]. Where and under what circumstances such a production may be practicable is something which I do not need to worry about for the time being.' Eight days previously he had written to Theodor Uhlig with a rather fuller and franker account of his festival plans: 'I shall then erect a theatre on the Rhine and invite people to a great drama festival; after a year's preparation I shall then perform my entire work within the space of four days. However wild this plan is, it is nevertheless the only one upon which I have set not only all my hopes and endeavours, but my whole life as well.'

And in the same month of November 1851, in Albisbrunn, Wagner drafted the prose sketch of *Die Walküre* and *Der Raub des Rheingoldes* ('The Rape of the Rhinegold'). Back in Zurich, in March 1852, he wrote the prose draft of *Das Rheingold,* and in May, while staying at the Rinderknecht boarding-house on the Zürichberg, the prose draft of *Die Walküre.* The libretto of *Die Walküre* was completed in June and that of *Das Rheingold* in October. In November and December he revised *Der junge Siegfried* and *Siegfried's Tod.* The libretto of the *Ring* was completed on 15 December 1852. The first private reading of the text took place only a few days later, on 18 and 19 December, at the Mariafeld estate which was the home of François and Eliza Wille. A public reading before a larger audience followed in February 1853 in the main hall of the Hotel Baur au Lac in Zurich; it was spread over four evenings.

In the final version of the text the basic tragic outline encompassing property, power and love, embodied in the figure of Wotan, is even more clearly defined than in the earlier prose draft. *Der Ring des Nibelungen* is a drama about Wotan, the supreme deity, and it is a drama about his guilt, which lies in his lust for power and in the theft of the ring. It is also a drama about his tragic dilemma that, as lord of treaties, he is also their slave; and ultimately it is a drama about his abdication as ruler of the world and of his conscious will for the end. Wotan's four great confrontation scenes, with Fricka and with Brünnhilde in Act II of *Die Walküre* and with Erda and with Siegfried in Act III of *Siegfried,* are the progressive stages in the development of this tragedy. Alberich, who renounces love in return for infinite power in the form of the ring, sins, it is true, but only against himself and his own free will. Wotan, however, lusted after power when 'the delights of young love faded', as a result of which he robs Alberich and falls victim to the latter's curse. *Das Rheingold* is like a 'peasants' trial' in its depiction of 'Wotan's guilt and fatal error and the urgent need for his renunciation' (Cosima Wagner's Diary, 12 December 1870).

Wotan is sufficiently far-sighted as to will his own destruction, which explains why Wagner saw him as 'the sum of the intelligence of the present, in contrast to which Siegfried is the man of the future whom we desire and hope for, but whom we cannot create; he has to create himself out of our own destruction' (letter to August Röckel of 25/26 January 1854). Siegfried, it is true, does not think in the same way as Wotan: he is 'all action', though he does 'recognize the

Municipal Theatre, Leipzig,
1878
Die Walküre
Producer: Angelo Neumann.
Costumes: Carl Emil Doepler
Scene between Wotan,
Brünnhilde and the Valkyries.
The earliest production
photograph of Act III. Since
Neumann ordered the sets to be
built in Coburg on the Bayreuth
model and since the Bayreuth
costume designer, Doepler,
copied the costumes for
Neumann from his Bayreuth
designs, the first Bayreuth
production must have looked
very similar to the one shown
here.

Grand Opéra, Paris,
12 May 1893
Die Walküre
A glimpse behind the scenes at
the Paris Opéra. The Ride of
the Valkyries was often staged
as a major spectacle. It was
generally performed by
experienced riders wearing
Valkyrie costumes: they
thundered past on their horses
across the back of the stage. In
this production, the Valkyries
crossed the stage on artificial
flying steeds, sliding down an
inclined track. In the centre of
the picture is the stage manager,
indicating the performers'
entries. Wotan is at the bottom
right-hand corner, waiting for
his own entry.

fate which he has taken on himself' (Cosima's Diary, 21 February 1872). Even Wotan's creatures, Brünnhilde, Siegmund, Sieglinde and finally Siegfried himself, all of whom are intended to carry out his will, become innocently guilty and fall victim to the curse and to the guilt of the gods which contaminates the world. In much the same way, Hagen is Alberich's agent, intended to avenge the wrong suffered by his father and to regain the ring for him, together with his right and power. Once she has discovered the connections between these events, Brünnhilde, in the final version of the libretto, consciously brings about the end of this guilt-ridden, power-hungry world, which love has destroyed; and she returns to the Rhinemaidens what is rightfully theirs, the golden ring. With that the ring loses its destructive force as a symbol of power. But music has the final say, with a *motif* of promise and hope.

It goes without saying that the foregoing is only a very rough outline of the meaning of the *Ring*. More than any other of Wagner's works, the 'world poem', as he called it, offers scope for the most varied interpretations. His characters are, so to speak, the signifiers in whom a large number of various motives are subsumed under a single principal motive, which is the immediate expression of the life of the character concerned *(Oper und Drama)*.

One might quote Thomas Mann's interpretation of the figure of Siegfried by way of example: 'A perspective opens up which reveals the first and earliest instance of men's dreaming in symbols: Tammuz and Adonis slain by the wild boar, Osiris and Dionysos who were torn limb from limb and who return as the crucified figure wounded in the side by a Roman spear so that he may be instantly recognizable – everything that was and always is, the whole world of beauty which has been sacrificed and murdered by winter's grief, is encompassed by this mythical gaze.' Wagner has not simply retold the ancient myths; he has recreated them by going back to their basic essentials in his 'primal myth'; and by grasping what is universal and exemplary at the basis of all cultures he has sketched out a complex but coherent account of the world, not in the form of an abstract theory or a philosophical system, but through the metaphoric imagery of the music drama. Quite justifiably, *Der Ring des Nibelungen* has been called 'the summation' of the nineteenth century. Wagner's own ontological experiences during these years of political and philanthropic commitment and the sense of failure which he suffered contributed decisively to the work's final form; but the biographical element which is so popular with all those who seek to interpret his works is of no use in the case of the *Ring*.

Oper und Drama contains an elaborate defence of Wagner's use of alliterative verse in preference to end-rhyme, the former, he argued, being capable of linking together 'linguistic roots of an antithetical expression of emotion'. Modulations in the music can then 'reveal such links to our feelings'. In alliterative verse, poetry and music are mutually dependent, which makes it the only suitable metre for the music dramatist who is the 'intentional portrayer of the involuntary' lying at the origins of all life in the shape of the will. Only the musician can fully realize the poet's intention, which he does 'by virtue of his ability to employ the primal relationships between musical sounds in such a way as to reveal to our feelings, with perfect unity, archetypally unified impressions.' This is certainly an ambitious theory and, in its way, just as ambitious as Wagner's attempt to realize it in practice; for he was concerned not only to revive an unusual metre for his unusual work, but also to invent a natural 'mythical' language. The fact that this has given rise to a number of questionable elements alongside a great deal that was extremely successful goes without saying, and Wagner's alliterative verse in the *Ring*, taken on its own simply as a

Metropolitan Opera, New York, 1912
Die Walküre
Brünnhilde: Margarete Matzenauer. Wotan: Hermann Weil
Typical both of the costumes and type of singers who could be seen before the First World War. Romain Rolland coined the rather malicious expression '100 kilo gestures' to describe their acting style and appearance.

Municipal Stages, Frankfurt am
Main, 1925
Die Walküre
Designer: Ludwig Sievert
Set-design for Act II. Sievert
retained this stylized mountain
gorge for all his productions of
the *Ring*. It was frequently
copied by others.

text, has been greeted with derision by whole
generations of opera-goers and has often
been parodied.

Almost a year passed between the completion of the libretto of the *Ring* and the beginning of the work's musical composition. The
move to a new home, conducting engagements, visits and travelling filled the whole of
1853. Was irresolution the reason for the delay? Were the musical ideas not yet mature?
Or was Wagner discouraged by the daunting
nature of the task ahead? When he wrote to
Franz Liszt that 'the music will proceed easily
and swiftly, since it is only a question of realizing ideas which are already fully formed,'

he was certainly underestimating the difficulties involved. The decisive stimulus came
in La Spezia, during the afternoon of 5 September 1853. Wagner's account of the moment in *Mein Leben* is the most famous of
what Carl Dahlhaus has called his 'genesis
myths':

[...] utterly exhausted, I stretched out on a
hard bed [...] and sank into a kind of som-
nambulistic state in which I was suddenly
overcome by the feeling that I was sinking
into swiftly flowing water. The rushing
sound of the water soon took on in my
mind the musical sound of the E flat major
chord surging incessantly in a figural *arpeg-*

gio [...] I awoke in panic from my half-slumber with the feeling that the waves were now billowing high above me. I realized at once that the orchestral prelude to *Das Rheingold,* which I had been carrying around within me without ever being able to locate it exactly, had dawned upon me.

Although Wagner returned to Zurich that very evening with the intention of making an immediate start on the composition, he nevertheless allowed a further two months to elapse before starting the composition sketch on 1 November.

What Wagner had been carrying around within him and what had suddenly dawned on him so clearly cannot be ascertained with certainty. It may well have been, in Carl Dahlhaus's words:

The lightning recognition that the watery depths in which the action of the tetralogy begins and to which, in a certain sense, it returns at the end, could be represented by a group of *motifs* which were able to form the origin and basic material for incalculable thematic derivatives. The musical vision [...] was at the same time a musico-dramatic vision which [...] in the picture that Wagner draws of the beginning both on stage and in the pit and which proved itself to be an inexhaustibly fertile source of ideas, presented the listener with a presentiment of the whole work.

In his *Epilogischer Bericht* ('Epilogue Report'), Wagner explained that his first task was to invent 'concrete nature *motifs* for *Das Rheingold,* 'which had to develop along increasingly

individualistic lines to become vehicles for the tendencies of passion contained in the remainder of the closely structured action as well as for the characters who find expression in that action.' It was a question of expressing the beginning and end of the world in music, the organic essence of nature and its process of cyclical change. Rather like the chorus in Greek drama, the orchestra is both a voice commenting on the stage action and its dramatic background; it recalls past events, betrays what is to come and interprets what is currently taking place. It was as a means of structuring the work that Wagner adopted the *leitmotif* technique. These *leitmotifs,* which have often been ridiculed as sign-posts, directional indicators or even as dog-tags, make the audience 'knowing', to quote Pierre Boulez. Wagner briefly characterized them as follows: 'the preliminary, absolute orchestral melody' relates to the verse melody of the singer 'as a *presentiment,* and from it is derived the "thought" of the instrumental *motif* as a *reminiscence.'* Wagner extended and enriched the tonal and expressive potential of the orchestra; Nietzsche wrote that 'he has given a language to everything in nature which until now had not desired to speak [...] In addition he immerses himself in the dawn and in forests, in mists, ravines, mountainous heights, the horrors of night and in radiant moonlight, and he observes in all of them a secret desire: they, too, desire to emit sounds.' He gives 'a resonant existence' to silent nature. It was with the famous F flat major chord that Wagner began the composition

of the prelude to *Das Rheingold* on 1 November 1853: 'My friend! I am in a daze! [...] A new world stands revealed before me [...]; I can see before me a wealth such as I never even dared suspect. I now consider my fortune to be immeasurable; everything seethes within me and creates music.' This was how he reported matters to Liszt. After an interval of five years he had again begun a major composition; and on 15 January 1854 he once again wrote to Liszt, informing him, '*Das Rheingold* is finished – but I'm finished, too!! [...] Believe me, no work has been composed like this before: I imagine my music to be terrible; it is a quagmire of dreadfulness and sublimity!' He had succeeded in performing 'the cruelly difficult task of creating a non-existent world'. And on 3 July, when he was working on *Die Walküre,* he again wrote to Liszt, 'I say! Things are really livening up now!' He was able to put the finishing touches to the composition sketch of Act I on 1 September. He began the second act on 4 September 'in an extremely bad mood', as he wrote to Hans von Bülow. He was afraid of the great scene between Wotan and Brünnhilde and was already considering whether he should perhaps dispense with it. It was difficult for him to continue working, given the 'desolation of his life' in Zurich. He felt 'quite ill', as he wrote to Princess Sayn-Wittgenstein in November 1854 and 'had to

break off completely'. At the end of the sketch for Act II he noted, '18 Nov. 1854 (that was an evil time!!!).' By 20 November, however, he had already begun Act III, the composition sketch of which he completed on 27 December. His work on the full score kept him fully occupied throughout the whole of 1855 and it was 20 March 1856 before the score was finally completed.

It was not until September 1856 that Wagner began Act I of *Siegfried.* The second act was started on 22 May 1857, his forty-fourth birthday. Since the Leipzig firm of Breitkopf & Härtel had declined to publish *Der Ring des Nibelungen,* considering it neither profitable nor promising any great public interest, and since Wagner was becoming increasingly preoccupied with *Tristan und Isolde,* he broke off the composition of Act II at the point, 'Dass der mein Vater nicht ist' ('That he is not my father') and wrote on the manuscript page of the score, 'When shall we see each other again?' In order, however, to prove to himself 'that it was not simply incipient exasperation' which was preventing him from completing the work, he finished the composition sketch of Act II before beginning *Tristan und Isolde.*

The interruption lasted twelve years, during which time he merely wrote out Act II in full score (1864/1865). It was not until 1 March

Théâtre National de l'Opéra,
Paris, 1948
Die Walküre
Producer: Pierre Chéreau.
Designer: Olivier Rabaud.
Conductor: Georges Sebastian.
Brünnhilde: Suzanne Juyol.
Sieglinde: Marisa Ferrer.
Siegmund: Charles Fronval
The Annunciation of Death in
Act II. Three-dimensional sets
with cloud projections.

Metropolitan Opera, New
York, 1948
Die Walküre
Producer: Herbert Graf.
Designer: Lee Simonson.
Conductor: Fritz Stiedry.
Wotan: Herbert Janssen.
Brünnhilde: Helen Traubel
Scene between Brünnhilde and
Wotan in Act II. A mountain
gorge, reminiscent of Ludwig
Sievert's designs.
Three-dimensional sets,
providing an opportunity for
effective entrances.

1869, at Tribschen, that he resumed work on the score. 'If it proves to be the case that this interruption has made no difference to the freshness of my conception, then I may well adduce this as proof of the fact that these conceptions have an everlasting life,' he wrote to King Ludwig on 23 February; and, again, 'true genius' proves itself 'not only in the comprehensive speed with which it conceives a great plan but, more particularly, in the passionate and, indeed, personal perseverance [...] which is required if the plan is to be fully realized.' He set to work on the Wanderer-Erda scene 'with a vague, sublime and terrible sense of awe'. 'Just like the Hellenes at the steaming crevice at Delphi, we here come upon the nub of the great world tragedy: the destruction of the world is at hand,' Wagner wrote to Ludwig on 24 February 1869. He completed the composition sketch on 14 June 1869 but took his time over preparing the full score since he was anxious to prevent the king from going against his wishes by commanding that this, his latest opera, should receive its first performance in Munich following the productions there of *Das Rheingold* (1869) and *Die Walküre* (1870). It was not until 5 February 1871 that he completed *Siegfried*.

Wagner began composing the final part of the tetralogy on 2 October 1869. In May and June 1856 he had written a new version of Brünnhilde's final oration and changed the title of the work to *Götterdämmerung*. He completed the composition sketch of Act I on 5 June 1870 and then laid the score aside for a year. It was at his birth-place of Leipzig, on 12 May 1871, that he announced that the first Festival would be held in Bayreuth in 1873. At this juncture not a single stone of the new festival theatre had been laid and the second and third acts of *Götterdämmerung* had not even

been written, quite apart from the fact that not a single penny had been raised for the whole undertaking. Between 24 June and 25 October 1871 Wagner drafted the composition sketch of Act II and that of Act III between 4 January and 9 April 1872. On 22 April of that year he moved to Bayreuth. The full score of the mammoth work was completed on 21 November 1874. 'Completed at Wahnfried. I've nothing more to say,' he wrote beneath the final bars.

'August 1867, *Ring des Nibelungen*. In the newly built festival theatre' was the entry in the plan Wagner drew up for King Ludwig II in January 1865, when he was still planning to complete *Der Ring des Nibelungen* before *Die Meistersinger von Nürnberg*. He gave Ludwig the manuscript scores of *Das Rheingold* and *Die Walküre* as birthday presents in 1865 and 1866. Although hopes for a festival theatre in Munich had to be abandoned, the king nevertheless wanted to see the *Ring*, following the first performances of *Die Meistersinger von Nürnberg*, and so he gave orders that the première of *Das Rheingold* should be staged as soon as possible. As late as February 1868 Wagner himself had suggested that each year one part of the cycle should be given a 'provisional' production in Munich, providing that the necessary modernization of the out-dated technical installations in the National Theatre was first taken in hand. The work of rebuilding the stage was carried out in 1869 and included enlarging the orchestra pit. At Wagner's suggestion Dr Reinhard Hallwachs was again entrusted with the production and Hans Richter was placed in charge of the musical side of the performances. Richter assembled a carefully chosen cast which included guest singers from other houses. Wagner, however, could not be persuaded to make the journey from Tribschen to Munich and to take part in the rehearsals. Throughout the spring and summer, the singers, scene-painters, stage technicians, producer and conductor all travelled to Switzerland in order to receive their instructions from Wagner. Because of the work of rebuilding the stage, the sets could not be tested until the beginning of August. Some of the new machines proved to be too slow for the scene changes, which had to be co-ordinated with the music to take place with the curtain up; and from that moment on the catastrophe simply took its course.

In accordance with Wagner's wishes, the dress rehearsal on 27 August was given before a specially invited audience who were admitted free of charge. It passed off as a kind of gala opening, certainly not as a routine op-

Bayreuth Festival, 1953
Die Walküre
Producer: Wieland Wagner.
Conductor: Joseph Keilberth.
Brünnhilde: Martha Mödl.
Wotan: Hans Hotter
Wotan und Brünnhilde in Wieland Wagner's first Bayreuth production of the *Ring*. Typical of the style of costumes, which were simple, un-Germanic and suggested by Greek sculpture.

Finnish National Opera,
Helsinki, 1959
Die Walküre
Designer: Paul Suominen
Sets for Act I. At the line,
'Winterstürme wichen dem
Wonnemond' ('Winter storms
have yielded to the month of
May'), no door flew open to
admit the moonlight and spring
night; instead the hut was
transformed into a forest.

Teatro alla Scala, Milan,
29 April 1968
Die Walküre
Producer: Peter Lehmann.
Designer: Jörg Zimmermann
The last production at La Scala
to employ the classical two-part
division of the stage into clearly
defined acting area and
backdrop for projections.

Royal Opera House, Covent
Garden, London, 1964
Die Walküre
Producer: Hans Hotter.
Designer: Günther
Schneider-Siemssen. Conductor:
Georg Solti
End of Act II, following
Hunding's fight with Siegmund.
Wotan is at centre-stage.
Three-dimensional sets with
projections on the backcloth. In
his later sets for the *Ring,*
Schneider-Siemssen generally
designed archaizing spaces
formed from light.

German Opera, Berlin,
26 September 1967
Die Walküre
Producer: Gustav Rudolf
Sellner. Designer: Fritz
Wotruba. Conductor: Lorin
Maazel. Fricka: Patricia
Johnson. Wotan: William
Dooley
Scene between Fricka and
Wotan in Act II. Sellner is
chiefly known for his directorial
work in the contemporary
theatre and in modern opera;
for his production of the *Ring*
he engaged the sculptor
Wotruba as designer. Wotruba
created block-like, abstract
spaces which gained a stark
three-dimensionality by means
of harsh contrasts between light
and shade.

eratic performance; but it was not a success. The event had aroused widespread interest and once again visitors had come from all over Europe, including Franz Liszt, Ivan Turgenev, the singer Pauline Viardot-Garcia, Camille Saint-Saëns, Jules Etienne Pasdeloup, Hermann Levi and Peter Cornelius. A particular stir was caused in the cafés around the opera-house by the presence of Judith Gautier-Mendès, one of the very first Wagnerians. Eduard Hanslick complained to his readers that *Das Rheingold* was the talk of the town: everyone was going on 'about swimming nixies, coloured steam, the castle of the gods and the rainbow' but 'only rarely about the music'. It was only too obvious that there had been insufficient rehearsals: everything gave the impression of being ill-prepared, both on stage and in the pit, in consequence of which there was a sense of disappointment that such considerable means had gone into producing such an insignificant result. The first performance was scheduled to take place on 29 August. Even before the dress rehearsal Franz Betz, who was singing Wotan, had apprised Wagner of the 'insane chaos' which reigned in the theatre: the best thing anyone could hope for was not to be laughed off-stage, but a fiasco was inevitable. Wagner sent a telegram to the king, asking him to postpone the première. Richter cried off and was immediately relieved of his post as court music director. The search for a new conductor began, but nobody had the courage to take over the task against Wagner's wishes. The king, furious at this 'revolt' against his authority, remained obdurate that the performance would go ahead as planned; he insisted that the artists should obey *him*, not Wagner. 'The behaviour of "Wagner" and his theatre rabble is perfectly criminal and utterly shameless,' he wrote to Lorenz von Düfflipp on 30 August; 'I have never before met with such impertinence.' And he ended by cursing 'the coterie of vulgarity and impertinence'. He toyed with the idea of withdrawing Wagner's salary.

The whole affair is generally regarded as an example of Wagner's insubordination and high-handedness towards his benefactor. But could it not more justifiably be seen as an example of a bold attempt to win emancipation on the part of an artist who wished most emphatically *not* to be a submissive courtier and a member of the 'theatre rabble', but who saw his own artistic demands as justifiable and who attempted to carry them through? Wagner himself arrived in Munich on 1 September with the intention of taking over one of the rehearsals, but the king, who had not

reacted to his telegram, prevented him from doing so. Wagner returned to Tribschen, following which Betz handed in his part. The intendant Perfall threatened to resign. The guest artists left. Press attacks and open letters accompanied the arguments, which took on the proportions of a scandal and an affair of state. A conductor was finally found in Franz Wüllner. 'Take your hands off my score!' Wagner wrote to him in Munich. 'I advise you to do as I say, my good man; otherwise you can go to hell! – Beat time in singing-clubs and choral societies.' But Wüllner refused to be intimidated by such abuse. Local singers from the Munich ensemble took over the parts of the guest artists. The first night was fixed for 22 September. The theatre was packed to the rafters, with the whole city curious to see the miracles of stage-craft that were promised. Even the by now obligatory parody of the work, renamed *Rhein Blech* ('Blech' is intentionally ambiguous: it means both 'brass' and 'rubbish'), had already taken place at the local puppet theatre.

In spite of all the imbroglios, the first night was a success. For the designers Heinrich Döll (Scene 1) and Christian Jank, aided by Angelo Quaglio (Scenes 2 and 3), the castle of the gods, Valhalla, and the bed of the Rhine had been particularly daunting challenges. The stage technicians Carl and Friedrich Brandt had solved the problems of the transformation scenes on an open stage by the use of steam lit by coloured lights and the swimming contraptions of the Rhinemaidens had been technically sound; but the practicable rainbow bridge over which the gods passed on their entry into Valhalla, had given too solid an impression and thus destroyed the illusion. Wagner had initially thought of commissioning the costume designs from academicians or painters; but the task was eventually entrusted to Franz Seitz. Wagner looked over his designs and improved a number of details. They turned out to be simpler and more characterful than those of the first Bayreuth performances seven years later. Not even the first night brought any peace. The tenor Heinrich Vogl, whose wife Therese had sung one of the Rhinemaidens, instituted an action for libel against the editor of the *Bayerisches Vaterland* for having written about 'an aquarium of whores' in which 'underwater females' were claimed to have swum around stark naked.

'Do you want my work as I want it? Or do you not want it like that?' Wagner had written to the king on 20 November 1869, after the opening performances had already taken

place. He could have no suspicion that Ludwig had already issued instructions for the first performances of *Die Walküre* to be staged the following December. All those who had proved themselves in *Das Rheingold* were entrusted with organizing the new production. Wagner wanted to make his cooperation provisional upon his being granted the same power of authority over the Court Theatre as he had enjoyed when *Tristan und Isolde* had first been performed. The intendant, Freiherr von Perfall, was scheduled to go on leave at this time. But the mutual trust which had formerly existed between Wagner and the king had now been undermined, and the return of the former to Munich was too much of a risk now that he was living with Cosima in Tribschen, her divorce from Hans von Bülow not yet having come through. Wagner suggested that Ludwig might be content with a dress rehearsal or a private performance and that the public performances should be called off; but all his entreaties were in vain. The whole 'disgusting business' took its course and the 'execution' of his new work (as he expressed himself to Franz Schott in letters of 17 April 1870 and autumn 1870) took place on 26 June 1870. Once again the composer was not present at the first night, which on this occasion aroused less interest and bore few marks of being sensational.

In general the new work was thought to be too long; and the second act in particular, with all its monologues, was felt to be a desolate waste land. As far as the Ride of the Valkyries was concerned, only a few 'screams' had been audible above the orchestral tumult. Several people were 'morally disgusted' by the ostensible lewdness of the story and were particularly disaffected by the mention of incest. There was unqualified praise for the skill of the Brandt brothers and the storm and tempest scenes left a deep impression by virtue of their new type of lighting effects and the dramatic scudding of clouds created by Angelo Quaglio. Grooms from the royal stables wearing appropriate costumes and riding real horses performed a dare-devil Ride of the Valkyries. Since the gas flames for the magic fire were too pale to make any impact, spirit was poured into buckets and set alight, causing flames to leap several feet into the air and giving off an intense heat. The inhabitants of the surrounding houses had protested against the dangers of these pyrotechnic displays and during the performances the audience was struck by such a sense of dread and terror that the ending of the work, with all its delicacy, totally failed to make any impression. At the performance on 17 July the audience applauded pointedly at the lines 'Bald entbrennt brünstiger Streit' ('Soon shall ardent battle be kindled') and 'Denn wo kühn Kräfte sich regen, da rat' ich offen zum Krieg' ('For where forces boldly stir, I openly advise war') in Act II, since it was just at this time that the first troops were being mobilized for the Franco-Prussian War.

Wagner in the meantime had realized that his 'most illustrious protector was now anxious only to receive the full score of *Siegfried* in order to carry out without delay exactly the same experiments on that work, too,' as he wrote to Franz Schott in the autumn of 1870. He wrote to the king, telling him that he felt like a father 'whose child has been torn from his arms in order to be handed over to prostitution' (1 March 1871). But the king in the meantime had already issued instructions for sets and costumes to be prepared for *Siegfried*. Enquiries about the production were sent from Munich, but Wagner answered them all by saying that he had not yet finished writing the opera, a claim which, at least from February 1871 onwards, no longer corresponded to the truth.

On 22 May 1872, Wagner's fifty-ninth birthday, the foundation stone of the Festival Theatre was officially laid. The king had turned down Wagner's invitation to attend. Building work proceeded briskly to begin with, but then repeatedly came to a halt each time the money ran out. Wagner had devised a system of financing the Festival by means of patronage certificates. These were shares to which people could subscribe and with which they acquired the right to attend performances of the Festival as patrons. In the end, however, Wagner was forced once again to appeal to Ludwig for financial support and the king wrote in reply his famous letter of 25 January 1874, indicating a change of heart on his part: 'No, no and again no! It shall not end like this! Help must be offered! Our plan must not be allowed to fail.'

The opening of the theatre was fixed for the summer of 1876. Preliminary rehearsals had begun the previous summer on 1 July 1875, first of all at Wahnfried with the singers and then with the orchestra in the as yet unfinished Festspielhaus. Wagner, as producer, took upon himself the laborious task of training his performers in his new style of singing and acting. It was not routine operatic gestures which he sought to achieve but a form of dramatic expression polished right down to the subtlest nuance. The difficulties involved can be seen from Julius Hey's detailed account of his rehearsals with Georg Unger, who was singing the part of Siegfried. There

State Theatre, Cassel,
25 March 1972
Die Walküre
Producer: Ulrich Melchinger.
Designer: Thomas Richter-Forgach. Conductor: Gerd Albrecht. Brünnhilde: Joy McIntyre. Siegmund: Karl Sablotzke
In attempting to expose the inconsistencies in the work, Melchinger began the series of constructive confrontations with the *Ring* which lasted throughout the 1970s. Stylization was out of the question since it would have meant both standardization and harmonization. Instead of a unified style, Melchinger preferred concrete images, each appropriate to the particular scene and intended to clarify the music. The production employed a mixture of styles, since the action was not historically fixed and could take place at any time, including our own age. The scenic elements reflect an anthology of styles from nineteenth-century art and from pop art, as is evident in the Annunciation-of-Death scene shown here.

Teatro alla Scala, Milan,
11 March 1974
Die Walküre
Producer: Luca Ronconi. Designer: Pier Luigi Pizzi. Conductor: Wolfgang Sawallisch
Act III, nominally the Valkyries' Rock, but designed here as a nineteenth-century interior, as in Act II. The Ride of the Valkyries was suggested by a monument, with the singing Valkyries lined up in front of it.

Bayreuth Festival, 1976
Die Walküre
Producer: Patrice Chéreau.
Designer: Richard Peduzzi.
Costumes: Jacques Schmidt.
Conductor: Pierre Boulez.
Wotan: Donald McIntyre
Scene from Act II. One of the
great illuminating moments in
Chéreau's staging of the work.
Wotan's self-accusation and
self-awareness in his
monologues are realized
visually through the stage
property of a mirror.

Bayreuth Festival, 1977–1980
Die Walküre
Producer: Patrice Chéreau.
Designer: Richard Peduzzi.
Costumes: Jacques Schmidt.
Conductor: Pierre Boulez
Magic fire: Wotan in front of
the fire-girt rock on which the
sleeping Brünnhilde lies. The
deployment of smoke in this
production was developed to
the level of a fine art.

were also problems with the sets and costumes. Wagner deliberately commissioned the sets not from any 'experienced scene-painter' but from a landscape artist who had some experience of working in the theatre, Joseph Hoffmann from Vienna. The theatre studios of the Brückner brothers in Coburg undertook the task of realizing his designs. On the whole, Wagner was impressed by Hoffmann's work, though he characteristically found fault with his 'neglect of the dramatic intentions in favour of his regard for arbitrary details of landscape scenery'. The hall of the Gibichungs in particular turned out to be too magnificently historicist for his

taste. He made it clear to Hoffmann that he had moved away from the period of 'medieval chivalry' in order to 'show *man* without all these conventional attributes' (letter from Malwida von Meysenbug to Emil Heckel, 1 December 1873).

From the costume designer Carl Emil Doepler Wagner expected 'a characteristic portrait realized by means of individual figures' and intended to 'present personal events from a culture [...] remote from our own experience' (17 December 1874). He stressed in particular that such iconographic models as those put forward, for example, by the painters Peter Cornelius and Julius Schnorr von

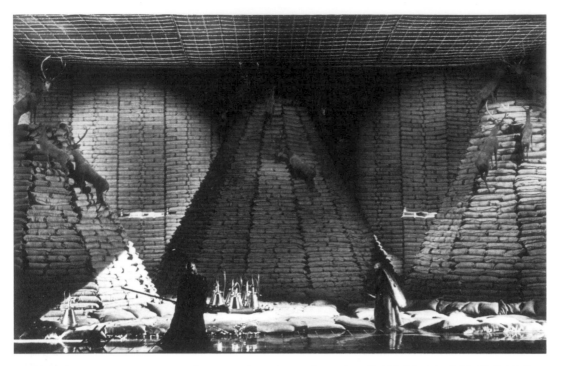

Carolsfeld in their own Nibelung fresco cycles, were no more worth considering than were the 'more recent depictions of a specifically Nordic mythology'. Wagner's mention of the fact that no attention had so far been paid to the 'brief references in those Roman authors who came into contact with the Germanic peoples to the latters' costumes' (he was thinking especially of Tacitus) had a disastrous effect upon Doepler. With archaeological meticulousness he proceeded to make copies of Germanic and Celtic ornaments, weapons and tools which he found in various museums. His costumes reduced Wagner's myth of the 'purely human' to the realms of the 'historically conventional'. They reminded Cosima 'of Red Indian chiefs': apart from 'their ethnographical absurdity' they bore in addition 'all the marks of provincial tastelessness' (Diary, 28 July 1876). There were endless difficulties. The dragon arrived from London only half-complete and the gas

Bayreuth Festival, 1876
Siegfried
Designer: Joseph Hoffmann
Set-design for Act I, Mime's
cave. Siegfried can be seen
forging the sword Nothung.

Bayreuth Festival, 1876
Siegfried
Designer: Joseph Hoffmann
Set-design for Act II, the depths
of the forest. The scene shows
Siegfried's fight with the
dragon. This scenic
arrangement, with the dragon
fight upstage at left and the
lime-tree downstage at right,
remained unchanged until as
late as the 1930s.

lighting in the auditorium was installed only at the last moment. In spite of all these problems the curtain went up on schedule on 13 August, before an international audience, even if technical breakdowns meant that the very first performance only narrowly avoided being turned into a fiasco. The German emperor was present, inspiring Karl Marx to make his much-quoted remark about Wagner 'the state musician'.

The rumours which even during the rehearsal period had come to public attention and reached the newspapers were largely concerned with the sensational new magic stage effects; that it was precisely these which did not always work perfectly naturally invited criticism. There is no doubt that the chief technician Carl Brandt brought off a great many highly sophisticated effects. The opening scene of *Das Rheingold*, with the rather unsafe swimming contraptions for the Rhinemaidens, together with the magic fire in *Die Walküre*, must have been highly poetic, whereas the coloured steam during the transformations, the use of spotlights to pick out individual characters or the magic lantern used to project the Ride of the Valkyries, while being technically innovatory, were not always felt to be successful solutions. But not even the very best stage technology of his day was equal to Wagner's theatrical vision.

Wagner was also disappointed with the conductor Hans Richter who, according to Cosima, was not certain of a single tempo. Wagner's 'ideal' had not been achieved. He was depressed because, as he told Ludwig in a letter of 25 August 1879, all the enormous effort which had gone into the production had once again produced only 'the birth of an ordinary child of the theatre'. None the less, he was determined to do 'everything differently' the following year, a resolve he was forced to abandon in view of the Festival's deficit of 148,000 marks. In spite of their criticism of points of detail, the experts were all agreed on the merits of the overall performance. The German emperor told Wagner, 'I did not believe that you would bring it off.' That was the prevailing opinion and an indication of the extraordinary and indeed unique results that Wagner had achieved in realizing his idea of establishing the Festival. The 'first circumnavigation in the realm of art' was how Nietzsche described the 1876 Festival.

Those theatre intendants who made the journey to Bayreuth felt that the vast and complex work could never be performed in their own repertory theatres. Only *Die Walküre* was given any chance of success, but Wagner stubbornly resisted all attempts to

perform this particular opera on its own. Nevertheless, he was finally forced to abandon his festival play to 'a vulgar theatrical career'.

Angelo Neumann, director of the Leipzig Opera, had attended the second Bayreuth *Ring* cycle and was one of the few people who considered that a complete performance was possible outside Bayreuth; he was even convinced that the work could be a box-office success. Wagner's initial reaction was to turn down the request which came to him from Leipzig, since he considered that the *Ring* was not yet finished and he intended reviving it in Bayreuth in 1877 in a carefully amended ver-

Royal Opera House, Berlin, 1913
Siegfried
Producer: Georg von Hülsen.
Designer: Hans Kautsky.
Conductor: Leo Blech.
Brünnhilde: Melanie Kurt.
Siegfried: Walter Kirchhoff
Brünnhilde's awakening in the new production by the General Intendant von Hülsen, mounted to mark the centenary of Wagner's birth. Stage reforms had already begun in the smaller theatres and in Vienna, but the Berlin Court Opera continued to be dominated by the Wagnerian style of the nineteenth century.

sion. It was only when the deficit forced him to abandon this idea that he agreed to Neumann's request. The scenery was ordered from the Lütkemayer studios in Coburg and the costumes were once again prepared by Carl Emil Doepler. Neumann, who was also the producer, strove for authenticity and Liszt reported to Wagner that some of the details of the Leipzig *Ring* of 1878 had been more successful than had been the case in Bayreuth. Neumann's achievement deserves to be all the more highly rated when one takes into account what sense of resentment the *Ring* was still exposed to among musicians and audiences. As early as the first Festival, the Viennese critic Ludwig Speidel had written that the German nation had nothing in common with this 'crying shame' and that, in the event of the Germans' deriving pleasure from the false gold of the Nibelungs, they could no longer be counted among the cultured nations of the earth. According to Neumann, the Leipzig Gewandhaus Orchestra considered that the music of the *Ring* was not 'worthy of the Gewandhaus'. In general there was a great deal about the *Ring* that people found objectionable. The intendant at Hanover, for example, believed that it was unfair to ask his audience to have to put up with love interest between siblings; he wanted to turn Siegmund and Sieglinde into cousins and to alter the text accordingly. Even then, he still appears to have been plagued by doubts, as a result of which he made enquiries of Hans von Bülow whether he might perhaps expose

himself to ridicule by staging the work. Bülow's telegram in reply consisted of just one word: 'Immortal.'

Complete cycles of the *Ring* were staged in Munich in 1878, in Vienna in the following year and in Hamburg in 1880. The success of the Leipzig production gave Neumann the idea of attempting a guest performance in the imperial capital of Berlin, since the local intendant Botho von Hülsen was known to want to perform only *Die Walküre* and even that only reluctantly. The performances, which were highly successful and much acclaimed, finally took place in May 1881 not, in the event, at the Imperial Opera-House but in the Viktoria Theatre. Even the arrival of the audience offered a remarkable spectacle, with the Berliners forming a guard of honour along the Unter den Linden while the members of the court drove to the theatre in carriages; and the same thing happened when Wagner himself arrived, having travelled expressly to Berlin for the performances. It was the first time that he had attended a *Ring* cycle outside Bayreuth. Therese Vogl, it may be added, was unable to perform her famous leap into the flames on the back of the horse Grane, something which had been the sensation of the Munich performances, since no suitable horse could be found in the imperial stables. But this was all to the good as far as Wagner was concerned, since he considered such acts to be no more than 'circus tricks'. He also turned down a request from the circus director Ernst Jakob Renz to turn the

Municipal Stages, Frankfurt am Main, 1925
Siegfried
Designer: Ludwig Sievert
Set-design for Act II, depicting Siegfried's fight with the dragon. Various attempts were made during the 1920s to move the dragon-fight out of the darkness at the back of the stage and to bring it downstage towards the footlights. The dragon, stage-centre, is seen from the back, it emerges from a trap.

State Opera, Berlin,
15 March 1926
Siegfried
Producer: Franz Ludwig Hörth.
Designer: Emil Pirchan.
Conductor: Erich Kleiber
Set-design for Act III, the Erda
scene. The design was more
impressive than the set itself.
Erda's costume was made of
rock formations out of which
the magically illuminated giant
head appeared like a spectral
mask.

Municipal Opera, Berlin, 1932
Siegfried
Siegfried's fight with the
dragon in Act II.
Three-dimensional sets. It had
now become traditional to show
not the whole dragon but
merely its crocodile-like head
which spewed fire and smoke.

Bayreuth Festival, 1934
Siegfried
Siegfried: Max Lorenz
At the Bayreuth Festival during
the 1930s Lorenz's name
became virtually synonymous
with the part: he established a
type of hero which for years
remained the ideal.

National Theatre, Munich,
22 December 1940
Siegfried
Producer: Rudolf Hartmann.
Designer: Ludwig Sievert.
Conductor: Clemens Krauss.
Mime: Erich Zimmermann.
Wanderer: H. H. Nissen
Scene between Mime and the
Wanderer in Act I.
The sets which Sievert and
other designers created for
Siegfried after the First World
War and during the 1920s were
not on the same high level of
imaginative stylization as their
other designs.

Municipal Stages, Danzig
Siegfried
Act I in Danzig: an example of
the widespread influence of
Emil Preetorius's style.

Teatro alla Scala, Milan,
22 March 1950
Siegfried
Producer: Otto Erhardt.
Designer: Nicola Benois.
Conductor: Wilhelm
Furtwängler. Brünnhilde:
Kirsten Flagstad. Siegfried: Set
Svanholm. Wanderer: Theo
Herrmann
Siegfried encounters the
Wanderer before a wall of
flames.

National Theatre, Mannheim,
2 November 1951
Siegfried
Designer: Rudi Baerwind.
Siegfried: Georg Fassnacht
One of the rare attempts after
the Second World War to
model the forest scene in Act II
on contemporary art. Painted
backdrops were also used in the
other parts of the cycle.

Bayreuth Festival, 1952
Siegfried
Producer and designer: Wieland
Wagner. Conductor: Joseph
Keilberth. Siegfried: Bernd
Aldenhoff
There is no forest, merely the
mouth of a cave lost in the
darkness behind the clearly
defined acting area, and out of
which the monstrous,
fire-spewing head of a dragon
looms like that of a dinosaur.

Bayreuth Festival, 1952
Siegfried
Producer and designer: Wieland
Wagner. Conductor: Joseph
Keilberth. Brünnhilde: Astrid
Varnay. Siegfried: Bernd
Aldenhoff
Siegfried and Brünnhilde,
following Brünnhilde's
awakening. One of the most
famous images in the New
Bayreuth style. The lovers stand
alone on the curved acting
surface, which represents the
world; they are surrounded by
the blue of infinite space. It was
a visual realization of Nietzsche's
account of this
scene: Here Nature arises – so
pure, lonely, inaccessible,
without desire, flooded by the
radiant light of love.'

Ride of the Valkyries into a brilliant number
for his equestrian performers.

Neumann brought his company to London
in May 1882, where they appeared at Her
Majesty's Theatre. In the meantime he had
purchased Bayreuth's stock of scenery and
costumes, having formed a plan to tour the
whole of Europe with his 'Touring Wagner
Theatre'. The sets were no longer of any value to Wagner, since the Festival Theatre in
Bayreuth had been closed since 1876. Neumann's *Ring* tour began in Breslau in September 1882 and ended in Graz in May 1883. It
was the biggest undertaking of its time in
terms of theatrical touring companies. A special train was required to transport the 134
members of the company and five railway
cars alone were needed for the sets, props,
costumes and musical instruments for the
sixty-piece orchestra. The tour went off very
successfully. The theatres visited were invari-

ably sold out in spite of the raised ticket
prices. The company visited Königsberg,
Danzig, Hanover, Bremen, Wuppertal-
Barmen, Dresden, Amsterdam, Brussels –
where the whole of the Parisian musical
world, including the composer Jules Mas-
senet, came to the performances – Aachen,
Düsseldorf, Mainz, Darmstadt, Karlsruhe,
Strasbourg, Stuttgart – where troops of
mounted policemen were required to preserve
order, the audience having queued all night at
the box-office – then Basle, Venice – where
the Erda scene in *Das Rheingold* had to be repeated, so prolonged was the applause – Bologna, Rome – where the performances were
given at the Apollo Theatre in the presence of
the King and Queen of Italy – Turin, Trieste
and Budapest. The differing sizes of the
stages and the often inadequate technical fa
cilities tested to their limits the inventiveness
and talent for improvisation of the stage tech-

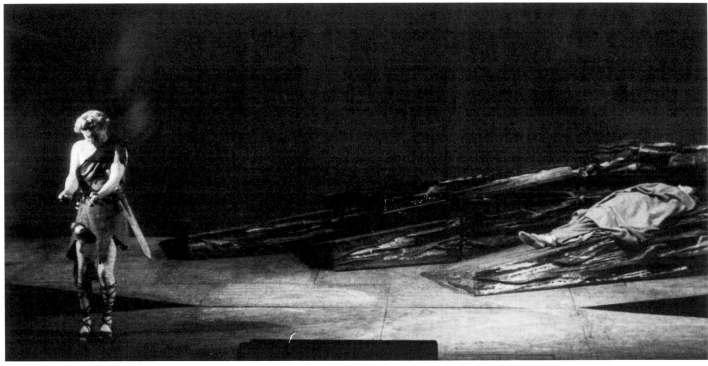

nicians. In addition, many theatres were initially reluctant to sign a contract with Neumann since rumours about the *Ring*'s technical difficulties were often exaggerated to the level of fable. The mere mention of coloured steam in particular must have struck terror into the hearts of all who heard the word. But the success of the venture encouraged theatre managers to attempt their own productions of the difficult work with their own resources, and in this way the *Ring* was finally able to win widespread acceptance.

In 1889 Neumann received an invitation to take the *Ring* on tour to St Petersburg and Moscow. The performances were conducted by Karl Muck and the audiences included the Tsar Alexander III and, in Moscow, Leo Tolstoi. As manager of the German regional

Royal Opera House, Covent
Garden, London, 8 June 1954
Siegfried
Producer: Rudolf Hartmann.
Designer: Leslie Hurry.
Conductor: Fritz Stiedry.
Siegfried: Set Svanholm
Scene from Act II, following
the dragon-fight. Rudolf
Hartmann has left an account
in his memoirs of the
difficulties posed by the dragon.
He was 'flabbergasted' when he
saw the dragon for the first
time, 'a biliously green giant
reptile' which could 'move its
head and jaws, lash the ground
with its tail, flash its eyes and
breathe smoke through its
nostrils'. Hartmann demanded
that the 'monster' should be
relegated to the back of the
stage and be barely visible in
the semi-darkness.

Royal Opera House, Covent
Garden, London, 8 June 1954
Siegfried
Producer: Rudolf Hartmann.
Designer: Leslie Hurry.
Conductor: Fritz Stiedry.
Brünnhilde: Margaret Harshaw.
Siegfried: Set Svanholm
Scene from Act III: Siegfried
finds the sleeping Brünnhilde.

German Opera, Berlin,
1 March 1967
Siegfried
Producer: Gustav Rudolf
Sellner. Conductor: Lorin
Maazel. Mime: Erwin
Wohlfahrt. Siegfried: Wolfgang
Windgassen
Scene from Act I. Fritz
Wotruba's blocks for Mime's
cave seem to create the
impression of flats.

theatre in Prague, Neumann also staged the *Ring* in the Bohemian capital and established the so-called May Festivals, devoted to performances of Wagner's works. This idea was then taken up by various other theatres, including, for example, Wiesbaden, Cologne and Zurich.

It was not until 1896, twenty years after the first performances there, that a new production of the *Ring* was staged in Bayreuth. Cosima, who was responsible for the production, wanted on the one hand a faithful re-adaptation of the original form of 1876 and, on the other, to alter what had not been a success on that occasion in accordance with her own ideas on the subject, ideas which she sought to legitimize by reference to Wagner's own statements on the matter. Unlike Wagner, she commissioned the design and execution of the sets from an experienced set-designer, Max Brückner in Coburg. He provided competent enough work, which was perfect from a purely pictorial point of view; but it was too much to expect that he would offer intellectual insights which would override the superficial and historical conventionalism of the work. Chamberlain spoke of the 'sufficiently well-known Brückneresque window dressings without a trace of inventiveness or genius'. But neither of these qualities had been demanded of him. It was precisely

their 'conscientious, affectionate regard for every detail of the poem' which Cosima praised, together, in particular, with 'their faithful recollection of details from 1876' (4 September 1894). Brückner's sketches are freely based on the 1876 designs, but without their sense of movement and drama. Everything about them gives the impression of being heavier and more massive; and, in his search for nuance, Brückner overindulged his well-known predilection for different shades of brown. What strikes us nowadays is the profusion of minute, naturalistic detail. Cosima paid particular attention to the costumes, determined that the fiasco of 1876 should not repeat itself. The costume sketches for the gods were designed by the painter Hans Thoma and those of the remaining characters by Arpad Schmidhammer. The attempts to reproduce a simpler and clearer line, without Doepler's 'ethnographical absurdities', are obvious.

Space does not allow mention of more than a handful of examples to show the extent of Cosima's concern for realism of details. For the Ride of the Valkyrics she used children wearing Valkyries' costumes and riding wooden horses which were drawn along in front of the backcloth. Children also played the gods in the *tableau* showing the final conflagration of Valhalla. At the end of Act II of

Royal Theatre, Stockholm,
2 April 1969
Siegfried
Producer: Folke Abenius.
Designer: Jan Brazda.
Conductor: Silvio Varviso.
Siegfried: Helge Brilioth
In this stylized new production
of the *Ring* at the end of the
1960s, the entire set for Act II
was dominated by the
suggestion of a lime-tree.
Similar to Wieland Wagner's
designs for his 1965 Bayreuth
production.

Royal Theatre, Stockholm,
2 April 1969
Siegfried
Producer: Folke Abenius.
Designer: Jan Brazda.
A characteristic feature of this
production were the sets by
Brazda, which made extensive
use of projections.

Götterdämmerung imitation sacrificial bullocks set on casters were wheeled in and even the rams which drew the chariot of Fricka (that 'divine privy councillor', to quote Eduard Hanslick) were present. Had it really not occurred to Cosima that the problems of such a work as the *Ring* could least of all be solved by recourse to stage realism? In this respect she was still completely imprisoned by the nineteenth century. Her real sphere of competence was her work with the singers and no one can underestimate her achievement in eliminating routine habits and slovenliness, together with the cult of the virtuoso and conceited star-performer. She demanded utter precision and refused to accept improvisation and spontaneity. For that reason her style has been condemned as mechanical and soulless, as mere drill and as a puppet-play. Her primary concern was the musical expression; and the text, which according to Wagner's definition was of fundamental importance in the music drama, had always to be intelligible.

Together with *Parsifal,* Cosima's *Ring,* more than any other of her Bayreuth productions, came to serve as a model for other theatres. The world's leading opera-houses engaged Bayreuth singers and relied upon the drawing power of the name of 'Bayreuth'. They commissioned their sets from Max Brückner, whose theatre workshop turned into a flourishing concern thanks to his links with the Festival. His sets were also diligently copied by other studios that specialized in multiple production techniques, with the result that sets for the *Ring* showed a certain uniformity of style all over the world.

Whereas the first complete cycle of the *Ring* was given at the Metropolitan Opera in New York in 1889, remaining in the repertory for decades as a vehicle for the great singers of the age, the Paris Opéra did not witness its first complete performances until 1911, when the work was sung in French. Paris did not hear it in German until 1929, and the Opéra did not give another complete cycle until 1955. In Germany, on the other hand, even the smaller municipal theatres showed remarkable willingness to tackle the problems involved in mounting the work. In his memoirs, Rudolf Hartmann has left a marvellous account of how the *Ring* was staged at the theatre in Bamberg in 1924 with limited means but a great deal of imagination and enthusiasm. The municipal electricians had to be called in; missing sets were replaced by black draperies and the local steam-engine

Royal Opera House, Covent
Garden, London, 17 September
1975
Siegfried
Producer: Götz Friedrich.
Designer: Josef Svoboda.
Costumes: Ingrid Rosell.
Conductor: Colin Davis.
Siegfried: Helge Brilioth.
Fafner: Matti Salminen
After Siegfried has defeated the
dragon, the giant Fafner
emerged from its interior,
rather like a soldier climbing
out of a tank. Other
productions during the 1970s
featured the dragon turning
back into Fafner after the battle
– Leipzig in 1975 and Bayreuth
in 1976. The forest was made
up of hundreds of green plastic
ribbons. The dragon was
shaped like a gigantic
many-legged insect which
attacked Siegfried with its
armour-plated claws.

Municipal Theatre, Leipzig,
25 October 1975
Siegfried
Producer and designer: Rudolf
Heinrich
Scene between the Wanderer
and Erda in Act III. According
to Joachim Herz, 'Wotan forces
Erda to rise up from the
ice-bound centre of the world
[…] Her eyes have long been
blinded.' Against non-commit-
ment – For imagination' was the
motto of both the producer and
the designer. The sets serve to
clarify the content. Turned into
a stone monument, Erda rises
out of the earth at Wotan's
command: the 'primeval mother's
wisdom' is at an end: the
downfall of the gods is at hand.

Bayreuth Festival, 1978
Siegfried
Production: Patrice Chéreau.
Designer: Richard Peduzzi.
Costumes: Jacques Schmidt.
Conductor: Pierre Boulez.
Siegfried: René Kollo
Brünnhilde's awakening in
Chéreau's production. Gwyneth
Jones's performance as
Brünnhilde in *Die Walküre*,
Siegfried and *Götterdämmerung*
between 1976 and 1980 left an
indelible mark on this
production.

National Theatre, Mannheim,
6 May 1979
Siegfried
Producer: Friedrich
Meyer-Oertel. Designer:
Herbert F. Kapplmüller.
Conductor: Hans Wallat.
Wanderer: Franz Mazura.
Mime: Jakob Rees
Mime's cave in Act I as a
mixture of machine room and
workshop, with Mime's
cooking-stove at centre stage.
Since the Cassel and Leipzig
productions of 1973 and 1975 it
has become traditional to
clutter Mime's cave with bits
and pieces of petty bourgeois
interior décor.

Gran Teatro del Liceo,
Barcelona, 1980/1981
Siegfried
Designer: José Mestres
Cabanes. Siegfried: Manfred
Jung
Cabanes's sets are completely
within the tradition of
nineteenth-century set-painting.
They were still in use in
Barcelona for the 1980/1981
performances of the *Ring*.

provided the steam necessary for the magic
fire, which proved so powerful that the entire
audience was drawn into the action and
Brünnhilde on her rock got decidedly hot.
Countless anecdotes have been handed down
about productions of the *Ring* in the course
of which the dragon or swimming apparatus
failed to work or else the anvil refused to split
when Siegfried struck it with his sword; and
legends have grown up around all the various
horses that have played the part of Grane. It
was only natural that these frequently inadequate efforts on the part of the theatres concerned should attract the attention of

cartoonists and wits. The work was said to
teem with bearskin-clad Teutons in horned
helmets and the notion of the 'Valkyrie' has
passed over into everyday language.

The style of set-design summarized here by
the name of Brückner was a late flowering
that marked the end of a grand tradition of illusionistic stage design which had been in existence since the time of the Baroque theatre
and which strove to create as life-like an impression as possible. It brought together for
the last time the sum total of all the possibilities of stage design known to the nineteenth
century. But those members of the audience

who sought the meaning of the work beneath the lavish and colourful spectacle increasingly felt a sense of unease at this style of design and acting, which was no longer appropriate to the work's significance, and which encumbered its intellectual and visionary levels with an abundance of stage effects and which mechanically translated the stage directions into unimaginative reality.

Romain Rolland, who attended the 1896 Bayreuth *Ring*, was struck by the 'conceptual greatness' of the subject, its 'complete, literary and philosophical component' and its 'universal significance'. He felt as though he were reading 'a second *Iliad*'. But the pleasure which these performances gave him was purely 'intellectual': these insights came to him not from the production but from the words and music. George Bernard Shaw, who was also a regular visitor to the Festival,

conceived of the *Ring* as a great socio-revolutionary parable in his *Perfect Wagnerite.* And Konstantin Stanislavski wrote that whenever people complained about the 'bombast' of Wagner's gods and heroes, it was not the characters who were to blame but only the style of acting. 'Even a Wagnerian god can be made plausible by virtue of a psychological grasp of his innermost nature and thus be transformed into an extremely effective stage figure whom we see related to us on a human level.'

Changes in the performing style of the *Ring* were not the result of any new or topical production ideas, nor of the style of acting then in fashion, but were based rather on attempts by contemporary set-designers to translate Wagner's visions *qua* visions into visual idioms appropriate to the times. Once again attention needs to be drawn to the im-

Teatro Communale, Florence, 25 January 1981
Siegfried
Producer: Luca Ronconi.
Designer: Pier Luigi Pizzi.
Conductor: Zubin Mehta
Scene from Act III. The mountainside in the form of a wide flight of steps broken by a huge pier-glass. At the top of the stairs is the rocky couch on which Brünnhilde lay sleeping. The horse Grane (a monumental statue) can be seen in multiple reflections on the mirrored wall at the back.

portance of Adolphe Appia, since in none of
Wagner's works have his fundamental ideas
been so influential as they have in *Der Ring
des Nibelungen*. Appia had drawn up his scen-
arios for the *Ring* as early as 1892. 'There is
no doubt that, far from enriching it, customary convention had merely violated his
[Wagner's] vision,' he wrote. As so often, Appia's forward-looking ideas arose out of the
inadequacy of contemporary theatre practice.
Appia's crucial recognition was that 'the music on its own and through itself never expresses the phenomenon, but rather the inner
nature of the phenomenon.' It was therefore
only logical that he should turn away from
naturalism on stage and from what he called
'the optical illusion of the stage'.

The task of the producer must be to express within the framework of the setting
fixed by the poet 'whatever corresponds to
the innermost nature of things as revealed by
the music.' The overall staging of the *Ring*
should resemble a 'modulation' capable of expressing the process of cyclical change in
nature and in human life. An essential requirement here was a 'dramaturgy of lighting'
since 'active, creative' light can 'fully and
vividly convey to us the eternal, changing picture of the physical world.' Now, this light pre-
supposes the practicability of a non-realistic
stage, in other words, 'three-dimensional
space'. It is here, and here alone, that the
three-dimensional actor can appear, not between canvas flats painted in a naturalistic
style. It is sufficient to include in this space
'evocative directional symbols', since only
suggestions can elucidate the 'random nature
of the visible setting of the plot', a point
which Appia supported by reference to
Schopenhauer. He called *Das Rheingold* an

esoteric work because the action takes place among gods, giants and dwarfs rather than among human beings. For that reason it demands a particular form, namely 'hieraticism' or, 'if one prefers, stylization' but 'without arbitrary digressions'. From the mythical beginnings on the bed of the Rhine the action develops towards the richly complex drama of *Götterdämmerung*, before ending once again with the 'hieratic elements' of *Das Rheingold.*

Cosima's frequently quoted dismissal of Appia ('Appia seems not to know that the *Ring* was performed here in '76 and that as a result there is nothing more to be discovered in terms of sets and production'; letter to Chamberlain of 13 May 1896) has been interpreted simply as narrow-mindedness on her part, which, from the point of view of posterity, is certainly not without justification. However, if one attempts to understand her reasons for desiring to realize her husband's wishes posthumously, then it becomes clear that we are dealing not simply with the diametrically opposed interpretations of two contrasting generations but with a fundamentally different approach to the work. Appia's ideas had no influence on Bayreuth until the composer's grandsons began to interpret 'the Master's wishes' according to their spirit rather than their letter.

Every designer concerned with stage reform inevitably relied heavily on Appia's ideas when turning away from the Bayreuth model, even if it is not always possible to trace a line of direct dependence. As had been the case with *Tristan und Isolde,* the initiative again came from the musical director of the Vienna Court Opera, Gustav Mahler. Mahler began a re-evaluation of the *Ring* in 1905 in collaboration with Alfred Roller. His involuntary departure from Vienna forced the abandonment of the project after *Die Walküre,* but the cycle was completed under the conductor Felix v. Weingartner in 1910. The break following Mahler's departure is unmistakable. This was the first time that any theatre had consciously rid itself of the Bayreuth yoke. There was no longer any sign of the horse Grane nor any rams for Fricka. The Ride of the Valkyries was suggested simply by projections of scudding clouds. The second act of *Die Walküre* must have been especially impressive with its vast, three-dimensional set modelled on the Dolomites, against which even the gods gave the impression of being small and lost. What was noticeable was the desire to illustrate the elementalism of nature by effective modern means. Was Mahler forced to abandon this attempt because he

was ahead of his time? Viennese audiences certainly found it difficult to accept the new style.

The same thing happened to Hans Wildermann in Cologne: he, too, had produced *Tristan und Isolde* for the town's Opera Festival in a style that was considered too daring, with the result that the following year's refurbishment of the *Ring* was not entrusted to him alone but divided among himself, the scenic artist Hraby and Heinrich Lefler. It was not until a number of years later that he was given sole overall responsibility when he designed the new productions at Dortmund in 1920/1921 and in Düsseldorf in 1926. Here, too, one sees in *Das Rheingold* the mystic abyss of the Rhine between the solid structures at the front of the stage and the background which was lit by projections; this was precisely the sort of design which Appia had insisted on. The first and second acts of *Siegfried* were designed in an entirely naturalistic way and it must be said that, as a general rule, all attempts to stylize the forest in Act II have been unsuccessful. The fact that at the end of the cycle, following the conflagration of Valhalla, Wildermann had a large cross projected onto the cyclorama says rather more about his own esoterically Christian tendencies than it does about the ending of the work.

It was evidently easier to try out new ideas on staging the *Ring* away from the main operatic centres. Ludwig Sievert, in collaboration with the producer Franz Ludwig Hörth, was the first to work out a consistently stylized interpretation of the work at Freiburg im Breisgau in 1912/1913. Sievert redesigned his sets for later productions in Baden-Baden in 1917, in Hanover in 1925 and in Frankfurt in 1926/1927, when the producer was Lothar Wallerstein; in the process, however, a great deal of their originality was eroded simply as a result of their being altered. Sievert first made continuous use of a revolving stage and cyclorama in his Freiburg production. In *Das Rheingold* the gods stood on the segment of a globe in an open space completely uncluttered by wings. His sets for *Das Rheingold* were intended to convey 'the vision of a mythical landscape'. It remains doubtful, none the less, whether the 25-foot deep stage of a spa theatre like the one at Baden-Baden was really able to give the impression of infinite space.

Between 1917 and 1921 Felix Cziossek designed a new production in Stuttgart which adhered neither to legend nor to history but which attempted to portray the myth through stage pictures and dramatic action. Leo Pasetti designed the sets for a new production at

Court Opera, Vienna,
14 February 1879
Götterdämmerung
Designer: Carlo Brioschi
Set-design for the Gibichung Hall in Act I. This design for the first Vienna production was stylistically independent of Bayreuth but orientated rather towards the brightly coloured and richly ornamental style that Brioschi lavished on the exotic settings of the grand operas he designed for Vienna. As in the 1876 production, however, the costumes were designed by Carl Emil Doepler.

Court Theatre, Cassel, 1890
Götterdämmerung
Designer: Oertel
Set-design for Act II, showing the banks of the Rhine in front of the Gibichung Hall. Backed by the authority of the 1876 Bayreuth production, this layout remained unchanged until the 1930s, and in some cases even longer. To the right are the corner pillars of the Gibichung Hall, with the banks of the river beside it and the Rhine in the background.

Bayreuth Festival, 1896 and later
Götterdämmerung
Producer: Cosima Wagner.
Designer: Max Brückner
A version of the closing scene in Cosima Wagner's 1896 production. The sets were in part substantially modified by Siegfried Wagner in the years which followed. Shown here are the ruins of the Gibichung Hall, with the Rhine behind it on the point of overflowing its banks; on the backcloth Valhalla and the gods are engulfed in flames. Until 1924 Bengal light (a type of flare) was used to create this effect.

the National Theatre in Munich in 1921/1922; the conductor was Bruno Walter and the producer Anna Bahr-Mildenburg, who had been a famous Isolde and Kundry in her day. She had undergone Cosima's tutelage and learned the latter's stylized repertory of gestures, which makes it all the more commendable that Pasetti stuck as closely to Appia as he did since in the Munich of these years the style of the original production was still felt to be valid. In 1903 the Prinzregententheater, a rival establishment to the Bayreuth Festival, had ordered sets from Brückner's workshop which were faithful in every detail to the Bayreuth originals and it wooed tourist audiences with this cachet. Pasetti was an artist whose importance continues to be underrated. He produced extremely artistic designs which, while based upon Appia's observations, were translated into his own individual images. The sets designed by Emil Pirchan for the Prussian State Opera in Berlin in 1928/1929, produced by Franz Ludwig Hörth, and those designed by Oskar Strnad for the Dresden Opera in 1930 were more obviously indebted to the stylistic movement of Expressionism with their highly significant qualities and their sharp contrasts of light and shade. The production by Hörth and Pirchan replaced the earlier one of

1912/1913, which had been designed by Hans Kautsky. Kautsky had remained deeply rooted in the nineteenth-century tradition of painted flats, although he attempted to employ contemporary technology, albeit with variable success. The entry of the gods into Valhalla, for example, was projected by means of a cinematograph onto the backcloth, but the jerky movements of the actors in the film were out of synchronization with the flow of the music and hence destroyed the illusion. The production of Pirchan and Hörth was a copy of their work at the New German Theatre in Prague in 1924, when Alexander von Zemlinsky had been the conductor. The production was notable for its successful synthesis of stage direction and sets. This consistency of style also extended to the costumes with their strongly symbolic colours, and new techniques of stage-craft were subordinated to the overall dramaturgy. In the transformation between Scenes 2 and 3 of *Das Rheingold,* for example, the gods were raised up into the flies while beneath them there appeared the underworld realm of Alberich. In the transformation following Scene 3 this set sank downwards below the stage. The Valkyries' rock no longer showed the gently flowing form which the *art nouveau* designers had favoured but was steep and

Court Opera, Vienna,
21 November 1910
Götterdämmerung
Designers: Anton Brioschi, Alfred Roller
Roller's set-design for the Gibichung Hall in Act I, in a rendering by Brioschi. Roller designed the sets for many of Gustav Mahler's new productions. Viennese audiences disliked his expressive hall with its total absence of Norse or Teutonic motifs. The 'mysterious log cabin' was described as a 'tap room', a 'shooting gallery' or a 'pavilion at the Boat Show'.

Royal Opera House, Berlin, 1913
Götterdämmerung
Producer: Georg von Hülsen.
Conductor: Leo Blech. Gutrune: Lilly Hafgren-Waag. Hagen: Paul Knüpfer. Gunther: Herr Wiedemann
The Gibichungs' scene in the new production by the General Intendant von Hülsen, mounted in celebration of the centenary of Wagner's birth. As in Bayreuth, the Hall is designed to be viewed from the front and is richly furnished with animal heads, Norse wood-carvings and carpets.

jagged. The fire which destroys the world at the end of *Götterdämmerung* and the Rhine's bursting its banks were described as 'miracles of staging'. Pirchan's concern was to interpret the images of the *Ring* as the 'revelation of the innermost vision of the very essence of the world'.

Saladin Schmitt and set-designer Johannes Schröder staged the *Ring* as 'Expressionist coloured-light music' in Duisburg in 1922/1923: brightly coloured images welled out of the darkness of the stage. The Valkyries' rock arose from below, was wheeled forward and then raised up further, whereupon it began to glow from within.

The Third Reich put an end to all these various and stimulating attempts at reform in Germany, and from 1933 onwards such productions were replaced by stagings that utterly reject those efforts at stylization that had been typical of the art movements now being dismissed as 'degenerate'; in their place there reappeared realistic, monumental and heroic landscapes, which as often as not gave the impression of being trivial and provincial rather than heroic. More than any other work it was the *Ring* which the Teutonic ideologues of the Nazi period adapted to suit their own particular ends in a way that was often quite grotesque. To cite only a single example: when a new production of the *Ring* was staged in Hamburg in 1937, produced by Oskar Fritz Schuh and conducted by Eugen

Jochum, an exhibition devoted to Germanic archaeological artefacts and ornaments was held in the foyer of the opera-house. Included in the display was a thatched farmhouse and a couple dressed in ancient German costumes. The way of life, the costumes and the arts and crafts of the Germanic tribes were thus revalued, and the picture of the barbaric and uncultured Teuton in his bearskin was corrected. What all this had to do with the *Ring,* remains a mystery.

In this context, it must also be emphasized that throughout this period Bayreuth, while serving the party leaders as a framework for large-scale spectacles and as a prestigious cultural signboard, refused to be coerced into toeing the party line; in the midst of state-decreed naturalism, the Festival attempted to go its own way, in spite of the extraordinarily violent attacks which were directed against the new production of the *Ring* in 1933 and 1934, a production that was felt to be too matter-of-fact. Emil Preetorius saw the events of the *Ring* as 'parables' in the widest sense and as 'archetypes of eternal events'. He avoided everything that could have been related to a historically identifiable period. The central problem for him was Wagner's requirement for a 'certain closeness to nature [...] as the appropriate complement to his insistently representational music'; this closeness to nature 'should certainly not be naturalistic in the banal sense of the word: Wagner's music demands these natural elements and events in the same sense that words demand them as a framework over which the whole work is extended.' Preetorius wished to move away from the world of 'naturalistic illusion' in the direction of 'a symbolically simplified form', something which, it must be admitted, he achieved to an exemplary degree in only a few scenes, since in Bayreuth, as was to be expected, he felt restricted by having 'faithfully to follow all of Wagner's directions for producing and staging the work'. It is true that he translated Wagner's stage directions into his own symbolic language, but the positioning of the individual units of scenery around the stage, which had been respected at Bayreuth ever since 1876, was something which for the most part he left unchanged. The Valkyries' fir-tree remained at the left of the rock; the Hall of the Gibichungs continued to be viewed head-on and the corner pillars and roof structure of the hall still stood at right in Act II of *Götterdämmerung.*

Götterdämmerung was the last performance to be given at the Vienna State Opera on 30 June 1944, under Hans Knappertsbusch,

State Opera, Berlin,
17 May 1929
Götterdämmerung
Designer: Emil Pirchan
Design for the Norns' scene of
the Prelude. Erda's daughters,
the three Norns, rose from the
ground as their mother, Erda,
had done in *Siegfried*. The
fir-tree under which the Norns
spin is in the middle.

National Theatre, Mannheim,
1932/1933
Götterdämmerung
Scene from Act III. This is how
especially smaller theatres
staged the dramatic collapse of
the world of the *Ring:* a few
falling beams and projections
on the backcloth. In the
foreground to the right and left
is the chorus which, according
to Wagner's stage directions,
watches 'with rapt emotion the
growing fiery glow in the sky'.

New Theatre, Leipzig, 1936
Götterdämmerung
Producer: Wolfram
Humperdinck. Designer: Karl
Jacobs
Siegfried moors his boat at the
Gibichung Hall in Act I, leading
Brünnhilde's horse, Grane – a
familiar sight to theatre
audiences throughout the 1920s
and 1930s.

New Theatre, Leipzig, 1936
Götterdämmerung
Producer: Wolfram
Humperdinck. Designer: Karl
Jacobs
Closing scene, with the
conflagration of Valhalla on the
cyclorama and the chorus with
hands raised in the air. The
three Rhinemaidens are
upstage, left.

250

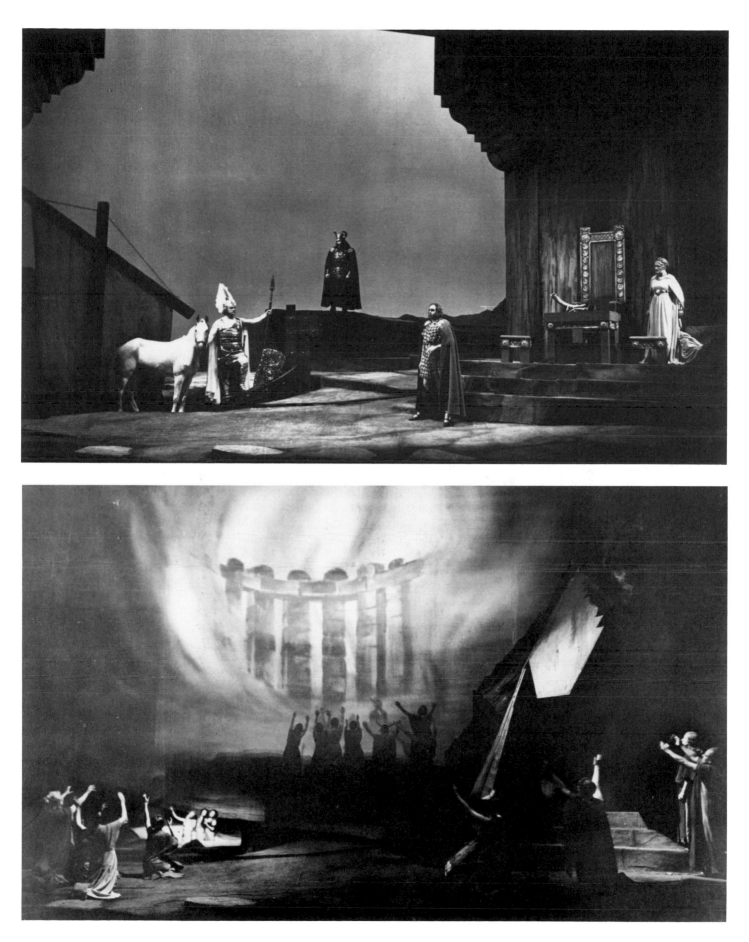

National Theatre, Munich,
29 July 1941
Götterdämmerung
Producer: Rudolf Hartmann.
Designer: Ludwig Sievert.
Conductor: Clemens Krauss.
Brünnhilde: Gertrude Rünger
A live photograph of
Hartmann's new production.

National Theatre, Munich,
29 July 1941
Götterdämmerung
Producer: Rudolf Hartmann.
Designer: Ludwig Sievert.
Conductor: Clemens Krauss.
Siegfried: Günther Treptow
Scene from Act III. Siegfried
and the Rhinemaidens in
Hartmann's new production,
with designs by Sievert.

Teatro alla Scala, Milan,
2 April 1950
Götterdämmerung
Producer: Otto Erhardt.
Designer: Nicola Benois.
Conductor: Wilhelm
Furtwängler
Scene from Act II. Arrival of
Gunther and Brünnhilde in
front of the Gibichung Hall.
Instead of the countryside
around the Rhine the set shows
a heroic, rocky landscape with
the Hall reminiscent of an
Etruscan tomb.

Teatro alla Scala, Milan,
2 April 1950
Götterdämmerung
Designer: Nicola Benois
Set-design for Act III, showing
the valley of the Rhine and
Siegfried's funeral march. An
atmospheric painting depicting
a heroic landscape lit by the
rays of the setting sun.

before total war forced the closure of the house. The world conflagration had become a terrible reality and many theatres (including the Vienna State Opera) were reduced to ashes.

Two productions deserve a mention here for having stood out from the general run of things, although neither of them had any lasting influence. The first was a production of *Das Rheingold* and *Die Walküre* at Basle in 1924/1925, produced by Oskar Wälterlin and designed by A. Appia, and the second the production of *Die Walküre* by Sergei Eisenstein at the Bolshoi Theatre in Moscow in 1940.

Appia had produced *Tristan und Isolde* in Milan in 1923, as a result of which Wälterlin invited him to collaborate on a new production of the *Ring* in Basle. He wanted to stage the work as a 'living present-day myth', since the *Ring* for him was 'not a museum of historical characters but something of the most topical relevance; [...] it expresses what takes place in life as an eternal human tragedy and what has once again become manifest within recent years in a gigantic way'. Appia was finally given a chance to stage the one work which had been the object of his most important deliberations. 'May he who has waited so

Metropolitan Opera, New York, December 1951
Götterdämmerung
Producer: Herbert Graf. Designer: Lee Simonson. Conductor: Fritz Stiedry. Gutrune: Regina Resnik. Siegfried: Set Svanholm. Hagen: Deszö Ernster. Gunther: Paul Schöffler
Scene from Act I. Another production where the hall is viewed head-on. The set consists of a framework of beams hung with curtains. This photograph was taken at a rehearsal, which explains why the singers are not wearing wigs.

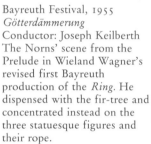

Bayreuth Festival, 1955
Götterdämmerung
Conductor: Joseph Keilberth
The Norns' scene from the Prelude in Wieland Wagner's revised first Bayreuth production of the *Ring.* He dispensed with the fir-tree and concentrated instead on the three statuesque figures and their rope.

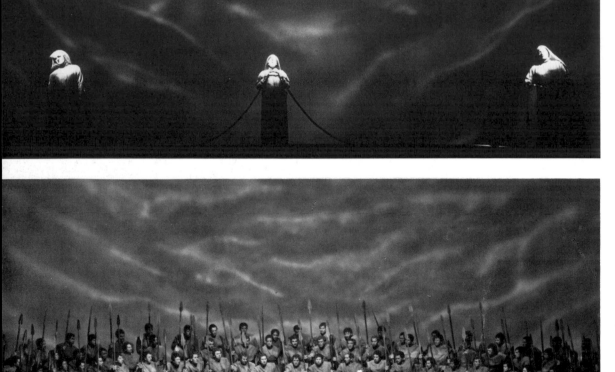

Bayreuth Festival, 1958
Götterdämmerung
Conductor: Hans Knappertsbusch. Gunther: Otto Wiener. Brünnhilde: Astrid Varnay. Hagen: Josef Greindl. Siegfried: Wolfgang Windgassen. Gutrune: Elisabeth Grümmer
Scene from Act II in Wieland Wagner's revised first Bayreuth production of the *Ring.* An empty space without any sign of the pillars of the hall. The circular shape is characteristic. The male chorus, identically attired, is positioned around the perimeter of the disc while the protagonists are placed in an area reminiscent of the *orchestra* of classical Greek drama.

Regional Theatre, Hanover,
7 September 1958
Götterdämmerung
Producer: Kurt Ehrhardt.
Designer: Rudolf Schulz
Scene from Act I. Extremely
simplified version of the
Gibichung Hall. The triangular
relationship between the
characters is symbolized by the
triangular arrangement of
beams suspended above the
stage.

Royal Theatre, Stockholm,
26 March 1970
Götterdämmerung
Producer: Folke Abenius.
Designer: Jan Brazda.
Conductor: Silvio Varviso
The Norns in the Prologue
stand like statues in front of the
'flickering tongues of fire' and
surrounded by a tangle of
ropes.

long be spared unduly bitter disappointment!' Wälterlin wished him, but in vain.

Even the technical facilities of the Basle stage made compromises necessary: there was still no cyclorama, something which was indispensable for Appia's three-dimensional effects. As a result he was forced to use footlights, which he had categorically rejected in his theoretical writings, and even the remaining lighting was deficient. There was no projection of Valhalla, which had to be painted on the backcloth. Scene-changes could not be effected without lowering the curtain and Appia, finally, had to manage without the rainbow. He had to make do with a system of ramps, cube-shaped platforms with cloth-covered sides and various draperies. Wälterlin, it is true, had spoken of the need for a 'disenchantment of the theatre', but audiences expected Appia to produce an authentic, rather than an improvised, realization of his ideas.

The question nevertheless arises whether things would have been different, and more successful, in a theatre which, from a technical point of view, had been better equipped.

Salzburg Easter Festival, 1970
Götterdämmerung
Producer and conductor:
Herbert von Karajan. Designer:
Günther Schneider-Siemssen.
Costumes: Georges
Wakhevitch. Hagen: Karl
Ridderbusch. Gunther: Thomas
Stewart. Gutrune: Gundula
Janowitz
Der Ring des Nibelungen
between symbolism and realism.
Sophisticated lighting plot. The
Hall on the vast stage of the
Festspielhaus modelled on the
stone circle at Stonehenge.

State Theatre, Cassel, 28 April
1974
Götterdämmerung
Producer: Ulrich Melchinger.
Sets and costumes: Thomas
Richter-Forgach. Conductor:
James Lockhart
The Hall of the powerful but
degenerate race of Gibichungs
in the architectural style of the
Berlin Reich Chancellery.

Municipal Theatre, Leipzig,
28 March 1976
Götterdämmerung
Producer: Joachim Herz. Sets
and costumes: Rudolf and
Reinhard Heinrich. Conductor:
Gert Bahner
Scene from Act II. The bridal
procession of Gunther and
Siegfried given the 'red carpet
treatment' in an iron-clad hall
(reminiscent of a factory) with
red carpets and hung with
banners, the colours and
insignia of which were a clear
reference to current political
events. Gutrune is downstage at
right wearing a modern
wedding gown. The steps and
platforms offered plenty of
opportunities for chorus
entrances and processions.

Municipal Theatre, Leipzig,
28 March 1976
Götterdämmerung
Conductor: Gert Bahner
For the first time ever, Wotan
appeared on the cast list of a
Götterdämmerung production.
Joachim Herz and Rudolf
Heinrich staged Siegfried's
funeral march as Wotan's
grief-stricken and melancholy
valediction to his heroic ideal.

Bayreuth Festival, 1977
Götterdämmerung
Producer: Patrice Chéreau.
Designer: Richard Peduzzi.
Costumes: Jacques Schmidt.
Conductor: Pierre Boulez.
Siegfried: Manfred Jung.
Brünnhilde: Gwyneth Jones.
Hagen: Karl Ridderbusch
The oath on the spear in Act II.
The intensely dramatic
performances of the singers
under Chéreau's guidance set
new standards of acting in the
staging of Wagner's works.

Bayreuth Festival, 1976–1980
Götterdämmerung
Producer: Patrice Chéreau.
Designer: Richard Peduzzi.
Costumes: Jacques Schmidt.
Conductor: Pierre Boulez.
Brünnhilde: Gwyneth Jones
Brünnhilde, a white bird in a world of darkness, an avenging angel and a goddess, sings her final peroration with the burning funeral pyre bearing Siegfried's body. As soon as the flames of Valhalla had burned themselves out, the chorus turned round and stared fixedly at the audience, listening to the closing music which, in Chéreau's words, was like an 'oracle' rising up out of the depths of the orchestra, as though from the depths at Delphi, and making a statement which might be interpreted as a question, as scepticism or as hope.

Appia had developed. He no longer sought after stylized effects but designed abstract, geometric spaces. He had worked during the intervening years with Jacques Dalcroze in Hellerau and Geneva. In the Basle *Das Rheingold* the Rhinemaidens performed a eurythmic dance wearing grey tunic-like garments. It may be that this whole experiment came too late for Appia. His ideas as expressed in *Die Musik und die Inszenierung* ('Music and Staging') were now almost thirty years old and it may well no longer have been his intention to put them into practice. His new style was considered too abstract, too cold and lacking in atmosphere. Plans for a complete cycle had to be abandoned in the light of public protests. Appia was never able to realize his entire *Ring* on stage.

When Sergei Eisenstein received a commission to stage *Die Walküre*, he had only ten days' preparation before rehearsals began. The first night took place on 21 November 1940. It was an official, political gesture towards the German Reich which in the summer of 1939 had signed a border and friendship treaty with the Soviet Union. Eisenstein wanted to produce an 'inner audiovisual unity in the performance': the 'pictorial music' demanded 'a visual form of imagery'. 'Visibility, objective realism, material perceptibility, topicality' and the mobility of people and sets were his key words. The performance was to be 'in its essence realistic, in its structure mythological, in its generalized forms epic and in the changing variety of its musical and visual depiction emotional.' Eisenstein wanted to set in motion, by dramatic means, 'those currents in the depths of our own consciousness in which our representational and poetic, sensory and mythological way of thinking is still very pronounced.' He set out from the principle that everything which is discussed or even mentioned in the course of the action should be made visible on stage, since, to a mythological way of thinking, the narrative was as representational as

State Theatre, Stuttgart,
18 December 1980
Götterdämmerung
Producer and designer:
Jean-Pierre Ponnelle.
Conductor: Silvio Varviso
Scene from Act I, Siegfried's
arrival. As produced and
designed by Ponnelle, the
Gibichung Hall became the
colourful tent of an oriental
potentate. The countryside
around the Rhine was realized
with a visual quotation of
nineteenth-century set-design.

Teatro Comunale, Florence,
13 June 1981
Götterdämmerung
Producer: Luca Ronconi.
Designer: Pier Luigi Pizzi.
Conductor: Zubin Mehta
The Gibichung Hall here
consists of five columns flanked
by two pillars. Siegfried enters
stage left. For his 1976
Bayreuth production Richard
Peduzzi also designed the
Gibichung Hall as a columned
loggia.

the fact *per se.* In addition, Eisenstein invented the so-called mimed choruses which translated the monologues into action.

Sieglinde's narration in Act I was mimed by a group of actors. Hunding was accompanied by a pack of hounds and Fricka by a group of rams in golden fleeces, half man and half sheep, reacting to her reproaches and reined in and whipped by her. During the Ride of the Valkyries the eight Valkyries prescribed by Wagner were encircled by additional groups of warrior maidens. The music for this scene was supposed to be broadcast through loudspeakers scattered around the auditorium, stairs and foyers; but this proved technically impracticable. The mimed choruses enveloped the leading characters as a mobile mass. Since at this mythical early stage of his development, man was not yet able to conceive of himself as an individual, the choruses were intended to act as a link between the principal characters and their environment, in other words nature. In his mythical state man is at one with nature, which is why nature interferes actively in men's affairs. In Siegmund's fight with Hunding, the cliffs rose into the air and subsided in accord with the actions of the singers. 'A mutually creative cross-fertilization between the cinema and the theatre' was intended to take place 'on the border between sound film and music drama, without suppressing the originality of either but bringing both to bear on the solution of new problems.'

Apart from *Parsifal*, it is the *Ring*, for which Wagner conceived his Festival Theatre, which has always been the chief work performed at Bayreuth. Since 1951 there have been only three Festivals when it was not staged, those of 1959, 1981 and 1982. The five post-war productions, each of which was constantly revised, improved and rethought, are of particular importance first and foremost because of the work's continuous presence in the repertory. They provided an impulse for new productions at other opera-houses outside Bayreuth and kept alive the debate about the *Ring* in particular. Wieland Wagner staged the cycle in Bayreuth in 1951 and 1965, Wolfgang in 1960 and 1970. In addition, there were guest performances and guest productions in Germany, Spain, Italy, Belgium, France and Japan. During its first two seasons at least, Wieland's 1951 production remained within the Bayreuth tradition of cautious stylization. The break with the past and a consistent use of Appia's ideas did not come until 1953/1954. Wieland sought the intellectual drama behind the external course of the action, a drama which, he argued, cannot take place in a realistic space and a particular locale, but in a world of symbols. This was also the first time that light, which can translate music into movement and colour, had been used consistently as a mode of expression. The style of acting was 'hieratic' in Appia's sense of the word. The characters were raised on the acting platform almost as on the cothurni of the Greek theatre.

In his Hamburg production of 1956, Günther Rennert and his designer Helmut Jürgens set out 'from the Bayreuth scene', but Rennert felt that 'the emblems and symbols had to be concretely expressed', since the theatre requires the 'object' which Bayreuth had abolished, 'the tangible symbol, tree, hearth, door [...] and all those other realities which are pregnant with meaning.' For Rennert, too, 'space, light and colour' were 'the most basic elements of today's music theatre [but] man in his real mass, his movements, his pantomimic and gesticulatory modes of expression still remains [...] the measure of all things, including the theatre.'

In much the same way, it was not principles but the human beings in the *Ring* which Wolfgang Wagner revealed in his 1960 production of the work. He, too, started out from the idea of a disc encompassed by the cyclorama which, like the classical *orchestra* of the Greek theatre, harmonized with the amphitheatre of the auditorium and symbolized the 'world', while at the same time opening up a new three-dimensionality to the abstract stage by combining the lighting plot with architectonic elements. In the tragedy of power and love, the only 'radiant couple' was Brünnhilde and Siegfried, set off from the others by their nearly white costumes.

It was 'inevitable' that in his 1965 production Wieland's path should lead him away from the empty stage 'towards abstract, three-dimensional forms and to "modernist" colourfulness'. He had discovered that the score of the *Ring* contained 'hieroglyphs and ciphers which Wagner had left to future generations to decode'; and he attempted to find 'an analogy for the musical ciphers in the score of the *Ring* in archetypal images'. Around the fixed acting platform he set up three-dimensional elements which were powerful symbols. Individual man, as he appears in the *Ring*, was 'depicted in all his archetypal modes of existence'; Wieland's concern was 'the constantly repeated clashes between the male and female principle of life'. The topicality of this principle lay in its timelessness.

Wieland had hoped that a sculptor such as Henry Moore might have designed archaic, three-dimensional sets for the *Ring*. For his 1967 production at the Deutsche Oper in Berlin, Gustav Rudolf Sellner was able to persuade the sculptor Fritz Wotruba to collaborate with him in his staging of the work. In their productions at the Metropolitan Opera in New York during the 1960s and at the Salzburg Easter Festivals between 1967 and 1970, Günther Schneider-Siemssen and Herbert von Karajan depicted the scene of action as superordinate to the individual. In their combination of painting, projections and three-dimensional scenery, these vast, soaring sets were an image and expression of the grandeur and elemental force of nature.

In his 1970 production Wolfgang perfected his projection techniques and the disc on which the action was played out, thus providing a new interpretation. At the beginning of *Das Rheingold*, the disc symbolized a dormant world which was still whole. Parallel to the development of the plot, the five basic elements forming the disc were tilted, separated, displaced and made to overlap, until they finally came together again in their original form during the closing bars of the work, as a symbol of reconciliation and hope for the *homo novus,* or new man. But the final question as to whether it would be 'Utopia or repetition' which emerged out of the catastrophe remained unanswered.

During the 1970s there began a new and exciting chapter in the interpretational history of the *Ring.* In the first instance it was the imminence of the 1976 celebrations to mark the centenary of the first Bayreuth performances which prompted a number of opera-houses to plan new productions of the complete cycle; and once again it was the smaller houses which first showed the initiative, beginning with Cassel in 1970, Leipzig in 1973, and then London and La Scala in 1974 and Geneva in 1975. The style of New Bayreuth, which had taken as its starting-point the timelessness of myth, now seemed not simply to have been outgrown: there was also a conscious effort merely to be different. The initial question was now where *Der Ring des Nibelungen* was set, at what period and in what place? The topicality of the work was no longer to be found in its timelessness but rather in its reference to a particular period. That required a concrete production style rather than an archaistic one, and a specific setting rather than the lack of one.

The new assessment of the nineteenth century, in which writers saw the roots and constraints of their own cultural and social conditions clearly laid out, now became the central focus of attention. The social questions of the nineteenth century, the history and criticism of ideology, determined the particular interpretation and the subsequent course of the work's reception and influence was also written into the production. The *Ring* was seen as a political parable or as an allegory; and the problem of the abuse of power, which had brought about world-wide catastrophes in our own time, was strongly emphasized. It was no longer possible to feel sympathy for Wotan as a god beset by classical tragedy: instead he was unmasked as a bankrupt and condemned as a criminal. The urge to provide enlightenment about *Der Ring des Nibelungen* has occasionally led producers into inflicting pedagogical methods on their audiences. The intellectual efforts to come to terms with the *Ring,* which had been made previously and often on a very high conceptual level, were to be made more radical: the audience had to be provoked. There is no doubt that this was connected with the revolt by the so-called generation of 1968 and its radical ways of thinking and behaviour.

The 1970s were also a decade of scandals provoked by the *Ring;* but such provocation also gave rise to bewilderment and thought-taking on the part of that segment of the public which willingly engaged in the distraction. The classics of the legitimate theatre were also radically interpreted during this period and rescued from their remoteness so as to be given a new relevance. *Der Ring des Nibelungen,* however, was not only taken seriously or unmasked; it was also discovered to be a piece of imaginative theatre, a great dramatic adventure. In the theatre, as in the visual arts, there was no longer any obligatory style. According to the point of departure adopted by the particular interpretation, the *Ring* was staged in the style of the period immediately after 1871; of the early years of the Industrial Revolution; of pop art; of the Third Reich; of German folklore; and of constructivism, in which collage techniques were used with the intention not only of producing a wealth of associations but also of drawing attention to the inconsistencies in the work.

Wolfgang Wagner deliberately entrusted the centenary production of the *Ring* in 1976 to a young team from abroad. The producer was Patrice Chéreau, the sets were designed by Richard Peduzzi and the costumes by Jacques Schmidt. The conductor was Pierre Boulez. The question which inevitably arose was: did this hundred-year-old work still have something to say to the new generation and, if so, what is it that it had to say? Chéreau's production attempted to stage the totality of the work by means of a complete translation of both words and music into a theatrical experience and into action and images on stage. This new way of looking at the work led to storms of protest during the first performances in 1976, disturbances such as had never before been witnessed in the Festspielhaus. By the time the production was last staged in 1980, it was being greeted by storms of applause which were equally unique in the history of the Festival.

The starting-point for Chéreau's interpretation was the conditions of individual freedom in any system of power, such as that wielded by Wotan and Alberich. Individual freedom is only permitted by the gods in so far as it helps them maintain or regain power. Even the freedom of the allegedly 'freest of heroes', Siegfried, is programmed by Wotan. 'Wotan needs freedom without conscience, without knowledge: he needs an unsuspecting stooge in order to remain essentially what he was before, the man who wields the power and who knows what is going on [...]. Siegfried can therefore no longer be the radiant hero': he is 'paralysed by ignorance about himself'.

In contrast to other producers, Chéreau took account not only of the work's political aspect, the exploitation and the abuse of power, but also of Wagner's counter-proposals for a more beautiful, youthfully optimistic mode of human existence as embodied in the love of Siegmund and Sieglinde, Siegfried and Brünnhilde. And he included, too, the sense of bitterness and grief which is felt when such love is destroyed, betrayed and cheated through its being sacrificed to the will to power. In Wagner's return to Germanic mythology, Chéreau saw an attempt to give a cultural basis and a past to a whole period of history and at the same time to depict by means of that mythology the attitudes of Wagner's own time. *Der Ring des Nibelungen,* for Chéreau, is an allegory of the nineteenth century which, 'in the guise of myth', tells us all about ourselves and speaks to our powers of recollection. His multi-layered view of the work was matched by a production style which made symbolic and referential use of pictorial elements from various historical periods and stylistic movements, combining them all in an interpretative whole which evoked a wealth of associations in the spectator.

It is striking that, since 1976, various attempts to stage the *Ring* have come to grief through being abandoned or postponed. One thinks in this context of Paris, Frankfurt, Nuremberg, Vienna, La Scala and Hamburg. The reason for this was not simply that the *Ring* was now regarded as a difficult work which placed heavy demands on the resources of any opera-house; it was also connected with the stylistic and interpretational problems of the work. In Vienna, for example, the ideas of Harry Kupfer (producer), Peter Sykora (sets) and Reinhard Heinrich (costumes) were rejected as being too progressive, whereas Filippo Sanjust's realization of the cycle was broken off after *Die Walküre* because it was felt to be too conventional. It appears that a certain sense of perplexity has set in. It remains to be hoped that this may lead in turn to a period of creative thought which will be the starting-point for new interpretations of the *Ring.*

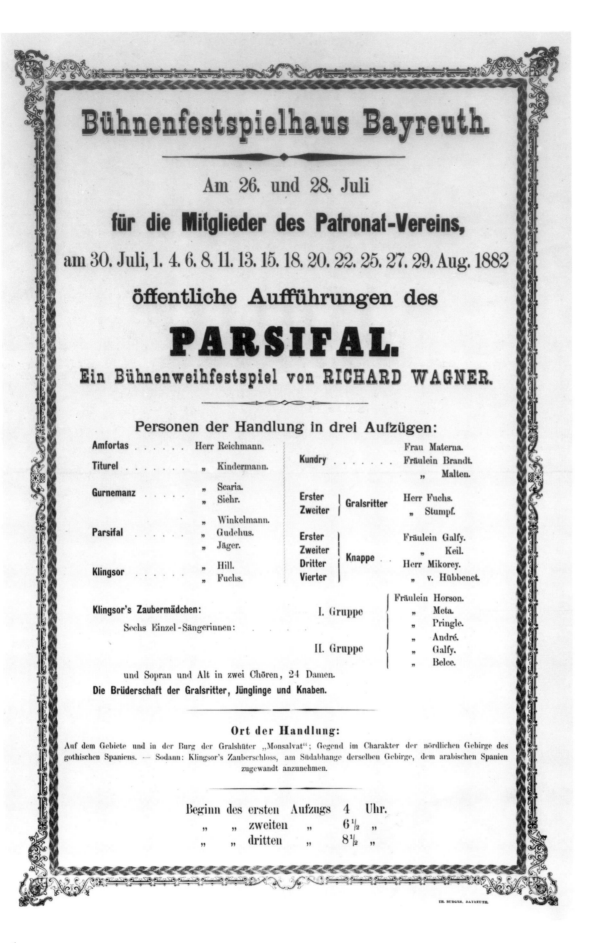

Parsifal

It was at the end of April 1857 that Wagner moved into the 'Asyl' beside the Wesendoncks' villa in Zurich.

In addition there now set in a period of fine spring weather; I awoke for the first time in the new house on Good Friday to be greeted by bright sunshine: the little garden had grown verdant, the birds were singing and I was finally able to sit on the turreted roof top of the house and enjoy the sense of calm which I had so longed for and which seemed so full of promise. Overcome by that feeling of calm, I suddenly told myself that today was in fact 'Good Friday' and I recalled how significant this reminder had once before struck me as being, in Wolfram's *Parzival*. Since that sojourn in Marienbad [...] I had paid no further heed to the poem; now the ideas which it contained pressed in upon me with overwhelming force and, starting out from that thought about Good Friday, I quickly conceived an entire drama which, divided into three acts, I immediately sketched in a few brief strokes.

Writers on Wagner have interpreted this passage from *Mein Leben* as proof of the unique position which *Parsifal* is said to hold in Wagner's creative output and of the seamless unity between life and art. Since the publication of Cosima's Diaries, however, we know that what we are dealing with here is in fact a 'myth of inspiration'. For, as Cosima noted on 13 January 1878, Wagner felt he had made a mistake in his biography: it was simply the peaceful atmosphere of the garden which recalled the mood of Good Friday. And, on 22 April 1879: 'In fact it is all as far-fetched as my love affairs, for it was not Good Friday at all – just a pleasant mood in Nature which made me think 'This is how a Good Friday should be.'

Mystification on the one hand and, on the other, the calm retraction of earlier claims are both characteristic, and not just of Wagner's own point of view; mystification and its decisive rejection have also determined the whole

remarkable history of the way in which this unusual work has been interpreted and of the influence which it has exercised. Wagner's familiarity with the subject, then, dates back to that Marienbad summer of 1845. Parzival and the grail then reappeared in the libretto of *Lohengrin*, in the *Wibelungen* essay and in the preliminary notes for *Tristan und Isolde*. The prose sketch which Wagner claims to have conceived in the Asyl in 1857 has, strangely enough, never come to light. Perhaps it existed only in Wagner's head? However this may be, in his letter to Mathilde Wesendonck of 1 October 1858, he speaks quite clearly of the contents of Act III, Good Friday morning, and on 2 March 1859, while working on *Tristan und Isolde* in Venice, he informed Mathilde, 'In particular, an original creature, a wondrously world-demonic woman (the grail messenger) is taking an increasingly lively and obsessive hold of me.' Mathilde Wesendonck had sent him San Marte's edition of *Parcival. Rittergedicht von Wolfram von Eschenbach* ('Parcival. Courtly romance by Wolfram von Eschenbach'), the second impression of which had appeared in 1858. It may well be that Wagner was already clear in his own mind about the 'ideas which it contained', but, as he wrote to Mathilde, the contents of Wolfram's rambling romance caused him even more problems than had been the case with any of his other medieval sources, since 'Master Wolfram' had taken the easy way out: he had 'understood absolutely nothing of the actual content' but had strung 'one incident to another and each adventure to the next [...] so that the serious reader is forced to ask himself what Wolfram actually had in mind.' 'Like a starling' he has mindlessly repeated 'the inferior French courtly romances'. Wagner certainly recognized that this Christian legend, like the others, was based on a 'foreign, pagan source', that the Spanish Moors had known it, that the Ka'aba at Mecca – a stone dating from the time of pre-Mohammedan religions – had been regarded as an object of venera-

Bayreuth Festival, 1882–1933
Producer: Richard Wagner.
Designer: Paul von Joukovsky
The temple of the grail in the
original production remained
unchanged for fifty-one years.
Above a hexagon supported on
columns and arches rises a
dome, its top out of sight. The
so-called choruses from on high
resounded from this dome. The
side aisles were used for the
chorus entrances. Italianate
Romanesque style of
architecture. The closing scene
of the work is shown here.

Bayreuth Festival, 1882–1933
Producer: Richard Wagner.
Designer: Paul von Joukovsky
The Good Friday Meadow in
the original production. Flowers
of roseate spring colours wind
around the huge tree trunks
and the meadow painted on the
backcloth is similarly strewn
with flowers. To the left is
Gurnemanz's hut, to the right
the scene of Parsifal's
anointing. There is no
three-dimensional scenery, only
open-work flats.

tion, and that in the Christian version of the legend, Joseph of Arimathea brought with him to France the chalice which had been used at the Last Supper and in which 'the indelible blood of the Redeemer himself was caught and preserved' at the Crucifixion. These passages from his letter to Mathilde show clearly to what extent the subject had already impressed itself upon Wagner and aroused his interest. But he was horrified to realize that, while making a supreme effort to write the music for the scene of Tristan's sufferings in Act III, he was again becoming involved in a 'fundamentally evil' task and that Amfortas's sufferings would mean 'an inconceivable intensification' of the anguish suffered by Tristan. He violently resisted the thought of embarking on such a task: 'And you expect me to carry out something like that? and set it to music on top of everything else? No thank you very much! Anyone who feels like doing so can get on with it; but I've no intention of saddling myself with it! ...' Wagner knew that he would have to 'compress' the whole complicated action, which Wolfram had described in several thousand lines, 'into three main situations of graphic substance, so that the profound and ramified content should emerge clearly and distinctly.' May God preserve him from such a task, he went on and concluded by taking his leave of the 'nonsensical plan; [the poet Emmanuel] Geibel can carry it out and Liszt can set it to music' (29/30 May 1859).

And yet the subject refused to stop haunting him. Parzival was stirring within him, he wrote to Mathilde from Paris at the beginning of August 1860. 'I can see more and more in it, with increasing clarity.' In the schedule which he drew up for King Ludwig II in January 1865, the first performances of the new work were planned to take place in 1872. 'How wonderful! – the king demands passionately to hear about Parzival,' he wrote in *Das Braune Buch* on 26 August 1865, and the following day he began to write out the full-length prose draft. On 30 August he added at the foot of the completed manuscript the remark, 'So! That was a help in time of need!!' The draft was then put to one side since Wagner's immediate concern was to complete *Die Meistersinger von Nürnberg* and *Der Ring des Nibelungen*.

'Parzival' remained the familiar form of address which Wagner used in his correspondence with the king. Throughout the turbulent period of preparations for the first Festival, Wagner continued to look forward to starting work on *Parsifal* (which was the spelling which he adopted from 1877 on-

wards). He had in fact hoped to present the finished poem to the king at Christmas 1876 but the problems which arose as a result of the deficit incurred by the first Festival prevented him from working in peace. When his publisher Ludwig Strecker visited Wahnfried on 10 January 1877 and asked about *Parsifal*, Cosima noted in her diary, 'Alas Parzival, when will thy star shine forth?' It was 25 January before Wagner finally disclosed to her, 'I'm going to begin *Parzival* and shan't let it out of my sight until it is finished.' Cosima was so happy that she broke into laughter. Between 25 January and 23 February Wagner worked on the great prose draft, parts of which were already in dialogue form. The libretto followed, between 14 March and 19 April. As he was working on it, Wagner recalled that it was fifteen years since he had last been engaged in a similar task, when he had composed the libretto of *Die Meistersinger von Nürnberg* in Paris. The composition and orchestral sketches, on which Wagner worked simultaneously, were both begun on 25 September 1877 and completed on 16 and 26 April 1879 respectively. And with that the main work on *Parsifal* was complete as far as Wagner was concerned. 'Over,' he wrote at the foot of the sketches. He began writing out the full score on 23 August 1879, while still in Bayreuth, continuing it during his long stay in Italy between January and Oc-

Adolphe Appia
Set-design for Act I, the forest of the grail's domain, 1896
Appia's most influential design. The forest is formed out of tree trunks which look like columns; only at the top is there any suggestion of foliage, which resembles the roof of the columned hall. At the back of the stage are the sacred lake and the gentle curves of a mountain slope.

tober 1880. Act II was started on 6 June 1881, again in Bayreuth, and completed on 20 October. He took up the third act on 8 November, during a further stay in Italy, this time at Palermo. The full score lay finished on his desk on 13 January 1882. The final words, 'Palermo, for you!' are dated 25 December 1881: Wagner had wanted to give Cosima the finished score for her birthday, which was why he had to anticipate his actual completion of the work.

Cosima's Diaries record Wagner's progress on *Parsifal* in minute detail. It must have been a time of happiness for Wagner, for on 5 January 1878 he told her, 'It was time that I was allowed for once to write a work under such good auspices.' He was afraid, however, of the big scene in Act II between Kundry and Parsifal, although he had previously written other scenes in a similar vein, including Venus's scene in *Tannhäuser*. Mozart, Wagner continued, had only composed one scene like that of the Commendatore in *Don Giovanni*. In comparison with Parsifal's outcry in the scene just mentioned, Tristan's curse had been a pure jest: 'Then you must quickly think up another work for the Society of Patrons,' Cosima replied jestingly (9 April 1878). Wagner also complained about the 'ghastly and bloody business demanded by the whole concentration of ecstasy'; but a sense of contentedness and the happiness of success prevailed. In Act I he made sparing use of 'sensuous intervals' but in the Flowermaidens' scene he again dipped into his 'old paint pot' (5 April 1878). In the course of composing the work he was to 'make use of eccentric colours', but his art consisted in his 'not allowing them to sound like eccentricities' (14 November 1881).

The Diaries, however, also reveal to us a further facet of Wagner's personality which is totally at odds with our traditional image of the solemn and vocationally inspired composer of *Parsifal;* and that is his 'ability to convert the most serious of things into nonsense in a flash' (6 August 1878). One should, Wagner maintained, be able 'to joke about the sublimest of things' (24 December 1877). His Grail March, for example, he described as 'the proper march for a spa', adding that he would have to go to Marienbad or Bad Ems in order to hear it (27 December 1877). 'I've got Amfortas to shut his mouth,' he announced to Cosima on completing the grail king's lament (18 January 1878). He called the world-demon Kundry his 'dear old primeval woman' (17 April 1878) and Klingsor a 'musico-dramatic horseradish'. On one occasion, when Wagner and Cosima were eating

Karlsbad wafers, he commented that his knights of the grail ought to have something similar since he couldn't give them bread and butter to eat, 'or they will start digging in and not want to leave' (23 September 1878). But when one of the chorus members made fun of the communion bread in the grail scene of Act I during a rehearsal, he was violently reproached for having done so.

Wagner called his work a *Bühnenweihfestspiel* ('Stage-Consecrating Festival Play'), extending and deepening the concept of the 'Stage Festival Play', a term he had already used for *Der Ring des Nibelungen.* The 'consecrating' or 'dedicatory' nature of the work lay in its particular subject-matter and the resultant performing style. His initial explanation of the sub-title was purely practical: since the 'mystically significant Love-feast' of his grail knights was not some popular fairground revel, he was obliged to think of his Festival Theatre as 'especially dedicated' to this type of representation. In the same way, the attitude towards their work on the part of the artists and technical staff, who were concerned not with personal acclaim but with the success of the venture as a whole, could only, Wagner felt, be described as 'having the effect of a benediction poured freely over everything without any directive from above' (*Schlussbericht* ['Final Report']).

Parsifal is Wagner's most radical attempt to restore to the superficial operatic stage of his own day the dignity and expressive power en-

Metropolitan Opera, New York, 24 December 1903 Designer: Hermann Burghart The temple of the grail in the New York première, an event described as 'The Rape of the Grail'; the sets themselves had been 'pillaged' from Bayreuth, the Viennese designer Burghart having based his own sketches on the Bayreuth model, although his temple was more richly ornamental and created an impression of greater magnificence.

Designer: Remigius Geyling. Set-design for the temple of the grail, 1912. It was made for an atelier in Vienna. Influenced by the gentle colours of the Vienna Secession and reminiscent of the light-temple fantasies by the German artist Fidus.

joyed by the classical Greek theatre in its handling of themes and its association with cultic ritual, and by the mystery plays of the Middle Ages and the sacred representations of the Baroque era. Mozart's *Die Zauberflöte,* with its ethical message and, in the realm of symphonic music, Beethoven's Ninth Symphony with its final chorus, were for Wagner the last links in this chain of western tradition. In his old age Wagner came to adopt a severely critical attitude towards his own secularized and materialistically orientated century that puts its faith in progress, science and capital and which he regarded as deeply inhuman. In writing *Parsifal* he hoped to provide a basis of humanity and to counteract egoism, which

had been raised to the status of a general principle, by postulating the concept of compassion for others weaker than oneself.

With its uncompromising demands for an intellectual component in art, *Parsifal* is also Wagner's criticism and counter-proposal to the art of his own time which, in his view, had been made subservient to capital and which had forgotten its true function in its obsessive pursuit of financial gain and success. Wagner must have been fully aware of the fact that this was not only a bold undertaking but a dangerous one, too, and he had doubts as to whether he should ever allow the work to be performed at all, since he feared it would never be understood or at least only by future generations. And it was not long before the first such misunderstanding arose. Nietzsche reproached Wagner for having prostrated himself before the Cross. *Parsifal* was called 'Rome on the stage', a 'Sacrilegious Festival Play' and an act of blasphemy. The former young revolutionary was said to have turned into a sanctimonius old man whose platform was that of founding a new religion. The essential mystery of redemption which, in Wagner's view, was fundamental to all the world's great religions was depicted in Christian imagery since it was Christianity which had shaped our own culture and which, as a result, was the most readily intelligible. But what is striking is Wagner's insistence upon the contrast between *Parsifal*, on the one hand, and ecclesiastical practice, on the other, and his refusal to accept a one-sided and dogmatically Christian interpretation of the work. Admittedly he made enquiries of the Munich priest Petrus Halm at the time of the first prose draft, in order to obtain precise details about the Catholic mass, but, while working on the score, he gave Cosima to understand that he was energetically 'averse to turning the Last Supper into a theatrical performance [of] the Mass' (2 September 1880). He was pleased that in *Parsifal* he had 'not depicted the action of the service in the Temple, but has concentrated everything into the blessing of the Grail' (16 June 1878). Although Hans von Wolzogen's article on *Parsifal* gave him some pleasure, he felt that Wolzogen had 'gone too far in calling Parsi-

fal a reflection of the Redeemer'; he had not for a moment thought of the Redeemer in this context (20 October 1878). Klingsor represented for Wagner 'the peculiar quality which Christianity brought into the world: just like the Jesuits, he does not believe in goodness, and this is his strength, but at the same time his downfall' (2 March 1878). A 'priest' was the 'most unbearable thing' he knew of; but none of that had anything to do with the 'symbol of redemption'. None the less, Wagner's conversations with Cosima included such concepts as 'the Last Supper' or 'High Mass' to describe the grail ceremony, which inevitably sowed the seeds of later confusion.

Wagner was fully aware of the similarities, differences and boundaries between religion and art and he explained them in an essay written in 1880, in other words while he was working on *Parsifal*. For Wagner both religion and art were initially and principally basic intellectual needs on the part of conscious man who was no longer on the same level as animals. It can be the function of art to grasp the 'mythic symbols' which religion 'wants to have believed to be true', according to 'their symbolic value'; and art, by depicting these mythic symbols as ideas, can reveal their 'deep, hidden truth'. The difference between the artist and the priest, however, lies in the fact that the priest's concern is to have 'religious allegories' regarded as 'actual truths', whereas the artist freely and openly passes off his work as his own invention. Once religion

Stadsschouwburg, Amsterdam, 20 June 1905
Designer: Hermann Burghart
The magic garden, as designed by Burghart for various opera-houses, including the Metropolitan in New York. Behind the tangle of foliage to the left is the entry to the castle in an Arabian style. Kundry's couch of flowers is at right. A garden with tropical vegetation and luxuriant tendril-like creepers which fell to the ground when the scene was transformed into a wilderness. More realistic than the Bayreuth sets in which the flowers were so large that the singers seemed to have grown out of them.

begins to lead a life which is purely artificial, in other words, once it starts to develop its 'dogmatic symbols' and in that way 'to conceal what is unique, true and divine', it readily makes use of art. The latter is intended 'to support the ostensibly real truthfulness of the symbol' by making 'fetishistic idols for sensuous worship'. That, however, is not the true function of art. Art alone is capable of grasping the essence of the 'allegorical image by means of its ideal portrayal', in other words 'ineffable divine truth'. Even these brief considerations prove how thoughtless it is to speak of *Parsifal* as a surrogate religion or an attempt to set up new gods.

Wagner, however, must have been aware that in composing such a work he had come up against the limits of what could be expressed in the theatre as well as the limits of what could be uttered in words. 'It is very remarkable; I have never before gone so far; my "ein andres ist's" ["another grace, a different one"] almost goes beyond the bounds of what is permissible,' he told Cosima in the context of Parsifal's mysterious words in Act II (18 September 1878). And, again, on the subject of the variously interpreted closing lines, 'He then hints at rather than expresses, the content of this work, "salvation of the saviour" – and we are silent after he has added, "good that we are alone"' (5 January 1882). Even in the prose drafts silence is striking. In his programme notes to the Prelude to *Lohengrin* and the Grail Narration, he had given all the relevant details; but now, when Parsifal asks about the grail, Gurnemanz answers, 'Das sagt sich nicht' ('That cannot be said'). This cryptic silence has of course contributed a great deal to the subsequent aura of mystery surrounding *Parsifal.*

'There are two worlds here locked in battle for ultimate redemption,' Wagner wrote to the king on 15 October 1878. It is a clash between the principles of good and evil, represented by the grail king Titurel and by Klingsor, the pagan magician who himself strives to gain control of the grail. Within this field of conflict Wagner has attempted to encompass a coherent plan of the world in which earlier non-Christian attitudes should also be included. In such 'profoundly significant mysteries', however, he could speak only 'in parables and through comparisons', he told Ludwig in a letter of 7 September 1865. The stage picture is here a symbol. The action, which contains a large number of significant motives, pointers and references, is held tightly together by means of the strict dramaturgic structure of the three acts. Wagner here employs the same basic dramaturgic model as that found in the morality plays of the Middle Ages and the Baroque, where it was used chiefly to depict the struggle between good and evil, virtue and vice, and where it was founded upon a conceptual basis common to various cultures. The conflict was exemplified in the image of the confrontation between a young hero and a seductively beautiful woman whom he has to resist (by making the right decision) if he

Municipal Theatre, Zurich, 13 April 1913
Kundry: Emmy Krüger.
Parsifal: Willy Ulmer
The Flowermaidens' scene in Gustav Gamper's plain and unpretentious sets. The magic garden without any tropical luxuriance; the Flowermaidens decked out with garlands, as usual.

wishes to achieve a true understanding of goodness and virtue.

Similarly in the dramaturgic structure of Wagner's *Parsifal*, the scene between Kundry and Parsifal is the peripeteia of the plot. In his instructions for the scenery, the iconographic model of the early morality plays is transparent. On the one hand there is the Christian grail castle, inaccessibly situated in the mountains of northern Gothic Spain, on the other, located on the southern slopes of these same mountains and facing Moorish Spain, Klingsor's magic garden with its tropical vegetation. In the great temple scene in Act I and in the Flowermaidens' scene in Act II, these two worlds are graphically depicted in all their polarity. Apart from these two poles, and to a certain extent mediating between them, is the third of the settings, the open spaces of innocent nature: the grail forest in Act I and the Good Friday meadow in Act III. It is here that Gurnemanz's scenes take place. Gurnemanz, although a knight of the grail, distances himself from the other knights. He instructs the squires and Parsifal and acts as mediator with Kundry, who also has access to this domain. And this is where the intellectual resolution of the conflict is achieved and a state of balance restored. This setting, too, has a deeper significance. From the time of Romanticism in art onwards, nature and landscapes were interpreted as forms of divine revelation, a theme which was repeatedly taken up throughout the whole of the nineteenth century: the workings of God's omnipotent power could be recognized in nature. Even the flowers in the magic garden, having smiled so seductively at Parsifal and then withered, are redeemed in the Good Friday meadow.

Parsifal is also a narrative story recounting the development of its eponymous hero. Parsifal arrives from nowhere and is confronted by two opposing worlds. At the beginning, certainly, he is a pure but still 'stupidly stumbling fool', who can only see and perhaps suspect, but who does not yet understand. He is not yet 'knowing': knowledge is something he learns through Kundry's kiss. It is at this point that the links between events become clear to him: he becomes 'worldly wise' and realizes he is a fool. His own experience of suffering makes him capable of fellow-suffering. He must travel 'the paths of erring and anguish' until he finds his way back to the grail. Only then can his acts of compassion redeem Kundry, Amfortas and the world of the grail. He has destroyed one of the two principles and transformed the other into a new synthesis. In Wagner's view compassion

was an active rather than a meditative quality. As he explained to Mathilde Wesendonck on 1 October 1858, 'Nothing leaves me colder than the complaints of a philistine when his peace of mind is disturbed: any sense of compassion here would be an act of complicity. Just as my entire nature involves rousing people from their base condition, so I feel the urge here to spur on others to feel the great suffering of life.' And two weeks before his death, he wrote to his son's tutor, Heinrich von Stein, that, in spite of the curse which lay on the world, it was still possible to 'give active examples of the most earnest recognition of the feasibility of deliverance'. This marks a major step forward from the tragedy of the *Ring*. Siegfried, who had wanted to become wise, perished, while Alberich survived. Parsifal, however, finds his way: a pure fool like Siegfried, he becomes wise through compassion towards others.

The character of Kundry is without doubt one of Wagner's most important creations and it is through her that one can expound the wealth of associations which have been woven into *Parsifal*. Almost everything about the subject suddenly became clear to Wagner when, in 1860, he realized 'that the fabulous, wild messenger of the grail must be one and the same character as the seductive woman of the second act,' as he wrote to Mathilde Wesendonck at the beginning of August 1860. When King Ludwig asked him the meaning of Kundry's kiss, he replied, in a letter dated 7 September 1865, 'I'm sure you know the serpent in Paradise and its tempting promise: *eritis sicut Deus, scientes bonum et malum.* Adam and Eve became "knowing"; they became "conscious of sin". The human race had to atone for this knowledge through suffering and misery [...].'

As a result of her curse, Kundry has to bear the sufferings of all mankind, being condemned to rebirth like the Wandering Jew (1865 prose draft). Ahasuerus had refused Christ a moment's rest as He bore the Cross to Calvary, and Kundry had laughed at Him when she should have felt pity. This is the radical counterpart of the attitude which forms the central theme of *Parsifal*. She is now forced compulsively to keep on repeating that accursed laughter: she is incapable of weeping, but can only scream, rage and rave. She is nameless, since she bears many names. Klingsor calls her 'arch she-devil', 'rose of hell', 'Herodias' and 'Gundryggia', names which indicate the way in which the figure of Kundry represents features of a basic type common to various cultures and periods. As a woman, she is mother, whore and serving

Municipal Stages, Freiburg im Breisgau, 4 January 1914 Designer: Ludwig Sievert Set-design for Act I. In the centre are two three-dimensional tree trunks; the one on the left was intended to rotate during the transformation scene and, together with the one on the right, to form the entrance to the castle of the grail. The only three-dimensional elements which the temple contained were also these two column-like trunks. The transformation was technically too complicated for the Freiburg stage and failed to work. In the foreground one can see a meadow full of crocuses; Gurnemanz and the squires are in the centre. Solemn atmosphere divorced from reality.

maid. She can be redeemed only by a man who resists her attempts to seduce him. Klingsor can use her for his own ends; having castrated himself, he is not subject to her curse and is her master because she has no power over him.

In her other, seductive, role Kundry must challenge the man and test him in order to ascertain if he can resist her. She despises the chaste knights of the grail, none of whom has been able to resist her until now. They, too, are weak and enslaved by her curse. She serves them by way of atonement, even though they treat her like an animal, Gurnemanz being the only one who attempts to understand this strange woman. The only emotions she expresses are wild grief and de-

rision. Parsifal is alone in resisting her and her promise that he will achieve 'divinity' and 'knowledge'. He becomes wise not through sin (as was the case with Adam and Eve, who allowed themselves to be deceived by the serpent's promise) but through compassion which he feels even for Kundry. The rose of hell, however, does not suffer eternal damnation, as did the she-devils of medieval morality plays. She is baptized and accepted into the temple of the grail: the feminine principle which she embodies is reconciled.

Even while he was still working on *Parsifal*, Wagner had come to realize that special conditions would be necessary for such a work to be performed. He had signed an agreement, dated 31 March 1878, with the administration of the Munich Court Theatre, releasing not only the Court Orchestra but the artists and technical crew as well, so that they would be available for Bayreuth. In return the Court Theatre was to receive 'unlimited performing rights' to the new work. In his letter of 28 September 1880, which he sent from Siena, Wagner presented Ludwig with a *fait accompli*, announcing that he had to dedicate a particular stage to his Stage-Consecrating Festival Play, 'and this can only be my Stage Festival Theatre which stands all on its own at Bayreuth. It is there and there alone that *Parsifal* may be performed from now on; in no other theatre shall *Parsifal* ever be offered as an amusement for the general public.' The only exceptions which Wagner was prepared to make were private performances for the king's pleasure.

Wagner justified his decision by arguing that 'a drama in which the most sublime mysteries of the Christian faith are openly enacted on stage' could not be presented 'in theatres like ours, alongside an operatic repertory and before an audience like ours'. He could not hold it against the church authorities if they objected 'to displays of the most sacred mysteries on those same boards upon which, yesterday and tomorrow, frivolity luxuriantly sprawls.' That, Wagner went on, was a 'sin comparable to the desecration of the Eleusinian mysteries'. A subordinate clause in Ludwig's reply showed that the king admitted the truth of Wagner's argument, and all earlier agreements with the Court Theatre were rescinded.

Wagner was appalled by the thought of a casual audience, paying admission and expecting to be entertained, although ultimately it was precisely this type of audience that he had to depend on. He preferred a public which shared the same 'emotional understanding' of the work and which was in sympathy with the feelings and impressions he wished to convey in the production. It was not a critical distance – which for Wagner indicated a lack of involvement – but agreement in feeling which he sought. That does not mean that he expected or presupposed uncritical admiration. As a practical man of the theatre, he was sufficiently critical himself to know what had not been a success. Throughout his life, performances of his works had been accompanied by noisy demonstrations of support and crude misconceptions, and *Parsifal* seemed to him unsuited to such fairground behaviour.

'Ah, just don't think of performing it,' was Wagner's constant cry while he was composing *Parsifal*, since, as he informed Ludwig in a letter of 1 March 1882, 'preparing such a work for performance' could not but involve 'terrible excitement'. Cosima recorded his famous remark, 'Oh, I hate the thought of all those costumes and grease paint! When I think that characters like Kundry now have to be dressed up, those dreadful artists' balls immediately spring into my mind. Having created the invisible orchestra, I now feel like inventing the invisible theatre' (Diaries, 23 September 1878). Wagner was painfully aware that in the case of *Parsifal* more than any other work his visions could only with difficulty be transformed into the material world of the contemporary stage. The king, who was unable to restrain his impatience to see the work performed, sent the set-designers Christian Jank and Heinrich Döll to visit Wagner on 9 November 1878. It was they who had worked on the earlier productions of his works in Munich. Wagner wanted to discuss matters with them before they set to work on their designs, in order to avoid any misunderstandings that might arise in the future. The 'gentlemen' already had 'their heads full of ornamental designs and distant perspectives'. Any further collaboration was out of the question.

As early as 1878 Cosima had wanted to surprise Wagner by presenting for his birthday sketches for the sets designed by a real artist. But Arnold Böcklin declined to become a Bayreuth scene-painter, as did the costume designer Rudolf Seitz and the architect and painter Camillo Sitte. Wagner's concern was to find collaborators who would attempt 'not to bring with them their *own* ideas but to begin by understanding *mine,*' as he wrote to Ludwig on 17 May 1881. In January 1880, while Wagner was in Naples, his circle of acquaintances was joined by the Russian artist Paul von Joukovsky (Zhukovskii). Joukovsky was neither a scene-painter nor had he any practical theatrical experience, but he was exactly what Wagner was looking for – somebody who was prepared to work in close contact with him and to produce sketches according to his own ideas; in other words, he would be 'an extension of Wagner's own hand'. On the occasion of a visit to the grounds of the Villa Rufolo in Ravello in May 1880, Joukovsky prepared sketches of the magnificent vegetation in the gardens and of the remains of the Saracen architecture there, since, as he wrote in the visitors' book, Wagner believed that he had found here Klingsor's magic garden. Joukovsky had to produce no fewer than seven coloured sketches before Wagner expressed

Court Opera, Vienna, 14 January 1914
Designers: Anton Brioschi, Alfred Roller
Roller's design for Klingsor's castle, in a rendering by Brioschi. The Viennese spoke of it as a 'medieval dungeon' and rejected it as too modernistic. A variation of the model designed by Appia in which the tower was also open to the sky. Influenced by the action of the scene, the dialogue between Klingsor and Kundry takes place at the bottom, and Klingsor observes Parsifal's impetuous approach; a genuine teichoscopy.

Costumes: Heinrich Lefler
Costume designs, 1913
From left to right: Flowermaiden; Kundry in Act II; Kundry in Acts I and III, realized by the Vienna Costume Atelier in 1913. The Flowermaidens' costumes very often showed the influence of contemporary fashions at this time. The Act II Kundry looks like one of Gustav Klimt's allegorical female figures, majestic and expressive of a sublime eroticism.

Municipal Stages, Frankfurt am Main, 2 January 1914
Designer: Heinrich Lefler
Set-design for the magic garden. Not tropical, but delicate, fragrant and unreal in the style of the Vienna Secession.

any degree of satisfaction. He was not interested in sets like those used in the spectacular fairy-tale plays which were the major theatrical attraction of the day. He imagined the flowers being so enormous 'that the maidens might seem to grow out of them'. They had not grown out of the ground, Wagner insisted, but had appeared as though at the wave of a magic wand.

Rather more successful was Joukovsky's attempt to design the temple of the grail. Only the most noble monuments to Christian architecture could serve as a model here, Wagner felt. When visiting Siena Cathedral in August 1880, he was moved to tears; it was the most profound impression a building had ever made on him. Once again Joukovsky prepared a sketch, which was very useful later on when he came to design the grail temple. But the set was not a copy of Siena Cathedral since it lacked, for example, the characteristic black-and-white horizontal bands of the pillars. It was more the sense of space and the structure of the dome above the crossing which served as a guide.

Klingsor's magic garden and the *Wandeldekoration,* or moving panorama, posed no particular problems as far as the visual ideas were concerned, and so they were designed by the Brückner brothers, who were also entrusted with the task of realizing the remaining settings. The *Wandeldekoration* was a piece of technical wizardry which impressed the audience deeply. Three painted strips of cut-out canvas, one behind the other, were unwound on rollers, like film-strips, and transformed the scene from the forest, rising through cliffs, to the temple of the grail. It was not intended merely as a decorative effect but was dramaturgically justified by Wagner. Like Parsifal, the spectator should be led imperceptibly, 'as though in a dream-like trance', along the trackless paths to the castle of the grail, paths which only those who were summoned by the grail could find. Gurnemanz's famous lines, 'Du siehst, mein Sohn, / zum Raum wird hier die Zeit' ('You see, my son, / here time and space are one'), should in this way be realized visibly on stage. During the very first discussions, the stage technician Carl Brandt, whom Wagner called his 'true scenographer', had pointed out that the musical interlude was not long enough for the scenery to be fully unwound. Wagner was beside himself with anger, claiming that he was now being expected to write music by the yard. During the rehearsals, E. Humperdinck, one of the musical assistants, put together a few extra bars of music; but in Act III the *Wandeldekoration* could not be used at all.

Wagner was also disappointed by the series of costume designs which Rudolf Seitz had delivered in response to the commission entrusted to him. In a letter to Daniela of 14 April 1881, Cosima called them 'magnificently contrived, indeed splendid, and impossible' and Wagner informed Ludwig on 17 May 1881 that Seitz had designed 'Flowermaidens like *café chantant* Valkyries, with indecent ballroom gowns such as might have been devised by the famous Parisian *haut couturier* Worth for the *demi-monde*.' Wagner wanted these costumes to be simpler, more characterful and poetic, 'chaste', as Cosima said. Joukovsky then tried to realize on paper Wagner's idea of having two calyxes form the costumes. Wagner joked about one of the designs, saying that these 'bean blossoms were Klingsor's kitchenmaids' (Diary, 24 July 1881). Titurel's magnificent regalia, as designed by Seitz, reminded Wagner of the King of Thule draining his last cup of wine. He preferred 'solemn simplicity' to 'grandiose effects'. He was extremely pleased with the costume sketch which Joukovsky produced for Kundry in Act II. He felt that, in fact, Kundry 'ought to be lying there naked, like a Titian Venus' but since that was out of the question, her nakedness 'had to be replaced by finery' (Cosima's Diary, 4 January 1881). Joukovsky had designed an ornate dress trimmed with large flowers; a wide band, embroidered with pearls and brightly coloured stones, was wound about her neck and bosom and served as an additional adornment. The costumes were made by a firm in Frankfurt and when they were finally tried out for the first time at one of the rehearsals, Cosima recorded the impression as follows: '(1) Horror, (2) absurd comicality [...], (3) earnest and worried efforts to alter them' (19 June 1882). As had been the case with *Der Ring des Nibelungen*, Wagner once again felt an inevitable sense of pain at seeing a work of bold imagination translated inadequately into the realities of the theatre, with its flat canvases, wood and fabrics. Only with immense effort could the sets and costumes be made to conform to his principle of solemn simplicity.

For audiences accustomed to judging historical sets and costumes according to their degree of magnificence, *Parsifal* must certainly have appeared plain and dignified. The extent to which Wagner was able to realize his stylistic intentions can only partially be reconstructed. The most important point here is his effort to overcome the triteness of stage realism in the magic garden and to achieve a style which one might describe as surreal. But for an audience brought up in the tradition of realism, such a style was by no means easy to understand. There were complaints about the enormous flowers which, it was argued, were simply not life-like, and about their intensely bright colours. But this is presumably exactly what Wagner wanted. The audiences would have preferred the sumptuously voluptuous magnificence of a Hans Makart, but Wagner was anxious to avoid any sense of sultry sensuousness and a brothel-like environment. His ideal was a totally unreal, ingenuously spontaneous, airy and substantial ambience of seduction, both on stage and in the orchestra – in other words, what Cosima described as the 'chaste' element in Wagner's art. The task of costuming the Flowermaidens had similarly caused a great deal of anguish, precisely because Wagner had no wish for overdressed fairies but rather a desire to create the surrealistic impression of singing flowers. Nor does the current tendency to dismiss the style of *Parsifal* as 'Nazarene or 'Oberammergau-esque' strike to the heart of the matter. Even if it is the case that Wagner, like the early Nazarenes, strove for a religious art of solemn simplicity, his artistic aims had nothing in common with the trivialized, Christian picture-book world into which the Nazarenes had sunk in the meantime and which during the late nineteenth century created a readily comprehensible and obligatory religious iconography, disseminated in popular tracts. These sentimental, gently transfiguring and mawkish images were admittedly carried over into religious dramas, passion plays and pageants and represented the only valid style for sacred drama, but Wagner stressed that it was impossible for *Parsifal* to contain 'a certain sentimentality'; what it *did* express was 'a divine wildness', as Cosima noted on 17 April 1879. And Parsifal was not to speak like a 'preacher': everything about him must be 'emotional' (30 September 1878).

Wagner was thinking rather of the sacred plays of the Baroque, the final great period of religious drama in its struggle to come to terms with existential issues. One need only think of the abrupt transformation of the magic garden into a desert, where the Baroque concept of *vanitas* finds expression in the stage setting. One illuminating remark in this context is Wagner's observation that everything in *Parsifal* is direct, in other words sensually perceptible. Heinrich Heine's comment on the Nazarenes may also apply to Wagner: 'It is not the outer barrenness and pallor which characterizes what is truly Christian but a certain inner effusiveness which, in music as in painting, can be neither

Costumes: Ewald Dülberg Costume designs for the Flowermaidens, 1914. The costumes shown here were designed for the Hamburg production of 1914 but were rejected as too bold and were never used. These Flowermaidens were no florally seauctive *art nouveau* beings but comparable rather to the women of Tahiti painted by Paul Gauguin.

National Theatre, Munich, 15 August 1924 Designer: Leo Pasetti Set-design for the Good Friday Meadow. This sketch is a compendium of all those pictorial elements used by set-designers in 1914 and later to create the Good Friday Meadow: green birches, alpine pastures rendered in the fresh colours of early spring and snow-capped mountains in the distance.

named nor studied' (*Lutezia*, 1842). But the most fundamental and decisive difference lies in the fact that the pictorial world of Nazarene art did not include depictions of suffering and pain, which is one of the basic themes of *Parsifal*.

As far as can be ascertained, Wagner must have attempted to translate into the style of acting his recognition that *Parsifal* was concerned with allegory and comparison. Otto Weininger, who attended performances of the work around the turn of the century, reported that the gestures 'were sketched rather than mimed'; even in those scenes which invited passionate outbursts everything had looked as though it were painted; there were no 'Othello contortions', as a result of which 'the symbolic character of the whole' had emerged 'with profound clarity'.

In his *Schlussbericht* Wagner spoke with pleasure of his rehearsals with the artists and technical crew: 'Experienced theatre managers asked me about the supreme power which had been organized right down to the smallest detail to cope with even the least demands and which was responsible for the amazingly reliable performance of all the scenic, musical and dramatic activities on, over, under, behind and in front of the stage; to which I could reply good-humouredly that it was all the product of anarchy, since everybody did what he wanted; in other words did what was right. There is no doubt about it: everybody understood what it was all about and the purpose of the desired effect of the whole undertaking.' Wagner was happy at finally being allowed to taste the joys of success once again.

The première, however, which took place on 26 July 1882 against a background of inclement weather, ended on a note of discord. After the second act Wagner had advanced to the front of his box and asked the audience not to applaud during the acts and to refrain from calling the singers out to take a curtain call. When the final curtain was greeted by total silence, Wagner went onto stage in an attempt to correct this misunderstanding but the singers had already returned to their dressing-rooms when the applause finally began. 'The journey home, taken up with this subject, is a vexed one,' Cosima reported. 'Once we are home it takes a very long time to calm R. down, since a host of different impressions are mixed up inside him.' Nobody applauded at all at the second performance and so Wagner delivered yet another speech, stating that he had no wish that his artists should be denied applause as a way of thanking them. It is reported that on one

occasion Wagner himself was shushed by the audience for applauding his Flowermaidens. He finally succeeded in making it known that there should be applause only at the end of each act. The tradition which Wagner introduced at this time, whereby the curtain was raised once again during the final applause in order to show the closing tableau, is still retained in Bayreuth to this day.

On the whole the performances were a great popular success. Even so critical a writer as Eduard Hanslick was forced to admit that, in spite of all his practical objections, Wagner was 'the greatest living opera-composer' and 'the world's leading producer'. At the last performance Wagner himself conducted, for the first and last time in his own Festival Theatre, taking over the baton for the final scene from the transformation music onwards. 'Well, that's what I wanted to say to you,' he is reported to have remarked afterwards and 'Until next year'. But it was his definitive farewell to the theatre: he died in Venice on 13 February 1883.

As a result of his death the 1883 performances of *Parsifal*, which he himself had prepared, became a sort of requiem in memory of the dead composer. Out of respect there was now no applause at all, which gave rise to a tradition which has been observed for decades, not only in Bayreuth but elsewhere. The stage play *Parsifal* was definitively transported into the sphere of a solemn divine service. Even the 1883 performances showed deviations creeping into the staging – Julius Kniese spoke of 'bad comedy acting' – so that the following year Cosima herself intervened. From a screened-off area on the stage, unseen by the others, she observed the rehearsals and performances and sent notes with corrections to the conductor Hermann Levi and the producer Anton Fuchs.

During the last year of his life, Wagner's relationship with King Ludwig II had become even more strained, since nothing could persuade Ludwig to attend a performance of *Parsifal* in Bayreuth. Wagner even had an extension specially added to the Festspielhaus with its own approach, so that the king could reach the theatre undetected. But Ludwig had hated 'driving round' the town, as he had been expected to do in 1876; he now spent most of his time in the mountains, away from Munich. He only wanted to see *Parsifal* privately performed for his own pleasure in his Court Theatre; and he insisted that the performances should not be in summer, as at Bayreuth, but in spring, preferably at Easter.

The king had an element from the stage-set of the Good Friday meadow erected in the

National Theatre, Munich, 15 August 1924
Designer: Leo Pasetti
Set-design for the magic garden. This magnificent sketch, which relies more for its effectiveness on the use of colour than on its handling of structural shapes, is reminiscent of Emil Nolde's flower paintings. It remains doubtful, however, whether the technical means available in the theatre were adequate to realize it on stage.

grounds of Linderhof: a hermit's cell in the middle of a pasture, which his gardeners had to transform into a field of flowers. Immediately after the 1882 Festival he gave orders for private performances to be staged in the spring of 1883. Wagner made it clear to him that such a demand was impossible since the moving panorama would have to be altered and was at present unusable. The king then postponed the performances until the spring of 1884 and stuck resolutely to his orders in spite of the objections raised by all those who were responsible and who pointed out the enormous difficulties involved in such an undertaking. The sets and costumes were transported to Munich in twelve huge goods wagons and stored in the Glass Palace, since there was not enough room for them at the theatre. The technical rehearsals alone took three days, with another four days given over to musical and stage rehearsals. The theatre was closed to the public for this entire period. The three private performances which were mounted exclusively for the king took place on 3, 5 and 7 May. At His Majesty's express command the whole expensive operation had to be repeated in November of the same year and in April 1885.

During the final years of his life Wagner anticipated with horror what the Wagnerians would get up to after his death. Even Cosima, who was so readily characterized as the guardian of the grail, complained bitterly about the 'temple guardians' and her unfortunate experiences with them. They now had a place of pilgrimage, complete with a temple and a tomb, and *Parsifal* was the accompanying requiem. It is true that it was Wagner himself who first put forward the idea of a select congregation: he did not want an audience intent solely on entertainment, but neither did he want a sect or religious community but, rather, a group of like-minded individuals. He was a practical man of the theatre and knew that *Parsifal* was not a religious ceremony but a stage play involving dramatic values and applause. But he was also aware of how delicate an issue this was and how great the danger of sinking into handy consumer mysticism and a devotional exercise. It is not a question of taking sides here if one claims that the history of reactions to *Parsifal* would never have taken this turn if Wagner had lived a few years longer and been able to take countermeasures against this line of interpretation. His death lent to that Bayreuth institution known as *Parsifal* an aura of reverence and awe, resulting in the work's being spiritualized and turned into an absolutist ideology. The concept of the grail, especially,

has caused a great deal of mischief. Many people were offended by it, while others regarded it merely as something risible. Wagnerians spoke the word with deep feeling, until it finally came to be devalued as a meaningless object of *kitsch*. The shops in Bayreuth which specialized in devotional objects also sold replicas of the grail chalice in which an electric light bulb caused the blood of Our Lord to glow red. The inane custom of naming one's friends after the characters in *Parsifal* which was followed even by Cosima, strengthened still further the sense of exclusivity and allowed these concepts to be used for all manner of ends.

At this time *Parsifal* could be staged only in Bayreuth and countless visitors have recorded their experiences and impressions of their journey and of the performances they attended. Their reactions range from rapture and emotion to open rejection. Alban Berg, who attended the 1909 Festival, felt like screaming with pain after the first act and rushed away 'alone into the fields'. Being of a sensitive nature, he saw that the dignity of so unique and overwhelming a miracle as *Parsifal* was demeaned by all the goings-on in the 'Festival Beer-Hall' and the 'Festival Eating House'. In 1891 Romain Rolland was moved to tears and wrote, 'It really is no longer a theatre, it is no longer art; it is religion and like unto God Himself.' The writer Theodor Fontane, on the other hand, fled from the theatre even before the end of the Prelude, when a blast from the tubas rang out as at the

Regional Theatre, Darmstadt, 19 April 1925
Designer: A. Pohl
Sets for the Good Friday Meadow in Act III. The slender trees are like graphic symbols. Gurnemanz's hut is stage centre, designed here as a rocky cave.

Bayreuth Festival, 1936
Producer: Heinz Tietjen.
Designer: Alfred Roller.
Conductor: Wilhelm
Furtwängler. Kundry: Martha
Fuchs. Parsifal: Helge
Roswaenge. Amfortas: Herbert
Janssen. Gurnemanz: Ivar
Andrésen
Closing scene of Act III:
Parsifal holds the grail and the
dove wings down from heaven.
Alfred Roller's sets were
composed of a circle of massive,
gleaming green columns rising
out of sight above the stage,
with no dome to round them
off. The red costumes of the
knights contrasted with the
green of the columns.

Last Judgement. But he was not sorry to have seen the sights of Bayreuth. Igor Stravinsky, whom Sergei Diaghilev invited to *Parsifal* in 1912, at the very time he was working on *Le Sacre du Printemps,* imagined himself to be in a crematorium. He refused to speak about the music, since by that time he felt himself to be too remote from it. He expressed his doubts, however, about the advisability of elevating a theatrical performance to the level of a church service. *Parsifal,* he went on, could not be compared with the mystery plays of the Middle Ages, since their religious ceremonies rested upon the fundamental principles of religion, and any aesthetic qualities they may have had were purely incidental. Similarly, the philosopher Friedrich Jodl, who in 1886 had been enthralled by the power of Wagner's artistic imagination, stressed that this 'can and must be only pretence'. Also worth noting is the judgement of the liberal thinker Friedrich Naumann in 1902. He considered it fortunate that 'in so much beauty that was to be both heard and seen, there existed genuine ideas.' The world of technology and commerce was here 'exposed to another world in which loftier powers hold sway than machines and money'. It would be wrong, he concluded, to 'seek a doctrine of redemption' in *Parsifal,* but audiences should surrender to this art 'because it is the best that we have and are ever likely to have.'

After the death of King Ludwig II in 1886, the Munich Court Theatre claimed for itself the performing rights of all of Wagner's works, including *Parsifal;* it was argued that the agreements with the king were no longer valid since he had been deposed and declared insane. This was the first assault on Bayreuth's exclusive rights to *Parsifal.* The performances were the Festival's chief attraction; the great stream of visitors and the financial success of the work – about which a great deal was said although few people had actually seen it – excited the interest of other theatre managers. When, in 1893, Angelo Neumann announced that in two years' time he intended bringing out his own production of *Parsifal,* Wagner having promised him the performing rights under certain conditions, the director of the Munich Court Theatre, Ernst von Possart, expressed his determination not to withhold the work from his own audiences a moment longer. And while the new Prinzregententheater was being specially built to house Wagner's operas in Munich, he again bruited this plan abroad.

Cosima was able to do little more than appeal to the edict issued by the late king for his own Court Theatre in Munich, but it seemed as though the debate which had been going on in the Reichstag since 1898 on the question of extending the period of copyright for works of fine art and of literature might bring about a change in the uncertain legal position. The issue was whether these works should be protected for fifty years following the death of the author, rather than thirty. Cosima addressed an initial appeal to the arts minister von Studt, in a letter dated 30 November 1899. Her primary concern was *Parsifal*: because of the work's unique content, 'which celebrates the most sacred mysteries of our faith in fervent reverence,' it ought, she argued, to be reserved for Bayreuth. She was hoping for a special law to protect *Parsifal*. When it became clear that such a plan was not going to succeed, she drew up a petition to the Reichstag dated 9 May 1901. It was an open letter calculated to create a considerable stir.

Cosima began by correcting some of the factually incorrect accusations which one of the members of the Reichstag, Eugen Richter, had made against her in the course of the debate. She then went on to ask that *Parsifal* might be viewed as Wagner's 'bequest to the German nation'. It was the task of parliament 'to right the wrong which has been done and to honour the greatest master by carrying out his final request.' It was certainly an impressive and proud demand, but what else could Cosima have done in such a situation? It was anything but usual at this time for a woman to step into the public gaze in this courageous way. The attacks on her were correspondingly violent; slogans such as 'Lex Cosima' and 'Lex Parsifal' began to circulate and the whole affair provided cartoonists with an inexhaustible supply of material.

The petition was accompanied by a formal protest from the Co-operative of German Composers and by a resolution passed by the general assembly of the combined Wagner Societies. During the summer months of the 1901 Festival an appeal was sent round unanimously demanding copyright protection for *Parsifal;* it was accompanied by a list of signatories. However, Cosima's petition found only limited support in parliament and not even the general terms of copyright were extended. The implications for *Parsifal* were that after 1913 it would have no choice but to embark on the course of a 'vulgar theatrical career'. Noteworthy in this emotionally charged war of words waged over Wagner's most conciliatory work was the voice of reason belonging to F. Kunert, a social democrat and editor of *Vorwärts,* who wrote to Cosima on 28 May 1901 that 'the best protection for *Parsifal* in the distant future' was 'not the family but the people, not the individual but humanity, which is capable of infinite change.' Until then the only occasions when *Parsifal* could have been heard outside Bayreuth had been concert performances of excerpts from the work, such as those given in Paris in 1903 under Alfred Cortot and at La Scala, Milan,

in the same year, when Arturo Toscanini performed the Prelude and third act in *forma d'oratorio*. It was also in 1903, on Christmas Eve, 24 December, that the first unauthorized performance of the work took place, at the Metropolitan Opera, New York. This infamous 'rape of the grail' was regarded by the Bayreuth Circle as proof of the greed for profit which typified 'the land of the dollar', a country which had no time for ideals. Cosima took the matter so seriously that she considered going to America herself in order to prevent the performances from taking place. However, there was nothing she could legally do, since the United States had not yet signed the Berne Convention covering the protection of works of art. Although she knew that she was wasting her time, Cosima instituted proceedings through an American lawyer, but lost the case.

The Met's new general manager and lessee, Heinrich Conried of Vienna, had gained an ally in Ernst von Possart, the Munich intendant. The producer Anton Fuchs, who had worked in Bayreuth, and the technician Karl Lautenschläger both came from the Munich Court Opera. The production was heralded as the most important event in the entire history of the American theatre (which at that time did not stretch back very far). Even the preparations caused a considerable stir. A fashionable new complaint raged throughout New York, 'Parsifalitis'. There are reported to have been Parsifal sweets, Parsifal ties, Parsifal cocktails and such like on sale. While the women were racking their brains about what to wear (the performance was scheduled to begin at five o'clock, which was too early to put on evening dress), soap-box clergymen were inveighing against the sacrilege and blasphemy of such a production. The New York Society for the Protection of Children demanded that the police should intervene to prevent the participation of a boys' choir.

Although ticket prices were doubled, the first-night audience is said to have numbered 7,000. In the first interval, which lasted almost two hours, crowds of patrons fought for tables at which to dine in the foyer, while the more distinguished members of the audience drove home to change hastily into evening dress. The lavish production was sent on tour around the country the following season, playing in some sixteen cities, including Boston, Dallas and San Francisco.

It was Conried's ambition to emulate the Bayreuth model as closely as possible, or even to surpass it. The very ritual which accompanied the course of the performances was copied: as in Bayreuth, trumpeters gave a sig-

Teatro alla Scala, Milan,
26 March 1948
Producer: Oskar Fritz Schuh.
Designer: Caspar Neher
Set-design for Klingsor's tower.
Neher's futuristic vision of a
cosmic magician entangling
Kundry (downstage right) in a
web woven from rays of light.
The tower is influenced by
medieval representations of the
Tower of Babel, and is
reminiscent of Fedorovsky's
Lohengrin model in Moscow in
1923.

nal that the individual acts were about to begin; the house lights were lowered and late-comers were not admitted once the performance had started. Never in the whole history of the Metropolitan Opera had the preparations on stage and the rehearsals been so intensive. Conried was particularly concerned not to present yet another of the traditional star-studded performances but a carefully rehearsed, musico-dramatic production such as had previously been achieved only in Bayreuth. His Parsifal, Alois Burgstaller, had already sung the role at Bayreuth in 1899 and 1902; he was a model pupil of the Bayreuth school of stylistic training and his participation in the New York production caused Cosima particular distress. Milka Ternina, who sang Kundry, had also appeared in the same role in Bayreuth in 1899 and Anton van Rooy, the Amfortas, was another Bayreuth regular. The conductor was Alfred Hertz.

The sets had been commissioned from the Burghart studios in Vienna. Once again they were inevitably modelled on those used at Bayreuth, especially for the scene of the temple of the grail. For Klingsor's magic garden there was an attempt to move away from Bayreuth in the direction of a more realistic set. Luxuriant garlands of flowers, life-like in size, hung from the trees like vines in a tropical garden; they crashed to the ground at Parsifal's final words. This scene was considered more successful than the enormous and garish flowers of its Bayreuth equivalent. Nor

were the Flowermaidens dressed like flowers but wore decorative garlands of flowers over their simple garments of veils. Klingsor was dressed in an oriental costume, his magic castle a solid and impressive structure with dragons and serpents rather like Castle Dracula. On the whole there was an attempt to reproduce a realistic narrative and acting style.

Reports confirm that the performances did justice to the solemnity and dignity of the subject and that in a number of details they were superior to Bayreuth. This claim was later seized on by way of subsequently justifying and advertising the event. Conried himself emphatically protested against accusations that he was concerned only to make money or create a sensation, rather than achieving a purely artistic success. That is certainly only partially true in the case of an undertaking like the Metropolitan Opera, which was forced to seek to make a profit and where a spectacular local première such as that of *Parsifal* was inevitably also calculated to be a box-office success. Equally predictable was Cosima's disapproval and the fact that her protest would heighten public interest in the production. But could any other reaction have been expected of her?

People have spoken and written *ad nauseam* about Cosima as the 'guardian of the grail'; she was caricatured as such and attacked for covetously refusing to allow *Parsifal* to be performed outside Bayreuth. But one must make allowances for the fact that it was not exclu-

283

sively material concerns and the defence of a lucrative monopoly which determined her actions, but first and foremost reasons of piety which encouraged her attempts to enforce Wagner's final request. Even though it may not be possible to condone her motives, her attitude nevertheless deserves our respect. From a financial point of view she would certainly have done better to have accepted Conried's offer of royalties and to have released *Parsifal* at a time when the work was on everyone's lips. For once the period of copyright had expired and every theatre in the land was performing the work, she no longer had any claim to a percentage of the box-office receipts. Arthur Seidl calculated that, as a result of this refusal, Wahnfried lost a seven-figure sum in royalties, but that is something which can no longer be proved.

The Munich writer Michael Georg Conrad wrote an idiosyncratic piece called *Der Gralsraub* ('The Rape of the Grail') in which he libellously attacked Conried as an unscrupulous speculator. Conried took him to court and Conrad was fined, which once again inevitably caused a great stir and excited the wrath of the Wagnerians.

Conried's success encouraged the impresario Henry Savage to organize a rival tour of *Parsifal* in an English-language production; the company visited forty-six towns and gave 224 performances. In this he surpassed Conried, and since the director of the Metropolitan Opera had included on his posters the claim that his own production was better than the one in Bayreuth, Savage wagered in return that *his* was even better than Conried's.

Shortly before the Netherlands signed the Berne Convention, Henri Viotta set about mounting a production of *Parsifal* for the Amsterdam Wagner Society. This society had been founded in the year of Wagner's death by a group of Dutch visitors to the Bayreuth Festival. In 1884 they organized their first concert and from 1893 onwards they put on performances of Wagner's works in their own productions. The performances of *Parsifal* were again preceded by a press war and by protests on the part of composers, conductors and Wagner Societies, but the legal position was clear, as Viotta, who was a lawyer, knew perfectly well. He himself conducted the Concertgebouw Orchestra and the chorus of the Wagner Society. Parsifal was sung by Ejnar Forchhammer, Kundry by Felia Litvinne and Gurnemanz by Robert Blass. The sets were once again provided by the Burghart studios and were copies of the same firm's designs for New York. The first night was a private performance given on 20 June 1905 at

the Stadsschouwburg; there were further performances on 22 June and in 1906 and 1908. Non-members were admitted with no further formality than the payment of a membership fee. Here, too, the organizers prided themselves on having staged a better production than in Bayreuth, and the character of the Stage-Consecrating Festival Play was also said to have been preserved.

A renewed, last-minute attempt was made on 28 November 1912 to stall proceedings, in the form of a parliamentary question demanding that a special law be passed relating to *Parsifal* which would make it impossible for 'this festival drama to be staged in unsuitable performances for purposes of profit'. Once again there was a considerable stir. Hermann Bahr wrote an article entitled *Parsifalschutz* ('Protection of *Parsifal*') and August Püringer called for the 'mobilization of the sleepy German spirit'. Püringer's appeal was displayed at the Festival, where it attracted the support of 18,000 signatories. But this final attempt failed, too, when the Reichstag met to debate the issue on 13 April 1913. From 1 January 1914 *Parsifal* was available to all.

Two voices worth noting in this chorus for and against copyright protection for *Parsifal*

Bayreuth Festival, 1954
Producer: Wieland Wagner.
Conductor: Hans Knappertsbusch. Klingsor: Gustav Neidlinger. Kundry: Martha Mödl
The scene between Klingsor and Kundry in Wieland Wagner's production. The scene interpreted as a symbolic space based on the meaning of the work. Klingsor is already in possession of the spear, which is a masculine symbol. With the aid of the feminine principle (Kundry and the Flowermaidens) he lures the knights into his power in order to gain possession of the feminine symbol, which is the grail. The set is a spider's web, a trap and a female symbol stretching out to infinity and drawing everything into it as though by suction. The part of Kundry is played here by Martha Mödl who, together with Astrid Varnay, was one of the great interpreters of the role in New Bayreuth.

Bayreuth Festival, 1958
Producer: Wieland Wagner.
Conductor: Hans
Knappertsbusch. Kundry:
Régine Crespin. Parsifal: Hans
Beirer. Gurnemanz: Jerome
Hines
Wieland Wagner's forest of the
grail, created without any
three-dimensional elements but
simply by means of light; it
breathed coolness, solemnity
and 'the forest's morning
splendour'. In the centre is the
permanent circular acting area.

are those of the critic Paul Bekker and the composer Arnold Schoenberg. Bekker wrote in the *Frankfurter Zeitung*, 'To bind a work of art to a particular place, unless there are compelling economic reasons for doing so, is tantamount to transforming a living force into a dead tourist attraction.' And Schoenberg, writing in the *Neue Musikzeitung*, recognized Bayreuth's moral right to *Parsifal*, but not its artistic one. He respected the feelings of reverence, but, he went on, Wagner's idea was no longer vital precisely because *Parsifal* had become an attraction for a type of audience such as Wagner had never envisaged. The whole world should be invited to tackle the problems 'of realizing *Parsifal* musically and on stage'. If the work was prevented from developing as a living organism no style could emerge. Bayreuth was preserving a tradition 'and tradition is the opposite of style'. He ended with the plea that *Parsifal* should be performed only on public holidays and that special performances should be organized with free admission for young artists. A similar decision was taken by the members of the Society of German Theatres at their general assembly in Weimar in 1913: *Parsifal* should not be accepted into the standard repertory,

and its particular character as a Stage-Consecrating Festival Play should be respected.

A private performance of *Parsifal* took place in Monte Carlo in January 1913, and on 13 April there was the first performance in Zurich, the period of copyright protection having already expired in Switzerland with the thirtieth anniversary of Wagner's death. The production was characterized on the whole as plain and straightforward, but dignified; and it stood out from the general hectic scramble which now overtook the work. The artist Gustav Gamper was the first to introduce Swiss alpine scenery into his designs for the Zurich production, an idea which many designers took up in the years which followed.

And now the great race got under way. Many theatres scheduled their local premières for New Year's Day, although that particular evening had until then traditionally been reserved for somewhat lighter forms of entertainment, as was the case, for example, at the Charlottenburg Opera in Berlin or the German Theatre in Prague. But the theatre which ran off with the prize was the Teatro del Liceo in Barcelona where, because of the difference in the hour between Germany and Spain, the première was able to begin quite legally at eleven o'clock at night on New Year's Eve. It lasted until five in the morning.

Within a month of the copyright expiry, *Parsifal* had been performed by about forty German theatres, which included not only the larger ones but also such smaller houses as those in Halle, Wuppertal-Barmen, Kiel, Mainz, Königsberg and Chemnitz. Abroad, the work could be seen in Vienna, Paris, where it was performed at three different theatres, London, Brussels, St Petersburg, Budapest, Madrid, Milan, Rome and elsewhere. Although prices were raised, audiences stormed the first performances. In Frankfurt ticket prices were raised to 120 marks, in Vienna they were quadrupled and in Dresden they were even quintupled, in spite of which the house was sold out four weeks in advance.

All these first nights were important social events. The one at the Vienna Court Opera was a sensation second only to those witnessed when Caruso was singing. Police were called in to control the vast concourse of carriages, and inside the theatre the women were resplendent in their boxes, wearing full evening dress and 'dripping with jewellery that represented entire fortunes'. London opera-goers travelled to Paris by special trains for the first performance in the French capital, since their own local première was not due to take place for another month. The German court theatres in towns such as Dresden, Weimar and Stuttgart withdrew to a discreet distance and announced their own productions for the coming Easter. There is no doubt that the unknown Stage-Consecrating Festival Play had become the talk of the town and a fashionable topic of conversation: theatre managers hoped that a work on which they did not have to pay royalties would be a box-office success. On the other hand, the keenness of the competition necessitated a certain care in preparing the performances and an intensive effort to come to terms with the technical and musical difficulties which the work posed. And once the first rush of sensationalism had passed and ticket prices returned to their former levels, it was felt as a positive gain that all those who were interested in music but who could not afford to journey to Bayreuth should now be able to see *Parsifal* in their own local opera-houses.

There was general agreement that Bayreuth's musical standards, which were the result of years of training and experience, could not be matched. But, from the point of view of design and stage technology, many pro-

ductions were felt to be superior to the Bayreuth staging, which by now was thirty-one years old. What was missed, particularly in the large towns, was the unique atmosphere of the secluded Festival Theatre, which encouraged a greater degree of concentration on the work. Many theatres imitated Bayreuth and covered over the orchestra pit; they also had the individual acts announced by fanfares, performed the work with the auditorium in darkness and introduced hour-long intervals. This in turn gave rise to a number of new problems: during the intervals in Vienna, there were successive attacks launched first on the cloak-rooms, then the surrounding cafés and finally the restaurants. A number of theatres prided themselves on having audiences well-bred enough not to applaud.

Stage designers were confronted by a difficult task, since until now there had been only the Bayreuth model. Their stylistic approach to *Parsifal* is marked by a vitality unique in Wagner's *œuvre*. Every stylistic movement was represented, from crass naturalism to stark symbolism. Some theatres, such as the one in Nuremberg, bet on an easy box-office success and offered exact copies of the Bayreuth sets. Typical of the work produced by a large and famous workshop are the designs which could be ordered from the Berlin firm of Baruch. Whereas the temple was based on the one to be seen at Bayreuth, the forest scenes showed the first signs of the new concept of nature which was beginning to find expression in contemporary art. They remained conventional in their disposition of the various elements around the stage, but were brighter and less solemn than the heavy Bayreuth landscapes rendered in the style of nineteenth-century painting. In the interest of sales, the workshops preferred to tread a middle pathway, still being able to appeal to Bayreuth, while at the same time showing a contemporary awareness and avoiding offence as a result of any daring stylistic innovations. International comparisons strikingly reveal that the temple scenes were far more richly ornamented, far more magnificent and mystical than in Bayreuth, something which was especially true of Barcelona, whereas the nature scenes turned out to be brighter, more idyllic and in the style of *art nouveau.*

Adolphe Appia, too, had joined in the general discussion about a new style for *Parsifal* with the designs which he published in the *Türmer* in 1912. He himself was never able to realize them in practice and it was not until 1964 that Max Röthlisberger based his own sets on Appia's designs for a production in Geneva. Whereas Appia's temple and magic

Vienna State Opera,
1 April 1961
Producer and conductor: Herbert von Karajan. Designer: Heinrich Wendel. Amfortas: Eberhard Waechter. Kundry: Elisabeth Höngen, Christa Ludwig
The temple in the great classical tradition with its circular shape, the columns merely hinted at, the dais in the centre and the knights of the grail kneeling in a circle. The vast space faded into semi-darkness and determined the impact of the scene. In this production the part of Kundry was taken by two singers, Elisabeth Höngen in Acts I and III, and Christa Ludwig in Act II.

State Opera, Hamburg,
12 April 1968
Producer: Hans Hotter. Designer: Rudolf Heinrich. Conductor: Leopold Ludwig
The designer attempted to break away from the traditional circular form and used pillars and arches as a suggestion rather than as a means of creating a recognizable space. The table was semi-circular, as usual, but the way it dominated the set evoked associations of Leonardo's *Last Supper.* Other designers invested the table with a similar meaning during the 1970s.

Bavarian State Opera, Munich,
15 April 1973
Producer: Dietrich Haugk.
Designer: Günther
Schneider-Siemssen. Conductor:
Wolfgang Sawallisch. Kundry:
Hildegard Hillebrecht.
Klingsor: Heinz Imdahl
Klingsor's magic castle as a
vision of desolation in the style
of Hieronymus Bosch. There is
also a visual quotation from
Pieter Brueghel's painting of
the Tower of Babel.

garden had very little influence, his designs for Klingsor's castle and, above all, the forest set in Act I achieved a far-reaching significance comparable to that enjoyed by his designs for *Das Rheingold* and for the Valkyries' rock.

Those independent set-designers who did not have to feel bound by the Bayreuth tradition attempted to rid themselves primarily of the notion that the second act had to be set in Moorish Spain. In particular, they did away with all the oriental clutter which littered Klingsor's castle and which only some of the larger theatres were able to afford; and in this they were encouraged by Appia. His set for Klingsor's castle was a boldly curving open tower made of rough-hewn square stone blocks seen in distorted perspective. From 1919 until the 1930s Appia's design for this scene was taken as the model, as, for example, by Joseph Urban at the Metropolitan Opera in 1919 and Giovanni Grandi at La Scala, Milan, in 1928. A more original course was that pursued by Erwin von Osen in Prague, where he created a modern stepped stage for a production conducted by Alexander Zemlinsky, and by Gustav Wunderwald at the Charlottenburg Opera, for which he designed a simple structure of steps and walls composed of square blocks that looked like stone.

Appia's most influential idea, however, turned out to be that of designing the smooth tree-trunks in the forest scene in such a way that they resembled columns; they created an atmosphere of solemnity and could be transformed into the columns of the temple of the grail. The aim here was to attune the audience immediately to the symbolic style of a mys-

tery play. Ludwig Sievert adopted this concept in Freiburg in 1913, as did Gustav Wunderwald in Berlin. In Breslau (modern Wrocław) Hans Wildermann designed the trees to resemble Gothic arches and retained this concept for the temple. The designs produced by Joseph Urban for the 1919 production at the Metropolitan remained in use until 1955; and Johannes Schröder employed similar designs for Saladin Schmitt's production at Bochum/Duisburg in 1921. And as late as 1972, in the sets designed for Antwerp by Rolf Christiansen, the slender green trunks of the forest scenes formed the pillars of the temple when the lighting on them changed to blue. This list could be infinitely extended. The logical conclusion of the idea was drawn by Günther Uecker in the abstract bars which he designed for Götz Friedrich's 1976 Stuttgart production. At the Budapest State Opera, where *Parsifal* had received its first local performance as early as 1914, the Secessionist artist Laszlo Markus designed a forest of palms that resembled a Gothic nave. The Grand Duke Ernst Ludwig of Hesse attempted to achieve a similar effect in Darmstadt in 1915 by means of solemn, dark cypresses, and Jürgen Rose's forest of cypresses for the 1979 Vienna production stands in the same tradition.

The sets for the spring-like Good Friday meadow showed all the wonderfully delicate colours of *art nouveau*. Fresh green-leaved birch-trees and broad meadow slopes studded with yellow spring flowers were now the new elements in set-design which appeared simultaneously all over Europe. Typical of this new style are the designs seen in

Leipzig, those produced by Heinrich Lefler for the Vienna Volksoper and those by Gustav Wunderwald for the Charlottenburg Opera. Gustav Gamper had already designed such a meadow for the Zurich production, where it had been dwarfed by snow-capped Swiss Alps; and Alfred Roller's 1933 Bayreuth designs reflected similar concepts. Günther Schneider-Siemssen also created a flower-spangled meadow for Herbert von Karajan's 1980 production at the Salzburg Easter Festival.

The basic structure of the Bayreuth temple, a central structure encircled by columns, remained the model for all other designs. It was altered to look more austere or more straightforwardly Romanesque, or else it was enlivened by brighter colours, but the possibilities of varying this basic design were limited. A few theatres found a way out of the impasse by taking too literally Wagner's remark that, for the solemn dignity of the grail temple, only the most noble monuments of Christian architecture were worthy of imitation. In their view the greatest authenticity would result from copying suitable buildings. The Brussels Opera sent its set-painter to Spain so that the monastery of Montsalvat could be rebuilt on stage on the basis of his sketches and be made to look as close to the original as possible. In Leipzig, the sculptor Max Klinger encouraged the designer to model himself on the architecture of San Vitale in Ravenna, as the best example of 'a serious and chaste architectural style from the early period of the Christian faith'. And in Hanover the stage was dominated by an exact replica of the crossing of Mainz Cathedral.

As it had done in Bayreuth, the moving panorama posed a considerable technical and financial problem. Smaller theatres such as the one at Weimar could not afford it and simply lowered the curtain during the transformation scenes, which was at least a more honest solution than that adopted by other financially limited theatres which used the Valhalla backdrop from their *Ring* productions for the distant view of the grail castle in Act I. The critics who were present poured scorn on the ensuing lack of style; on the whole they were of the opinion that only the best equipped theatres should attempt a work such as *Parsifal.* But even there the ambitious plans often went awry. In Vienna, for example, it was hoped to use motion-picture projections, but in the end the designer had to make do with a steam curtain and gauzes, a technical solution which had first been tried out in Zurich. The opera-house in Frankfurt, being well-to-do, was able to afford a new, expensive moving panorama.

Once the early mood of sensationalism had died away, *Parsifal* again returned to a life of comparative calm. This was less the result of any loss of interest in the work than because of the outbreak of the First World War. For the 'iron cure' of the European nations, where even the theatres took a staunchly warlike stance, *Parsifal's* message of compassion was no longer appropriate. The work was now performed only on special occasions, such as at Easter.

Royal Opera House, Copenhagen, 5 December 1977 Producer: Harry Kupfer. Designer: Peter Sykora. Costumes: Reinhard Heinrich. Conductor: Wolfgang Rennert. Parsifal: Peter Lindroos. Amfortas: Ib Hansen. Gurnemanz: Ulrik Cold Grail scene in Act I. Two angels with a fiery sword realized in the style of the Nazi sculptor Arno Breker, expressing the fascist attitudes and militancy of the order of the grail knights and contrasting with the true symbol of compassion, the figure of the crucified Saviour, from which the order has grown estranged.

In Bayreuth the original staging of the first production remained unchanged until 1933, a total of fifty-one years. During the final year, Cosima's daughter Daniela, who had been present at the first performances in 1882, was in charge of the production. During the intervening years, the magic garden had been redesigned in accordance with Siegfried Wagner's impressionistic sketches of 1911; a new tower had been built for Klingsor in 1925 and, finally, in 1927 the eternally problematical second act had been entirely rethought. But the temple of the grail, which had remained unaltered since the first performances, had become in the meantime a reverentially protected monument as well as a curiosity.

It was predictable, therefore, that Winifred Wagner would encounter violent opposition to her plan to drop the old production from the 1934 Festival. As in 1913 there was again a good deal of talk about sacrilege and crimes committed against the work. In 1913 it had been a question of protecting *Parsifal* from 'the outside world'; but now the work had to be 'defended against Wahnfried', to quote the leader of the protest, Paul Pretsch. His appeal, which was also printed in *Le Figaro* in Paris, was signed by about 1,000 people, headed by Cosima's daughters Eva and Daniela, together with Richard Strauss and Arturo Toscanini. Pretsch demanded that the sets, which were claimed to be an integral part of the work and on which 'the eye of the Master had rested', should be retained and that *Parsifal* should be preserved as a unique 'memorial' 'in the original 1882 format'.

The theatre, however, is not a memorial but an art form which of necessity has to change. What the signatories of Pretsch's petition failed to realize was that, even if the sets had remained the same for decades, the spirit and atmosphere of the 1882 staging could not but be affected by all the changes of cast which had taken place. Alfred Roller, now seventy years old and regarded as a doyen of stage design, was commissioned to design the sets for the new production, but in the event he was able to satisfy neither the old-guard Wagnerians nor the advocates of a new production. His Viennese style had scarcely developed since 1914. Here, too, his temple, with its circle of thick, shiny green columns, turned out to be too confining and too solid, and the Good Friday meadow was again a mountain setting showing an alpine pasture in spring. In 1937 the twenty-year-old Wieland Wagner designed new sets with a Romanesque temple and with elements of Moorish architecture in the magic garden,

but not even this solution turned out to be convincing. On the whole these years were dominated by a spacious, clearly monumentalizing style which was neutral and which possessed neither the stylistic variety nor the personal, expressive charm of many of the designs seen in 1914 and during the 1920s.

Writers today often like to argue that *Parsifal* was one of the favourite operas of the Third Reich and that it was particularly frequently performed at this time, a claim supported by the figure of 102 performances a year between 1933 and 1939. Given the large number of theatres, however, this works out statistically at an average of between two and three performances a year per theatre, which was no more than usual. This calculation also includes figures for 1933, the fiftieth anniversary of Wagner's death and 1938, the 125th anniversary of Wagner's birth, when a number of theatres mounted complete cycles of his works. Nor is it tenable to argue that *Parsifal* contains the seeds of the Third Reich's ideology of the purity of the blood and the cult of a master race, and that Wagner prepared the ideological ground for the Nuremberg Laws which were designed to keep the race pure. Wagner's Christian and pacifist message, which preached reconciliation and compassion, was the diametrical opposite of the aggressive Nazi ideology. To assert this is not to defend or justify Wagner but rather to point out the necessary differences. *Parsifal* posed greater problems than Wagner's other works to those who wished to make it relevant to the age; and before the war it was suggested by the *Reichskulturkammer* (Chamber of Culture) that theatre managers should remove *Parsifal* from their repertory.

The Festival reopened on 30 July 1951 with Wieland Wagner's new production and with it there began the era of the so-called New Bayreuth. The aim was a radical break with a tradition which was felt to be a burden, and an intensive, intellectual attempt to come to terms with Wagner's works. Wieland's *Parsifal* was of decisive influence in forming the style of New Bayreuth and laid down international standards for as long as it remained in the repertory. The sets of this production appear to us today to be classically beautiful and it is impossible to appreciate what a revolution they betokened at the time. Wieland's temple of the grail, which consisted of only four narrow columns that emerged glowing golden-red from the surrounding darkness, became the epitome of the New Bayreuth style. For Wieland the sets were 'strictly speaking nothing less than an expression of

Grand Théâtre, Geneva,
29 January 1982
Producer: Rolf Liebermann.
Designer: Petrika Ionesco.
Conductor: Horst Stein.
Kundry: Yvonne Minton.
Klingsor: Franz Mazura
Klingsor's magic castle as a
huge atomic reactor: Klingsor is
the Lord of the Spear, in this
case an atomic bomb.

mother–Saviour–Klingsor–Titurel (or of
the archetypes swan–dove–spear–chalice)
Parsifal's mental and spiritual development
takes place within a perfectly reflecting arc,
where the turning-point is Kundry's kiss:
mystical centre, climax, nadir and circle of
the path of salvation, at one and the same
time. The absolute parallels between the
fates of Kundry and Amfortas and those
between the 'white' magic of Titurel and
the 'black' magic of his antagonist Klingsor
emerge in this way as a matter of course.
Gurnemanz stands outside the scheme, fulfilling his task as the grail's doctrinalist and
evangelist beyond the calvary of the others'
struggling souls.

It was the set for Act II which Wieland most
frequently and fundamentally altered, clearly
showing the influence of various contemporary artists such as Jackson Pollock. In the
mid-1960s, in collaboration with Pierre Boulez, he began the comprehensive task of reviving *Parsifal* both musically and on stage. His
death in 1966 prevented the plan from being
completed, at least as far as the staging was
concerned. His production continued to be
performed until 1973, a total of twenty-two
years. In that time it came to be regarded as a
classic realization of the work; its style was
imitated elsewhere and internationally it gave
rise to a virtually uniform series of designs.
And once again history repeated itself in a
way that was 'peculiar to Bayreuth', in the
form of a desire to preserve this production as
a memorial and obituary for Wieland.

Wolfgang resisted these demands and insisted upon the need for a new critical look at
the work, a task which he proceeded to take
upon himself. In planning his approach to his
1975 new production, he took as his starting-
point Wagner's own characterization of
Parsifal as a 'fundamentally evil task'. The
term was applied in the first instance to Titurel's institutionalized world of the grail. It
was a critical view of the world of the grail
which was totally new, not just in Bayreuth,
and it gave an important stimulus to other interpretations of *Parsifal* throughout the
1970s.

Alienation from the grail's original ideal
has brought the elitist all-male society to a
state of desolation. In striving for personal
perfection, the knights, as guardians of the
symbols of compassion, have themselves lost
all sense of compassion. Titurel's inhuman insistence upon asceticism is to blame for Klingsor's failure and forces him to pervert the
world of the grail. Parsifal, coming from outside, becomes capable of compassion and of
understanding his fellow men as a result of

the changing moods of Parsifal's soul'. That
was why the Good Friday meadow could no
longer be a natural romantic setting since this
scene was concerned with 'the emergence of
three living and suffering individuals into a
state of ultimate spiritual clarity and a recognition of ultimate cosmic relationships.'
These insights of depth psychology provided
Wieland with a 'human explanation of the action and the characters'.

In the so-called *Parsifal* Cross, which dates
from 1952, Wieland offered a graphic depiction and explanation of his analysis. It
formed an 'objective basis for the structure of
the work'. In the field of conflict created by
the poles

his sorrowful process of learning. He resolves the polarity of Titurel's and Klingsor's worlds, which had been mutually dependent in their paralysis and distortion, and he brings about a new synthesis. The ending for Wolfgang was not a restoration of the original state of things. The grail and spear were no longer locked away but were revealed to all. Wolfgang decided not to have Kundry die in the temple; for the grail community had eliminated the feminine principle to its own detriment. The fundamentally evil work was provided with an open ending and with the 'principle of hope'.

The symmetry in the structure of the sets for the three acts had a dramaturgical function for Wolfgang. He, too, set out from the traditional circular form of the temple, such as had been seen at Bayreuth ever since 1882. In the world of Klingsor, the perversion of this principle, the circular form was broken. The circular form did not harmonize but made plain the inner unity and mutual dependence of the two worlds. The nature scenes stood outside these two architectonically characterized worlds, visibly embodying Wagner's demand that 'the purely human be kept in a state of harmonious balance with the eternally natural'. The transformation scenes, which took place on an open stage, were particularly impressive: the walls of foliage faded away, to be replaced by pillars which closed like vices around the grey stone hall of the grail; at its lowest point stood the shrine in which the grail was kept locked away.

By the early 1970s the abstract phase in art seemed already to be *passé* and this was as true of the set-designs for *Parsifal* as it was elsewhere. There was now an attempt to locate the work in a particular period and in a fixed setting, so that it should not become lost in some remote and ill-defined region. Günther Schneider-Siemssen created an *art nouveau* temple for Dietrich Haugk's 1973 Munich production, while Jürgen Rose's designs for the temple in the Paris production of 1974 and in the Vienna production of 1979 consisted of two large solid symbols, a plain cross and an altar. In Hamburg the painter Ernst Fuchs carried over on to the stage the very personal, brilliantly colourful mysticism of his neo-surrealist style.

For his 1976 Stuttgart production Götz Friedrich decided against commissioning work from a set-designer, since he felt that the latter's traditional use of historical quotations and stylistics would be unconvincing in a work such as *Parsifal*. He chose instead to collaborate with Günther Uecker, an artist known for works employing nails. Working with the materials familiar to him, Uecker created cool, severe spaces in which the ossification and empty rituals of the worlds of the grail and of Klingsor were visually evoked. 'We cannot stylize reality until we have painfully torn it apart,' Friedrich said. Criticism of the world of the grail became a leading idea in the minds of many producers during the 1970s, the most extreme example being Harry Kupfer's 1978 Copenhagen production. At the end the grail king, Amfortas, died; but Parsifal, instead of succeeding him, left the temple, taking Kundry and the two symbols of compassion, the grail and the spear, with him. He invited the knights to follow, a handful of whom agreed to do so, while the others remained behind in perplexed confusion.

When Rolf Liebermann chose *Parsifal* to make his production debut in Geneva in 1982, he set out from the diametrically opposite point of view, the restitution of the world of the grail. The action began after the atomic bomb had fallen; the temple lay in ruins and knights and squires began again at a primeval stage of evolution. Klingsor was in possession of the spear, a destructive atomic weapon. At the end the temple was splendidly rebuilt. Suffering was interpreted here not as something existential, but as a consequence of catastrophe.

The fact that the Stage-Consecrating Festival Play has lost some of its 'sacredness' in the course of its performing history has not been a bad thing. Quite the opposite: by way of compensation, *Parsifal* has gained in contemporary relevance. Today, at a time when there is a universal search for human alternatives in an inhuman world, its message of compassion as a social requirement can be a 'counter-proposal': 'criticism and Utopia at one and the same time in a world which needs redemption as much today as it ever did, since its process of humanization still lies in the future,' to quote Hans Küng. In this way *Parsifal* can be seen neither as a surrogate religion nor as a means of solving life's problems, but as a work which provides insights and stimuli. Here, too, Wagner's desire was 'to spur on'. Seen in this light, *Parsifal* still has its future before it.

Select Bibliography

Adorno, Theodor W., *Versuch über Wagner.* Frankfurt, 1952

Appia, Adolphe, *Die Musik und die Inszenierung.* Munich, 1899

Bablet, Denis, *Le Décor du théâtre de 1870 à 1914.* Paris, 1975

Barz, Paul and Götz, Friedrich, *Abenteuer Musiktheater. Konzepte, Versuche, Erfahrungen.* Bonn, 1978

Baumann, Carl-Friedrich, *Bühnentechnik im Festspielhaus Bayreuth.* Munich, 1980

Dahlhaus, Carl, *Richard Wagners Musikdramen.* Velber, 1971

Deathridge, John, *Wagner's Rienzi, A Reappraisal Based on a Study of the Sketches and Drafts.* Oxford, 1977

Diebold, Bernhard, *Der Fall Wagner. Eine Revision.* Frankfurt, 1928

Eisenstein, Sergei, *Über Kunst und Künstler.* Transl. from the Russian by Alexander Kaempfe. Munich, 1977

Fetting, Hugo, *Die Geschichte der Deutschen Staatsoper.* Berlin, 1955

Gedenkboek der Wagner vereeniging. Haar geschiedenis in beeld 1884–1934. Amsterdam, 1934

Gregor-Dellin, Martin, *Richard Wagner. Sein Leben. Sein Werk. Sein Jahrhundert.* Munich – Zurich, 1980

Grossmann-Vendrey, Susanna, *Bayreuth in der deutschen Presse. Vol. 1: Die Grundsteinlegung und die ersten Festspiele, 1872–1876. Vol. 2: Die Uraufführung des Parsifals 1882.* Regensburg, 1977

Hartmann, Rudolf, *Das geliebte Haus. Mein Leben mit der Oper.* Munich – Zurich, 1975

Hommel, Kurt, *Die Separatvorstellungen vor König Ludwig II. von Bayern.* Munich, 1963

Irmer, Hans-Jochen and Stein, Wolfgang (eds.), *Joachim Herz, Regisseur im Musiktheater.* Berlin, 1977

Jubiläumsausstellung 100 Jahre Wiener Oper am Ring (catalogue). Vienna, 1969

Kapp, Julius, *Geschichte der Staatsoper Berlin.* Berlin, n. d.

Karbaum, Michael, *Studien zur Geschichte der Bayreuther Festspiele.* Regensburg, 1976

Kaut, Josef, *Festspiele in Salzburg. Eine Dokumentation.* Munich, 1970

Kindermann, Heinz, *Theatergeschichte Europas.* Vols. 8–10, Salzburg, 1968, 1970, 1974

Kirchmeyer, Helmut, *Musikkritik. Das zeitgenössische Wagnerbild in Dresden.* (Studien zur Musikgeschichte des 19. Jahrhunderts, Vol. 7.) Regensburg, 1972

Kloss, Erich (ed.), *Briefwechsel zwischen Richard Wagner und Franz Liszt.* Leipzig, 1910

Kloss, Erich (ed.), *Richard Wagner an seine Künstler.* (Bayreuther Briefe, Vol. 2.) Berlin – Leipzig, 1908

Kolodin, Irving, *The Metropolitan Opera 1883–1935.* New York, 1936

Kügler, Ilka-Maria, 'Der Ring des Nibelungen', in *Studie zur Entwicklungsgeschichte seiner Wiedergabe auf der deutschsprachigen Bühne.* Ph. D. thesis, Cologne, 1967

Loewenberg, Alfred, *Annals of Opera 1597–1940.* Totowa, New Jersey, 1978

Mack, Dietrich, *Der Bayreuther Inszenierungsstil.* Munich, 1976

Mack, Dietrich (ed.), *Theaterarbeit an Wagners Ring.* (Schriften zum Musiktheater, Vol. 3.) Munich – Zurich, 1978

Mayer, Hans, *Richard Wagner in Bayreuth 1876–1976.* Stuttgart, 1976

Mayer, Hans, *Richard Wagner in Selbstzeugnissen und Bilddokumenten.* Hamburg, 1959

Müller, Karl Hermann, *Wachet auf! Ein Mahnruf aus dem Zuschauerraum für Richard Wagners Bühnenbild.* Leipzig, 1935

Neumann, Angelo, *Erinnerungen an Richard Wagner.* Leipzig, 1907

Newman, Ernest, *The Life of Richard Wagner.* 4 vols., New York, 1960

Niessen, Carl, *Johannes Schröder, ein Meister der Szene.* Hamburg, 1963

Panofsky, Walter, *Wieland Wagner.* Bremen, 1964

Petzet, Detta and Michael, *Die Richard-Wagner-Bühne Ludwigs II.* Munich, 1970

Prawy, Marcel, *Die Wiener Oper.* Vienna, 1969

Preetorius, Emil, *Geheimnis des Sichtbaren. Gesammelte Aufsätze zur Kunst.* Munich, 1965

Programmes of the Bayreuth Festivals 1951–1982

Röckl, Sebastian, *Ludwig II. und Richard Wagner.* 2 vols., Munich, 1913

Säuberlich, Hartmut, 'Die Dekoration der frühen Tannhäuser-Aufführungen' in *Maske und Kothurn,* fasc. 2, Vienna, 1962, pp. 74 ff.

Schäfer, Walter Erich, *Wieland Wagner.* Tübingen, 1970

Sievert, Ludwig, *Lebendiges Theater.* Munich, 1944

Steinbeck, Dietrich, *Inszenierungsformen des 'Tannhäuser' (1845–1904). Untersuchungen zur Systematik der Opernregie.* Regensburg, 1964

Steinbeck, Dietrich, *Richard Wagners Lohengrin-Szenarium.* (Kleine Schriften der Gesellschaft für Theatergeschichte, fasc. 25.) Berlin, 1972

Strecker, Ludwig, *Richard Wagner als Verlagsgefährte. Eine Darstellung mit Briefen und Dokumenten.* Mainz, 1951

Tintori, Giampiero, *Duecento anni di Teatro alla Scala. Cronologia opere, balletti, concerti 1778–1977.* Milan, 1978

Wagner, Cosima, *Die Tagebücher 1869–1877, 1878–1883.* Ed. and annototed by Martin Gregor-Dellin and Dietrich Mack. 2 vols, Munich, 1976–1977

Wagner, Cosima, *Das zweite Leben. Briefe und Aufzeichnungen 1883–1930.* Ed. Dietrich Mack, Munich, 1980

Wagner, Richard, *Sämtliche Schriften und Dichtungen.* 16 vols., Leipzig, n. d.

Wagner, Richard, *Mein Leben.* Ed. Martin Gregor-Dellin. 2 vols., Munich, 1969

Wagner, Richard, *Das Braune Buch. Tagebuchaufzeichnungen 1865–1882.* Ed. by Joachim Bergfeld, Zurich–Freiburg im Breisgau, 1975

Wagner, Richard, *Dokumente und Texte zu 'Rienzi, der Letzte der Tribunen'* (Sämtliche Werke, Vol. 23.) Ed. Reinhard Strohm, Mainz, 1976

Wagner, Richard, *Dokumente zur Entstehung und ersten Aufführung des Bühnenweihfestspiels Parsifals.* (Sämtliche Werke, Vol. 30.) Eds. Martin Geck and Egon Voss, Mainz, 1970

Wagner, Richard, *Lohengrin.* Ed. Michael von Soden, Frankfurt, 1980

Wagner, Richard, *Die Meistersinger von Nürnberg. Texte, Materialien, Kommentare.* Ed. Attila Csampai and Dietmar Holland, Hamburg, 1981

Wagner, Richard, *Sämtliche Briefe.* Ed. for the Richard-Wagner-Familien-Archiv Bayreuth by Gertrud Strobel and Werner Wolf. 4 vols., Leipzig, 1967 (in progress)

Richard Wagner an Mathilde Wesendonck. Tagebuchblätter und Briefe 1853–1871. Ed. Wolfgang Golther, Leipzig, 1916

Richard Wagner und König Ludwig II. Briefwechsel. 5 vols., ed. by Otto Strobel, Karlsruhe, 1936–1939

Wagner, Richard, *Bayreuther Briefe (1871–1883).* Ed. Carl Friedrich Glasenapp, Berlin – Leipzig, 1907

Richard Wagner an seine Künstler (1872–1883). Ed. Erich Kloss (Bayreuther Briefe, Vol. 2), Berlin – Leipzig, 1908

Wagner, Richard, *Letters. The Burrell Collection.* Ed. John N. Burk, New York, 1950

Wagner, Wieland (ed.), *Hundert Jahre Tristan. Neunzehn Essays.* Emsdetten, 1965

Wapnewski, Peter, *Der traurige Gott. Richard Wagner in seinen Helden.* Munich, 1978

Westernhagen, Curt von, *Die Entstehung des "Ring". Dargestellt an den Kompositionsskizzen Richard Wagners.* Zurich – Freiburg im Breisgau, 1973

Wolff, Stéphane, *L'Opéra au Palais Garnier 1875–1962.* Paris, 1962

Zelinsky, Hartmut, *Richard Wagner – ein deutsches Thema. Eine Dokumentation zur Wirkungsgeschichte Richard Wagners 1876–1976.* Frankfurt, 1976

Zuckerman, Elliott, *The First Hundred Years of Wagner's Tristan.* New York – London, 1964

The extracts from *Cosima Wagner's Diaries,* edited and annotated by Martin Gregor-Dellin and Dietrich Mack, translated and with an introduction by Geoffrey Skeleton, New York–London, 1978–80 are reproduced by kind permission of the publishers, Messrs. William Collins Sons & Co Ltd, London and Harcourt Brace Jovanovich, Inc, New York.

General Index of Names

Index of Richard Wagner's Stage Works

listed chronologically with theatres in order of production

Photo Credits

The author and publisher would like to thank all those who provided the material for the illustrations. The numbers refer to the pages.

Amsterdam, Toneel Museum 74, 270
Bad Berneck, Bild-Archiv Handke 15
Barcelona, Archivio Monsalvat 241 b.
Bayreuth, Bildarchiv Bayreuther Festspiele (Photos Siegfried Lauterwasser, Wilhelm Rauh, Jean-Marie Bottequin) 12, 24, 27, 28, 31 t., 38, 40, 41 b., 43, 44, 45 b. (Photo Günter Dietel), 53, 55 b., 60, 67 t., 71, 86, 90, 100, 108, 112, 121, 123 b., 127 t., 130, 147 (Photo Scheer), 153, 155 b., 158, 159, 167, 173 b., 175 (Photo Ramme), 176, 179, 180 b., 186, 192, 194 t., 195 t., 200 t., 201, 204, 206 t., 207, 208, 209, 215, 219, 223 b., 226, 227, 229 b., 232 b. left, 234 b., 235, 240 b., 243, 246, 247 b., 248, 254 m., b., 258, 259, 264, 266, 271, 284, 285
Bayreuth, Wilhelm Rauh 21
Bayreuth, Richard Wagner Gedenkstätte 18, 211 t., 214 b., 220 b., 281
Berlin, Ilse Buhs 221 t., 237
Berlin, Komische Oper 187 (Photo Arvid Lagenpusch)
Berne, Schweizerische Theatersammlung 141 t. (Photo Leo Hilber), 198, 214 t., 267
Brunswick, R. Winkler 107
Brussels, Théâtre royal de la Monnaie 116 t. (Photo Henri Vermeulen)
Budapest, National Opera 152 (Photos Eva Keleti)
Cologne, Theatermuseum des Instituts für Theaterwissenschaft, Cologne University 29, 33 b., 48, 63, 69, 73, 75, 76, 78, 79, 81 m., b., 105 b., 111 m., 120, 134, 135, 138, 139, 141 b., 144 b., 170, 171 t., b., 195 b., 199 t., b., 213, 233 t., 245 b., 249 t., 251 t., 273, 275 m., b., 277, 279
Copenhagen, Royal Opera 115, 289 (Photo Rigmor Mydtskov)
Darmstadt, Theatersammlung der Hessischen Landesbibliothek 77, 111 t., 280
Dresden, Erwin Döring 95, 156 t.
Düsseldorf, Jürgen Theis 148
Florence, Maggio Musicale 150, 228 b. (Photos Marchiori), 242, 260 b.
Frankfurt am Main, Günter Englert 89 b.
Fuldatal, Photo Sepp Bär 54, 225 t., 256 b.
Geneva, Claude Gafner 291
Graz, Opernhaus 109
Hamburg, Gert von Bassewitz 124 t.
Hamburg, Hamburgische Staatsoper, Bildarchiv 51 (Photo Peyer)
Hamburg, Elisabeth Speidel 287 b.
Hanover, Landestheater 255 t. (Photo Kurt Julius)
Hanover, Peter Lehmann 210 b.
Hanover, Opernhaus, Niedersächsisches Theatermuseum 65 (Photo Ulbricht), 286 (Photo Hoerner)
Helsinki, Finnish National Opera 116 b., 220 t. (Photo Taisto Tuomi)
Kiel, Joachim Thode 206 b.

Lausanne, Marcel Imsand 203 b.
Leipzig, Städtisches Theater 177, 202 (Photos Helga Wallmüller), 240 t., 257
London, Wilfried Newton 236
London, Royal Opera House Covent Garden 239 (Photo Stuart Robinson)
London, Donald Southern 203 t.
London, Reg Wilson 155 t.
Mannheim, Joachim Sipos 241 t.
Mannheim, Theatersammlung des Reiss-Museums 234 t., 250 b.
Mainz, Renate Schäfer 36 b.
Milan, Archivio Fotografico Ricordi 32, 42, 72
Milan, Teatro alla Scala, Archivio Fotografico 34, 55 t., 110, 117, 119, 127 b., 149, 221 b., 225 b., 233 b., 252 b., 253, 283
Milan, Teatro alla Scala, Museo Teatrale 143, 169 t. right, b.
Moscow, VAAP 217 (Photos Evgenii Fedorovskii)
Munich, Bayerische Staatsoper 232 b. right, 252 t., m.
Munich, Rudolf Betz 118
Munich, Jean-Marie Bottequin 260 t.
Munich, Deutsches Theatermuseum 16, 68, 103 b., 105 t., 133, 162, 165 t., 193
Munich, Sabine Toepffer 49 b., 57 b., 123 t., 124 b., 180 t., 288
New York, City Opera 173 t.
New York, Metropolitan Opera 57 t., 83 t. (Photos Sedge Lebland), 83 b., 93 (Photos J. Heffernan), 218 b., 223 t., 254 t.
New York, The Metropolitan Opera Guild 196, 212
Paris, Michel Szabo 228 t.
Paris, Bibliothèque Nationale, Musée de l'Opéra 33 t., 41 b., 64, 67 b., 87, 103 b., 106, 195 t. right, 211 b.
Paris, H. Roger-Viollet 172 t., 218 t. (Photos Lipnitzki-Viollet)
Prague, National Theatre 49 t., 185 (Photos Josef Svoboda), 140, 197
Rome, Camillo Parravicini 113
Salzburg, Archiv der Salzburger Festspiele 144 t. (Photo Ellinger)
San Francisco, Opera 91 (Photo Carolyn Mason Jones), 125, 205 (Photo Ron Scherl), 145 (Morton Photo), 216
Seattle, Opera 156, 207
Stockholm, Royal Theatre 83 (Photo Ena Merkel Rydberg), 183, 238, 255 b.
Überlingen, Siegfried Lauterwasser 35, 36 t., 151, 181, 256 t.
Vienna, Elisabeth Fayer 89 t., 123 m., 154, 200 b., 287 t.
Vienna, Theatersammlung der Österreichischen Nationalbibliothek 31 b., 45 t., 47 t., 81 t., 104, 111 b., 114, 137, 146, 165 b., 169 t. left, 172 b., 194 b., 232 t. left, 245 t., 247 t., 249 b., 250 t., 269, 275 t.
Warsaw, Teatr Wielki 58 (Photo Leon Myszkowski)